SPIRIT-FILLED LIFE®

NEW TESTAMENT COMMENTARY SERIES

JOHN

SPIRIT-FILLED LIFE®

NEW TESTAMENT COMMENTARY SERIES

JOHN

JONATHAN DAVID HUNTZINGER

JACK W. HAYFORD AND DAVID P. SEEMUTH
GENERAL EDITORS

NELSON REFERENCE & ELECTRONIC
A Division of Thomas Nelson Publishers
Since 1798
www.thomasnelson.com

Spirit-Filled Life New Testament Commentary Series: John
Copyright © 2006 by Jonathan David Huntzinger

Published by Nelson Reference and Electronic, a Division of Thomas Nelson, Inc., P.O. Box 141000, Nashville, Tennessee 37214.

Book design and composition by Mark McGarry, Texas Type & Book Works

Spirit-Filled Life New Testament commentary series: John/Jonathan David Huntzinger
Jack W. Hayford and David P. Seemuth, general editors
ISBN 0–7852–5254–1

Printed in the United States of America
1 2 3 4 5 6 7 — 10 09 08 07 06

To Penney, with all my love.

Contents

FOREWORD

Welcome to the Spirit-Filled Life® New Testament Commentary Series. It has been my desire to combine solid biblical scholarship with a passionate embrace of kingdom living principles in a format accessible to pastors, students, and other readers of God's Word. If you have picked up this commentary you probably wish to become a more equipped servant of God through the thorough understanding of the Spirit's revealed Word to us.

God has led me at this stage of life to pour myself into the training of people fit for the task of kingdom ministry. Of course, this does not mean ministry in the "professional" sense. Ministry (service for the Master) occurs when people are moved by the Holy Spirit to advance as equipped warriors in a spiritual battle with evil forces to help deliver people from the realm of darkness and bring them into the kingdom of the Beloved Son of God. We know that this refers to outreach and evangelism. But such ministry extends far beyond that. People must embrace the fullness of the kingdom of God for every aspect of life. Only by Spirit-filled living and moving will people be able to comprehend and connect with such a life. And only by Spirit-filled ministry will such work occur in the lives of others.

Key to the advancing of such kingdom ministry is the ministry of God's Word. To this end I have brought together individuals of significant biblical scholarship who also have an understanding of what it means to live the Spirit-filled life in order to form the Spirit-Filled Life® New Testament Commentary Series. It should come as no surprise that biblical scholarship and an understanding of the Spirit-filled life are put together. Solid intellectual discovery of the Word of God leads to conclusions about the Spirit-filled life consistent with experience of God's empowering Spirit. The two are not to be in conflict. And they are not, in fact, in conflict. God's truth in the revealed Word (given by the Holy Spirit) is the same truth given in Spirit-empowered living. The Holy Spirit is the common denominator!

In this series you will find:

- A commitment to renew our confidence in God's Word through solid scholarship in tune with current issues in New Testament studies
- A commitment to realized kingdom living through practical insights and application of God's Word
- A commitment to reflect the inspiration of the text through seeing the Holy Spirit as Author even though God used human writers
- A commitment to reveal kingdom principles God has built into the Scriptures

Of course we know that the real purpose for knowing God's Word is to be transformed and equipped by it. We are not simply to accumulate intellectual facts about the Word. The end of study is not knowledge but knowing God by His Holy Spirit. This series will help you do just that.

So, it is my joy to present these commentaries to you for your edification. May God use these to build you up for His service.

—Jack W. Hayford

PREFACE

My earliest recollection of reading the Gospel of John goes back to junior high school when I read through the Gospels in my *Good News for Modern Man* paperback. The stick-figure drawings and Jesus' command, "Lazarus, come out!" remain vivid in my memory.

The reading of the Gospel of John that is given here is the result of much reflection since that time as well as the wisdom and generosity of others.

In particular, my appreciation for the importance of signs in John and the way in which they may be interpreted was gained while auditing Dr. Colin Brown's Gospel of John graduate seminar at Fuller Theological Seminary in the mid 1990s. His careful reading of Scripture and disorienting mastery of secondary literature and issues related to John helped me understand more about the Gospel than I knew existed prior to that time! My own thoughts and insights on the story of Jesus in the Gospel emerged later in discussions with students while teaching my Johannine Literature and Gospel of John classes at The King's College and Seminary.

Though there are many good books on the Gospel of John, it is my hope that busy readers will find this one accessible and useful for understanding John's presentation of Jesus. The focus throughout is on the sign-story of Jesus that John tells and the continuity of this story with that of Old Testament Scripture.

I would like to thank Daniel Partner for his careful reading and editing of the manuscript and the editorial staff at Thomas Nelson for allowing me the freedom to write this volume on John, a book that I refer to in classes as The Gospel of the New Creation. Also, I would like to thank Chancellor Jack Hayford for inviting me to contribute to the Spirit-filled Life New Testament Commentary series.

My wife, Penney, read much of the commentary and listened to my explanations of many passages, and invariably would ask helpful questions like, "What does this *mean*?" Her questions and thoughts sharpened my own thinking and writing.

It is to her, the one whom I love, that this commentary on John is dedicated.

Jon Huntzinger
The King's College and Seminary
Spring 2006

INTRODUCTION

The First and Final Words

The final words of the Gospel of John could perhaps be the first written about John's gospel: "There are also many other things that Jesus did, which if they were written one by one, I suppose that even the world itself could not contain the books that would be written" (21:25). Books, commentaries, and dissertations about the fourth gospel fill library shelves; courses on John are prominent in colleges and seminaries, film and dramatic presentations based on John are produced every year, and a search of the Internet reveals thousands of entries on the subject. John's gospel has inspired Christian believers and challenged biblical scholars since the time of its composition. Why does it inspire? Why does it challenge? The reasons are many and varied:

- The figurative depiction of Jesus in the Gospel of John sparks the imagination. In it Jesus is the Bread of Life, the Good Shepherd, and the Vine with the branches. John presents these and a variety of other pictures that describe Jesus Christ.
- John's fascinating prologue asserts, "The Word was in the beginning with God," linking Jesus to the genesis of all things. In this way, the book presents Jesus against the background of universal history.
- Memorable phrases, verses, and passages from this book remain in the mind long after they have been read: "For God so loved the world that He gave His only begotten Son;" "God is Spirit, and those who worship Him must worship in spirit and truth;" "He who is without sin among you, let him throw a stone at her first;" "Jesus wept;" "Behold, the Man."

- John describes miracles that are not found in the synoptic Gospels; for example, the turning of water into wine and the raising of Lazarus from the dead. These cause us to wonder, *What do these things mean?*
- The many references to times, places, and customs animate first-century Galilee, Judea, and Jerusalem.
- Jesus' embrace of His passion reveals that His death was not a mere human tragedy. Thus, He declares to Pilate, "You could have no power at all against Me unless it had been given you from above."
- Throughout his gospel, John asks the reader to believe in Jesus Christ, calling for an immediate and personal response to the truth of the gospel.

The Gospel of the New Creation

Bible readers commonly see a connection between John 1:1, "In the beginning was the Word" and Genesis 1:1, "In the beginning God created the heavens and the earth." John establishes this connection to show that the preexisting Word of God has become incarnated in the person of Jesus. This commentary builds upon John's observation, his gospel through the account of the creation narrative in Genesis. Simply stated, John views the ministry of Jesus as God's new work of creation among mankind. He intends his gospel to serve as a testimony to God the Creator who has provided a new beginning for all people through Jesus Christ. Several features of the Gospel of John support this reading:

- The prologue (1:1–18) provides the perspective from which the rest of the book should be viewed. That is, its first verses establish the thematic focus of John's presentation of Jesus throughout the book. As with all well-written literature, the introduction speaks of what will follow and is inextricably related to it. By introducing Jesus as God's Word and by referring to Him in terms of God's light and life, John sets not only the beginning but also the entirety of Jesus' ministry against the background of divine creation.
- The division of Jesus' ministry into seven miracles or signs corresponds to the seven days of creation described in Genesis 1:1–2:3. God accomplishes His work in six days and enjoys the result of His creative efforts on the seventh. The seventh day is firmly bound to the previous six in that the rest God enjoys is the culmination of all that He has done up to that moment. Therefore, Jesus' seven miracles

described by John reveal the new creative work of God among His people. The number seven is important in the Gospel of John; but why not three miracles or twelve signs? Seven represents completion or wholeness within Jewish tradition because of its relation to God's work in creation. Thus, the seven miracles of Jesus represent the complete work of God in the ministry of Jesus Christ. Having introduced his gospel with reference to Genesis 1:1, John uses the creation account of Genesis 1:1–2:3 to provide the thematic context for Jesus' ministry and to reveal it as God's new work of creation.

- John reports the descent of the Spirit upon Jesus at the beginning of His public ministry in order to show that a new work of creation has begun. In the beginning, God created by His word with the Spirit. The Spirit is present when God speaks creation into existence (Gen. 1:2). By describing Jesus as God's Word upon whom the Spirit descends and remains, John prepares his readers to view the ministry of Jesus as the beginning of a new creative work of God.

- John presents Jesus as One who offers the "eternal life" of God to the people of God. Whereas the synoptic writers emphasize the kingdom of God in Jesus' teaching, John draws attention to the promise of eternal life (3:15; 5:39; 10:28; 17:3—see also 1:4; 5:21; 6:63; 8:12; 10:15; 11:25). By showing that eternal life is a central theme of Jesus' ministry, John emphasizes the goal of God's new creative work. It is not in creating the firmament above or the waters and dry land below that moves God to cease and to rest; it is not the creation of lights in the great spaces or the creation of living creatures in the earth that represents the crowning achievement of His wisdom and power; it is the creation of Adam into whom God breathes the breath of life (Gen. 2:7). John picks up on this emphasis from Genesis and shows the apex of Jesus' ministry is the offering of the eternal life of God to humanity. This eternal life, the life of the new creation, is manifested in the miracles of Jesus and exemplified in His person.

- Throughout his gospel, John identifies Jesus as the *I am* of God. At first, one may associate this with Moses' experience of the burning bush (Ex. 3:13, 14). There, God revealed Himself to Moses as the *I am*. Many have remarked that Jesus' use of this designation shows Him to be the new deliverer of the people of God. This is certainly true. However, by delivering the Hebrew people out of slavery in Egypt, God gives them a new life. This is seen in God's promise to give Israel a land flowing with milk and honey (Ex. 3:8, 17)—an abundant new life in a new land. This new life in Canaan is reminiscent of the life that God intended for Adam in the Garden of Eden. Similarly, the

I am statements in John reveal Jesus to be the One who offers humanity the life of God. Jesus is not only the Resurrection and the Life and the Way of Life, He is the Light of the World to generate life, the Bread of Life to nourish life, the Good Shepherd to sustain life, and the Vine through which life flows (6:34; 8:12; 10:11, 14; 11:25; 14:6; 15:1–5). All of these designations speak of Jesus as the means by which God's creative life comes to His people.

- Chapters 7–9 of the Gospel of John draw attention to the issue of sin. Not only does Jesus offer forgiveness for the sin of the woman caught in adultery (8:1–12) and dismiss the notion of sin in the condition of the man who was born blind (9:3), but He also addresses the problem of sin and refutes accusations of sin in His own life (8:21–36, 46). The extended emphasis of sin in John's gospel shows the influence of the creation account in Jesus' ministry. The reason that Jesus came to offer the life of God is because sin has been with us from the beginning. Eternal life begins when one accepts forgiveness of sin.
- John's record of Jesus' teaching about the Spirit (14:15–18; 15:26, 27; 16:13, 14) also recalls the creation account in Genesis. As already noted, the creation of mankind is the highest expression of God's wisdom and power. Yet, God did not create Adam to be a trophy. He created him in His image to be His representative in the earth (Gen. 1:26, 27). God's intention was that Adam, into whom He breathed the breath of life, would perform His will (Gen. 2:7). Therefore, in John, Jesus says that He will send the Spirit of Truth to be with and in the disciples after He is gone (14:17). The purpose for this is that they might be His representatives in the world.
- The disciples' participation in God's new creation has its beginning in Jesus' command, "Receive the Holy Spirit" (20:22). Christ imparts the fresh breath of God to the disciples in order that they also may minister the life of God. This authority recalls that God breathed life into Adam giving him the authority and privilege to participate with God in His creation (Gen. 2:7, 8, 19, 20).

The Old Testament Story of Redemption and the Narrative Outline of the Gospel of John

John interprets the life and ministry of Jesus as the new creation of God in view of the Old Testament story of creation. He uses the Old Testament story of redemption as an outline of Jesus' signs and teachings. So, John selects those miracles, teachings, and stories that recall God's redemptive activity for Israel. John compresses the redemption of God as seen in the Law and the Prophets into the ministry of Jesus. Several points of agreement between John's record of the ministry of Jesus and the Old Testament story are noted in the table below.

THE OLD TESTAMENT	JOHN'S GOSPEL
God creates heaven, earth, and mankind by His word. He speaks creation into existence (Gen. 1, 2).	God's Word is present in the beginning by which He creates the world (John 1:1–5); this Word has become flesh in the person of Jesus (1:14).
God establishes a covenant with Abraham and preserves it through Jacob/Israel (Gen. 25:24–34; 27–33). He reveals Himself to Jacob and changes his name to Israel (Gen. 32:22–33), the name by which the people will forever be known.	Jesus reveals Himself to Israel (a son of Israel, a leader and teacher of Israel, and a daughter of Jacob/Israel) (1:47; 3:1, 10; 4:7–26).
God delivers His people from servitude. He gives signs by which they may believe His promise and feeds them during their sojourn in the wilderness despite their complaints (Ex. 3–20).	Jesus gives signs by which the people may believe His teaching. He feeds 5,000 men and contends with the murmuring of certain leaders. In this way, Jesus shows Himself to be the deliverer of God's people (4:43–7:52).
God makes a covenant with the people and gives them laws by which they are to live in relationship with Him as well as with one another. Failure to live in accordance with these laws is sin and results in judgment. Yet, the heart of the covenant and its laws is mercy and God's love (Ex., Lev., Deut.).	Jesus addresses the problem of sin and speaks about forgiveness and judgment. Not only does He draw attention to the intention of the law in the covenant, but He also exemplifies the covenant in His life and ministry (8:1–9:41).
The people struggle with sin through the period of Judges and Kings. Without an understanding of God and without direction from their leaders, they face the prospect of exile. God condemns the leadership of the people, describing them as false shepherds who destroy the flock. He promises to be a shepherd to them (Jer. 23; Ezek. 34).	Jesus is the Good Shepherd who gives life in the midst of death. He warns of false shepherds who, rather than help the sheep, harm them (10–11).
Through the prophets, God speaks of a day of judgment that He calls "the Day of the Lord." After this judgment, however, He promises salvation and says He will send the Spirit upon all people (Joel 2, 3).	From the beginning of His ministry Jesus alludes to His "hour." It is the moment of His glorification. As He prepares for His death (and resurrection), He says that His "hour" has come and He speaks of the coming of the Spirit (12–17).

Though these parallels should not be overdrawn, they illustrate that the broad contour of John's gospel follows that of the Old Testament story of redemption. John shows that in Jesus Christ, God is present to save His people even as He has been present to save throughout earlier generations. What is the nature of this salvation? It is nothing less than a return to a relationship with God as planned from the beginning. John describes this relationship in terms of eternal life.

The Evidence of Irenaeus

Many students of John are surprised to learn that the earliest documented use of his gospel are in the second-century writings of Gnostic such as Valentinus. Justin Martyr is one of but a few orthodox church fathers to allude to John during this time. However, by the end of the second century church leaders were commonly using the Gospel of John. For example, it is the foundation of Tatian's Diatesseron, an early harmony of the four Gospels. The most important source of historical information on the Gospel of John during this time is the theologian Irenaeus (b. A.D. 130), a second-generation disciple of John who claimed a lineage of faith to him through Polycarp, the bishop of Smyrna (d. A.D. 156). Irenaeus writes, "Polycarp also was not only instructed by apostles, and conversed with many who had seen Christ, but was also, by apostles in Asia, appointed bishop in Smyrna, whom I also saw in my early youth, for he tarried [on earth] a very long time" (*Against Heresies*, 3.3.4). In a letter to a wayward colleague Irenaeus elaborates on this relationship with Polycarp and his connection to John:

> I remember the events of those days [in Polycarp's house] more clearly than those which happened recently, for what we learn as children grows up with the soul and is united to it, so that I can speak even of the place in which the blessed Polycarp sat and disputed, how he came in and went out, the character of his life, the appearance of his body, the discourses which he made to the people, how he reported his intercourse with John and with the others who had seen the Lord, how he remembered their words, and what were the things concerning the Lord which he had heard from them, and about their miracles, and about their teaching, and how Polycarp had received them from the eyewitnesses of the word of life, and reported all things in agreement with the Scriptures. (*Ecclesiastical History*, 5.20.5, 6)

Like most early church leaders, Irenaeus carefully linked his teaching with earlier instruction that he believed went back to the apostles. He saw himself as a link in a chain of custody that preserved the teachings of and traditions of the apostles. Undoubtedly, he assiduously assessed the traditions he received and the sources from which they came. With respect to John, he is confident in his source, which is Polycarp, since Polycarp had been with the apostles.

Irenaeus' testimony is the basis for the assertion that John wrote the gospel that bears his name. In a brief discussion concerning the circumstances of the composition of the four Gospels Irenaeus writes, "Afterwards, John, the disciple of the Lord, who also had leaned upon [Jesus'] breast, did himself publish a gospel during his residence at Ephesus in Asia" (*Against Heresies*, 3.1.1.). When commenting on the church in Ephesus, Irenaeus refers to John: "The church in Ephesus, founded by Paul, and having John remaining among them permanently until the times of Trajan, is a true witness of the tradition of the apostles" (*Against Heresies*, 3.3.4). Thus, Irenaeus asserts that the apostle John authored the book that bears his name and lived in Ephesus through the end of the first century.

The Gospel of John was especially useful to Irenaeus in his debate with sectarian teachers. He believed that John originally wrote this gospel to refute the teachings of certain men. "John, the disciple of the Lord, preaches this faith, and seeks to remove that error which by Cerinthus had been disseminated among men . . . that he might confound them, and persuade them that there is but one God." Irenaeus also drew from its authority to refute heterodox views of God and His Word (*Against Heresies*, 3.11.1). What was the content of these views? According to Irenaeus, some asserted that the Word did not enter the world. Others contended that the Word did not become incarnate and did not suffer. They said the Word was like a dove that came upon Jesus and ascended once it had made the fullness of God known to Him. Numerous additional views proliferated. Irenaeus gives his assessment of these views when he writes, "For if any one carefully examines the systems of them all, he will find that the Word of God is brought in by all of them as not having become incarnate . . . The Lord's disciple [John], pointing them all out as false witnesses, says, 'And the Word was made flesh, and dwelt among us'" (*Against Heresies*, 3.11.2).

From Irenaeus we also learn that a primary matter of debate between the early church and sectarian interpreters concerned the nature of God as Creator and the manner in which He created heaven and earth. Many of these men contended that God had created through intermediaries and used John's gospel to support their view that the logos (Word) of God was one such intermediary. For Irenaeus, John's contention that Christ is the Word of God by which all things were created reveals the fundamental nature not only of Christ as God's Word but also of God Himself as Creator who has initiated a new beginning through Jesus Christ. This shows that early in the history of the interpretation of John's gospel, certain men were attempting to modify or even reject John's assertion that the new creation of God begins and ends with Jesus Christ.

The Question of Authorship

Though Irenaeus and other church fathers point to the apostle John as the author of the book that bears his name, many New Testament scholars are not persuaded by his testimony. The reasons for their caution are listed below, but the basic question concerning the authorship of the Gospel of John may be posed in the following manner: "Does the Gospel of John essentially reflect the nature of Jesus' ministry as recalled and interpreted by one of His closest disciples, or does it reflect the experience and interpretation of the early church community?" More simply, "Is this gospel about Jesus or is it about the church?" Some will say that it is about Jesus. Others will say that it addresses the situation of the early church and the issues they were confronting at the end of the first century.

The two positions noted here need not be viewed as mutually exclusive. John's gospel certainly is about the ministry of Jesus. At the same time, it has been written to address the needs of the disciples of Jesus in the last decade of the first century. Nonetheless, the position that one takes on this question affects how he or she answers other questions such as the authorship of John. Some reasons scholars question the traditional view of authorship are as follows:

- The church fathers in the first half of the second century (A.D. 100–150) rarely cite or allude to John's gospel. This is hard to explain if the apostle John is its author. New Testament scholar C. K. Barrett says that this point is "no common argument from silence."[1] For example, the church leader Ignatius fails to name John or his gospel in his letter to the Ephesians. Why would he not acknowledge John if he were in Ephesus as Irenaeus claims? Barrett concludes from this, "If [the gospel] was written by an apostle, it was not known to have been so written . . . [It] is hard to see why, if it was, it was not published under his name."[2]
- Some early church evidence points away from the apostle John to another church leader who shared the same name. The church historian Eusebius quotes Papias, a contemporary and colleague of Polycarp, to show that there were two Johns in Ephesus and that he [Papias] knew John the elder not John the apostle:

I shall not hesitate to append to the interpretations all that I ever learnt well from the presbyters and remember well, for of their truth I am confident . . . But if ever anyone came who had followed the presbyters, I inquired into the words of the presbyters, what Andrew or Peter or Philip or Thomas or James or John or Matthew, or any other of the Lord's disciples, had said, and what Aristion and the presbyter John, the Lord's disciples, were saying. (*Ecclesiastical History*, 3.39)

Thus, Irenaeus is mistaken when he says that Papias also knew John. Papias knew what others had told him about John. (See *Against Heresies*, 5.33.4.) Moreover, Irenaeus sometimes conveys fanciful information in his writings, such as his assertion that Jesus was nearly fifty years old when He was crucified (*Against Heresies*, 2.22.6). If he is mistaken about such matters as Papias' relationship with John, he is not unimpeachable as a source of information about John. Without the testimony of Irenaeus, the external evidence for the view that John the apostle composed this gospel is weak.

- The theological presentation of the Gospel of John is so unlike that of the synoptic Gospels (that is, Matthew, Mark, and Luke) that it is difficult to conceive a disciple of Jesus composing it. For example, the content of Jesus' teaching presented by John diverges from that preserved by the synoptic writers. Whereas Matthew, Mark, and Luke emphasize the kingdom of God in the teaching of Jesus, in John, Jesus says relatively little about the kingdom. In the synoptic Gospels Jesus teaches in parables. In John, He teaches in discourses. Also, too many important events recorded in the synoptic Gospels, such as the temptation of Jesus, His transfiguration, and the Last Supper, are not recorded by John. The argument is that a disciple of Jesus would not have ignored the most basic instruction in Jesus' teaching ministry, failed to account for the way He taught others, or overlooked such crucial and definitive events of His ministry as the writer of John does.
- Important historical information given by John does not correlate with that provided by the synoptic writers. For example, John reports that Jesus was crucified on the Day of Preparation when the Passover lambs were being sacrificed in the temple (18:28, 29; 19:14, 31, 42). Thus, the meal reported in 13:1–30 was not the Passover. The synoptic writers place the Crucifixion on the day following the Passover meal (Matt. 26:17–19; Mark 14:12, 42; Luke 22:7–13, 15). Jesus had already celebrated the Passover with them when He was crucified. Since the

synoptic writers agree with each other, it is more than likely that John is mistaken. Yet, how can it be that a disciple who was present at the meal is mistaken on this matter? The answer is that he would not. Thus, the writer of this gospel cannot be John.

- The Gospel of John reveals no stylistic difference between the speech ascribed to Jesus and that of John himself. What John says about Jesus sounds just like Jesus' conversation and discussion with those around Him. Had the apostle John written this gospel, he would have been careful to distinguish Jesus' words from his own.

- This gospel reveals the hand of an editor in the text. Some of the content of this book no doubt originates with the apostle John, but it took its final form over an extended period as the apostle's followers developed it. Thus, its final editorial form is not the work of John, though he undoubtedly inspired it. Rather, it is the contribution of an unknown disciple or disciples. Many contemporary New Testament scholars hold this view of this gospel's composition and authorship.

These arguments against the traditional authorship of John's gospel cannot be casually dismissed. It is easy to understand why many wonder if the apostle John really did write the Gospel of John. Nonetheless, these points may be answered with the following observations:

- At first, the early church fathers may have been cautious to cite or to refer to John's gospel because of its popularity with heterodox teachers such as Valentinus. John's presentation of Jesus as God's Word from the beginning appealed to these teachers and led them to use it in support of their own views of Jesus. Though this negative use of this gospel caused church leaders to be wary of using it themselves, by the end of the second century men like Clement of Alexandria not only accepted it based on its apostolic authority but also without hesitation pronounced it as inspired by God. Moreover, we possess only a small sampling of the documents written and circulated from this period. It is estimated that of all the holdings in the famous library at Alexandria in the second century B.C. only five percent have been preserved. The point is that the present absence of materials from the ancient world is not evidence that none existed.

- Two answers may be given to the assertion that there were two Johns in Ephesus. First, Eusebius quotes Papias to discredit the view that the apostle John wrote the book of Revelation. Eusebius did this because he had a negative view of the Revelation because of its flamboyant language and so wanted to sever its connection with the beloved apostle. Based on Papias' statement quoted above, he reasons that there were two Johns in Ephesus, the lesser of whom wrote Revelation (*Ecclesiastical History*, 3.39.5–7). He says that Papias knew the elders but not the apostles and that he knew John the elder but not John the apostle. This John wrote the book of Revelation. Though Eusebius' interpretation of Papias' words appear sensible, it actually represents a misinterpretation of his statement. Eusebius draws a distinction between the elders and the apostles where Papias does not. For Papias, the words of the elders are equivalent to the teaching of the apostles: "I inquired into the words of the presbyters [elders], what Andrew or Peter or Philip or Thomas or James or John or Matthew . . . had said" (*Ecclesiastical History*, 3.39.7). Here the elders are apostles. Thus, when Papias next refers to "Aristion and John the elder" he likely means "Aristion and the aforementioned John." The two references to "John" represent a categorical way of referring to the one apostle who once taught along with the other apostles and still teaches as a leader in the church.[3] Second, among early writers there is no record or description of anyone other than John as the author of the gospel attributed to him. Church fathers are unanimous in their view that the apostle John wrote this book. If someone other than John wrote it, we should expect to find a stronger historical tradition concerning such a person. Yet, none exists. It is unlikely that such an author has been universally shunned in church tradition in favor of the apostle John.

• John's presentation of a different portrait of Jesus than that offered by the synoptic writers is intentional. Early fathers such as Clement of Alexandria recognized this to be the case. The structure and message of John focuses on the signs performed by Jesus—miraculous acts that point to truths about Jesus and the significance of His ministry as the new work of creation by God among His people. Rather than recount events that Matthew, Mark, and Luke had already recorded, John selects other events that fulfill his desire to show the ministry of Jesus as the new creative work of God through Him and set it within the context of God's salvation history.

• The celebration of Passover and Unleavened Bread lasted eight days. The large number of people who traveled to Jerusalem for the festival sometimes made it necessary for priests to slaughter lambs for Passover on days other than Passover. John's "Day of Preparation" may well refer to a day after the first day of the festival when sacrifices continued to be performed. The meal indicated by John in chapter 13 would then have been the Passover or first meal of the festival.[4] Therefore, the information John gives about this meal and the subsequent crucifixion does not contradict the presentation of these events in the synoptic Gospels.

- It is not surprising that the language of Jesus' teachings in this gospel is similar to John's since John presents these teachings in translation from Aramaic. In addition, it has been suggested that the language of Jesus in John reflects the personal and conversational speech used by Jesus with His disciples in private, not His more formal, public style of speaking.

- Finally, it is not remarkable that John's colleagues would assist him in the preparation of his gospel, even posthumously. Anyone would perform such a service for an esteemed friend and mentor. It was common practice at this time for amanuenses or secretaries to assist in the writing of documents. Their admiration for John and his teaching would have constrained them from attempting to add to or detract from his gospel in any way that would distort it. Minor revision does not constitute authorship. With regard to the view that this gospel was developed in stages over time, note that any developmental theory of composition is simply a theory. Moreover, to attribute this book to the apostle John is not to say that he wrote it at a single sitting without assistance. There is no way to determine the length of time involved in its composition.

The Historical John

In his commentary on the Gospel of John, published more than 120 years ago, New Testament scholar B. F. Westcott makes five time-honored observations about its author.[5] He says that the writer was a Jew from Palestine who knew Jesus and was one of His apostles. Westcott reckons that this is John and thus is the author of the book that now bears his name. But who is this person whose book about Jesus Christ is being read 1,900 years after it was written? There are several answers to this question:

- John was a friend to Jesus. It is likely that he is the "beloved disciple" mentioned in the Gospel of John—an otherwise unidentified follower who leans upon Jesus at the meal before His passion (13:21–25), stands with Mary at the cross (19:25–27), runs to the tomb upon hearing Mary Magdalene's report (20:1–10), and is the object of Peter's interest (21:20–25). The most convincing evidence in favor of the apostle John is the way John the Baptist is introduced in the book. Matthew, Mark, and Luke introduce the forerunner of Jesus as "the Baptist" or "the one who baptizes" (Matt. 3:1; Mark 1:4; Luke 3:2, 3). The Gospel of John, however, introduces him simply as John (1:15, 19) without any additional description (compare 1:26, 31, 33). The author identifies no one else by that name, including himself. The best explanation for this is that because he is the author, he identifies himself in some other way. The question remains: "Why would John write of himself in such an indirect manner?" Some find it implausible that John would describe himself as beloved since this seems to be immodest. But, this may be nothing more than a description of how John felt about himself. He was not more loved than his fellow disciples, but like them had experienced the overwhelming love of God in Christ Jesus. The synoptic Gospels complement this view of John by showing him to be one of Jesus' inner circle who witnesses the raising of Jairus' daughter (Mark 5:37; Luke 8:51), sees Him transfigured on the mountain (Matt. 17:1; Mark 9:2; Luke 9:28), and remains close to Christ in Gethsemane while He prays (Matt. 26:37; Mark 14:33).

• John was a man of conviction, emotion, and ambition. According to Luke, he resists the ministry of the exorcist and is angered by the Samaritan response to Jesus (Luke 9:49–56). Mark introduces John as a "son of thunder" who covets a place of authority in the kingdom (3:17; 10:35–45). Irenaeus supports the view that John possessed a fiery, strong disposition. Here is his report of John's reaction to the Gnostic teacher Cerinthus: "John, the disciple of the Lord, going to bathe at Ephesus, and perceiving Cerinthus within, rushed out of the bathhouse without bathing, exclaiming, 'Let us fly, lest even the bathhouse fall down, because Cerinthus, the enemy of the truth, is within'" (*Against Heresies*, 3.3.4). Though contemporary readers may smile at a story of the apostle running away from a public bath in a dramatic gesture of mock fear to show his disapproval of the Gnostic teacher—it reveals that some in the early church remembered John as one who was passionate for the truth of God.

• John possessed an eye for detail. He describes the layout of the temple (10:23) and the geography of Jerusalem (5:2; 9:11; 18:1, 2, 15, 28; 19:13, 17, 41), Judea (3:23; 11:18, 54), and Galilee (1:28, 44; 4:5,6; 12:21). Also, his gospel is filled with references to time (1:39; 2:1, 12, 20; 4:6,

43; 5:5; 11:6, 49; 18:2; 21:11) and other data that reveal a personal knowledge of the recorded events. Thus, John describes a whip of cords with which Jesus assaults the vendors and money changers in the temple (2:14, 15); the barley loaves that feed 5,000 (6:13); the incredulous observation of the people that Jesus was not even fifty years old (8:57); the value of the oil used to anoint Jesus (12:5); the fact that the fire in Caiaphas' courtyard as made of coals (18:18); and the weight of the spices brought by Joseph and Nicodemus (19:39).

- John was a leader in the early Christian community. The authority granted to his gospel by the early church points to someone who had not only been with Jesus but who had exerted influence in its midst. Polycrates, the bishop of Ephesus (A.D. 189–198) makes the interesting comment that John was a priest "wearing the breastplate," as well as a martyr and teacher who died in Ephesus (Eusebius, *Ecclesiastical History*, 5.24). Though we cannot be certain what Polycrates means when he says John was a priest who wore the breastplate, it is likely a figurative expression that refers to John's ministerial role in the church and the authority he possessed as one of the apostles, possibly the last remaining apostle, who had been with Jesus during His earthly ministry.

- Finally, John is an evangelist who wants others to know Jesus as he knows Him. Through Jesus, he has experienced the new life of God and wants others to experience it as well. This is illustrated by another early Christian story about the apostle John as told by Clement of Alexandria and preserved by Eusebius (*Ecclesiastical History*, 3.23): While visiting churches in Asia Minor, John proclaimed the message of salvation to a young man who later turned away from it and became a robber. When John discovered this, he sought out the young man and patiently restored him to the Lord and to the church.

John's Ambition

Why did John write his gospel? As noted above, John writes so that others may know Jesus as the One who offers the eternal life to mankind just as God intended from the beginning. He shows that the redemptive love and work of God as recorded in the Old Testament story of salvation was present in Jesus. Such a message has broad significance: it possesses meaning for Jews because it presents Jesus through the lens of the Torah and the Prophets; it appeals to Gentiles because it depicts Jesus in the universal context of God's divine plan as the answer to their concern about fate and the caprice of their pagan gods.

The apostle himself said that he wanted to inspire faith in others (20:30, 31). Because of two different textual readings of the verb believe in verse 31, there are two possible meanings. Most texts show the verb as aorist tense (*pisteusēte*, πιστεύσητε) while others show it to be present tense (*pisteuēte*, πιστεύητε). The aorist tense indicates that John wrote to engender new faith while the present tense signifies that he wanted to nurture the already discovered faith of those who heard or read his gospel. Regardless of the tense of the verb, the intent is clear. The purpose of John's gospel is to pronounce publicly Jesus as the divine Son of God who offers the eternal life of God to all who will believe in Him. For those unfamiliar with Jesus, it serves to establish the truth of this promise and enable them to believe. For those who already know Jesus, the gospel sustains such faith in them.

In addition, John writes to answer the question that Jesus posed to His disciples in Caesarea Philippi: "Who do you say that I am?" (Matt. 16:13–20; Mark 8:27–30). Of course, Peter was the first to answer at that time: "You are the Christ, the Son of the Living God." Jesus acknowledges Peter's answer and confirms the revelatory nature of his confession: "Flesh and blood has not revealed this to you but my Father in heaven" (Matt. 16:17). Peter was the first of the disciples to confess Jesus' identity. In writing his gospel, John was the last to do so. John not only agrees with Peter's confession that Jesus is the Son of the Living God, but he expands upon it by asserting that Jesus brought to mankind the eternal life of God.

John's Testament and Testimonial

John's gospel may be seen as a type of testament—the last word about Jesus' ministry that establishes His identity for the ages. Jewish literary testaments in the ancient world took the form of deathbed admonitions or exhortations by famous biblical figures to sons, friends, followers, and others about ethical and eschatological matters. John's gospel is certainly not one of these! Yet, it does represent John's view of Jesus at the end of his long life and ministry. It functions as an exhortation to others to believe in Jesus Christ. It is John's definitive presentation of Christ's work on earth in view of God's redemptive activity throughout history.

This gospel may also be seen as a testimony given in a court of law. In ancient Rome, personal, written documents were uncommon and most people did not possess the variety of identification papers that we have today. Then, people were identified by the testimony of others. John gathers an impressive list of witnesses to identify Jesus as the Son of God. He presents the testimony of these people to persuade the world that Jesus Christ embodied God's intervention into human affairs. Furthermore, he asserts that this testimony is true. Any other is inadequate and false.

John gathers both human and divine testimonies. The human testimony involves numerous people who identify Jesus according to categories with which they were familiar. These include the Baptist (1:6–8, 19–36), disciples like Peter (6:68, 69), Thomas (20:28), and Martha (11:27), those touched by His ministry such as the Samaritans (4:29, 42) and the man born blind (9:17), as well as the crowds in Jerusalem (7:40–42). God the Father, who sent Jesus into the world (3:34; 8:26; 7:28, 29, 33) and bears witness through Jesus' words (7:16, 8:28, 12:49 50, 17:8, 14) and works (5:36, 7:16; 10:32, 38, 14:10), gives the divine testimony. Moreover, John calls upon Scripture to testify to the identity of Jesus (5:39, 40, 46; 2:17; 12:37–41; 19:36, 37).

This table lists twelve witnesses who testify on Jesus' behalf in John's gospel.

The Topic of the Testimony	The Witness	The Passage	The Identity of Jesus
The Word of God	The Apostle John	1:1–5	The beginning of life with God
The Lamb of God	John the Baptist	1:6–8, 19–36	God's Sacrifice for sin
The Son of God/ King of Israel	Nathanael	1:49	The One through whom God's promises are realized
Teacher from God	Nicodemus	3:1–21	The Teacher who brings eternal life
The Messiah/ Savior of the World	The Samaritan Woman	4:29, 39–42	The One who reconciles mankind to God
The Messiah/ Prophet to Come	The Jewish People	6:14, 15; 7:40–41	The One who speaks for God
The Messiah/ Son of the Living God	Peter	6:67, 68	The One designated to complete God's purpose
The Prophet/ Healer	Man Born Blind	9:17	The One who reveals God
The Messiah/ Son of God	Martha	11:27	The One who gives life in the midst of death
The King of Israel	The Multitude	12:13	God's promised ruler
The King of the Jews	Pilate and the Roman soldiers	18:37; 19:3, 14, 19	The King who suffers on behalf of His people
The Lord and God	Thomas	20:28	The One who is worthy of worship

Note: The human testimony for Jesus is not unanimous. Certain Jews, for example, ask if Jesus is not the son of Joseph, revealing that they think He is simply another man (6:41, 42).

Finally, John has Jesus testify for Himself by recording the signs that He performs and the statements that He makes concerning Himself. The *I am* statements, as already noted, declare that the creative life of God is experienced through Jesus; the signs reveal the nature of the creative life-giving work of God in Him.

John among the Evangelists

Does John know the synoptic Gospels exist when he writes his own? Has he read and studied them? Has he developed his gospel with an eye toward the writings of his fellow evangelists? Biblical scholars have viewed John as both dependent on the synoptic Gospels and independent of them. Barrett, for example, believes that John knows Mark's gospel and is dependent on it for his basic presentation of Jesus' ministry.[6] Others believe that John is independent of the synoptic gospels, does not know of their existence, and thus produces a unique account of Jesus' ministry distinct from theirs. Which of these views is correct? Given that he wrote at the end of the first century from Ephesus, a major Christian community, it is reasonable to assume that John is not ignorant of Matthew, Mark, and Luke. But, is John dependent on the three synoptic Gospels? On one hand he is, because he consciously includes and excludes information about Jesus in response to the information they contain. However, he is not dependent on them for his gospel's organization, content, or interpretation.

John's depiction of Jesus is similar to that of the synoptic writers in the following ways:

- Jesus begins His ministry after being baptized with the Holy Spirit at the Jordan River.
- He then calls disciples and then teaches them about God the Father and His kingdom.
- He instructs the crowds that follow Him. This teaching occurs in synagogues as well as in other private and public venues.
- He performs miracles that draw the attention of others and cause them to inquire into His identity. All four Gospels record the miraculous feeding of 5,000 men (John 6:1–14; Matt. 14:13–21; Mark 6:30–44; Luke 9:10–17).
- This ministry occurs in Galilee as well as in Judea and culminates in

Jerusalem where Romans put Him to death with the support of certain temple leaders of the city. After His death, Jesus is resurrected and appears to His disciples.

John's view of Jesus diverges from that of the synoptic writers in many ways:

- As noted above, the outline of Jesus' ministry in John's gospel follows the Old Testament pattern of redemption as He moves between Galilee and Jerusalem.
- The synoptic evangelists locate Jesus' ministry in Galilee and describe but one trip to Jerusalem whereas John shows Jesus in Jerusalem on several occasions, at least three of which are for the festival of Passover (2:13–22; 5:1; 12:1).
- Important events common to John and the synoptic Gospels are set at different times in Jesus' ministry. Jesus' demonstration in the temple, for example, occurs at the beginning of Jesus' ministry according to John (2:13–21) but during the week of His passion according to the other three evangelists (Matt. 21:12–17; Mark 11:15–19; Luke 19:45–48).
- The synoptic Gospels indicate that Jesus' ministry occurred over the course of a single year. John describes a ministry that spanned at least three years.
- The content of John's gospel includes miracles not mentioned in the synoptic Gospels, such as water turned to wine, the healing of the man born blind, and the raising of Lazarus (2:1–12; 9:1–12; 11:1–44)
- John mentions events like the washing of the disciples' feet (13:1–17) and Jesus' interrogation by Pilate (18:28–19:16) that the other three evangelists omit.
- The synoptic writers describe numerous events in the life and ministry of Jesus that are absent in John. The most important of these is the narrative of the Last Supper. Matthew, Mark, and Luke describe this meal that Jesus ate with His disciples the night before His crucifixion. John, however, makes only a passing reference to a meal (13:2, 18–30). He describes Jesus with His disciples, washing their feet, and teaching them about the Holy Spirit, but he does not elaborate on a last meal.
- The content of Jesus' teaching in the Gospel of John concerns His relationship to God, the importance of belief, the nature of truth, and the origin and gift of eternal life. The synoptic Gospels show that the

primary theme of Jesus' teaching is the kingdom of God. For them, Jesus' miracles confirm the presence of the kingdom in His ministry and life. For John, however, the miracles are signs pointing to the fact that Jesus is the "one who has been sent by the father." This expression is unique to John and occurs more than thirty times in his gospel.

Ultimately, John is independent of the synoptic writers in the composition of his gospel. Though he may have been aware of their writings when he wrote, John draws from his own recollections to testify of Jesus to others. However, to say that John writes out of his own experience is not to suggest that he does not make use of other sources. Does John consult other written accounts? Does he recall popular oral traditions? This cannot be precisely determined. Some scholars say that John makes slavish use of a so-called signs source, a discourse source, and a passion source.[7] This is unlikely. His gospel is original to his own understanding and experience with Jesus. So, he records seven signs to recall the creative activity of God and organizes the ministry of Jesus according to the Old Testament story of redemption. John is not academically dependent on outside sources for his presentation of Jesus. Rather, he draws on his own memory to meet the need of his community for encouragement in the faith.

John the Theologian

As mentioned above, John depicts the ministry of Jesus as a new beginning for all people. In Him, God has begun a new work of creation by which men and women may experience eternal life. Moreover, the Old Testament story of God's redemptive work among His people as told in the Law and the Prophets provides the general framework in which John declares the good news. John also weaves several theological themes through his gospel that unify its different sections and focus attention on features of Jesus' life and ministry he considers vital. These themes include:

- Jesus is the *logos* (Word) of God. Not only so, He also speaks God's word to the people.
- Jesus' place of origin and ultimate destination are described. Jesus both descends into the world and ascends from it. He is not of this world.
- Light and darkness are figurative images that speak of the realm of God and the realm of the world. Jesus is the Light of God that has entered into the world.

- Jesus tells of His "hour." This describes the definitive moment of His earthly ministry in His passion and the triumph of His resurrection.
- God's glory is manifested in Jesus' death on the cross. The most severe symbol of brutality and shame in the ancient Roman world is the means by which God's essential nature is revealed.
- Knowledge describes Jesus' understanding of His mission and the ways of God His Father; lack of knowledge speaks of the limited understanding of others concerning Him. Whereas Jesus knows all things, He remains unknown to many people.
- Jesus exemplifies the truth of God and desires for people to experience truth in Him. For John, truth is not an ideal but a person.
- Belief in Jesus is the key theme in John's gospel. Everything that Jesus says and does reveals His identity to others for engendering faith in them.

John's theological themes all point to Jesus. For him, theology is not an abstract intellectual exercise but an encounter with the living God through Jesus Christ His Son.

A principal feature of John's presentation of Jesus is his emphasis on the Spirit. This emphasis may be seen in the presence of the Spirit at key moments in Jesus' life as well as in Jesus' consistent and extensive teaching about the Spirit during the course of His ministry. The Spirit comes upon Jesus at His baptism at the Jordan (1:32, 33), is present to perform the signs of the new creation in His ministry, is the subject of His last remarks to the disciples before His crucifixion, and is imparted by Him to His disciples after His resurrection (20:22, 23). The significance of the Spirit's presence is discussed in the following chapters, but note that the Spirit is present with Jesus throughout His ministry. Jesus' ministry may be called a Spirited ministry.

Also, the Spirit is prominent in Jesus' thoughts and the frequent subject of His instruction. Jesus speaks of the Spirit to Nicodemus (3:3–8), the Samaritan woman (4:20–24), unnamed disciples (6:63), worshipers at the temple during the feast (7:37–39), and the twelve disciples (14:15–18; 15:26; 16:5–15). He speaks of the Spirit in relation to new birth and the kingdom of God, true worship of God, and the giving of the eternal life of God. Jesus also speaks of the Spirit in connection with His own ministry and the future ministry of the disciples with respect to sin, judgment, righteousness, and the ministry of forgiveness. John shows that the Spirit is a vital thrust of

Jesus' teaching. The theological teaching of Jesus that we find in John is profoundly pneumatological.

Theology and History in the Gospel of John

Does John's theology make his gospel as reliable as a historical book? One of the earliest descriptions of this gospel is attributed to Clement of Alexandria (d. A.D. 215) in the latter part of the second century. In a passage preserved by Eusebius (*Ecclesiastical History*, 6.14), Clement makes the tantalizing observation that John composed a "spiritual gospel" (*pneumatikon euangelion*, πνευματικὸν . . . εὐαγγέλιον). John was the last of the four Gospels to be written and was evidently composed to complement the "facts" (*sōmatika*, σωματικά) presented by Matthew and Mark (6.14). What does Clement mean when he says that John wrote a spiritual gospel? Does he mean that it contains more insight into the spiritual nature of Jesus' life and ministry than the other gospels? That it is more attentive to the divine essence than the human nature of Jesus' life? Does he mean that John focuses on the internal dimension of Jesus' life and ministry even as the other evangelists focus on the external?

Many biblical scholars interpret Clement's statement as meaning John's purpose is theological rather than historical. John is not so much interested in giving an historical record of Jesus' miracles and teachings as he is in interpreting Jesus as God's Word and describing the implications this has for mankind. This view is supported by the fact that Clement was a noted philosopher who undoubtedly was interested in John's theological interpretation of Jesus. Whether or not Clement believed John had no interest in the historical nature of Jesus' ministry is another matter.

John Calvin is representative of biblical scholarship's view of theology and history in John's gospel. He writes:

> [The synoptic gospels] are certainly not silent on Christ's coming into the world to bring salvation, to atone for the sins of the world by the sacrifice of His death and, in short, to perform all the duties of a Mediator; just as John also devotes part of his work to historical narration. But the doctrine that points out to us the power and fruit of Christ's coming appears far more clearly in him than the others. And since they all had the same object, to show Christ, the first three exhibit the body, if I may be permitted to put it like that, but John shows his soul.[8]

Here Calvin reveals the long influence of Clement's second-century observation. Whatever Clement intended to mean by the word spiritual, he understands the Gospel of John to be a work by the Spirit. Thus, he writes, "Last of all . . . encouraged by his pupils and irresistibly moved by the Spirit [*pneumati thephorēthenta*, πνεύματι θεοφορηθέντα], John writes a spiritual gospel" (*Ecclesiastical History*, 6.14). For Clement, John's presentation of Jesus' ministry is ultimately a divine work that originates in the Spirit of God.

The question of history and theology in John has been debated vigorously for a long time and will continue to be debated. All history involves interpretation and John makes it clear that he is interpreting Jesus Christ when he writes, "These are written that you may believe that Jesus is the Christ, the Son of God, and that believing you may have life in His name" (20:31). John writes in order to persuade others of his conviction that Jesus is the Messiah, the Son of God, who inaugurates a new creation through His life for those who believe in Him. This does not mean that he has created facts, changed facts, or distorted facts related to the historical story of Jesus. There is no question that John is interested in facts because he concludes his writing with the following affirmation: "This is the disciple who testifies of these things, and wrote these things; and we know that his testimony is true" (21:24). Whether John or a disciple of his wrote these words, the assertion is that the facts contained in the book are true. John describes the ministry of Jesus and presents himself as its witness. In this way, he testifies to the historical Jesus he knew.

Like the other evangelists, John is not so distracted by his proclamation about Jesus that he is careless about the history upon which it is based. The four Gospels, including John, are not historical romances.[9] So, what kind of interpretation is involved in John's gospel? It is biblical-testimonial interpretation; interpretation in the service of exhortation that makes known the historical reality of the divine life of God in Jesus Christ against the background of God's redemptive activity in the Old Testament. Such interpretation can be judged in the following ways:

- The clarity with which John shows the correlation between Jesus' ministry and the work of God in the life of the people of Israel. Does John successfully present the miracles and teachings of Jesus in a way that recalls God's work among His people as recorded in the books of the Old Testament?
- The reliability with which John presents and preserves his information about Jesus. Is John consistent in what he asserts about Jesus and

the evidence he gathers to support his assertion?

- The efficacy of John's message upon those who first read and studied it. Though initially used by sectarians to promote their views of God and His Word, John soon was accepted and recognized as authoritative by the church for the establishment of faith and teaching. It is not likely that people in the ancient world would have accepted John's account of Jesus if it were not grounded in plausible historical truth and did not affect the reality of their own lives in a dramatic positive way. The disgrace of crucifixion would have deterred them from accepting anything less.

The reader of John's gospel must ask himself or herself: "Did God really enter history in the person of Jesus to initiate a new work of creation among receptive men and women? Did He do so to initiate new creation in me?" It is appropriate that people grapple with this question today even as those who first heard Jesus had to decide for themselves the nature of His identity and truth of His claims. According to the Gospel of John, Jesus required a response when He lived among the people of Israel. Today a response to this gospel is required of those who read and study it. Is this depiction of Jesus a historical romance or is it a true historical testimony of the life of God in Jesus Christ?

The Last Shall Be First

It is interesting to note that the last of the four gospels to be written (A.D. 90–100) has the oldest surviving extant manuscripts. The earliest New Testament manuscript is the Rylands Papyrus 457 of John 18:31–33, 37, 38, dating to A.D. 125–150. A second early manuscript is the Egerton Papyrus. This gospel-like document contains several allusions to John and dates to the second century. According to early church fathers, John was the last of the four gospels to be written (*Ecclesiastical History*, 3.24; 6.14). This, along with the fact John seems to know the synoptic Gospels, points to a date after the composition and circulation of these gospels. Thus, John was likely written toward the end of the first century after the synoptic Gospels and prior to the estimated date of the John papyri. The church fathers also place John in Ephesus in the last decades of the first century (Ireneaus, *Against Heresies*, 3.1.1, 3.3.4). While other locations have been suggested (such as Antioch and Alexandria), this early church information along with John's intention to counter certain false views of Jesus (according to Irenaeus) makes Ephesus a likely place for this gospel's origin.

QUESTIONS FOR PERSONAL REFLECTION AND GROUP DISCUSSION

1. What evidence does John present to show that the ministry of Jesus represents God's new work of creation among men and women?
2. How does John outline his presentation of Jesus' ministry?
3. What kind of man was John?
4. What type of gospel does John write?
5. What is John's attitude toward the facts of Jesus' ministry?

CHAPTER 1

THE WORD IN THE BEGINNING

John 1:1–34

The First Word (John 1:1–2)

The first verse of the Gospel of John is similar to that of Genesis; they both refer to the beginning. Unlike the Gospels of Matthew and Luke, which begin with accounts of the birth of Jesus, or Mark, which introduces Jesus at the moment of His baptism, John escorts the reader to the beginning of time and space when there was simply the Word. John does not describe a so-called big bang, or narrate a struggle of cosmic forces or deities in the heavens. Instead, he observes with remarkable understatement: "In the beginning was the Word." Thus, John reveals that before there was even one human word, before the ten "words" of the Decalogue were spoken to Moses (Ex. 19), before a single word was spoken by one of God's prophets, there was the Word with God. People use words to communicate and to perform tasks. We use words to share information or to express our thoughts, feelings, and ambitions; on the other hand, we use words to build relationships and to accomplish goals. In a very real sense our words represent us when we speak them and are a verbal extension of ourselves to others. By opening his gospel with a reference to the Word that was *with* God in the beginning that also *is* God, John boldly says that God's Word is the extension of God Himself. The thoughts, feelings, and ambitions of God are bound up in His Word, able to accomplish all of His purposes.

> *In the beginning was the Word, and the Word was with God, and the Word was God. He was in the beginning with God (vv. 1, 2).*

John begins his gospel with a statement about the Word of God in the form of a brief chiasmus—a literary device in which the words of parallel lines are reversed.

WHAT IS A CHIASMUS?

A chiasmus is not only a literary device in which the words of parallel lines are reversed; it may also describe the structure of larger literary units. A literary unit is a chiasmus when its elements (lines, sentences, paragraphs or even larger sections) are arranged in sequential inverted order (A, B, C, C1, B1, A1) to establish their correlation and to give emphasis to the elements at the center of the structure. John makes frequent use of this device in his gospel.

This technique is used to draw attention to an opposing relationship of parallel thoughts. For this reason the lines should be read "inside-out." So, John 1:1, 2 reads this way:

> A.   In the beginning was the Word.
> B.   The Word was with God.
> B1.   The Word was God.
> A1.   He was in the beginning with God.

Thus, clauses B and B1 emphasize the Word's relation to God while clauses A and A1 set the Word in the beginning. The chiasmus of these opening verses highlights the fact that the Word has been an extension of God from the beginning.

The Logos in the Gospel of John

The Greek word that John translates as "word" in verse one is *logos* (ὁ λόγος), a common Greek noun that, depending on its context, also may be translated into English as "matter," "speech," or "expression." Greek philosophers generally used the term to signify rational explanation and regarded it as the means by which the material and moral order of the universe was established and could be understood. The Jewish philosopher Philo used *logos* in a variety of ways. Primarily, he used it to describe the rational aspect of God's mind by which He created heaven and earth. This meant that the universe itself had a rational structure. Secondarily, he used it to describe the rational aspect of humanity by which the universe may be known. John is not constrained by these notions of *logos*. For him *logos* is not exclusive rationality or order or universal structure. Rather, the *logos* is personality— a self-expression of God that has existed from the beginning and was in the beginning. But this is not all. John also uses the term throughout his gospel.

In fact, he uses it thirty-five times outside of chapter one, most often in reference to Jesus' teaching. This use of *logos* suggests that John intends to connect "the Word in the beginning with God" with the word spoken by Jesus throughout His ministry. John shows that the Word present at creation continues to perform the creative will of God through Jesus' own teaching. Below is a selection of passages in John that link *logos* with Jesus.

Passage	Logos and Jesus in the Gospel of John
2:22	The disciples remember and believe the logos Jesus spoke about Himself concerning His death and resurrection.
4:39–42	Many Samaritans believe the logos the woman speaks about Jesus as well as the logos Jesus speaks about Himself.
4:50, 51	The nobleman believes the logos Jesus speaks and discovers that his son has been healed.
5:24; 8:31–37, 43; 12:48	Those who hear and believe the logos of Jesus will have eternal life and be His disciples. However, there are some who refuse to receive His logos and others who do not understand it. Those who reject Jesus will be judged by His logos.
6:53–60	What Jesus says about His flesh and blood is a hard logos.
7:40	The logos Jesus speaks about rivers of living water cause some of the people to declare that He is a prophet.
8:51–55	Those who keep Jesus' logos will not experience death; Jesus keeps the logos of His Father.
14:23, 24	Loving Jesus is defined as keeping His logos; the logos Jesus speaks is from God His Father.
15:3	The logos of Jesus makes His disciples clean.
15:20	The disciples are to remember the logos that Jesus has spoken to them about persecution.
17:6–20	The disciples have kept God's logos. Jesus prays for those who hear the logos of the disciples.

Several points can be made in view of the connection between the *logos* and Jesus:

- As already noted, the *logos* in the beginning continues to be spoken by God through Jesus and His own *logos*. God remains active in His creation to forge relationships with people in this way.
- The *logos* of Jesus refers to His teaching. It stands for specific instruction given by Jesus concerning God His Father and the eternal life that He offers (5:24; 7:40; 8:51–55).
- The response of faith to the *logos* of Jesus releases the creative power of God into people's lives. The Samaritans declare Jesus to be the Savior of the World when they hear and believe the *logos* of the woman about Jesus and that of Jesus about Himself (4:37–41); the nobleman believes the *logos* of Jesus and finds that his son is healed (4:50). Jesus promises that everyone who hears and believes His *logos* will receive eternal life (5:24); those who reject His *logos*, however, will not receive life but will experience judgment instead (12:48).
- Jesus' *logos* should not be regarded as mere human instruction or communication. It serves to fulfill the very purpose of God. Some of the strongest statements made by Jesus to His opponents and by His opponents to Him in John originate in the fact that Jesus claims that His *logos* is that of God (8:37–47). His *logos* has divine origins.
- Fifth, the disciples who have heard and accepted Jesus' *logos* (2:22) will themselves speak the *logos* to others (17:20). The work of new creation that starts with Jesus and His *logos* will continue in the ministry of His disciples as they declare His *logos* to others.

The Creative Word (John 1:3–5)

John understands the *logos* or Word of God to be the self-expression of God in the beginning. This is not all. John further defines this Word with several additional observations about it:

- The Word is the source of all created things.
- Life exists in the Word.
- The Word is light that provides life for all people.
- The Word that is light shines in darkness.
- The Word that is light is not comprehended by the darkness.

John builds on his initial statement that the Word was with God in the beginning by asserting that the Word was instrumental in creation, especially in giving life to mankind. He draws on the imagery of light to describe both the nature of the Word as well as the function of the Word in creation. The phrase, "And God said," occurs ten times in Genesis chapter one, emphasizing the fact that God created through His Word. (See Gen. 1:3, 6, 9, 11, 14, 20, 24, 26, 29.) It is not a coincidence that John asserts that "all things were made through [the Word]." How does God create? He creates by speaking His Word. The Word of God is a creative Word.

THE ORDER OF CREATION

As illustrated in the table below, John follows the order of creation in Genesis 1 in describing the Word of God. In the opening verses of the Bible we read that God first creates the environment in which life will exist and then creates the life to live in that environment. After this, He creates mankind who is dependent on the totality of creation for survival. Thus, the order of creation moves from the physical environment to life to human life. Likewise, in verses three and four of John 1, the activity of the Word is described in a similar way. First, John says that all things were created through the Word and, second, he observes that the Word possesses the life for mankind. Not only is John's dependence on Genesis evident, but also his intention to emphasize the life-giving capacity of the Word.

Genesis	The Creative Activity of God	John	The Work of the Word
1:1–19	God creates the physical environment for the creatures of the sea, air, and land.	1:3	All things were made by the Word.
1:20–28	God creates all life, culminating in human life.	1:4	In [the Word] was life that is the life of mankind.

All things were made through Him, and without Him nothing was made that was made (v. 3).

John highlights the creative work of the Word with both a positive and a negative statement. "All things were made through Him" represents a positive observation on the work of the Word; "without Him nothing was made that was made" is the same observation made in a negative way. This type of *contrast parallelism* emphasizes the basic fact that the Word creates.

In Him was life, and the life was the light of men (v. 4).

John relates the Word to both life and light. These complementary themes are developed throughout the rest of his gospel. By presenting life and light as equal and mutual aspects of the Word, John can assert that "the life [of the Word] was the light of men." Later in the gospel, Jesus identifies Himself as both life and light to all people when He says He is "the Light of the World" who gives to those who follow Him "the light of life" (8:12). This linkage of life and light sets Jesus' ministry against the background of creation in which both light and life are prominent. There, God's first act is to create light, which He separates from the darkness and names day (vv. 3–5). After forming the water and dry land, God creates initial life when He brings into existence plants and various kinds of animals. He then creates Adam and breathes "the breath of life" into him (2:7). Thus, the creation account in Genesis shows that light is the context of God's life-creating work. According to John, the life-giving nature of Jesus' ministry issues from the fact that He is the Word of God who is the light of men. Jesus Himself said that He is the Light of the World. This description of God's Word as light is not unique to John. The psalmist makes the same observation when he writes, "Your word is a lamp to my feet and a light to my path" (Ps. 119:105). Later he states, "The entrance of your word [into the psalmist's life] gives light" (v. 130). Of course, his use of "word" in these verses is in reference to the law of God, which is his delight (vv. 70, 77, 174) and worth more than silver and gold (v. 72). Nonetheless, the law of God that the psalmist describes as God's word is viewed by him as light. Likewise, when he petitions God, "Revive me according to your word" (vv. 25, 107; 116) and "Strengthen me according to your word" (v. 28), he is recognizing the life-giving capacity of God's word as expressed in His law. This declaration is explicit in his claim, "Your Word has given me life" (v. 50). Thus, the psalmist describes God's Law, which is an expression of His Word, both as light and life-giving. It is in line with this tradition that John declares the Word to be both life and light.

And the light shines in the darkness, and the darkness did not comprehend it (v. 5).

John extends his figurative use of light as an expression of God's Word by saying that while it shines in the darkness it is not comprehended by the darkness. In this way he contrasts the positive statement of the Word in verse four ("the life [of the Word] was the light of men") with this negative observation. John typically uses contrast to give definition to a matter or subject under discussion. Light and darkness is one example of such dualism in John. Other examples include knowledge and ignorance, truth and falsehood, belief and unbelief, that from above and that from below. These will be discussed as they appear in the gospel.

The Greek word that is translated "comprehend" (*katalambanō*, κατα-λαμβάνω) occurs three times in John's gospel and fifteen times in the New Testament, often with the meaning of "grasp" or "catch." It suggests the ability or power to take possession of something. Its meaning here is not only that darkness cannot make sense of the light; rather, it cannot take control of the light (as to extinguish it, for example). This notion is present in Jesus' declaration, "A little while longer the light is with you. Walk while you have the light, lest darkness overtake you" (12:35). Here *katalambanō* is translated by "overtake." The word is also used to describe the adulterous woman as one who is "caught" in her sin (8:3). In these three passages John uses this term to speak of exertion or control. Darkness may be the antithesis of light, but it is not equal to the light and cannot control the light. In these verses John reveals that in the coming of the Word as light a new day of creation has dawned. The light remains separate from the darkness and represents the beginning of a good and wondrous work of God.

Ignorance and Knowledge in the Gospel of John

Though darkness cannot control the light, the light remains unknown to the world and, in effect, is darkened to it. Here in chapter one and elsewhere in the gospel, John uses irony to describe Jesus and His ministry. Everything has been made by God's Word, which is light, yet the world does not know the light of its creation. The light of God's Word has been eclipsed in the world. John draws attention to this lack of knowledge in chapter one.

First, he says that the world does not know the light that made it (v. 10). Second, he quotes John the Baptist as saying that the hoped-for deliverer of the people is in their midst but not known to them (v. 26). And, third, he quotes the Baptist himself saying that he did not know this Word until He was revealed to him (v. 31). A lack of knowledge is descriptive of the general condition of the world into which God's Word comes as light. In 1:26, 35 the word *know* translates the Greek word *oida* (οἶδα) a distinctive linguistic expression for John in that he uses it more than eighty times in his gospel. In fact, he uses this word more than Matthew, Mark, and Luke combined. In general, *oida* is distinguished from *ginōskō* (γινώσκω) another Greek word for "know" that refers to knowledge obtained through insight or close observation. However, *oida* connotes relational knowledge like that which issues from personal relationship.[10]

Chapter one makes clear the fact that the world does not know and does not stand in relation to the Word of God. The light shines in the darkness, the darkness cannot control it, and still the light is not known. Because the world does not know the light, it follows that it does not know Jesus (17:25) nor the Spirit (14:7). In fact, John's gospel depicts widespread ignorance of Jesus. At first Nicodemus does not know or understand Jesus' teaching (3:10, 11) and the Samaritan woman does not know His identity until He reveals that He is the Messiah (4:11, 25). The blind man does not know who healed him when he is questioned (5:13). Many think they know Jesus but in reality they do not. Unnamed people in Jerusalem claim to know Jesus, but He says that though they may know where He lives they do not know His Father (7:26–29; 8:14, 19). Not surprisingly, His opponents do not know Him. How can they? They do not keep His words and do not know His Father (8:55). Moreover, Nicodemus' question, "Does our law judge a man before it hears him and knows what he is doing?" indicates that the leadership does not fully understand the nature of Jesus' ministry (7:51). And the fact that the leaders ask, "Who are you?" reveals their ignorance of His nature and teaching (8:25–27). The only thing they are certain about is that Jesus has a demon (8:52). Not all are ignorant, however. Peter knows that Jesus is the Messiah (6:69) and Jesus says that the disciples know that He has come from the Father and done the will of the Father (17:7, 8, 25).

To accept Jesus' words is to enter into a state of understanding. He says, "You will know the truth and the truth will set you free" (8:32). It results in knowing the Father (14:7) and issues in eternal life (17:3). Full understanding will come to the people when Jesus is lifted up and glorified (8:28). Though the world does not know Jesus, Jesus knows the world. John observes that Jesus knows all things (21:17). This includes people. He knows all men (2:24, 25): He knows the evil intention of His opponents (5:42), the desire of the people to make Him a king (6:15), and the murmuring of certain disciples (6:60). But His knowledge of people is not wholly defensive. He also knows His sheep (10:14, 27; 13:18).

Not only does Jesus know the nature of men and women, He knows His Father as well. Jesus knows the One who sent Him (7:29; 8:55; 10:15) and He is confident that His Father hears Him (11:42) since He and His Father are one (10:38). Furthermore, Jesus knows the purpose of His Father and He knows that He has fulfilled God's purpose in His death (19:28). Thus, Jesus knows both the nature of men and women as well as the purpose of God His Father. How is this possible? It is possible because Jesus is the Word of God who has become flesh.

The Light and the Word (John 1:6–18)

The role of the Baptist is clearly defined by John in this passage. He is a witness to the light of God's Word so that people may believe. A witness is needed because the world does not know the Light even though it was made by the Light. Those who believe in the light will become children of God since they are born by the will of God and not the will of the flesh (vv. 12, 13). This leads to the astonishing statement, "The Word became flesh and dwelt among us" (v. 14). Not only did the Word become flesh, but the glory of God was manifested in the presence of those who knew the Word.

There was a man sent from God, whose name was John (v. 6).

The Baptist is introduced as John, "a man sent from God." Only his first name is given. As mentioned in the introduction, if the apostle John did not write the gospel we would expect some designation or title to be given to the Baptist to distinguish him from the apostle. In any case, he joins a long list of messengers and prophets in the Bible, beginning with Moses, who are described as coming from God to speak God's message to His people. Jesus is described in a similar manner throughout the gospel as one sent by the Father. God speaks His Word, He sends His messengers, and He initiates a relationship with His people.

This man came for a witness, to bear witness of the Light, that all through him might believe (v. 7).

In the ancient world, people were dependent on the witness of others for the purpose of personal identification in formal proceedings. The verb *martyreō* (μαρτυρέω) is used more than thirty times in John's gospel with the basic meaning of "bear witness." Initially it is used as a job description for the Baptist (vv. 7, 8, 15, 32, 34). He is sent to identify the Light of God so that people may believe in the light. This implies that they would not be able to identify the light for themselves otherwise.

He was not that Light, but was sent to bear witness of that Light (v. 8).

John repeats himself when he says that the Baptist gives witness to the Light of God but that he himself is not the light. Why does he do this? It is possible that there were people at the time of the apostle who still identified with the Baptist. When Paul first arrived in Ephesus in the mid-fifties he encountered disciples who were unfamiliar with the apostolic teaching about the Holy Spirit. They only knew John's baptism. After Paul's instruction, they were baptized in the name of Jesus and filled with the Spirit (see Acts 19:1–7). A tradition related to the ministry of the Baptist may have continued, however, and would explain the Gospel of John's emphasis on the supportive nature of the Baptist's ministry. Regardless, John clearly describes the role of the Baptist as being a witness to the Light.

> *That was the true Light which gives light to every man coming into the world (v. 9).*

The Light to which the Baptist is a witness is the true (*alēthinos*, ἀληθινός) Light. Throughout his gospel John uses the adjective *true* (and its cognate *alēthēs*, ἀληθής) to indicate what is genuine in nature and revelatory of God. Moreover, for John, *true* signifies what is eternal and changeless. Several examples of its use in John make this clear:

- First, by revealing Himself in the Son, God shows that He is true (3:33; 7:28; 8:26; 17:3). The eternal and changeless nature of God is revealed in Jesus.
- The testimony about Jesus is true in that it consistently supports what He says about His relation to God (5:31–37; 8:13–18; 21:24).
- Jesus is the true Bread from heaven (6:32) whose flesh and blood is true food and drink (6:55). He is true in that He offers the eternal life of God to the world.
- Jesus is the true Vine in which the disciples are grafted as branches and have life in Him (15:1).
- In John 1:9, the Baptist speaks of the authentic Light not an artificial light; a light that discloses the reality of God in the world.

> *He was in the world, and the world was made through Him, and the world did not know Him. He came to His own, and His own did not receive Him (vv. 10, 11).*

John's statement here extends his earlier observation in verse five. There he says that the Light shines in the darkness but is not controlled by it. Here he

THE LIGHT IN THE WORLD

In verse five John remarks that "the darkness did not control [the Light]; in verse ten he says that "the world did not know [the Light]"; and in verse eleven he observes that "His own [those things created by the Light] did not receive Him." John has carefully sharpened the focus of the relation of Light to that which is not Light in these verses.

- Darkness does not control the Light (v. 5).
- The world does not know the Light (v. 10).
- His own did not receive Him who is the Light (v. 11).

John moves from showing the relation of Light to undifferentiated darkness, then to the world, and finally to God's beloved people. In the present state of things there is no relation between Light and God's creation. The world into which the Light shines is utterly dark.

says that Light was in the world—even made the world—yet was not known by the world or by "His own" (which refers specifically to those things created by the Light).

> *But as many as received Him, to them He gave the right to become children of God, to those who believe in His name: who were born, not of blood, nor of the will of the flesh, nor of the will of man, but of God. And the Word became flesh and dwelt among us, and we beheld His glory, the glory as of the only begotten of the Father, full of grace and truth (vv. 12–14).*

In the nadir of darkness, those who receive the Light and believe in His name are given the right to be children of God. The conferral of childhood upon those who know God is described elsewhere as an act of love (1 John 3:1). The Greek word that is translated "right" is *exousia* (ἐξουσία) a term that often has the meaning of power. The Word that is light gives power to be children of God to those who believe in the name of the Light. Such power is not their possession, of course, but belongs to God. Those who become children of God do so by the creative power of His Word. Verse thirteen describes those who believe in the name of the Light as those born of God. Such birth is not a natural birth—it is not by blood, the will of the flesh, or the will of man. It is divine birth that originates with God.

The Word that was in the beginning with God took on human form and lived among men and women. John uses the Greek verb *skēnoō* (σκηνόω) to indicate the physical presence of the Word among the people. Other than its use in the book of Revelation, this is the only use of the verb in the New Testament. Its Old Testament usage suggests the meaning of "dwell in a tent," which, when used of God, figuratively describes His presence among His people as in the Exodus from Egypt. For John, the human-bound Word of God makes known the revelation of God among the people in the course of their deliverance.

This incarnated Word is described as "only begotten," translating the Greek *monogenēs* (μονογενής). John uses this term not to signify the birth or generation of the Word, but to mean that the Word is one of a kind or unique. He uses the term four times to describe Jesus' relationship to God (1:14, 18; 3:16, 18; see also 1 John 4:9). The Word is unique in that it is eternally related to God ("the Word was God") and inextricably joined to mankind ("the Word became flesh"). It is also unique due to its status as the only Word that reveals God to the world. For this reason John says that it is replete with grace and truth. It is full of grace because God has forever joined His Word to the world of human experience. It is full of truth, since the Word is the authentic expression of God.

In these verses (vv. 12–14), John adroitly links new birth among those who receive the Light of God with the incarnation of the Word of God. He reveals that new birth in God is possible only through the birth of the Word among people. He accomplishes this by using contrast parallelism, a literary technique that binds together seemingly opposing ideas. In this instance, the truth that children of God are not born of flesh but God's will (or Spirit, according to 3:5–8) is contrasted with (and bound to) the truth that the Word of God has become flesh to reveal God's glory. Children of God are not born of the flesh, They are born by the will of God (vv. 12, 13) The Word of God becomes flesh, revealing God's glory (v. 14)

> *John bore witness of Him and cried out, saying, "This was He of whom I said, 'He who comes after me is preferred before me, for He was before me'" (v. 15).*

The Baptist's witness includes the observation that the One who follows him was before him in the sense that He was first. All words, all messages, all prophets come after the first Word of God.

> *And of His fullness we have all received, and grace for grace. For the law was given through Moses, but grace and truth came through Jesus Christ (vv. 16, 17).*

God's grace is not only amazing but also abundant in that it has been given to all people out of the fullness of the Word that has become human. John finally identifies this Word as Jesus Christ through whom the grace and truth of God is given. Moreover, he compares the grace of Jesus to the Law of Moses. Just as the Law of Moses represented the way of life provided by God for His people to live as His people, so also the grace and truth of Jesus is the way of life now available to all.

> *No one has seen God at any time. The only begotten Son, who is in the bosom of the Father, He has declared Him (v. 18).*

The unqualified relationship between Jesus and God is emphasized in several ways in this verse. First, no one has ever seen God. The Greek grammar is emphatic. John's statement is particularly striking in that it is made in the context of his reference to Moses who, according to the book of Numbers, spoke with God face to face (12:8; see Deut. 34:10; compare Ex. 33:20). Jacob declares that he saw the face of God and lived (Gen. 32:30). Though these references may be regarded as figurative, John infers that the Son has seen the Father. Second, the metaphor of sonship and fatherhood is used to describe the special relationship between Jesus and God. This metaphor had a long history of use prior to this time in reference to the people of Israel and God. The idea of sonship first describes the people of God who are delivered from servitude in Egypt. In fact, the people in bondage are described as God's firstborn son (Ex. 4:22) who are called out of Egypt (Hos. 11:1). Also, a number of passages describe God as a father (Ps. 68:5; 103:13; Is. 63:16; 64:8; Mal. 2:10). The fact that John uses this metaphor as an initial way of speaking of Jesus and God draws attention to intimate relationship shared between them. Third, not only is Jesus a Son to God His Father, but He is the *monogenēs* Son—the unique Son from the bosom or heart of God, meaning the Son represents the affection of God's desire and intention of His will.

A Witness to the Word (John 1:19–28)

John records the testimony given by the Baptist about Jesus. His testimony is given to priests, Levites, and Pharisees, all of whom are religious leaders who have genuine interest in the Baptist and his message. Not only does he understand his role and status in relation to Jesus, but he also understands Jesus' role and status as well, as indicated by his identification of Jesus as "the Lamb of God" and "Son of God."

*Now this is the testimony of John, when the Jews sent priests and
Levites from Jerusalem to ask him, "Who are you?" (v. 19).*

Religious leaders connected with the temple in Jerusalem have come to ask
the Baptist, "Who are you?" His activity and teaching concerning the Word
of God has gained their attention.

The Jews in the Gospel of John

The priests and Levites do not approach the Baptist on their own initiative.
They are sent by the Jews in Jerusalem to gather information about him. This
is John's first reference to people he describes throughout his gospel simply
and sometimes provocatively as "the Jews." Who are these people? Scholars
have closely studied this and have reached different conclusions. Their difference of opinion is due to the fact the expression *the Jews* is used in a variety of ways in the Gospel of John. Sometimes it is used to define the festivals
of the people, as in "the Passover of the Jews" (2:13; 6:4; 11:55), or traditional
customs and practices, like "the purification of the Jews" (2:6). Scholars see
the use of the term in such passages as descriptive of the ethnic or national
roots and the geographic origins of these festivals and traditions. Other
times the term is used in relation to Jesus as when He is called the King of
the Jews (18:33; 19:19, 21), which some understand as "the king of the people
of Judea." He tells the Samaritan woman that "salvation is from the Jews"
(4:22) in the sense that the origin of messianic aspirations lies with the people of Judea. Most often, however, "the Jews" describes a faction of people
with whom Jesus has an antagonistic relationship (though there are occasions when the reference speaks of those who believe in Him). Their hostility toward Jesus is such that John says they accuse Him of being demon possessed (7:20; 8:48, 52; 10:20, 21) and attempt to kill Him on several occasions
(5:15–18; 7:1, 16–19; 8:59; 10:31–39).[11]

Who are these people who oppose Jesus? Is the term *the Jews* a general reference to ethnic Jews? Is it a reference to people who live in Judea? May it be
a specific reference to religious people like the Pharisees? These references
are unlikely. First, many Jewish people are intrigued by Jesus' teaching and
miracles and declare that He has come from God. Not all Jews respond to
Jesus in a uniform way. Some believe while others do not. Second, though
many Pharisees strongly oppose Jesus and are depicted as antagonistic
toward Him, not all are so described. Nicodemus, for example, is sympa-
thetic to Him (3:1, 2; 7:50, 51; 19:39–42). Thus, it is unlikely that the term *the
Jews* is a cipher for the people in general or the Pharisees in particular. It is

more likely that John usually, though not exclusively, uses the term *the Jews* to describe the temple leadership in Jerusalem. This leadership would include top officials with a vested interest in the temple, but not limited to any particular group such as the Pharisees or Sadducees.

What does John reveal about these people?

- He introduces the Jews as being from Jerusalem (1:19). It seems that they are headquartered there. Jesus hesitates to go to Jerusalem for one of the festivals because of His concern for the Jews who, apparently, reside there (7:1, 11) and He leaves Jerusalem to get away from them (11:54).
- They possess an exceptional degree of authority. Not only are they able to send priests and Levites to question the Baptist (1:19) but they inspire fear in others. The people are afraid (7:13), the parents of the blind man who is healed are afraid (9:22), and Joseph of Arimathea, who asks for the body of Jesus in secret, is afraid of the Jews (19:38). Even Nicodemus, described by John as a ruler of the Jews, approaches Jesus at night out of fear for what his colleagues might say and do (3:2).
- The Jews are offended by Jesus' action in the temple and challenge His claim that the temple will be destroyed and rebuilt in three days (2:13–22). Those who were responsible for the operation of the temple would be particularly alarmed by such talk.
- Jesus most often encounters the Jews when He is in Jerusalem. (An exception is John's reference to the Jews in 6:41–59.) They surround Him when He is in Solomon's Porch in the temple for the Feast of Dedication and ask if He is the Messiah (10:22–24) and they criticize the healings that are performed on the Sabbath near the temple (5:1–18; 9:13–34). Furthermore, they are present when Lazarus is raised from the dead in Bethany, a village two miles outside the city.
- John shows the prominence of the Jews in Jesus' interrogation before Pilate (18:31, 38; 19:7). Only top leadership would have such access to the Roman governor.

Why not call these people "the authorities" or even "the temple elites"? It may be that John draws from the understanding that they had of themselves. That is, the temple leadership and administration in Jerusalem saw themselves as representatives of the people due to their supervision of the ritual worship and management of the most treasured symbol of God's presence in the nation—the temple. They saw themselves as stewards of Judaic identity in the nation through their special status and role among the people. In their eyes they were *the* Jews among the Jewish people. Thus, John often uses the term *the Jews* to speak of the temple authorities who are largely opposed to Jesus' ministry.

> *He confessed, and did not deny, but confessed, "I am not the Christ." And they asked him, "What then? Are you Elijah?" He said, "I am not." "Are you the Prophet?" And he answered, "No." Then they said to him, "Who are you, that we may give an answer to those who sent us? What do you say about yourself?" He said: "I am the voice of one crying in the wilderness: 'Make straight the way of the LORD' as the prophet Isaiah said." (vv. 20–23).*

It is uncommon to answer the question, "Who are you?" by stating who you are not. Yet, this is how the Baptist answers the question posed to him. By answering in this way, he continues to assert the preeminence of the One who comes after him. The Baptist says, 1) he is not the Christ, the Messiah, 2) he is not Elijah, and 3) he is not the Prophet.

- John the Baptist is not the Messiah who will fulfill the expectations of the people and deliver them from their oppressors. The popular eschatological view of the Messiah among the people was that he would be a political or military figure who would expel the Romans from the land and establish a government of equity and blessing. Most views of the Messiah drew from Psalm 2 and its description of an anointed king who would rule over Israel at the end of days. Some believed this royal figure would come from the royal line of David (Ps. 17).

- He is not Elijah. A considerable tradition of belief had developed around this classical prophet due to the fact that he was caught up into heaven by a chariot of fire (2 Kin. 2:9–11). The people expected him to return and continue his ministry of miracles in their midst. The prophet Malachi wrote that Elijah would appear before the Day of the Lord and establish peace among God's people: "I will send you Elijah the prophet before the coming of the great and dreadful day of the Lord. And he will turn the hearts of the fathers to the children, and the hearts of the children to their fathers" (4:5, 6). Others said that he would restore the tribes of Jacob (Sirach 48:10).

- He is not the Prophet. Moses had spoken of one who would follow him and speak God's words to the people as Moses spoke God's word (Deut. 18:15–19). Of course, the words of Moses brought deliverance to the people from Egypt and pointed to a new way of life in the land of Canaan. The people looked forward to this prophet who would speak such words to them and deliver them as Moses did their ancestors.

The Baptist's answer is loud and clear: I am not your deliverer! The temple emissaries from Jerusalem ask again, "Who are you?" To which the Baptist responds, "The voice of one crying in the wilderness, make straight the way of the LORD." By reciting from Isaiah (40:3), the Baptist does place himself within a *tradition* of deliverance.

Originally, this passage from Isaiah represented a promise of deliverance for a people in exile. The prophet declares that their deliverance is imminent (v. 2) because the way has been prepared for the Lord to come to them (vv. 3, 4). With these words from Isaiah, the Baptist identifies himself as one whose message is given during a time of exile before the coming of the Lord. The Baptist not only identifies himself with the prophet of exile but he identifies the people of his own time with the people of exile. The people of his time are in virtual exile. He declares that their deliverance is at hand with the coming of the Lord. Their deliverer is on the way. In addition, by identifying himself with the prophet Isaiah, the Baptist identifies himself with Isaiah's God who is depicted in this passage (Is. 40) as One whose word is eternal (v. 8), who cares for His people as a shepherd (v. 11), and as One who has created all things by His Spirit (vv. 12–14, 21–23, 26–28). Isaiah envisions the God who will deliver His people from exile as a Creator of heaven and earth. By bringing His people back from exile He performs a new act of creation among them. The ministry of the Baptist anticipates yet another new act of creation by the One who will come after him.

> Now those who were sent were from the Pharisees. And they asked him, saying, "Why then do you baptize if you are not the Christ, nor Elijah, nor the Prophet?" John answered them, saying, "I baptize with water, but there stands One among you whom you do not know. It is He who, coming after me, is preferred before me, whose sandal strap I am not worthy to loose." These things were done in Bethabara beyond the Jordan, where John was baptizing (vv. 24–28).

The Jews from Jerusalem who have sent the priests and Levites include Pharisees.

The priests and Levites ask why John baptizes. He seemingly ignores the question by answering that he baptizes with water. Certainly, they can see this! Yet, the oblique nature of his response does represent an answer to their question. He has already identified himself as one who prepares the way for the Lord, meaning his baptism with water is preparatory ministry for the greater work of God's deliverance. This deliverance will come through One who is already present among them but not known to them. What did John's baptism represent? The priests and Levites were familiar with the various washings established in the Torah and practiced by the people. For example, the priests traced their own ritual washings back to Aaron (Ex. 30:17–21; 40:30–33) and they knew the purification requirements of people who were viewed as impure or unclean (Lev. 17:15, 16). Their response to the Baptist indicates that his ministry of baptism would make sense to them if he were the Messiah, Elijah, or the Prophet. Since he declines to identify himself in any of these ways, they are perplexed. What is the Baptist doing? It is possible that John's baptism has some connection to the purification washings required for Gentile converts to Judaism. Even as non-Jews would undergo ritual washings as part of their conversion to their new faith, so also the people coming to the Baptist are being washed as they repent of their sins as a sign of renewed commitment to their old faith. Of course, if John's baptism has any connection with Gentile washing it has been developed by him to emphasize repentance and forgiveness of sins (Matt. 3:1–12; Mark 1:4, 5; Luke 3:3–14). For the Baptist, repentance meant a return to the covenant of Moses. Repentance was the acknowledgement of the primacy of God's Word in the Torah of the covenant and a commitment to living according to its guidelines.

Nonetheless, the priests and Levites do not understand why the Baptist does what he does if he is not the Messiah or the Prophet. They see such baptism in terms of God's final work of salvation by His anointed representative while the Baptist sees it in terms of preparation for God's great work of deliverance. The Baptist sees himself as less than a servant to the Deliverer who will come after him since he is not worthy to untie His sandals. Once again, the emphasis is not on the Baptist but on the One who comes after him. This One is preferred to him (v. 15), is present but not known to them (v. 26), and is of such status that he is not worthy to loosen His sandals (v. 27). The Gospel of John places this initial account of the Baptist in Bethabara, a town east of the Jordan River. One ancient map locates the town on the west side of the river. The oldest manuscripts of John give the name of this place as Bethany.

The Lamb of God (1:29–31)

In this brief section, the Baptist identifies Jesus as the Lamb of God who prepares for public ministry by submitting to baptism in the Jordan River. The sacrificial nature of Jesus' life and ministry is indicated by the Baptist's pronouncement. It should be noted that he does not say "the One who will become God's lamb." Jesus is already the Lamb of God. In that the Word from the beginning has become flesh, the sacrificial work of Jesus has already begun.

> *The next day John saw Jesus coming toward him, and said, "Behold! The Lamb of God who takes away the sin of the world! This is He of whom I said, 'After me comes a Man who is preferred before me, for He was before me'" (vv. 29, 30).*

Upon seeing Jesus, the Baptist identifies Him as "the Lamb of God who takes away the sin of the world." This identification is meaningful for several reasons.

- The sacrificial nature of Jesus' life and ministry is recognized and announced by the Baptist. Lambs were offered every morning and evening as part of the temple worship (Ex. 29:38–42; Num. 28:4). They were sometimes offered as freewill offerings (Lev. 22:23), burnt offerings (Gen. 22:7, 8), peace offerings (Lev. 3:1–7), and as an atonement for sin (Lev. 5:6; Num. 6:12–14).
- The sacrifice of lambs was integral to the celebration of Passover (Ex. 12). So common was the sacrifice of lambs in ancient Israel that it was used to describe the suffering and death of an innocent person (2 Sam. 12:1–6; Is. 53:7). Even Jeremiah the prophet describes himself as a lamb led to the slaughter (Jer. 11:10). Such a title would cause people to think of their dependence on God's grace through the various sacrifices for maintaining their relationship with Him. It would cause them to reflect on their national story of deliverance that was commemorated annually at Passover when they would sacrifice lambs as their ancestors did at the beginning of the Exodus.
- This connects Jesus' ministry with that of the Baptist. Whereas the Baptist called the people to repentance—a turning back to God through the Mosaic covenant—the Lamb of God is the means by which this covenantal relationship may now be experienced. For this reason, the One who follows the Baptist is greater than the Baptist since He fulfills the promise of the Baptist.

- Jesus is *God's* Lamb. The Baptist's pronouncement clearly reveals that
  the lamb is not provided by the people or the nation. Even as God
  has spoken His Word in the darkness, so also He has provided His
  Lamb for the sins of the people. This recalls the ram that God provided for Abraham in place of Isaac on the mountain (Gen. 22:1–14).
  What He did for Abraham, He now does for all those who identify
  with Abraham by providing His own Lamb.

*"I did not know Him; but that He should be revealed to Israel,
therefore I came baptizing with water" (v. 31).*

The Baptist is not unlike those who have come to question him or even the
world in general. He did not know anything about the One who would follow him and succeed him except that He must be revealed *to Israel*. This reference is important in that it connects the appearance of Jesus, the Word
from the beginning, with Nathanael, Nicodemus, and the Samaritan woman
who follow in John's narrative. The Word of God in Jesus must be revealed
to Israel as represented in these three individuals just as God revealed
Himself to ancient Israel through His Torah. The One who follows the
Baptist is identified as "a Man." The word translates the Greek *anēr* (ὁ ἀνήρ;
male or husband), meaning that he is not to be regarded only as the ideal or
representative human, but that he is fully human. This identification affirms
John's earlier statement that "the Word became flesh and dwelt among us"
(v. 14) at the same time it anticipates Pilate's declaration to all the people,
"Behold, the Man" (*anthrōpos,* ὁ ἄνθρωπος; 19:5). From birth to baptism to
crucifixion, Jesus is a man who lives a human life and dies a human death.
This depiction of Jesus by John stands alongside the Jesus who is the Word
from the beginning through whom all things were made. The wonder of the
divine Word of God that is also a man who lives in the world is the subject
of John's gospel and is to be the object of all people's faith. The Baptist links
his ministry of water baptism to the revelation of God's Word in Jesus. The
message of repentance and ministry of baptism prepared the way for the
coming of God's Word in Jesus as the Lamb of God to bring about a new
deliverance for God's people.

The Spirit and the Word (1:32–34)

The Word from the beginning is about to be spoken in an unprecedented
and unique way to God's people. The very breath or Spirit of God comes
upon the Word at this moment of renewal and restoration. Not only does the

Spirit meet the Word in the person of Jesus, but Jesus will baptize with the same Spirit. The new work of creation will continue among Jesus' own followers.

And John bore witness, saying, "I saw the Spirit descending from heaven like a dove, and He remained upon Him" (v. 32).

John begins his gospel with an account of the Word. In fact, the first eighteen verses should be viewed as an extended description of the Word. Now John begins his narration of Jesus' public ministry by introducing the Holy Spirit. Even as the Word was in the beginning with God, so the Holy Spirit of God is with Jesus at the beginning of His ministry. Interestingly, John does not record Jesus' baptism; rather, he reports what the Baptist says about it. The Baptist bears witness that he saw the Spirit come from heaven and rest on Jesus. Significantly, the Spirit *remains* (*menō*, μένω) on Him. The Greek imperfect tense of *menō* is used by John to highlight the permanent presence of the Spirit with Jesus during the course of His ministry. This fact is repeated in verse 33. The coming of the Spirit was not a momentary, inspirational event, but the beginning of an abiding relationship between Jesus and God's Spirit for the purpose of eternal life.

The Word that was with God and was indeed God has come in the person of Jesus who has the very Spirit of God abide with Him as He begins His ministry of signs and teaching. New life comes by God's Word and God's Spirit. Genesis 1 describes God as creating by His Word. The phrase *and God said* is the expression that introduces the creative acts of God in the first chapter of the Bible. Such speech comes by God's *ruah* (רוּחַ)—His breath or Spirit—which is described as present in the beginning (1:2). Thus, God's Word must be exhaled or released by God's Spirit. Try sounding out words without releasing your breath when speaking the words. It cannot be done! People sound words only by releasing their breath when speaking. John uses this imaginative way of thinking about God's creative activity to define the ministry of Jesus. Jesus is the Word of God upon whom the Spirit of God remains. In this way John shows that Jesus' ministry is a new act of God's creation in which God's Word is spoken by His Spirit to bring new life into the world that has fallen into darkness and ignorance.

"I did not know Him, but He who sent me to baptize with water said to me, 'Upon whom you see the Spirit descending, and remaining on Him, this is He who baptizes with the Holy Spirit'" (v. 33).

The Baptist restates what has just been observed in verses 31 and 32 with one additional note: the One who comes after the Baptist is a greater Baptist since He baptizes with the Holy Spirit. What does it mean to "baptize with the Holy Spirit"? According to John, it is both related to but different from that of the Baptist. Whereas the Baptist used water to represent the cleansing act of obedience and return to God, Jesus by the Spirit offers the eternal life of God to those who will receive it. The Baptist calls men and women to return to their God through baptism in water. Jesus will usher men and women into the experience of eternal life through baptism in the Spirit. Baptism with the Holy Spirit confers the very presence of God upon those who know and follow Him in His ministry.

The Baptist has already said that he "did not know [the Word that has become flesh]." The knowledge he possesses has come through divine revelation. What does he know? He knows that Jesus will baptize with the Holy Spirit. The fact that the Baptist does not name God but refers to Him as "He who sent me" reveals his reverence for the God of Israel. It is a circumlocution or indirect way of speaking of what is holy. This is not the only event in which God speaks in a voice that is unmistakably His own. Here the Baptist says, "He who sent me to baptize with water said to me, 'Upon whom you see the Spirit' . . . this is He who baptizes with the Holy Spirit." Later, after Jesus enters Jerusalem to the acclamation of the people, "a voice from heaven" declares that God's name has been and will continue to be glorified (12:28, 29).

"And I have seen and testified that this is the Son of God" (v. 34).

The chiastic[12] structure of verses twenty-nine through thirty-four depicts Jesus as both the Lamb of God and the Son of God who has the Spirit. First, John the Baptist proclaims that Jesus is the Lamb of God (vv. 29, 30) and states that he does not know Jesus but his baptism prepares for the Lamb's coming to Israel (v. 31). Next, John says he saw the Spirit descend upon Jesus like a dove (v. 32). Then the Baptist repeats that he does not know Jesus and mentions the baptism with water a second time (v. 33). In the same verse he again tells of the Spirit's coming upon Jesus and of baptism. But this is a different baptism—that of the Holy Spirit—and a different Baptizer—Jesus Christ (v. 33). Finally, John the Baptist returns to his original statement that Jesus is the Lamb of God (v. 29) in a modified form testifying that Jesus is the Son of God (v. 34).

The structure of John 1:29–34 and the fact that the Baptist twice says the Spirit comes upon Jesus indicate that this gospel is intent on presenting Jesus as the Spirit-anointed Lamb of God who is God's Son. Also note that the last title John the Baptist confers upon Jesus at the inauguration of His ministry

---

THE EFFICIENCY OF THE BIBLE

The Scriptures are remarkable for the economical way in which they present the revelation of God. John 1:29–34 accomplishes much in relatively few words. These verses first contrast the ministry of John the Baptist with that of Jesus Christ. Whereas John baptizes with water, Jesus baptizes with the Holy Spirit. Although Jesus' baptism follows after John the Baptist's, Jesus' baptism surpasses John's. This information is vital if one is to know Jesus Christ. But, as if this were not enough, these verses also present a concise yet complete picture of Jesus:

- As God's sacrifice for sin, Jesus is the Lamb of God (v. 29).
- For the accomplishment of God's purpose, Jesus is anointed with the Spirit. That is, He is the Christ (vv. 32, 33).
- In relationship to mankind, Jesus baptizes with the Holy Spirit to give eternal life (v. 33).
- In relationship to God, Jesus is the Son of God (v. 34).

---

is that of God's Son. From this point forward, the Word of God, the Light of God, and the Lamb of God is identified as simply the Son or the Son of God. This underscores the strong familial relationship of Jesus and God. In fact, Jesus refers to God as His Father 100 times in John's gospel whereas He identifies God as Father less than fifty times in the other three Gospels combined.

As God's Son, Jesus possesses God's authority (5:21–23) and nature (10:36). He comes from God, is loved by God (3:35; 5:20), and reveals God to others (12:45; 14:9). He does the will of God (4:34; 5:19; 6:38) and presents the salvation and life of God to them (3:16; 6:40; 11:27). In addition, the glory of the Son is closely related to that of the Father (11:4; 14:13; 17:1, 5). Jesus is the Lamb of God as well as God's own Son. He is God's sacrifice on behalf of the people and God's familial representative among the people. By introducing Jesus in this way, John shows that God withholds nothing of Himself from Israel as He seeks to establish a new beginning with the beloved nation. This is strikingly evident in the fact that Jesus will baptize the people with nothing less than the Spirit of God.

The Spirit, the Dove, and the New Beginning

The Spirit is described as descending from heaven like a dove. The synoptic Gospels join John in recounting this coming of the Spirit upon Jesus (Matt.

3:16; Mark 1:10; Luke 3:22). That all four Gospels use the imagery of a dove to describe the Spirit at Jesus' baptism speaks to the significance of this symbol.

A key for understanding this significance is found in the narrative of Noah and the Great Flood in Genesis 6–9. The flood account may be interpreted as a second creation story. Not only does it speak of God's judgment upon mankind for rampant corruption and violence (6:11–13) but also it points to a new beginning for men and women. In bringing an end to human wickedness, God begins the work of new life. This idea is substantiated in the promise God makes to Noah once the waters have receded. Not only will He spare mankind in the future but He also commands Noah, "Be fruitful and multiply" (9:1). He gives all animals "into Noah's hand" (v. 2) and affirms the fact that "in the image of God He made man" (v. 6). Thus, the result of the Flood is that mankind made in God's image has power and responsibility over the animals and is given an opportunity to begin again. Not only will the human race increase, but also the land itself will produce life. God promises that there will be seedtime and harvest as long as there is an earth (8:22). Clearly, God's action in the Flood is not only to judge the wickedness of mankind but also to return men and women to a status of relationship as intended in the beginning when God made Adam in His image (1:26, 27), gave him dominion over the animal kingdom (vv. 26, 28), and told him to "be fruitful and multiply" (v. 28).

In addition to this, the situational context of God's promise to Noah resembles that found in Genesis 1 as well as the baptism accounts of the Gospels. In Genesis 7, everything is submerged in water (vv. 17–24). Nothing remains except the ark on top of the water. This picture of deep water over the earth recalls the description of the beginning of creation in Genesis 1:2: "The earth was without form, and void; and darkness was on the face of the

The Divine Intention in Genesis 1	The Post-Flood Promise of Genesis 9
vv. 26, 27: God declares His intention to make Adam in His image.	v. 6: God confirms that Noah and his family are made in His image.
vv. 26, 28: Adam is given power and responsibility over God's animal creation.	v. 2: The animals are given into the hand of Noah for food. This right comes after Noah has tended to and protected the animals during the Flood.
v. 28: Adam is commanded "to be fruitful and multiply."	vv. 1, 7: Noah and his family are commanded to "be fruitful and multiply."

deep. And the Spirit of God was hovering over the face of the waters." God creates when there is no structure to the earth and light is absent; nothing but darkness and water. Likewise, the baptism of Jesus in the Jordan River is set by John against the background of darkness and ignorance (1:4, 5, 10, 11).

The presence of the dove in the story of the Great Flood speaks of God's creative activity. As the waters begin to recede, Noah releases a dove to fly over the water (8:8–12). When it returns with an olive leaf, he knows land is emerging from the flood. When the dove fails to return, he knows that the land can support life once again. The picture of the dove over the water of the flood points in two directions. It points in the direction of Genesis 1 where the Spirit of God hovers over the waters at the moment of creation. The word used in Genesis 1:2 (*rahaph*, רָחַף) typically describes the motion of a bird in the air, like one guarding her young in a nest. It also points in the direction of the Gospels. The Spirit comes as a dove upon Jesus who is being baptized in the water of the Jordan River. The figure of the dove and the water of the Jordan recall the narrative of the Flood (Gen. 6–9) and that of creation (Gen. 1). By linking Jesus' baptism with this imagery (1:32, 33), John intentionally places the beginning of His ministry in the context of God's creative and recreative work. All three passages speak of God at work in creation and recreation. Just as God's Spirit hovers over the waters at the beginning of all things, and the dove (as a symbol of God's Spirit) goes out over the water as the flood subsides in a new beginning for Noah, so also the Spirit descends from heaven as a dove upon Jesus at His baptism in the Jordan to begin a new work of creation through Him. God's intention for mankind to be fruitful and to exercise authority according to His purposes finds a new beginning in the ministry of Jesus.

QUESTIONS FOR PERSONAL REFLECTION AND GROUP DISCUSSION

1. How does John use the word *logos* in his gospel?
2. To whom does John normally refer when he uses the term *the Jews* in his gospel?
3. How does the Baptist identify himself to temple emissaries?
4. What is the meaning of his response to the temple emissaries?
5. In the Gospel of John, what is the significance of Jesus' baptism with the Spirit?
6. What four-fold identity does John ascribe to Jesus in his account of Jesus' baptism?

CHAPTER 2

An Israelite, a Teacher of Israel, and a Daughter of Jacob

John 1:35–4:42

According to John, during the early public ministry of Jesus three people come to Jesus. All three are identified with Israel's patriarch Jacob. Jesus greets Nathanael as "an Israelite who has no deceit;" he recognizes Nicodemus as "a teacher of Israel;" he implicitly accepts the Samaritan woman's assertion that Jacob is the father of her people. This shows that, in John's opinion, Jacob is an important figure for understanding Jesus' ministry. Jacob is the one through whom the God's promises of land, people, and blessing are affirmed and perpetuated. These three, who are related to Jacob by title or claim, are heirs of these promises. By including these stories at the beginning of his gospel, John professes that the promises of God to His people are fulfilled in the person and ministry of Jesus.

Naming Peter (John 1:35–1:42)

John begins his account of Jesus' public ministry by recalling His initial meeting with Simon. This is an unusual event because Jesus gives a new name to this man whom he has never before met. What does this mean? By renaming Simon, Jesus not only confers a new identity upon him but also points to his future role in the redemptive work of God. This act reveals that, through Jesus, God's new work of creation among His people has begun.

> *Again, the next day, John stood with two of his disciples. And looking at Jesus as He walked, he said, "Behold the Lamb of God!" The two disciples heard him speak, and they followed Jesus (vv. 35–37).*

John the Baptist looks intently at Jesus before he repeats his declaration that Jesus is the "Lamb of God". The Greek word *emblepō* (ἐμβλέπω) suggests that the Baptist carefully regards Jesus before making his open pronouncement. Two of John's disciples then follow Jesus. A disciple (*mathētēs*, ὁ μαθητής) is one who learns from another. Such learning was not limited to the acquisition of knowledge about the Torah but involved an overall worldview and the practical interpretation of such knowledge in everyday life. These two disciples have learned from the Baptist and now go to learn from Jesus.

> *Then Jesus turned, and seeing them following, said to them, "What do you seek?" They said to Him, "Rabbi" (which is to say, when translated, Teacher), "where are You staying?" He said to them, "Come and see." They came and saw where He was staying, and remained with Him that day (now it was about the tenth hour) (vv. 38, 39).*

The Baptist's disciples address Jesus as "rabbi," which in Hebrew means "my great one." It is a title of respect. Since the highest form of worship among the ancient Hebrew people was the study of Scripture, rabbis were honored as great men because they devoted their life to the Torah as an act of worship and to living out its precepts in the community. John translates the term *rabbi* for his readers as "teacher," indicating that such men were known for imparting their knowledge of Torah to others. Apparently, some among his readers did not know its meaning. It need not be assumed, however, that everyone in John's audience was a Greek or Roman and ignorant of the title's meaning. John's translation of the term only indicates that some within the community (or in the greater audience that he hoped to reach with his gospel) are unfamiliar with it. John however writes for a community which generally knows the Old Testament.

The Baptist's disciples remain with Jesus until that evening. The Jewish day at this time was divided into two twelve-hour periods. Since the Baptist makes His comment about Jesus sometime in the morning (*tē epaurion*, Τῇ ἐπαύριον; v. 35), and His disciples later follow Jesus to the place He is staying, it is likely that the tenth hour marks a time later in the day.

> *One of the two who heard John speak, and followed Him, was Andrew, Simon Peter's brother. He first found his own brother Simon, and said to him, "We have found the Messiah" (which*

is translated, the Christ). And he brought him to Jesus. Now when Jesus looked at him, He said, "You are Simon the son of Jonah. You shall be called Cephas" (which is translated, A Stone) (vv. 40–42).

John introduces Andrew as the brother of Simon Peter. Such an introduction points to Peter's importance among the disciples. After meeting Jesus, Andrew goes to Simon first to tell him about the Messiah. Some ancient texts of this passage indicate that Andrew went early in the morning to tell Simon about Jesus, obviously eager to share his discovery with his brother.

Jesus perceptively looks at Simon (*emblepō*—the same word used in verse thirty-six to describe the Baptist's behavior) and renames him Cephas, an Aramaic term meaning "rock." Peter is the Greek form of this name. John not only records the titles given to Jesus by others, but he shows that Jesus bestows titles as well. Peter is not a simple nickname. It represents the identity that Jesus gives to Simon, having discerned his nature. Jesus sees Simon as a man formed and given life by God and He asserts His unique authority by giving him a new name. He announces God's purpose and will for Simon by naming him Peter.

The Old Testament recounts two important stories in which God gives new names to men. Both of these speak of these men's participation in His redemptive work. In the first, God renames Abram as Abraham because he will be "a father to many people" (Gen. 17:1–8). In the second, a man wrestles with Jacob at the Jabbok River and gives him the new name of "Israel" ("he who prevails with God") when he is victorious (Gen. 32:27, 28). This man was God Himself. Israel, the name given to Jacob, will be the national name by which God's people will be known in history to the nations of the earth.

JESUS' TITLES IN JOHN 1

The titles given to Jesus in John 1:35–41 are remarkable and relate directly to the characters present at the time:

- Lamb of God–To John the Baptist, Jesus is God's response to human sin.
- Rabbi–For John's disciples, Jesus is a Teacher who knows the Scriptures.
- Messiah–For Andrew, who has been with Jesus but for one day, Jesus is the Anointed One of God who has come to save Israel.

Peter the Rock

Presumably, Jesus could have given Simon any number of names. Yet, He chooses to call him Peter, meaning "rock." Why this name? Is it to signify the strength of his character? The firmness of his convictions? No, Jesus calls Simon a rock to anticipate his part in the new salvation of God that is emerging in His ministry.

The terrain and geology of the land of ancient Israel is remarkable for its stony soil and its rocky hills and mountains. It is not surprising, then, that the biblical writers draw upon this omnipresent feature of the land in their writing to speak of security, stability, and strength. Often the biblical writers use the imagery of rock to describe their God. In particular, "rock" (*sur*, צוּר) is used to identify the God of Israel (*Yahweh*, יהוה) as the One who saves and delivers His people.

This is evident in several Old Testament passages:

- In the Song of Moses (Deut. 32) the psalmist recounts the deliverance of the people from Pharaoh and describes their wilderness experience. Throughout this passage God is described as a rock (vv. 4, 15, 18). He is the rock of salvation (v. 15), the rock who gave the people birth (v. 18), and the rock who defended them from ten thousand (v. 30). There is no other rock like the rock of Israel (v. 31).
- God is the rock who delivers David from his enemies (2 Sam. 22). David declares, "The Lord is my rock (here the Hebrew word *sala'* [סֶלַע] is used) and my fortress and my deliverer . . . the God of my strength (*sur*)" (vv. 2, 3). He praises the rock of his salvation who delivers him from all who oppose him (v. 47).
- Several psalms attributed to David from the Book of Psalms also depict God as a rock who saves and protects His people (18:2; 31:3; 61:2; 62:6, 7; 94:22; 144:1). There is no one like the God of Israel who has delivered the people from slavery (18:31, 46). Psalm 71 gives an extended description of God as the rock (v. 3) of His people who saves and protects them and is worthy of praise. In addition, rock is used to describe the God of Israel who is a redeemer and the portion of the people forever (Ps. 19:14; 78:35).

The figurative use of rock (*sur*) in the Old Testament when applied to God is consistently associated with salvation and deliverance. Jesus gives Simon a name that links him to the God who delivered His people from bondage in Egypt, who is praised for delivering David from his enemies, and who is the redeemer of His people throughout eternity. He anticipates Simon's future participation in God's redemptive work among His people. John's inclusion of this event complements that found in Matthew where Jesus says to Simon, "You are Peter and upon this rock I will build my church" (16:17, 18).

Jesus and Jacob's Ladder (John 1:43–51)

Just as Andrew finds his brother Simon to tell him about the Messiah, so also Phillip finds Nathanael to say that he has met the One written about by Moses and the prophets. Both Andrew and Phillip perceive that Jesus is not just another rabbi. With such declarations they reveal Him to be greater than the Baptist who already has said that he is not the Messiah, Elijah, or the Prophet foretold by Moses.

Jesus responds to Nathanael in the same way that He does to Simon. He identifies him as an "Israelite who has no deceit." This is a curious declaration about an otherwise obscure disciple. Nonetheless, John introduces Nathanael as one who comes to Jesus with interested skepticism.

The placement of this short narrative passage about Nathanael after the testimony of the Baptist and prior to Jesus' first sign at Cana signifies its importance in imparting greater insight into Jesus' identity. John has already

NATHANAEL'S GROWTH OF FAITH

Nathanael's growth from doubt to belief may be outlined in the following way:

Nathanael's Growth of Faith	Jesus Names Nathanael
Nathanael doubts Phillip's report that Jesus of Nazareth, the son of Joseph, is the One about whom Moses and the prophets wrote. He says, "Can anything good come out of Nazareth?" (v. 45).	Jesus sees Nathanael and identifies him as "an Isrealite . . . who has no deceit" (v. 47). He shows that He knows Nathanael's nature and what kind of man he is.
Nathanael accepts Jesus' identification. His skepticism is challenged. "How do you know me?" (v. 48)	Jesus says that He saw Nathanael under a fig tree (v. 48).
Nathanael manifests faith in Jesus when he declares Him to be the Son of God and King of Israel (v. 49).	Jesus promises that Nathanael will see heaven open and angels ascending and descending on the Son of Man (v. 51).

presented Jesus as the Word of God, the Light of the World, the Lamb of God, and the Messiah. Here, Jesus is the One about whom Moses and the prophets wrote, the Son of God and King of Israel. John attaches all of these titles to Jesus before He begins His ministry of signs. They all describe the One through whom God will perform a work of new creation. By naming Nathanael and Peter, Jesus shows that He possesses authority to enact the new creation and enable the new disciples to participate in it.

> *The following day Jesus wanted to go to Galilee, and He found*
> *Philip and said to him, "Follow Me." Now Philip was from*
> *Bethsaida, the city of Andrew and Peter (vv. 43, 44).*

This is the third day after the Baptist announced someone greater than he was coming. Jesus finds Philip and commands him to follow. The imperative form of the verb (*akolouthei*, ἀκολούθει) corresponds to the imperative of verse thirty-nine ("come"). Jesus does not ask Philip to follow; He instructs him to follow. Philip, along with Andrew and Peter, resides in Bethsaida, a small village whose name means "house of the fishermen" on the eastern shore of the Sea of Galilee.

> *Philip found Nathanael and said to him, "We have found Him*
> *of whom Moses in the law, and also the prophets, wrote—Jesus*
> *of Nazareth, the son of Joseph." And Nathanael said to him,*
> *"Can anything good come out of Nazareth?" Philip said to him,*
> *"Come and see" (vv. 45, 46).*

Whereas Andrew claims that he has found the Messiah, Philip declares that he has found "Him of whom Moses in the law, and also the prophets, wrote." Moses looked forward to a prophet like him who would speak the words of God to the people (Deut. 18:15–22). What kind of words did God speak through Moses? He spoke words of deliverance from bondage and a new life with God as well as words of responsibility about how to live as His people.

Philip identifies Jesus as the son of Joseph from the town of Nazareth. Like all men of His time and culture, Jesus would be known as the son of His father. This identification does not impress Nathanael. This anticipated prophet possesses no special familial heritage. He is but one man from among the people. The reference to Nazareth elicits skepticism from Nathanael. He is doubtful that any good can come from this nondescript village. "Can anything good come out of Nazareth?" Of course, his response is ironic since Jesus is the One through whom God performs a new work of creation and who will certainly do good. Just as God declares His creation to be good (seven times in Genesis 1; vv. 4, 10, 12, 18, 21, 25, 31), so also the new work of creation that God will perform through Jesus will be good.

> *Jesus saw Nathanael coming toward Him, and said of him,*
> *"Behold, an Israelite indeed, in whom is no deceit!" (v. 47).*

What does Jesus mean when He addresses Nathanael as "an Israelite who has no deceit"? The key for understanding this unusual expression is found in the story of the patriarch Jacob (Gen. 25:19–33:20). In this extraordinary narrative, twin boys are born to Rebekah and Isaac. The second of these grasps the heel of his brother in birth, thus giving him the name Jacob, which means "one who grabs the heel" or "one who deceives." Though the blessing and birthright of Isaac normally would go to Esau as the eldest son, according to the custom of the time and culture, Jacob with the help of his mother conspires to deceive his father and win the blessing and birthright for himself. He flees to Padam Aram (the land north of Canaan) to escape the wrath of his brother and to live with his father's family. While there he is deceived by his relative Laban into marrying his oldest daughter when he wanted to marry his youngest. After many years Jacob journeys back to Canaan.

During his return, he camps along the Jabbok River where he encounters a "man" with whom he wrestles during the night (Gen. 32:22–32). The result of this obscure ordeal is that Jacob is given the new name of Israel because he "struggled with God and with men and prevailed" (Gen. 32:28). This new name succinctly describes Jacob's life. It has been one of deception, struggle and, now, victory. As a result of his experience with Laban and with the "man" at the river (an indirect manner of speaking of God) Jacob has been transformed. He has become Israel. He is no longer a man of deceit, but a man prepared to grapple with the consequences of his actions as he moves forward to meet Esau (Gen. 33:1–17).

With this background in mind, Jesus' description of Nathanael as "an Israelite who has no deceit" may be understood. Like Jacob, Nathanael is a man who has encountered God and who has been changed by the encounter. He has prevailed in his struggle with God and, as a result, has achieved solid standing in his relationship with God and with people. Also like Jacob, he is representative of those who find their true identity in God's promises and purposes. Thus, an Israelite who has no deceit such as Nathanael is a person who, like Jacob, has been changed by God so that he might be used by God for His purposes because the deceit, the dimension of human failure, has been drawn out of him through experience and divine grace.

> *Nathanael said to Him, "How do You know me?" Jesus answered and said to him, "Before Philip called you, when you were under the fig tree, I saw you." Nathanael answered and said to Him, "Rabbi, You are the Son of God! You are the King of Israel!" (vv. 48, 49).*

When Jesus remarks that He has seen Nathanael under a fig tree, the true Israelite responds by saying that Jesus is the king of Israel. Jesus' remark likely alludes to Micah's prophecy of God's kingdom (4:1–5) which describes the worship of the nations in the latter days at the house of the God of Jacob (v. 2) when the way of God will be taught and the nations will be at peace as "everyone will sit under his vine and under his fig tree, and no one shall make them afraid" (vv. 2–4). As noted above, Nathanael is a man who has matured in his relationship with God and men; he is at peace and does not live in fear. He anticipates the future work of God as described by Micah. Jesus recognizes this basic truth about him and Nathanael responds by declaring that Jesus is his King. The true Israelite has found his King in Jesus. What does this mean?

Since Israel did not exist as an independent nation at this time and there was no one who was acclaimed to be the king of the people, Nathanael's response identifies Jesus with the hope of the people for the future establishment of God's kingdom in their midst as indicated by Micah's prophecy. (The Romans allowed the title of king to be used by the Herodian family as a reward for their allegiance to the emperor, but it did not signify a true possession of independent royal authority on their part.) In this way the title was viewed in relation to the promises given to Abraham and Jacob that included land, descendents, and blessing to the nations. As the King of Israel, Jesus serves as steward of God's promises to the people.

John develops the theme of kingship throughout his gospel (6:15; 12:13–15; 18:33–40; 19:1–16, 19–22) and shows that it was a basic way that the people and leadership viewed Jesus.

> *Jesus answered and said to him, "Because I said to you, 'I saw you under the fig tree,' do you believe? You will see greater things than these." And He said to him, "Most assuredly, I say to you, hereafter you shall see heaven open, and the angels of God ascending and descending upon the Son of Man" (vv. 50, 51).*

Jesus, in turn, prophesies that Nathanael will see "angels ascending and descending upon the Son of Man." Here the reference is to Jacob's vision at Bethel as he escaped to Padan Aram from Esau. In a dream the patriarch sees a ladder extend from heaven to earth with angels climbing up and down on it (Gen. 28:10–22). Jacob's ladder signifies the revelatory work of God in his life; it is a sign of God's activity in the affairs of His people through Jacob. Through this revelation God verifies to Jacob the promise He made to Abraham of land, descendents, and blessing (Gen. 12:1–3) when He says, "Your descendents shall be as the dust of the earth . . . and in you and in your seed all the families of the earth shall be blessed" (Gen. 28:14). By alluding to Jacob's ladder, Jesus says that Nathanael will see the revelation of God in His ministry and God's intention to bring heavenly blessings to His earthly people. Throughout the gospel, John shows Jesus to be the One closely related to heaven. (See 1:32, 33; 3:3; 3:13, 14; 3:31; 6:32–58; 8:23; 11:41; 12:28, 29; 18:36; 19:11; 20:17.)

Jesus' title for Himself is *the Son of Man*. He uses this expression because it points in two directions, both of which are integral to His own self-understanding. First, it points in the direction of the human community of belief to which He is related. The clearest example of this may be found in the book of Ezekiel where the prophet is addressed by God as "son of man." The prophet is a son of man in that he is representative of his community; he shares in their hopes and experiences their failures. His identity is inextricably related to that of his people which, in his case, was the community in exile during the sixth century B.C.. So also, Jesus personally identifies with His people Israel. He is One who shares the hopes and experiences the anguish of those with whom He lives.

The title *Son of Man* also points to God. The exilic visionary Daniel sees "one like the son of man" (7:13) enter into the very presence of God and receive that which exclusively belongs to God and cannot be shared with another—God's glory, honor, and kingdom (7:14). By referring to Himself as the Son of Man," Jesus identifies Himself as this being who shares in the privileges and honors of God. This One will one day return on clouds of glory to establish the rule of God among people. Notably, Jesus alludes to this passage when He stands before the high priest the early morning of His crucifixion (Matt. 26:27; Mark 14:62; Luke 22:69).

Nathanael will experience the revelation of God through Jesus who, as the Son of Man, identifies with both the human race as well as with the God of heaven and earth. Jesus embraces the whole of human temporal experience while, at the same time, He shares in the glory of the Ancient of Days.

The New Wine of Salvation (John 2:1–12)

Jesus attends a wedding where He turns water into wine. This is the first of seven miracles recorded by John in his gospel. This miracle is significant in that it represents the salvation of God's relationship with men and women through His Son.

Signs in the Gospel of John

John describes the miracle at the wedding in Cana as the beginning of signs (2:11). In fact, he regards all of Jesus' miracles as signs, even though he does not use the word (*sēmeion*, σημεῖον) to describe each one as such. Nonetheless, he uses the word *sign* throughout his gospel to describe the miraculous work

ELIJAH AND THE MIRACLE OF OIL AND FLOUR

The miracle of water into wine is reminiscent of that performed by Elijah at the beginning of his prophetic ministry (1 Kin. 17:1–16). In this story, God speaks to the man from Tishbe (in Gilead east of the Jordan River) and directs him to the town of Zarephath (a town along the Mediterranean coast between Tyre and Sidon) where he replenishes the flour and oil of a widow and her son by speaking God's word. Because of this word, as well as the woman's obedience, a miraculous increase of flour and oil keeps them from starvation. The abundance of God is manifest in a time of draught, revealing God's ability to provide despite the desperate circumstances. This story shares several points of agreement with the miracle of wine at Cana:

- Elijah's ministry begins with the miracle of flour and oil just as Jesus' ministry begins with the miracle of wine. Both ministries are defined from the beginning, in part, by the miracle-working power of God.
- Each miracle is creative in nature. By increasing the supplies of flour and oil, God (through Elijah) creates more of these food staples without the grain and olives from which they are made. He provides food in the midst of drought. By making wine out of water, Jesus immediately creates what can only occur over time through natural processes. Jesus makes wine when there is no wine.
- Each miracle represents the saving activity of God. Without flour and oil the widow and her son will die; without wine the wedding celebration will fail. The widow and her son are saved from certain death, even as the wedding celebration is saved from shame and ridicule.

of God in Jesus. The miracle of wine, the healing of the young boy, and the feeding of 5,000 men are specifically described as signs (2:11; 4:54; 6:14). In addition to this, many people, including Nicodemus and other Pharisees, use the word *sign* to describe Jesus' miracles (3:2; 7:31; 9:16; 11:47). Not all come to faith as a result of these miraculous signs, however (12:37). Still, the enthusiastic welcome given to Jesus as He approaches Jerusalem is due to the signs He has done (12:18). John concludes the gospel by saying that Jesus did many more signs than the ones he has recorded (20:30).

Why does John describe Jesus' miracles as signs? Why not "marvels" or "wonders"? The reason is simple. A sign is anything that possesses meaning greater than the thing itself. It may be a word, an act, an event, an image, anything, that signifies something in addition to its normal meaning. For this reason, a sign requires more than the ordinary interpretation given to it by those present at the time the word is spoken, the act is performed, the event experienced, or the image presented. For John, Jesus' miracles not only benefit those who experience them but they also reveal the true identity of Jesus and the meaning of His ministry. They are performed not to surprise people and elicit wonder nor are they done simply to bless people. John does not record these miracles to show that Jesus possesses the power to perform mighty works. Rather, he records them to show that Jesus is present to manifest the new creation of God and to inspire faith in Him.

This table identifies the seven signs Jesus performs that represent the new creation of God:

Passage	Key Text	Miracle	Significance
2:1–11	2:10	Jesus turns water into wine.	God's relationship with men and women is renewed in Jesus.
4:46–54	4:48, 50	Jesus heals an official's son.	Jesus speaks words of life.
5:1–14	5:7–9	Jesus heals an old man.	Jesus renews life.
6:1–15	6:9–10	Jesus feeds 5,000 men.	Jesus provides the basic needs of life for God's people.
6:16–24	6:20	Jesus walks on the water.	The natural creation submits to Jesus' authority.
9:1–41	9:24–25	Jesus gives sight to a blind man.	Jesus restores the natural function of the man's eyes.
11:1–44	11:43	Jesus raises Lazarus.	Jesus brings life out of death.

John does not interpret Jesus' miracles as done only for the benefit of those who experience them. They reveal Him to be God's deliverer who inaugurates new life among the people of Israel.

> *On the third day there was a wedding in Cana of Galilee, and the mother of Jesus was there. Now both Jesus and His disciples were invited to the wedding (vv. 1, 2).*

Cana was a small village in Galilee that was home to Nathanael (21:2). Though the ancient site cannot be definitively located, it was likely several miles north of Nazareth. Having promised Nathanael that "you shall see greater things than these . . . you shall see heaven open, and the angels of God ascending and descending upon the Son of Man" (1:50, 51), Jesus begins to fulfill His word by performing a miracle in his hometown.

> *And when they ran out of wine, the mother of Jesus said to Him, "They have no wine." Jesus said to her, "Woman, what does your concern have to do with Me? My hour has not yet come." His mother said to the servants, "Whatever He says to you, do it"* *(vv. 3–5).*

When the wedding host runs out of wine, Jesus' mother approaches Him about this. Jesus responds by saying that His "hour" has not come (2:4). Interestingly, He makes the same remark to His brothers when they urge Him to perform more miracles in public so that He will become known to the world (7:6, 8). Both times family members urge Jesus to act in conformity with their desires. These desires are admirable, but they do not represent God's desire for His Son. This is indicated by Jesus' retort to His mother, "What does your concern have to do with Me?" (2:4).

While it is obvious that Mary expects something to be done, Jesus' response seems to contradict her expectation. What are we to make of this? First, the word "woman" is a neutral term. It was a common expression and should not be interpreted as either harsh or endearing. What she wants cannot be managed by the son of Joseph. It can be accomplished only by the Spirit-anointed Son of God. Thus, Jesus responds to her not as her natural son, but as One who possesses the authority to provide the wine needed by the wedding party. Second, Jesus' hour has not arrived. Throughout the gospel Jesus' "hour" refers to His passion and resurrection when the full purpose of God to undo the effect of sin is manifested. (See 7:31; 9:16; 11:47; 12:37;

20:30.) To submit to this hour, not to turn water into wine, is the essential reason for His presence and ministry.

> *Now there were set there six water pots of stone, according to the manner of purification of the Jews, containing twenty or thirty gallons apiece. Jesus said to them, "Fill the water pots with*

THE SIGNS IN THE EXODUS

John is not the only biblical writer to view and describe the works of God as signs. Throughout the Old Testament God's miracles are described as signs. The Hebrew word ʾt (אוֹת) often describes God's miraculous activity to confirm His presence in their midst, generate faith in His people, or remind them of His relationship with them through the covenant. In other words, signs reveal who God is to His people as well as His plans for them. Ancient Israel knew God through His activity on their behalf.

A good example of this is the story of the Exodus, which could be entitled, "Signs and Deliverance." From beginning to end this story consists of a series of signs, all of which reveal God to be the deliverer of the people:

- God commands Moses to help Him deliver the people from their servitude in Egypt and He promises a sign to confirm this deliverance. The sign is the worship the people will give God on the mountain (Ex. 3:7–12).
- Moses performs two miracles that are signs for the people, convincing them of his message to them. A rod changes into a snake and his hand becomes leprous (4:1–9, 17, 28–30).
- The plagues that afflict the Egyptians are signs to Pharaoh by which he may know that God wants His people released (7:3).
- The people smear blood on their doorframes in obedience to God's command. This is a sign to them of God's momentous and awful final act of deliverance (12:13).

Throughout this story God's actions are described as signs. These events are not interpreted only as astonishing phenomena by which the people are delivered from servitude. Rather, they show God to be their deliverer who does such great things because He loves them (Deut. 7:7, 8). In Deuteronomy 4:32–40 the people are challenged to keep God's commandments because of the great things that God has done for them. The deliverance of the people is described as being done by "trials, by signs, by wonders, by war, by a mighty hand and an outstretched arm, and by great terrors" (v. 34).

water." And they filled them up to the brim. And He said to
them, "Draw some out now, and take it to the master of the
feast." And they took it. When the master of the feast had tasted
the water that was made wine, and did not know where it came
from (but the servants who had drawn the water knew), the
master of the feast called the bridegroom. And he said to him,
"Every man at the beginning sets out the good wine, and when
the guests have well drunk, then the inferior. You have kept the
good wine until now!" (vv. 6–10).

Jesus has the servants fill six stone purification jars with water. When the master of the feast tastes the wine, he exclaims that the groom has saved the best for last. John includes this comment in his account to reveal Jesus as the wine of God that has been saved for the present hour. This "wine" saves the celebration of relationship between God and mankind that God intended to have from the beginning.

The reference to six stone jars is likely a historical detail recalled by John that speaks to the veracity of the story. The jars would have contained water for ritual washing important to observant Jews at the time. By washing with this water the people of the household maintained good standing before God according to tradition and the law (Num. 19:9; 2 Chr. 30:19). The jars indicate that this family would have kept the Sabbath, adhered to dietary requirements, and participated as much as they were able in the festivals of the people in Jerusalem. They would have worshiped God with daily prayers and they would have faithfully read the Scriptures.

Some scholars believe that the six jars represent the six days of creation in which God worked and celebrated the world He made. Others see the miracle as a type of messianic feast, in which Jesus the Messiah celebrates God's saving work among the people. Since each stone jar contained twenty to thirty gallons of water, Jesus produces 120–180 gallons of wine for the celebration.

John records this miracle to show that the future period of blessing announced by the prophets is present in Jesus. In that the wine signifies the goodness of God and the immanence of the Spirit, the wine Jesus produces at Cana is symbolic of this goodness and God's Spirit present in His ministry to restore the marriage of men and women to God as it was in the beginning.

This beginning of signs Jesus did in Cana of Galilee, and mani-
fested His glory; and His disciples believed in Him. After this He
went down to Capernaum, He, His mother, His brothers, and
His disciples; and they did not stay there many days (vv. 11, 12).

WORD STUDY: WINE

The Greek word *oinos* (ὁ οἶνος) describes wine of all kinds. Wine was processed in late summer and early fall and involved (1) the production of must by treading grapes in stone vats; (2) straining and boiling the must; and (3) a first and second fermentation. A staple of the diet of the people at the time of Jesus, it was also an essential element of the temple ritual (Num. 15:1–10; 28–29).

Biblical writers identify wine along with oil and rain as symbols of the future blessings God will bestow upon His people (Joel 3:18; Is. 25:6). In particular, it symbolizes the restoration of Israel after judgment (Jer. 31:12; Joel 2:19, 24; Amos 9:13, 14). The prophet Joel, for example, foretells a future period of abundant oil, wine, and rain to be followed by a period of the Spirit (2:19, 21–24). In these verses from the Gospel of John, wine is a symbol of the renewal of God's blessing that anticipates the giving of His Spirit (2:28, 29).

John's remarks here reveal his understanding of Jesus' miracles. They "manifest His glory," meaning they reveal the life-giving presence of God in Jesus' ministry that elicits faith from others. Again, Jesus does not perform miracles simply to bless others. He does them so that the glory He has from His Father may be revealed and that this revelation will enable others to believe that He has come from His Father.

The Glory of God in the Gospel of John

The word *glory* has special significance in the Gospel of John. It uses the noun (*doxa*, ἡ δόξα) nearly twenty times in reference to the revelation of God in Jesus and the verb (*doxazō*, δοξάζω) more than twenty times with the general meaning of "glorify."

John's first use of *doxa* establishes its basic meaning throughout his gospel. He writes that when the Word of God dwelled among people "we beheld His glory, the glory as of the only begotten of the Father, full of grace and truth" (1:14). For John, glory is the exalted expression of God's being in Jesus, revealing grace and truth (*charitos kai alētheias*, χάριτος καὶ ἀληθείας). His meaning may be understood by considering the Hebrew expression "goodness and truth" (*hesed we'emet*, חֶסֶד וֶאֱמֶת) in Exodus 33–35. This narrative describes the renewal of God's covenant with Israel. In it God promises His presence to Moses only to have Moses ask Him to show His glory (*kābōd*, כָּבוֹד). Moses' request indicates that he desires something more than a divine manifestation; he wants to encounter God Himself. God appears, shows His glory, gives His words to Moses, and proclaims that He is "abounding in goodness and truth" (Ex. 34:6, 7).

What does God show when He shows His glory? He displays the full manifestation of His goodness and truth in time and place that results in the renewal of His covenant with His people. God does not appear to Moses through the medium of a natural phenomenon or in some limited, constrained capacity. He appears in His fullness. For this reason He can declare that He abounds in goodness and truth. That is, He relates to Moses and His people not in the way that they deserve, but according to His own personal and immediate nature and capacity. He relates with goodness or mercy (*hesed*)—understanding their fallen and alienated condition—and with truth (*emet*)—the means by which His people may have a relationship with Him despite their alienation.

Likewise, Jesus manifests God's immediate, personal presence to the people with grace—understanding their condition (2:24, 25)—and with truth—the means by which they can now have relationship with God. He represents God's compassionate response to His people's fallen and alienated condition (17:5; 5:17).

God's glory is revealed in the miracles of Jesus. The goodness or grace of God and His truth is manifested in the provision of wine for the wedding, the healing of the boy, and the strengthening of the lame man. It is displayed in the feeding of thousands and the gift of sight to the blind man. And it is most dramatically attested in the raising of Lazarus. Upon receiving the news that Lazarus is sick (*astheneia*, ἡ ἀσθένεια), He informs the disciples that the sickness will not result in death but in a display of God's glory (11:4); that is, a display of His goodness and truth. Later Jesus says to Martha, "Did I not say to you that if you believed you would see the glory of God?" (11:40).

In fact, the entirety of Jesus' ministry reveals God's glory. This may be detected in Jesus' final prayer to the Father when He says, "I have glorified You upon the earth, completing the work You have given me" (17:4). Jesus has manifested the goodness and truth of God in His healing and miracles. The final and greatest expression of such glory is His death and resurrection which, remarkably, represents the authority, majesty and love of God brought to bear upon the hopeless condition of His people for their salvation.

The Sign of Jesus' Death (John 2:13–25)

Jesus travels to Jerusalem for the first of three Passovers recorded by John following "the beginning of signs" in Cana (also 6:4; 12:1). After He drives out the money changers from the temple some demand the meaning of His actions:

"What sign do You show to us, since You do these things?" Jesus answers by saying, "Destroy this temple, and in three days I will raise it up" (2:18, 19). His comment refers to the temple of His body but the people misunderstand His remarks to be about their center of worship (2:19–21). Jesus' resurrection becomes a sign to the disciples when they recall what He said at this time (v. 22), yet His demonstration in the temple is not described as a sign. This is because His actions there are not intended to arouse faith in Him.

Jesus desires the temple to be a place of worship rather than a center of commerce. He reacts to the vendors at the temple despite the fact they and the money changers performed a necessary service for pilgrims who traveled to Jerusalem from distant countries. In order to purchase animals acceptable for sacrifice, they were required to exchange their local coinage for Tyrian which was the standard currency held in reserve by the temple. The vendors who sold animals for sacrifice were licensed by the temple and, thus, required Tyrian currency to be used. The city-state of Tyre was a center for trade and banking throughout the eastern Mediterranean at the time of Jesus and their currency was highly valued.

In the synoptic Gospels, this action occurs during the week prior to Jesus' crucifixion (Matt. 21:12–17; Mark 11:15–19; Luke 19:45–58). John, however, reveals that this event or one similar to it occurred much earlier in Jesus' ministry. It represents the first of many conflicts between Jesus and the temple officials.

> *Now the Passover of the Jews was at hand, and Jesus went up to Jerusalem (v. 13).*

Passover was one of the three primary feasts (along with Pentecost and Tabernacles) celebrated annually by Israel. Every Jewish male was expected to travel to Jerusalem to participate in its festivities at least once in his lifetime. Its importance should not be minimized since it was the national festival of remembrance commemorating each spring the deliverance of their ancestors from slavery in Egypt. The celebration was based on the story recorded in Exodus and enforced the notion that God was a deliverer and they were a delivered people. Because of the Roman presence in the land at this time, such a memory would have provided hope and inspired many to look not to the past acts of God but to His future activity on their behalf.

> *And He found in the temple those who sold oxen and sheep and doves, and the money changers doing business. When He had made a whip of cords, He drove them all out of the temple, with*

*the sheep and the oxen, and poured out the changers' money and
overturned the tables (vv. 14, 15).*

Jesus' action in the temple stands in juxtaposition to the miracle He performed in Cana. There He filled empty purification jars with wine to save the
feast from shame; here He acts against the perceived impurity of the temple
system of sacrifice and its empty worship. His demonstration is symbolic
since the large number of booths and vendors in the temple precincts would
have made it impractical for Jesus to have physically cleared the temple of all
such people.

*And He said to those who sold doves, "Take these things away! Do
not make My Father's house a house of merchandise!" Then His
disciples remembered that it was written, "Zeal for Your house
has eaten Me up." So the Jews answered and said to Him, "What
sign do You show to us, since You do these things?" Jesus
answered and said to them, "Destroy this temple, and in three
days I will raise it up." Then the Jews said, "It has taken forty-six
years to build this temple, and will You raise it up in three days?"
But He was speaking of the temple of His body (vv. 16–21).*

THE SIGNIFICANCE OF PSALM 69

In the aftermath of Jesus' actions in the temple, the disciples recall Psalm 69. His violent
response to the vendors and His strong declaration, "Do not make My Father's house a house
of merchandise," is seen as a fulfillment of Psalm 69:9: "Because zeal for Your house has
eaten me up." Jesus' disciples recalled this psalm because it enhanced their understanding of
Jesus' actions at the temple when He overturned tables, cried out for true worship, and spoke
of His future death.

It would be a mistake, however, to limit the importance of this psalm to this connection
only. This is because the entire psalm describes the alienation of one who has been zealous
for God's house yet is opposed and rejected by others. The psalmist declares, "Those who
hate me without a cause are more than the hairs of my head" (v. 4). Such a depiction would
have been read by the disciples as accurately describing the real opposition faced by Jesus
during His ministry. His enigmatic remark, "Destroy this temple, and in three days I will raise
it up," alludes to such opposition and rejection. The disciples recalled Psalm 69, therefore, not
only because it described Jesus' anguish over the temple but also because it described the
alienation and rejection of Jesus by those He came to save.

By interfering with the business-as-usual activity of the temple and declaring, "Do not make My Father's house a house of merchandise," Jesus dramatically expresses His anger with its formality of worship. He is exasperated with a sacrificial system that is operating like any other commercial enterprise. The essence of worship that was intended to give vitality to the ritual of sacrifice is largely ignored by those who supervise and maintain it. Psalm 69:30, 31 portrays desirable worship: "I will praise the name of God with a song, and will magnify Him with thanksgiving. This also shall please the Lord better than an ox or bull." Jesus' desire for true worship rather than perfunctory sacrifice is described in this psalm.

Therefore, when He had risen from the dead, His disciples remembered that He had said this to them; and they believed the Scripture and the word which Jesus had said (v. 22).

In His final discourse with the disciples before His crucifixion, Jesus promises to send the Holy Spirit who will help the disciples recall the things that Jesus had taught them (14:26). John's remark here speaks of this activity in the lives of the disciples after Jesus' ascension and glorification. It also reveals that the word of Jesus is viewed by the disciples as possessing equal authority to that of Scripture, which at that time was the Law and Prophets.

A Teacher of Israel Learns about the Spirit and the Son (John 3:1–21)

In this passage a rabbi approaches Jesus with questions about His ministry. In return he receives instruction on birth from above, the kingdom of God, the work of the Spirit, and the nature of God's love exemplified in the life of the Son.

Nicodemus recognizes that Jesus performs "signs" (3:2). He senses meaning in Jesus' ministry but he is unable to interpret His actions (such as the demonstration in the temple). He perceives the presence of God in Jesus but cannot conceive His identity. He asks, in essence, "What is the meaning of Your ministry?" Jesus' response to him, "Unless one is born again, he cannot see the kingdom of God" (v. 3), directly addresses this implied question by asserting that the significance of His ministry is its revelation of God's kingdom. This revelation, however, cannot be apprehended without one being born "from above" (*anōthen*, ἄνωθεν). Jesus tells Nicodemus, in other words, that he cannot understand the meaning of what God is doing in His ministry apart from a new beginning that has divine origin.

This new beginning is the work of the Spirit. In fact, Jesus speaks of being "born by the Spirit" three times (vv. 5–8):

- He links being born by the Spirit with entry into the kingdom of God (v. 5).
- He notes that being born by the Spirit is a work of the Spirit and not a human accomplishment (v. 6).
- He concludes that being born by the Spirit is a divine work that cannot be assessed by human deduction (v. 8).

This work of the Spirit is closely related to Jesus' own ministry (vv. 13–18). Not only is the Spirit integral to His ministry—indeed, there is no ministry apart from the Spirit—but the goal of the Spirit's work (the new birth) is linked to that of Jesus (eternal life). Jesus says that belief in Him as the Son of God who will be lifted up like Moses' serpent in the wilderness results in eternal life. Thus, the new birth of the Spirit (vv. 3–8) is grounded in the death of the Son of Man that makes possible eternal life for the whole world (vv. 10–19).

JESUS TEACHES THE TEACHER

The question and answer session between Jesus and Nicodemus is outlined in the table.

Nicodemus' Questions	Jesus' Teaching
Nicodemus recognizes that there is more to Jesus' good works than the works themselves. God is with Jesus is some special way. What do the signs mean? (v. 2).	One must be born from above to understand that the signs speak of the nature of the kingdom of God (v. 3).
Nicodemus asks how is it possible to be born from above (v. 4).	Being born by God's Spirit (from above) is the only way one can see God's kingdom (vv. 5–8).
Nicodemus still does not understand how one may be born of the Spirit (v. 9).	Birth from above by the Spirit is possible through the raising up of the Son of Man. Faith in Him results in eternal life. Jesus challenges Nicodemus to believe this teaching (vv. 10–21)

There was a man of the Pharisees named Nicodemus, a ruler of the Jews. This man came to Jesus by night and said to Him, "Rabbi, we know that You are a teacher come from God; for no one can do these signs that You do unless God is with him" (vv. 1, 2).

The fact that Nicodemus approaches Jesus at night has two levels of significance. First, he is hesitant about being seen with Jesus in public. Eventually, he will speak in His defense before his colleagues in the Sanhedrin (7:49–52) and he will join Joseph of Arimathea to bury Jesus' body after His crucifixion (19:38–42). At this time, however, Nicodemus is wary to be associated with this teacher who performs signs. Second, the darkness represents his own ignorance of Jesus and His teaching. Though he is a teacher of Israel, Nicodemus does not comprehend the meaning of Jesus' signs. The reference to darkness connects this story with John's introduction. There he writes, "The Light shines in the darkness, and the darkness did not overcome it" (1:5). Though he should understand the ways and means of God, Nicodemus is representative of the Israel that does not know the Light that has been sent to it (1:10). Jesus is the Light; darkness is human ignorance of His identity. Nicodemus may be moving toward the Light and desire to know about the Light, but he still does not know the Light. Shortly, Jesus will say to him, "The Light has come into the world, and men loved darkness rather than Light" (3:19).

Jesus answered and said to him, "Most assuredly, I say to you, unless one is born again, he cannot see the kingdom of God." Nicodemus said to Him, "How can a man be born when he is old? Can he enter a second time into his mother's womb and be born?" (vv. 3, 4).

Jesus' statement, "Most assuredly" (*amēn amēn legō soi*; ἀμὴν ἀμὴν λέγω σοι), is emphatic.[13] It draws attention to the fact that the following teaching belongs to Jesus only. He has not received it from other teachers or acquired it during the give and take of public discourse. He has not learned it from tradition. It issues from His own understanding of the work of God and His relation to God and, thus, is unique to Him.

Jesus says that the ability to see and know God's work is dependent upon birth from above. That is, divine birth. Already John has observed that those who believe the Word are born of God (1:12, 13). God's kingdom is unlike any human kingdom. At this time in human history every man, woman, and child belonged to a kingdom; everyone lived under the authority of a king. They will not be confused by Jesus' expression. They know that the location of one's birth determines the realm of authority in which they live. Moreover, they understand that birth from above means birth under the rule and authority of God. Jesus says that one must be born in God's kingdom if one is to understand the nature of God's rule.

Nicodemus' response, "How can a man be born when he is old," is often viewed as naïve and indicative of his woeful understanding of the nature of the kingdom of God. This is not the case. Nicodemus intentionally shifts the focus of what Jesus has said about birth from above to the ridiculous notion of a second physical birth. In typical rabbinic manner, Nicodemus raises an impractical or improbable consequence of Jesus' assertion in order to elicit further explanation from Him. Jesus understands this and replies that this new type of birth is not something that a person can will for himself or herself. Only God can give it (1:12, 13). Still, Nicodemus thinks that this is something one can personally accomplish: "Can he enter a second time into his mother's womb and be born?" Jesus' point is that only those who have life from God can able to understand the significance of His ministry (which is from above by the Spirit). Birth from above is new life and is God-given.

> Jesus answered, "Most assuredly, I say to you, unless one is born of water and the Spirit, he cannot enter the kingdom of God. That which is born of the flesh is flesh, and that which is born of the Spirit is spirit. Do not marvel that I said to you, 'You must be born again.' The wind blows where it wishes, and you hear the sound of it, but cannot tell where it comes from and where it goes. So is everyone who is born of the Spirit." Nicodemus answered and said to Him, "How can these things be?" (vv. 5–9).

Jesus again says, "Most assuredly, I say to you." This indicates that teaching is His own; not dependent on others.

The statement, "Unless one is born of water and the Spirit," is often interpreted as an allusion to baptism. However, Jesus' words recall what John the Baptist has already reported: He baptizes with water but Jesus baptizes with the Spirit. The words *water and Spirit* represent the new creative work of God in Israel and by extension the whole world. By saying that one cannot enter into God's kingdom apart from water and Spirit, Jesus means this: One cannot have a place under the rule of God unless one has first turned to God in expectation of deliverance from sin—signified by John's baptism of water—and has embraced Jesus' ministry, which results in the baptism of the Spirit. This means that God's kingdom cannot be experienced apart from a return to devotion to God and a response to God's work in Jesus Christ.

Jesus elaborates on what He means by "born from above" saying, "That which is born of the Spirit is spirit." He links birth from above with the work of the Spirit, which He compares to the wind that freely blows. Just as Nicodemus cannot tell the origin of the wind or its final destination so also he cannot restrict the nature of the Spirit's work in the new birth. In other words, the work of the Spirit cannot be reduced to human expectations.

What does Jesus mean by the phrase *the wind blows where it wills*? He is making an allusion to the role of the Spirit in the creative work of God. Throughout the Old Testament, God's work of creation and renewal (or recreation) involves water and Spirit (*ruah*). The creation of heaven and earth, for example, begins as the *ruah* (Spirit) of God moves over the waters (Gen. 1:2). Likewise, when God restores the earth after the devastation of the flood a *ruah* (wind) blows across the waters (Gen. 8:1). And when the Hebrew people flee Egypt to begin a new life in Canaan they cross through the Red Sea as a strong *ruah* (wind) drives back the water (Ex. 14:21). In these passages *ruah* speaks of wind that moves over the water. Jesus' expression *the wind blows where it wills* recalls the creative and redemptive activity of God in these passages in anticipation of a new beginning for Israel. He tells Nicodemus that God is at work by His Spirit to deliver His people in whatever manner He chooses.

This causes Nicodemus to abandon his rhetorical discourse with Jesus and plainly say, "How can these things be?" In other words, "How is it possible to be born from above by the Spirit?"

> *Jesus answered and said to him, "Are you the teacher of Israel, and do not know these things? Most assuredly, I say to you, We speak what We know and testify what We have seen, and you do not receive Our witness. If I have told you earthly things and you do not believe, how will you believe if I tell you heavenly things? No one has ascended to heaven but He who came down from heaven, that is, the Son of Man who is in heaven. And as Moses lifted up the serpent in the wilderness, even so must the Son of Man be lifted up, that whoever believes in Him should not perish but have eternal life" (vv. 10–15).*

Jesus describes Nicodemus as "the teacher of Israel." As noted above, the title is significant in that it identifies Nicodemus as a man responsible for instructing others about the way of relationship with God.

For the third time Jesus says to Nicodemus, "Most assuredly, I say to you." He does not refer to tradition; He does not cite rabbis. Jesus uses the first person plural pronoun "We" to indicate that His teaching also belongs to God His Father. He speaks from His own experience with God as One anointed with the Spirit. Yet, people do not believe the witness that He shares with God. This is not surprising since John has already stated that "Light shines in the darkness, and the darkness did not overtake it" (1:5), "He was in the world . . . and the world did not know Him" (1:10), and "there stands One among you whom you do not know" (1:26). Jesus has taught earthly things without being believed and, thus, does not expect to be believed when He teaches heavenly things. If people do not believe the evidence of His ministry that is given by the Spirit, then how will they believe what He says about the Spirit?

Jesus specifically identifies Himself as One sent from heaven who will eventually return to heaven. His return to heaven, however, is contingent upon being lifted up like Moses' serpent in the wilderness. Jesus alludes to the story in the book of Numbers (21:4–9) that describes God's judgment of the people in the wilderness for their complaint and unbelief. When the people repent God instructs Moses to make a bronze serpent and raise it on a pole so that they may look on it and live. Nicodemus would have known the story but he would have been perplexed by Jesus' identification with the serpent. That Jesus would make such an allusion is important for several reasons. First, it identifies His ministry with the deliverance of the people from servitude in Egypt. Second, the Hebrew people experienced judgment because they accused God of leading them to death. They disbelieved the good intentions of God because of their hard circumstances. This describes the prevailing condition of people at the time of Jesus (1:5, 10, 11). Third, just as the image of the serpent represents the life of God for His people in the midst of potential death, so also Jesus represents the eternal life of God in the midst of darkness. Jesus says that God did not send His Son into the world to judge the world; He sent His Son to save the world. His death will be a sign to the people of the mercy and love of God and will result in eternal life for those who believe. This is the second time that Jesus has made reference to His future death and resurrection as a sign to the people from God (see 2:18–22).

> *"For God so loved the world that He gave His only begotten Son, that whoever believes in Him should not perish but have everlasting life. For God did not send His Son into the world to condemn the world, but that the world through Him might be saved. He who believes in Him is not condemned; but he who does not believe is condemned already, because he has not believed in the name of the only begotten Son of God. And this is*

the condemnation, that the light has come into the world, and
men loved darkness rather than light, because their deeds were
evil. For everyone practicing evil hates the light and does not
come to the light, lest his deeds should be exposed. But he who
does the truth comes to the light, that his deeds may be clearly
seen, that they have been done in God" (vv. 16–21).

God's desire is for His people to experience life rather than death. Belief in His Son, who is the Word empowered by the Spirit, results in everlasting (*aiōnios*, αἰώνιος) life. But what kind of life is everlasting life? Is it life that goes on and on and on and on? For John, everlasting life is life that is lived in the very presence of God as it was initially experienced by Adam in the beginning. It is relational life that is totally dependent upon God. Everyone who believes that Jesus has come from heaven (v. 13) will not perish as Adam perished for his disobedience but will enjoy the life that God gives. The verb "perish" (*apollymi*, ἀπόλλυμι) most often describes complete loss or total destruction when used in the New Testament, making it an appropriate antonym to everlasting life.

Jesus does not bring God's judgment or condemnation to the world. The world already is spinning in darkness and confusion. Instead, Jesus brings the Light and life of God to it. To believe in Jesus is to be released from the darkness of the world, but to reject Him is to remain in the darkness. For those who receive the Light, God gives eternal life; for those who reject the Light, He allows them to remain in the darkness of their disbelief. Judgment and condemnation means that people experience the consequences of their choices even as Adam received the consequences of his in the beginning. Just as Jesus' miracles are signs that reveal His identity and reflect God's good work among His people, so also the deeds of men and women are signs that reveal their belief or unbelief. Evil deeds reveal love for darkness whereas deeds of truth manifest a love for the Light. Since Jesus is the Light of God (8:12; 9:5) the works that one does reflect the nature of one's relationship to Him: those who do evil works hate the Light; those who do good works love the Light. Nicodemus initially approaches Jesus and lauds His miracles as signs that reveal Gods presence with Him. Jesus now concludes their discussion by asserting that the works people do reveal whether or not they have a relationship with Him as the Light. Belief in Jesus will find expression in the things that one says and does.

In this discourse Jesus reveals that the signs He performs represent the presence of the eternal life of God. This cannot be understood apart from birth by the Spirit, which is related to belief in the lifting up of Jesus. To believe in Him as the One lifted up for the people like the serpent in the wilderness results in everlasting life. It undoes the work of the serpent in the Garden that resulted in the expulsion of Adam from the direct presence of God and issues in life lived in the presence of God like Adam first enjoyed. For John, this discourse is an important feature of his presentation of Jesus as the beginning of a new creation.

The Final Testimony of John the Baptist (John 3:22–36)

The Baptist was the first to speak of Jesus when he identifies Him as the Lamb of God, Son of God, and the One who will baptize with the Holy Spirit (1:29, 33, 34, 36). Now that Jesus has been baptized, has performed signs among the people, and has spoken of His role in the new creation of God, the Baptist says, "He must increase, but I must decrease." This means that the signs Jesus performs and the teaching that He gives take precedence over John's ministry. John, the voice in the wilderness, has completed his task of making the way of the Lord straight (1:23). The Baptist also acknowledges Jesus' superiority by repeating the teaching He has given to Nicodemus.

> *After these things Jesus and His disciples came into the land of Judea, and there He remained with them and baptized. Now John also was baptizing in Aenon near Salim, because there was much water there. And they came and were baptized. For John had not yet been thrown into prison (vv. 22–24).*

Though Jesus has begun His ministry, the Baptist continues to baptize in the Jordan River. Jesus has instructed Nicodemus that people cannot enter the kingdom of God unless they are born of water and Spirit. So, John the Baptist's ministry of water baptism prepares people for the ministry of the Spirit that Jesus offers. The Gospel of John observes that the Baptist had at this time not yet been imprisoned by Herod. This reveals that the ministries of John and Jesus overlap for a certain period of time. Contrast this with Matthew who depicts Jesus' public ministry as occurring after the Baptist is imprisoned (Matt. 4:12).

> *Then there arose a dispute between some of John's disciples and the Jews about purification. And they came to John and said to him, "Rabbi, He who was with you beyond the Jordan, to whom you have testified—behold, He is baptizing, and all are coming to Him!" (vv. 25, 26).*

The disagreement about purification between the Baptist's disciples and certain Jews leads to John's final words about Jesus. This event is included here to underscore Jesus' superiority over the Baptist. It is a continuation of the discussion between leaders from Jerusalem and the Baptist described earlier (1:19–28). At that time they wanted to know who John was and why he baptized. Now they want to know about Jesus' baptism. We are not told what is the specific disagreement between them. The gospel simply says that it is about purification. More than likely the disagreement concerns the efficacious nature of the Baptist's ministry. By baptizing with water, the Baptist may have been seen as performing a type of purification; that is, a ritual cleansing that enabled people to remain in good standing before God. The Jews may have objected to such an action because the water of the Jordan was not clean and would hardly have been regarded as an appropriate medium for purification. In any case, the discussion shifts from the Baptist's baptism to that of Jesus.

> *John answered and said, "A man can receive nothing unless it has been given to him from heaven. You yourselves bear me witness, that I said, 'I am not the Christ,' but, 'I have been sent before Him'" (vv. 27, 28).*

The Baptist attests that Jesus' ministry is divine in origin and alludes to the descent of the Spirit upon Jesus at His baptism (1:32, 33). God is at work in His miracles and message. Moreover, he repeats that he is not the anointed One who will deliver the people (1:20–28).

> *"He who has the bride is the bridegroom; but the friend of the bridegroom, who stands and hears him, rejoices greatly because of the bridegroom's voice. Therefore this joy of mine is fulfilled" (v. 29).*

The Baptist describes his role to Jesus as that of a friend to a bridegroom. Such a person was responsible for organizing the wedding and for overseeing its festivities. This released the groom to give his attention to the bride. The Baptist experiences joy—the sense of complete fulfillment—because he has prepared the way for Jesus' ministry to Israel. These words recall the wedding at Cana where, by turning water into wine, Jesus saved a marriage celebration and showed that He has come to renew the marriage relationship between God and His people. The miracle announced the good news that God has drawn close to His people in Jesus Christ to save them in the most intimate way possible. By comparing the ministry of Jesus to a marriage celebration, the Baptist says that Jesus is the groom to Israel and affirms the meaning of the miracle at Cana.

> *"He must increase, but I must decrease" (v. 30).*

Though his ministry has prepared for Jesus' own ministry and has complemented it, the Baptist observes that a new era has begun. The period of preparation has passed; the friend of the bridegroom has fulfilled his duties. It is now time for the bridegroom to receive His bride. In the ancient world, the vows, songs, and dances at weddings observed the reception of the bride by the bridegroom. For this reason, the bridegroom was featured in the festivities. Due to the presence of the bridegroom, the time for celebration has arrived.

> *"He who comes from above is above all; he who is of the earth is earthly and speaks of the earth. He who comes from heaven is above all. And what He has seen and heard, that He testifies; and no one receives His testimony. He who has received His testimony has certified that God is true. For He whom God has sent speaks the words of God, for God does not give the Spirit by measure. The Father loves the Son, and has given all things into His hand. He who believes in the Son has everlasting life; and he who does not believe the Son shall not see life, but the wrath of God abides on him" (vv. 31–36).*

The "increase" of Jesus is apparent in the Baptist's teaching at this point. He now teaches what Jesus teaches. John's narrative reports that the Baptist teaches what Jesus has already taught Nicodemus. By recounting these remarks, John shows the ascendancy of Jesus' ministry and underscores the importance of Jesus' instruction to the teacher of Israel about birth from above, the Spirit, and His own place in the salvation of God.

Jesus at Jacob's Well (John 4:1–42)

Now the Samaritan woman meets Jesus at Jacob's Well. The two engage in a meaningful conversation about Jesus' identity and its significance for her and her people. The story is surprising for several reasons:

- The social conventions of the time segregated men and women in public and disapproved of personal conversations between them.

The Baptist's Teaching	Jesus' Teaching
"He who comes from above is above all . . . He who comes from heaven is above all" (v. 31).	"Unless one is born from above, he cannot see the kingdom of God" (v. 3).
"What He has seen and heard, that He testifies; and no one receives His testimony" (v. 33). "For He whom God has sent speaks the words of God . . . The Father loves the Son, and has given all things into His hand" (vv. 34, 35).	"We speak what We know and testify what We have seen, and you do not receive Our witness" (v. 11).
God does not give the Spirit by measure (v. 34).	"The wind blows where it wishes . . . so is everyone who is born of the Spirit" (v. 8).
He who believes in the Son has everlasting life. (v. 36).	"For God so loved the world that He gave His only begotten Son, that whoever believes in Him should not perish but have everlasting life" (v. 16).

- These same conventions were such that most Jews shunned Samaritans and most Samaritans detested Jews.
- The conversation includes such important topics as the history of a people, the nature of worship, and the coming of the Jewish Messiah.
- This story shows Jesus moving across gender, ethnic, and historical-religious boundaries to talk about the new work that God is performing in His life.

Plus, a number of features connect this story with those of Nicodemus and Nathanael:

- Like Nathanael and Nicodemus the woman comes to Jesus. Jesus is at the well when she comes to draw water from it.
- Her initial response to Jesus involves a question. Nathanael wonders, "Can any good thing come out of Nazareth?" (1:46). Nicodemus implicitly asks, "What does your ministry mean?" (3:2). The Samaritan woman wants to know, "How it is that You, being a Jew, ask a drink from me, a Samaritan woman?" (4:9).
- As a result of her conversation with Jesus, the woman grows in her understanding of who He is and learns about eternal life.
- Jesus has already told Nicodemus that God sent His Son so that people may have eternal life through the Spirit and has promised

Nathanael that He would see heaven open. He now tells the
Samaritan woman that He offers the water of eternal life and makes it
possible for people to worship God in the Spirit.

John includes this encounter in his gospel to show that the eternal life of
the new creation is for all people. It is not limited in any way by gender, eth-
nicity, or background. He recalls this story because the woman is a daughter
of Jacob (Israel) who experiences the new life of God as such a daughter
should through her belief in Jesus.

Jesus identified Himself to Nicodemus as the Son of God who will be lifted up so that God's people may be born from above and experience eternal
life. Here He identifies Himself to the woman as the Messiah who offers living water that issues in eternal life. He accepts the woman though she has

A TEACHER OF ISRAEL AND A DAUGHTER OF JACOB

The Samaritan woman is the last person one would expect Jesus to speak to after conversing
with a teacher of Israel. The differences between the woman and Nicodemus are striking and
would be apparent to many of John's first-century readers. Yet, Nicodemus and the woman
share a common bond in that both are related to Jacob/Israel. The woman claims to be a
daughter of Jacob (4:12) while Nicodemus is "a teacher of Israel" (3:10). Jesus speaks to both
of them about the life of God which can be theirs through Him, the One who will be lifted up
and who is God's Messiah.

A Daughter of Jacob	A Teacher of Israel
A Samaritan woman	A Jewish man
She remains unnamed throughout the story.	Nicodemus is identified by name several times in John's gospel (3:1, 4, 9; 7:50; 19:39).
The woman is unlearned.	Nicodemus is a learned teacher.
The woman possesses no social status as an unmarried woman.	Nicodemus possesses high social status as a "ruler of the Jews."
The woman has low standing in her community; she has been married five times and lives with a man to whom she is not married.	Nicodemus is upstanding and obeys not only the Torah but also the traditions of the fathers.

been married five times and, in so doing, He accepts her people. The woman is a representative of the Samarian people as a whole.

Jesus addresses this woman's need, which is also the need of her people, by declaring that the true worship of God is not be limited to a particular place. He has already demonstrated the inadequacy of the temple as the locus of Israel's worship by overturning the tables of the moneychangers. Now Jesus reveals that the worship of God is not bound by time or place— it is in spirit and in truth (4:21–24). Worship was one of the issues that separated the Jews and the Samaritans at this time. The Samaritans used a different Scripture than the Jews and had built a temple on Mt. Gerizim where they worshiped God. Overriding this conflict, Jesus says that the true worship of God occurs in spirit and truth.

Next, Jesus acknowledges His messianic role to the woman. In this role He speaks figuratively to His disciples of a human harvest (4:27–38). The Samaritans' belief shows that this harvest is already being gathered. Jesus tells this "daughter of Jacob" that she and her people will once again enjoy true worship of God and many of her townspeople believe in Him. In this way He fulfills the promise made to Nathanael and manifests the truth of His teaching to Nicodemus.

A Samaritan Woman Meets the Messiah

The story of the Samaritan woman traces the progression of her knowledge of Jesus Christ. Though she does not know Him at the beginning, by the end she suspects that He is the Messiah. The question that Jesus asks His disciples in Mark 8 and Matthew 16, "Who do you say that I am?" is answered by this woman when she gives a testimony about Jesus to her village: "A man who told me all things that I ever did" (4:29, 39).

> *Therefore, when the Lord knew that the Pharisees had heard that Jesus made and baptized more disciples than John (though Jesus Himself did not baptize, but His disciples), (vv. 1, 2).*

Here John uses the term *Lord* in reference to Jesus. This is the Greek word *kyrios* (ὁ κύριος), which translates the Hebrew name for God used in the Old Testament. Its use here reflects John's exalted understanding of Jesus.

Jesus has His disciples continue the ministry of baptism practiced by the Baptist. Water baptism signified a return to God and His covenant and fidelity to relationship with Him. Jesus does not baptize with water; as the Baptist has already announced, He will baptize with the Holy Spirit (1:33).

Jesus' Words	Samaritan Woman's Response
"Give Me a drink" (v. 7). Jesus initiates a conversation with the woman.	"How is it that You, being a Jew, ask a drink from me, a Samaritan woman?" (v. 9). She points out the boundaries (ethnic, gender) that separate them and interprets His request against this background.
"If you knew the gift of God, and who it is who says to you . . . you would have asked Him, and He would have given you living water" (v. 10). Jesus says that she does not know Him despite her observation.	"Sir, you have nothing to draw with . . . Where then do You get that living water? Are You greater than our father Jacob?" (vv. 11, 12). She responds to what Jesus says about "living water" as well as to what He says about Himself. In other words, "Who are You?"
"Whoever drinks of the water that I shall give him will never thirst . . . [it] will become in him a fountain of water springing up into everlasting life" (vv. 13, 14). Jesus answers her question, "Who are You?" by saying He is the One who gives everlasting life.	The woman desires to have what Jesus offers, "Give me this water" (v. 15), and thereby to know who He is.
"Call your husband . . . You have well said . . . for you have had five husbands" (vv. 15–18). Now that Jesus has introduced Himself to the woman (as the One who gives everlasting life), He reveals knowledge of her.	"I perceive that you are a prophet. Our fathers worshiped on this mountain" (vv. 19, 20). The woman interprets Jesus as a prophet (she is growing in her knowledge of Him) and thus asks Him an important question (in the form of an indicative statement), "Where does worship of God occur?"
"You will neither worship in this mountain nor in Jerusalem. . . . True worshipers will worship the Father in Spirit and truth; for the Father is seeking such to worship Him. God is Spirit and those who worship Him must worship in Spirit and truth" (vv. 21–24). Jesus answers her question by saying that worship is an activity of the Spirit. In other words, worship will not be confined to a place or a tradition but will occur anywhere it is offered by people renewed by His Spirit.	The woman says that Jesus is talking about the time of the Messiah (v. 25).
Jesus identifies Himself as the Messiah (v. 26). He has fully introduced Himself to the woman.	The woman tells her townspeople that she believes she has met the Messiah (vv. 28–30). She now knows Jesus.

He left Judea and departed again to Galilee. But He needed to go
through Samaria. So He came to a city of Samaria which is
called Sychar, near the plot of ground that Jacob gave to his son
Joseph (vv. 3–5).

Jesus' demonstration in the temple and His discussion with Nicodemus occur while He is in Jerusalem for Passover. After this, He returns to Galilee and decides to travel through Samaria. Most observant Jews would travel back and forth between Galilee and Judea along the King's Highway that ran north and south through the Jordan River valley. Though the route was longer than the one that passed through Samaria, it allowed them to avoid contact with the Samaritans.

The location of Sychar is disputed. It is possibly in ancient Shechem, in the central mountains of Samaria where Jacob possessed land. (See Gen. 33:19; 48:22; Josh. 4:12; 24:32.)

Now Jacob's well was there. Jesus therefore, being wearied
from His journey, sat thus by the well. It was about the sixth
hour (v. 6).

Jacob's well represents the place where Jacob settled with his family. Historically, it is Jacob's residence.

By observing that Jesus was weary, John subtly but firmly asserts the humanity of Jesus. In other words, the Word of God became flesh (1:14). Also, by noting that Jesus' encounter with the woman was at the sixth hour (noon) John reveals that this is an eyewitness report.

A woman of Samaria came to draw water. Jesus said to her,
"Give Me a drink." For His disciples had gone away into the
city to buy food. Then the woman of Samaria said to Him,
"How is it that You, being a Jew, ask a drink from me, a
Samaritan woman?" For Jews have no dealings with Samaritans
(vv. 7–9).

Jesus is alone at Jacob's well and asks a Samaritan woman to give Him some water. Since He is weary it would not be unusual for one to make such a request, except for the fact the social conventions of this time discouraged all public contact between men and women, Jews and Samaritans.

WHO WERE THE SAMARITANS?

When the conquering Assyrians forcibly removed many northern Israelites to other provinces under their control, they relocated other peoples to the northern kingdom. This occurred in 722 B.C. (The biblical view of this event is recorded in 2 Kings 17.) These new settlers were encouraged to intermarry with the remaining Jews as part of the Assyrian policy of assimilation. Over time the people of Israel's northern kingdom thoroughly intermarried with the foreigners who settled in their land. This people of mixed blood were despised by the Jews of Judea.

To make matters worse, the Samaritans built a temple on Mt. Gerizim and developed their own version of the Pentateuch (the five books of Moses). The people of the southern kingdom of Judah, who were known as Jews after the Babylonian Exile of the early sixth century B.C., were highly critical of these innovations. After all, God had ordained His worship in Jerusalem and had given the Law to Moses. Moreover, when many of these Jews returned to Judea from exile in Babylon in the mid-sixth century B.C., they were opposed by the surrounding peoples, including the mixed people of the former northern kingdom of Israel—now Samaria. Therefore, by the time Jesus arrived in Samaria, the hostility between these two peoples had existed for hundreds of years.

> *Jesus answered and said to her, "If you knew the gift of God, and who it is who says to you, 'Give Me a drink,' you would have asked Him, and He would have given you living water." The woman said to Him, "Sir, You have nothing to draw with, and the well is deep. Where then do You get that living water? Are You greater than our father Jacob, who gave us the well, and drank from it himself, as well as his sons and his livestock?" Jesus answered and said to her, "Whoever drinks of this water will thirst again, but whoever drinks of the water that I shall give him will never thirst. But the water that I shall give him will become in him a fountain of water springing up into everlasting life." The woman said to Him, "Sir, give me this water, that I may not thirst, nor come here to draw" (vv. 10–15).*

Jesus tells the woman that He offers living water that quenches the true human thirst and issues in eternal life. Later, He will repeat this when He stands in the temple and proclaims, "He who believes in Me . . . out of his heart will flow rivers of living water" (7:38).

What is this water? John explains that it is the Holy Spirit (7:39). Thus, when Jesus says that if the woman knew Him, she would receive living water, He means that He offers eternal life through God's Spirit. Only the Spirit of God can satisfy the greatest human needs and desires and only Jesus can give the Spirit.

Jesus' use of water as an image of the Spirit has precedence in the Old Testament. Several passages describe water as being a primary feature of the Spirit in the future Day of the Lord. For example, God declared to the people in exile, "I will pour water on him who is thirsty, and floods on the dry ground; I will pour My Spirit on your descendents, and My blessing on your offspring" (Is. 44:3). Here, water is an image of the Spirit that God will give to His people when He brings them back from their banishment. The prophet Zechariah later declared that in the Day of the Lord, "A fountain shall be opened for the house of David . . . for sin and for uncleanness" (13:1) and, "Living waters shall flow from Jerusalem" (14:8). Though Zechariah does not explicitly describe the Spirit, he announces the cleansing and life-giving work of God that is indicative of the Spirit. The living water of which Jesus speaks is the Spirit who brings the life of God to all people.

The woman understands more of Jesus' words than one might expect. This is indicated by her question, "Are You greater than our father Jacob?" She wonders how Jesus can make such a claim since it signifies a greater promise than the blessing given to Jacob who, as she says, "Gave us the well, and drank from it himself, as well as his sons and his livestock." Jesus elaborates, saying that He offers the water of eternal life. God promised Jacob that he and the nation that would be generated by his offspring would enjoy blessing, descendents, and land. Jesus promises the woman that she can enjoy the blessing of God's Spirit and eternal life through Him.

> *Jesus said to her, "Go, call your husband, and come here." The woman answered and said, "I have no husband." Jesus said to her, "You have well said, 'I have no husband,' for you have had five husbands, and the one whom you now have is not your husband; in that you spoke truly" (vv. 16–18).*

Popular tradition claimed that the Samaritans traced their mixed lineage to five different peoples (2 Kin. 17:24). Therefore, Jesus' observation that the woman has had five husbands has significance beyond her experience. He speaks to her as a representative of her people. What Jesus says to her about living water, He says to all Samaritans.

At the end of the preceding section of his gospel, John described Jesus as the bridegroom to God's people (3:29). Here the bridegroom issues what might be described as a marriage proposal to the Samaritan people. He offers a life with God to a woman who has experienced nothing but matrimonial failure. By setting this encounter alongside the Baptist's statement that Jesus is the bridegroom, John creatively presents Jesus' ministry as marriage celebration in which, through Him, people enter into a relationship with God and enjoy life by the Spirit.

> *The woman said to Him, "Sir, I perceive that You are a prophet. Our fathers worshiped on this mountain, and you Jews say that in Jerusalem is the place where one ought to worship." Jesus said to her, "Woman, believe Me, the hour is coming when you will neither on this mountain, nor in Jerusalem, worship the Father. You worship what you do not know; we know what we worship, for salvation is of the Jews. But the hour is coming, and now is, when the true worshipers will worship the Father in spirit and truth; for the Father is seeking such to worship Him. God is Spirit, and those who worship Him must worship in spirit and truth" (vv. 19–24).*

The Samaritan woman asks an implied question with her statement about the two places of worship revered by the two peoples. Worship was a primary matter of dispute between Jews and Samaritans. Jesus says that worship will be given anywhere the Spirit is present. This complements His remarks about living water that leads to eternal life. Whoever has this water, which is the Spirit, will worship God with their very lives. God desires worship that is grounded in a shared relationship. Because God is Spirit, He desires worship from those who have the living water—that is, the Spirit.

Jesus' action in the temple and His remarks here reveal His extraordinary understanding of the nature of worship. Worship is not about giving the right sacrifice at the right time, nor is it about being in the right place at the right time. Worship is about enjoying the Spirit as "a fountain of water springing up into everlasting life" (v. 14). This nourishes others and blesses God. Such worship is performed in truth; it will be given with gratitude for the living water that makes such worship possible.

> *The woman said to Him, "I know that Messiah is coming" (who is called Christ). "When He comes, He will tell us all things." Jesus said to her, "I who speak to you am He" (vv. 25, 26).*

The woman remarks that Jesus is speaking of the age of the Anointed One of God, the Messiah, who will restore life to the people and lead them in worship of God. To this Jesus says that He is that Anointed One; the Messiah. This remarkable statement reveals that the Light is shining in the world for all to see.

> *And at this point His disciples came, and they marveled that He talked with a woman; yet no one said, "What do You seek?" or, "Why are You talking with her?" (v. 27).*

The disciples are surprised (*thaumazō*, θαυμάζω) and possibly disturbed to discover that Jesus has been conversing with a Samaritan woman. Jesus has ignored social customs by speaking in public with a Samaritan woman.

> *The woman then left her waterpot, went her way into the city, and said to the men, "Come, see a Man who told me all things that I ever did. Could this be the Christ?" Then they went out of the city and came to Him (vv. 28–30).*

The woman reports her conversation to the leading men of her town. Is it possible that Jesus is the Messiah? Like Andrew who quickly goes to Peter to tell him about Jesus and Philip who urges Nathanael to observe Jesus for himself, the Samaritan woman recounts her experience to the townspeople. Like Peter and Nathanael, they go to Jesus to see and hear for themselves.

> *In the meantime His disciples urged Him, saying, "Rabbi, eat." But He said to them, "I have food to eat of which you do not know." Therefore the disciples said to one another, "Has anyone brought Him anything to eat?" Jesus said to them, "My food is to do the will of Him who sent Me, and to finish His work. Do you not say, 'There are still four months and then comes the harvest'? Behold, I say to you, lift up your eyes and look at the fields, for they are already white for harvest! And he who reaps receives wages, and gathers fruit for eternal life, that both he who sows and he who reaps may rejoice together. For in this the saying is true: 'One sows and another reaps.' I sent you to reap that for which you have not labored; others have labored, and you have entered into their labors" (vv. 31–38).*

The disciples return with food for Jesus to eat. He tells them that He "has food to eat of which you do not know." This figurative expression is similar to the one He has made to the woman, "Whoever drinks of the water that I shall give him will never thirst" (v. 14). Because the disciples place a literal interpretation on Jesus' words, they misunderstand His meaning. This is a problem that Jesus will face throughout the course of His ministry. Time and again those who hear Him misunderstand His words (6:41–66; 8:48–59).

Jesus explains that He is nourished by doing God's will. He frequently uses this expression to describe God's role in His ministry. God has taken the initiative and sent the Son into the world. (See 3:17; 5:24, 27; 6:29, 38, 40, 44, 57; 7:18, 28, 33; 8:18, 29, 42; 11:42; 12:44; 13:20; 14:24.) And what is God's will? It is the harvesting of the fields; the ingathering of Israel into the kingdom. God does not wish that people be scattered from His presence, but that they be brought together to enjoy His presence. Just as many participate in the harvest of grains and fruits in season, many will also participate in the will of God. He tells the disciples that they have a part in reaping God's harvest and informs them they will enter into the labor of others. This recalls the labor of Israel's ancient prophets as well as the recent ministry of John the Baptist.

> *And many of the Samaritans of that city believed in Him*
> *because of the word of the woman who testified, "He told me all*
> *that I ever did." So when the Samaritans had come to Him, they*
> *urged Him to stay with them; and He stayed there two days. And*
> *many more believed because of His own word. Then they said to*
> *the woman, "Now we believe, not because of what you said, for*
> *we ourselves have heard Him and we know that this is indeed*
> *the Christ, the Savior of the world" (vv. 39–42).*

The Samaritans' response is evidence of the harvest to which Jesus refers. Moreover, their confession of Jesus as "the Christ, the Savior of the world" affirms His words to Nicodemus that "God so loved the world" and "God did not send His Son to condemn the world, but that the world through Him might be saved" (3:16, 17).

This section of John's gospel (1:35–4:42) concludes with the affirmation of Jesus as "the Savior of the world." This is significant because the stories of Nathanael, Nicodemus, and the woman at the well are all connected to the story of Jacob. This story emphasizes the promise of God to the patriarchs— that He will give them land and descendents. God promised Abraham many descendents (Gen. 12:2; 15:5; 17:5–7). God told Jacob that his descendents will be "as the dust of the earth" (Gen. 28:14). Jesus recalled this promise in mentioning the open heaven to Nathanael. He informed Nicodemus that the world (the dust of the earth) will experience the salvation of God. This is seen in the Samaritans' response to Jesus' message. Their belief is evidence that the promise of God to Abraham and Jacob are fulfilled in the ministry of God's Son.

QUESTIONS FOR PERSONAL REFLECTION AND GROUP DISCUSSION

1. What does Jesus mean when He names Simon as *Peter*?
2. Why does John use the word *sign* to describe Jesus' miracles?
3. What are the seven signs that Jesus performs? What do these mean?
4. What does Jesus mean when He tells Nicodemus that "the wind blows where it will"?
5. Nicodemus and the Samaritan woman could not be more different. How are they different?
6. Why does John group together the stories of Nathanael, Nicodemus, and the Samaritan woman?

CHAPTER 3

JESUS AND THE NEW EXODUS

John 4:43–7:52

The previous section of John's gospel drew upon the story of Jacob to give meaning to Jesus' encounters with Nathanael, Nicodemus, and the Samaritan woman. The events in this section are framed by the story of Israel's Exodus from Egypt. It begins with Jesus' observation that the people need signs in order to believe in God. He consents to their need and heals a young boy and an old man. He also performs a miracle by feeding 5,000 men with five loaves of bread and two fish. Throughout these events many oppose Jesus and speak against Him. The need for signs, the healing of the boy and the man, and the feeding miracle, along with the murmuring response of the people, recall the great act of deliverance in the Exodus. John has already shown that Jesus has come to fulfill the promises of God to Abraham and Jacob. In these verses, he shows that Jesus has come to lead the people in a new exodus—not to the physical land of promise but into the very presence of God.

A People in Need of Signs (John 4:43–54)

News about Jesus has circulated among the people of Cana. When He returns there from Jerusalem (v. 46) a royal official approaches Him on behalf of his ill son. Jesus announces the need for signs and says that the people will not believe without them. This is not a negative remark. It is a simple observation of a fact: humans depend upon signs to believe. As with the previous sign at Cana, this one results in faith: "So the man believed the word that Jesus spoke" (v. 50).

Jesus' statement here recalls the importance of signs in the deliverance of the Hebrew people from servitude in Egypt. As noted in chapter two, the

Exodus may be viewed as a series of signs that God performed as He led the people from Egypt into Canaan. The signs declare God's nature and ability to fulfill His promises. Without signs Israel cannot believe. Therefore, Jesus performs signs that speak of the nature of God in His ministry. The healing of the royal official's son is one such sign.

> *Now after the two days He departed from there and went to Galilee. For Jesus Himself testified that a prophet has no honor in his own country. So when He came to Galilee, the Galileans received Him, having seen all the things He did in Jerusalem at the feast; for they also had gone to the feast (vv. 43–45).*

Jesus travels to Galilee from Samaria and returns to Cana. There He testifies about Himself and decries the lack of honor He has received from His own people. What has prompted this pronouncement? Why does John include it here? More than likely, the reference to a prophet not having honor in his own hometown recalls Jesus' recent experience in Samaria. The Samaritans asked Him to remain with them longer and He complied. John reports that as a result, "many more believed in His word" and declared Him to be the Savior of the world (vv. 40–42). They honor Jesus by their response to His word even though His word had been met with skepticism by the people in Jerusalem.

Whereas John reports what Jesus said without quoting Him, the synoptic writers quote Jesus directly (Matt. 13:57; Mark 6:4; Luke 4:24). John inserts this observation about a prophet's honor into his narrative not only because it reflects on Jesus' reception in Samaria, but it prepares the reader for His reception by the Galileans.

> *So Jesus came again to Cana of Galilee where He had made the water wine. And there was a certain nobleman whose son was sick at Capernaum. When he heard that Jesus had come out of Judea into Galilee, he went to Him and implored Him to come down and heal his son, for he was at the point of death (vv. 46, 47).*

A royal official intercepts Jesus in Cana on behalf of his sick son in Capernaum. This man is likely an official of Herod Antipas whose government was centered there. The synoptic writers usually describe such people as Herodians (Matt. 22:16; Mark 3:6; 12:13). This man has traveled to Cana to solicit Jesus' help on behalf of his son who is about to die.

Then Jesus said to him, "Unless you people see signs and won-
ders, you will by no means believe" (v. 48).

As noted above, it is not necessary to read impatience or exasperation into
this statement. Rather, Jesus acutely recognizes the human need for external
confirmation to believe in the goodness of God.

The nobleman said to Him, "Sir, come down before my child
dies!" Jesus said to him, "Go your way; your son lives." So the
man believed the word that Jesus spoke to him, and he went his
way. And as he was now going down, his servants met him and
told him, saying, "Your son lives!" Then he inquired of them the
hour when he got better. And they said to him, "Yesterday at the
seventh hour the fever left him." So the father knew that it was
at the same hour in which Jesus said to him, "Your son lives."
And he himself believed, and his whole household. This again is
the second sign Jesus did when He had come out of Judea into
Galilee (vv. 49–54).

The official implores Jesus to come and heal his son. When Jesus responds by
saying, "Go your way, your son lives," the man believes the word of Jesus and
goes away. John emphasizes the fact that the man's son lives by repeating the
statement three times: Jesus tells the father, "Your son lives" (v. 50), the man's
servants report to him, "Your son lives" (v. 51), and John reports the recollection of the words of Jesus, "Your son lives," by the father as he returns to
his home (v. 53). Jesus' word not only brings physical life to the royal official's
son, even more it prompts faith in the father and the people of his household
(v. 53). Such faith, as indicated in the stories of Nicodemus and the woman
at the well, results in eternal life. The miracle is not just that the son has been
saved from death, but that the entire family has come to faith in Jesus Christ
and has experienced eternal life through Him. It shows that Jesus is the One
who gives the signs and speaks the words that restore physical life and
bestows eternal life on those who believe.

John notes that the son recovers at the seventh hour (the early afternoon)
at the time the royal official approached Jesus. This precise reference to time
indicates first-hand information of the miracle. Each of the stories recorded
by John up to this point have included similar references to place and time:
Jesus attends a wedding in Cana on the third day; Nicodemus approaches
Jesus at night while He is in Jerusalem; Jesus is by Jacob's well in Sychar at
the sixth hour when a woman comes to draw water. This type of informa-

tion not only speaks to the veracity of the events reported—John knows his subject well—but it also allows the reader to place himself or herself in the narrative and visualize the events.

Deliverance and Dishonor (John 5:1–47)

This passage continues and complements the previous story of the healing of the royal official's son. It also reveals the centrality of honor in relation to Jesus:

- Jesus introduces the subject of honor when He says that a prophet is not honored in his own country (4:44). The Greek word for "honor" (*timē*, ἡ τιμή) is uncommon in the Gospels. It is used twice in Matthew and once by John with the general sense of estimation or value. The verb form appears six times in John, four times in 5:23 alone. Such infrequent use points to its importance in this passage.
- The lame man does not recognize his healer until Jesus reveals Himself in the temple (v. 13).
- The healing introduces hostility to Jesus because it occurs on the Sabbath (vv. 16, 18). Jesus is criticized rather than honored for the miracle.
- The Father reveals everything to Jesus and has given all judgment to Him for the express purpose that He will receive honor.

Like the healing of the official's son, the healing of the man at the Pool of Bethesda is a sign representative of the restorative work of God in the deliverance of the Hebrew people in Egypt. John sets these two accounts of healing side by side in order to emphasize the liberating nature of Jesus' ministry. Just as he placed Jesus' conversation with Nicodemus alongside that of the Samaritan woman, so also John juxtaposes these two healings in order to accentuate this aspect of His ministry. The accounts are different and, at the same time, complementary. Both healings occur as a result of the word or command of Jesus and both result in restored life. All human life, young and old, is honored by Jesus.

The first miracle occurs after John announces that a prophet is without honor in his hometown and still results in belief. The second miracle leads to opposition and Jesus' declaration that the honor of God the Father is related to the honor of the Son. Thus, the notion of honor is the context for these healing stories.

COMPARISON OF TWO HEALINGS	
Royal Official's Son	**Man at the Pool of Bethesda**
A Roman official approaches Jesus on behalf of his son.	Jesus approaches a man by the Pool of Bethesda in Jerusalem.
By definition, the son is a young man.	The man at the pool has been an invalid for thirty-eight years. He is an older man.
The son is at the point of death; his condition is critical.	The man has struggled with his infirmity for a long time. His condition is chronic.
The father believes the word of Jesus: "Your son lives." This illustrates grace without works in keeping with Paul's ministry to the Gentiles (Eph. 3:8).	Jesus commands the man to "rise, take up your bed and walk." This illustrates grace with works in keeping with James' ministry to Israel's Twelve Tribes (James 1:1; 2:14–26).
John records Jesus' words three times indicating the power of His resurrection on the third day.	John records Jesus' command three times indicating that the man is healed by Christ's resurrection life.
The royal official and his household believe in Jesus just as the Philippian jailer and his family are saved by faith (Acts 16:31).	The man reports to the Jews that Jesus healed him. This leads to opposition because the healing occurred on the Sabbath.

After this there was a feast of the Jews, and Jesus went up to Jerusalem. Now there is in Jerusalem by the Sheep Gate a pool, which is called in Hebrew, Bethesda, having five porches. In these lay a great multitude of sick people, blind, lame, paralyzed, waiting for the moving of the water. For an angel went down at a certain time into the pool and stirred up the water; then whoever stepped in first, after the stirring of the water, was made well of whatever disease he had. Now a certain man was there who had an infirmity thirty-eight years (vv. 1–5).

John again gives the time and place of a miracle performed by Jesus. The feast of the Jews may refer to Passover. If so, this is the second Passover that John describes in his gospel.

The Pool of Bethesda was located north of the Temple Mount. There is some variance in the ancient texts concerning the name of the pool, likely the result of transliteration from Aramaic into Greek. The two most prominent names found in these texts are Bethesda and Bethzatha. Since Bethzatha (place of olives) was the name for the newer part of Jerusalem in the first century, located north of the temple, and Bethesda (house of mercy) accords well with the tradition of healing associated with the pool, it is not surprising that both names are attested in the early editions of John.

The name Bethesda is derived from the Hebrew *hesed* and has a rich range of meanings, including mercy, lovingkindness, and covenantal love. The name is particularly appropriate in that a large number (*plēthos*, πλῆθος) of sick people have gathered around the pool in need of God's mercy. They are helpless and wait for the waters to move so that they may be healed. This notion of mercy was closely related to God's deliverance of His people from Egypt as indicated in the "Song of Moses" (Ex. 15:1–18) which describes God as a warrior who battles on behalf of His people and who does so because of His *hesed*. "You in Your mercy (*hesed*) have led forth the people whom You have redeemed; You have guided them in Your strength to Your holy habitation" (15:13). God leads the people forward in His mercy. The background to the song is the parting of the water of the Red Sea and the destruction of Pharaoh's army. Thus, the condition of the people at the pool is not unlike that of the numerous Hebrew people in Egypt who are delivered from their sorrows or pains through the waters of the sea (Ex. 3:7–9). They need the water to move so they may be healed from the oppression of Egypt.

John reports the tradition of an angel stirring the waters as a fact. He does not question its genuineness. Why does he report such a curious folk-belief? As noted in the previous paragraph, he does so in order to link the healing of the man to the story of the Exodus. The popular acceptance of this story may be seen in the number of people who waited by the water for it to move. In fact, a tradition of healing associated with the pool is reported as late as the second century with the Greek god of healing Asclepius.

A man with an infirmity or weakness (*astheneia*)—a related word to that used of the royal official's son in 4:46—is one of the many people at the pool. He has been afflicted for thirty-eight years. Since the average lifespan at this time was forty years, the man had been an invalid for most if not all of his life. As one of the many people who are weak and sick and in need of the divine *hesed* of God, the man's condition and situation is not unlike that of his ancestors in Egypt who were sick and oppressed and in need of divine deliverance. The man had known suffering for most of his life even as the Hebrew people had known only sorrow during their many years of servitude in Egypt.

> *When Jesus saw him lying there, and knew that he already had been in that condition a long time, He said to him, "Do you want to be made well?" The sick man answered Him, "Sir, I have no man to put me into the pool when the water is stirred up; but while I am coming, another steps down before me" (vv. 6, 7).*

When Jesus asks, "Do you want to be made well?" He assesses the man's faith. The man only bemoans the fact that he cannot get into the water before the others. His response, "I have no man to put me into the pool" (v. 7), indicates that he needs someone to carry him into the water before he can experience healing. This recalls the need of the people in Egypt for a deliverer who will lead them out of bondage. It also recalls the pessimism of the Hebrew people as they stand at the edge of the Red Sea with the Egyptian army in furious pursuit: "It would have been better for us to serve the Egyptians than that we should die in the wilderness" (Ex. 14:12).

> *Jesus said to him, "Rise, take up your bed and walk." And immediately the man was made well, took up his bed, and walked. And that day was the Sabbath. The Jews therefore said to him who was cured, "It is the Sabbath; it is not lawful for you to carry your bed." He answered them, "He who made me well said to me, 'Take up your bed and walk.'" Then they asked him, "Who is the Man who said to you, 'Take up your bed and walk'?" (vv. 8–12).*

John draws attention to Jesus' command, "Rise, take up your bed and walk," In that the man repeats the phrase to the Jews and then the Jews repeat it (vv. 8, 11, 12). This emphasis underscores the fact that Jesus' words bring healing to the man. John has already depicted him as despondent, "I have no man to put me into the pool." Now Jesus commands the man's healing despite his despondency.

One of John's stylistic traits is his repetition of key points or features in a passage or several passages. Here, John repeats the fact that Jesus commanded the man to take his bed and walk. The healing results from Jesus' words. It does not result from the man's faith though he does respond to Jesus' words. In the healing of the royal official's son (4:46–54), Jesus' promise, "Your son lives," is repeated three times. This unequivocally asserts that Jesus' words give life to the boy.

John notes that the healing occurs on the Sabbath. This fact is important because traditional teaching limited activity on this day. For some, carrying one's mat or giving unusual care to the weak or infirm on the Sabbath was improper. They maintained that this one day was for worship of God rather than serving the needs of people. Those needs could be met on any of the other six days of the week. Though rabbinic teaching allowed for the care of people who were gravely ill, it was ambivalent about special treatment for chronic ailments.

> But the one who was healed did not know who it was, for Jesus had withdrawn, a multitude being in that place. Afterward Jesus found him in the temple, and said to him, "See, you have been made well. Sin no more, lest a worse thing come upon you." The man departed and told the Jews that it was Jesus who had made him well (vv. 13–15).

Jesus withdraws without revealing His identity to the man. He later finds him in the temple and exhorts him not to sin. Such failure may result in a more severe affliction. John gives close attention to the problem of sin later in his gospel. Here, the story suggests that the longstanding condition of the man is not unrelated to his standing before God. That Jesus finds the man in the temple indicates he has learned this truth and worships God for his healing. The man then tells the leaders of the temple that Jesus healed him. Like those before him, he testifies to the good work of Jesus.

> For this reason the Jews persecuted Jesus, and sought to kill Him, because He had done these things on the Sabbath (v. 16).

Opposition arises because the healing occurred on the Sabbath. The opposition is not due to jealousy or simple callousness; rather, it is related to the interpretation of work that some placed on Sabbath activities. The opposition is severe. The leaders of the temple desire to put Jesus to death.

The Gospel of Mark records a healing in a synagogue on the Sabbath with a similar reaction among some of the people. Jesus makes two statements that reveal His approach to the issue of Sabbath. First, He says, "The Sabbath was made for man, and not man for the Sabbath" (Mark 2:27). In other words, the Sabbath should benefit men and women. Second, He asks, "Is it lawful on the Sabbath to do good or to do evil, to save life or to kill?" (3:4). His question implies the Sabbath was established to do good and to save life. The Sabbath, like the days of creation, is a time to do good. Jesus' remarks connect the Sabbath to creation and indicate that it should be a day of revitalization and renewal. Thus, He interprets the Sabbath as a blessing for people as well as a time of worship of God and counters that of some who viewed the Sabbath exclusively in terms of service to God.

> *But Jesus answered them, "My Father has been working until now, and I have been working." Therefore the Jews sought all the more to kill Him, because He not only broke the Sabbath, but also said that God was His Father, making Himself equal with God (vv. 17, 18).*

Jesus equates His ministry with the work of God. This upsets the leaders of the temple, John reports, because in their view Jesus claims equality with God with such a statement. By asserting that God, His Father, had been working in His ministry up to this point, Jesus says that the things He does, God does. This would have been unthinkable for some, since Jesus did not honor certain traditions of the time, like the observance of the Sabbath, which they regarded as a measure of fidelity to the Law of Moses. Such behavior would have disqualified Jesus from any special relationship with God in their eyes.

Opposition to Jesus in the Gospel of John

John does not flinch from reporting the distressful fact that Jesus experienced violent opposition from the beginning of His ministry. In his introduction, John writes, "He came to His own, and His own did not receive Him" (1:11). This serves as a summary statement for John's portrayal of antagonism and conflict over the course of Jesus' ministry. Jesus consistently encounters opposition and rejection from others. But why is there such strong opposition to Jesus when He is performing signs that speak of the new creative work of God? John gives several clues in the first chapters of his gospel.

After His first miracle, Jesus goes to Jerusalem where He physically protests against the business activities that were being conducted there. The response to this behavior is forceful: "What sign do You show to us, since You do these things?" (2:18). The leaders are incredulous. Such activity would have been darkly interpreted by those responsible for the administration of the temple. Jesus then travels to Samaria where He claims the day is near when worship will not be centered in Jerusalem's temple or in any other temple and says that the eternal life of God is available to all. He remains two days with the Samaritans who were despised by the Jews and later says that a prophet has no honor in his hometown. Later he heals a man on the Sabbath, disregarding certain religious traditions of the period. In short, Jesus' violent action in the temple, His ministry among the Samaritans, and His violation of Sabbath prohibitions alienates many people. This disaffection is so great that certain leaders conspire to put Jesus to death.

John records these events to prepare the reader for the hostile resistance to Jesus' ministry. He reports that certain leaders "sought to kill Him" (5:16) and "sought all the more to kill Him" (5:18) because of the healing on the Sabbath. This would not have been the exclusive reason they wanted Jesus dead, but it represents the last of several events that would have hardened their views about Him.

MURDEROUS CONSPIRACY IN JOHN'S GOSPEL

John reports several occasions in which the Jews conspire to put Jesus to death. These include:

- Jesus refrains from going to Jerusalem to celebrate the Feast of Tabernacles because the temple leadership desires to kill Him (7:1, 2).
- He knows about these plans when He asks, "Did not Moses give you the law, yet none of you keeps the law? Why do you want to kill Me?" (7:19).
- Other people ask, "Is this not He whom they seek to kill?" (7:25).
- The threat of imminent harm is present throughout Jesus' ministry (7:30, 44, 45; 8:20).
- Jesus' teaching concerning Abraham incites the Jews to stone Him (8:48–59).
- His description of His relationship to God as that of Son to Father causes people to pick up stones against him (10:30–39).
- When Jesus raises Lazarus from the dead the leadership under Caiaphas decides that Jesus must die: "From that day on, they plotted to put Him to death" (11:53).

After Caiaphas has made up his mind that Jesus must die, Jesus Himself speaks of His impending death (12:20–36) and He alludes to it in His discourse with His disciples on the eve of His crucifixion (16:16–24).

The sad irony of this opposition to Jesus is that while some desire His death, He openly offers the eternal life of God to them. John's gospel moves along these two lines of thought. On one hand, Jesus reveals the intent of God to give life to His people through His Son. On the other, people resist Jesus' teaching and signs and desire to see Him dead. John's gospel traces the coming of the Light of God into the world even as it outlines the attempt of darkness to extinguish this Light.

Then Jesus answered and said to them, "Most assuredly, I say to you, the Son can do nothing of Himself, but what He sees the Father do; for whatever He does, the Son also does in like manner. For the Father loves the Son, and shows Him all things that He Himself does; and He will show Him greater works than these, that you may marvel. For as the Father raises the dead and gives life to them, even so the Son gives life to whom He will. For the Father judges no one, but has committed all judgment to the Son, that all should honor the Son just as they honor the Father. He who does not honor the Son does not honor the Father who sent Him (vv. 19–23).

Verses nineteen to thirty record what Jesus says to the Jews who want to kill Him for violating the Sabbath. His remarks may be organized by the three times He says, "Most assuredly, I say to you" (vv. 19, 24, 25) and "Do not marvel" (v. 28). As noted above, the expression, "Most assuredly, I say to you," introduces insight and knowledge unique to Jesus. His first use of the expression here leads to the claim that He does what He sees God His Father doing. This is possible because the Father loves Him and reveals everything to Him. Jesus then says that even as the Father gives life to the dead, He, too, gives life. This authority is given so that the Son will receive the same honor as the Father. If the Son is not honored, neither is the Father. Thus, in these verses Jesus says three things about God His Father: God loves the Son; God gives life to His people through His Son; and God has given judgment to the Son.

Jesus here speaks of God His Father as the God of resurrection: "For as the Father raises the dead and gives life to them." It is God's intent to give life. Like God, Jesus also gives life. He made this claim earlier when He told Nicodemus that, like the serpent in the wilderness and as God's only begotten Son, He offers eternal life (3:16). He also told the woman at the well that He gives the water that spouts into eternal life (4:14).

Even though He has come to offer eternal life to the people, Jesus says that all judgment has been given to Him. However, He has already told Nicodemus that the Son did not enter the world in order to condemn it (3:17, 18). So, how should His statement here be understood? Remember that Jesus also told Nicodemus that people's deeds link them to either light or darkness (3:19–21). In other words, people identify themselves with the light or the darkness by their actions. Jesus judges whether or not the deeds that people do identify with Him or not. The judgment concerning whether or not people know Jesus Christ is established by their response to Him.

Jesus' ambition is to do what He sees God the Father doing. God's ambition is for His Son to be honored. To reject Jesus' teaching, to disbelieve His miracles, to oppose Him is to dishonor Him and, in so doing, to dishonor God. It shows that one identifies with darkness rather than light.

> *"Most assuredly, I say to you, he who hears My word and*
> *believes in Him who sent Me has everlasting life, and shall not*
> *come into judgment, but has passed from death into life" (v. 24).*

Jesus asserts ("Most assuredly, I say to you") that acceptance of His teaching (word) and belief that God sent Him results in eternal life. This is identification with light rather than darkness.

> *"Most assuredly, I say to you, the hour is coming, and now is,*
> *when the dead will hear the voice of the Son of God; and those*
> *who hear will live. For as the Father has life in Himself, so He*
> *has granted the Son to have life in Himself, and has given Him*
> *authority to execute judgment also, because He is the Son of*
> *Man" (vv. 25–27).*

Yet again, Jesus asserts that the time has arrived when those who are dead will hear Him and live. He offers life because He is the Son of Man with the authority to judge. Who are "the dead"? They are those like the Samaritans who do not have life with God through His covenant. For the Jews to whom Jesus is speaking only those who live in conformity with God's covenant are alive. Life comes through God's covenant. Jesus says that life comes through Him as God's Son. Thus, those like the Samaritans live because they believe in the word of Jesus (4:39–42).

Why does Jesus say that it is as the Son of Man that He carries out God's judgment? Two reasons may be given. First, as the Son of Man, Jesus relates to all people: those of the covenant as well as those outside of it. As One who knows the nature of men and women, Jesus judges such people (compare 2:24, 25). Second, the Son of Man is the One who possesses the privilege and authority of God, according to Daniel 7:13, 14, who will rule God's kingdom and execute God's judgment on His behalf.

> *"Do not marvel at this; for the hour is coming in which all who*
> *are in the graves will hear His voice and come forth—those who*
> *have done good, to the resurrection of life, and those who have*
> *done evil, to the resurrection of condemnation. I can of Myself*
> *do nothing. As I hear, I judge; and My judgment is righteous,*

because I do not seek My own will but the will of the Father who sent Me" (vv. 28–30).

Jesus' statement is imperative: "Do not marvel." Not only will those who are dead, those who are outside the sphere of God's covenantal blessing, find life in Him, but those who have physically died will also hear His voice and some will rise to life while others will rise to judgment. Thus, Jesus extends what He says about people like the Samaritans who are dead to God in the covenant to the future day of resurrection and judgment.

It is important to follow the development of Jesus' remarks in these verses. In verses twenty-five to twenty-seven He speaks of the present ("the hour is coming, and now is") when the dead (people like the Samaritans) hear His words and live. He merely states what is already happening in His ministry as exemplified by the Samaritans' belief in His word (4:39–42). Jesus then broadens His discussion to the future (5:28–30). Not only does He offer the life of God now, but He will offer the life of God in the resurrection. At that time, all who have died ("all who are in the graves") will hear His voice. They will be judged by their own works: good works reveal their relation to the light; evil works reveal their preference for darkness (3:19–21).

"If I bear witness of Myself, My witness is not true. There is another who bears witness of Me, and I know that the witness which He witnesses of Me is true. You have sent to John, and he has borne witness to the truth. Yet I do not receive testimony from man, but I say these things that you may be saved. He was the burning and shining lamp, and you were willing for a time to rejoice in his light. But I have a greater witness than John's; for the works which the Father has given Me to finish—the very works that I do—bear witness of Me, that the Father has sent Me. And the Father Himself, who sent Me, has testified of Me. You have neither heard His voice at any time, nor seen His form. But you do not have His word abiding in you, because whom He sent, Him you do not believe. You search the Scriptures, for in them you think you have eternal life; and these are they which testify of Me. But you are not willing to come to Me that you may have life. I do not receive honor from men. But I know you, that you do not have the love of God in you. I have come in My Father's name, and you do not receive Me; if another comes in his own name, him you will receive. How can you believe, who receive honor from one another, and do not seek the honor that

comes from the only God? Do not think that I shall accuse you to
the Father; there is one who accuses you—Moses, in whom you
trust. For if you believed Moses, you would believe Me; for he
wrote about Me. But if you do not believe his writings, how will
you believe My words?" (vv. 31–47).

In these verses, Jesus speaks to the Jews about witnesses. He defers from giving testimony on His own behalf since such testimony was not viewed as
valid at this time. The Jews he addresses are the same ones who sent associ-
ates to John the Baptist to inquire about Jesus (3:25–36; 1:19–28). They are the
temple leaders in Jerusalem. Jesus acknowledges that the Baptist is a witness,
the burning and shining lamp, of a greater Light, but He also says that there
is a greater witness.

Jesus points to the miracles He does as evidence of God's authority in His
ministry. They reveal that God is at work in what He says and does. Thus,
God the Father is a witness to Jesus. By rejecting Jesus, the temple leaders
reject God's witness in Him. "But you do not have His word abiding in you,
because whom He sent, Him you do not believe." The living word of God is
absent in their lives because they reject the Word of God sent to them in the
flesh.

The Jews diligently study the Scripture but they fail to see that Jesus is the
embodiment of its teaching. For this reason they fail to understand the
Scripture's primary function: to reveal the intention of God to give eternal

---

THE TESTIMONIES ON BEHALF OF JESUS

John has already presented several witnesses on behalf of Jesus. He himself is one of these,
declaring Jesus to be the Word of God from the beginning by which everything was made,
which became flesh and dwelt among us (1:2, 3, 14), and who is "the true Light which gives
light to every true man coming into the world" (1:9). Other witnesses are:

- John the Baptist who proclaims that Jesus is greater than he, that He is the Lamb of
  God upon whom the Spirit of God descends, and the Son of God (1:27–35).
- Those who become disciples of Jesus say that He is the Messiah, the One of whom
  Moses wrote (1:41, 45).
- Nathanael, who hears Philip's testimony, says that Jesus is the Son of God and the King
  of Israel (1:49).
- The despised Samaritans who laud Him as the Messiah, the Savior of the world (4:42).

life, the life as it was in the beginning, that is now present in Jesus' ministry. By refusing to acknowledge that the life of God is offered in and through Jesus, the leaders withhold honor from Him. Though God wants to honor them—that is, He wants to restore them to the place of relationship that He intended in the beginning—they prefer the honor that they receive from one another. By placing the traditions of their ancestors before Jesus, the Jews place human honor before divine honor.

Jesus says that the Jews "are not willing to come to Me." Unlike Andrew and Philip, Nicodemus and the Samaritan woman, and even the royal official, all of whom approach Jesus and believe in Him as a result of their encounter, the leaders stay away and remain in unbelief. Moreover, He says that they do not have the love of God in them. Since God's love is manifest in Jesus (3:16) and reflects His primary feeling toward Jesus (5:20), to reject Him is to reject God's love.

Jesus concludes His remarks to the Jews by referring to Moses. He will not accuse them; Moses will accuse them. How will Moses do this? As the author of the Torah, Moses was the authority under which these people lived. The commandments, the laws, the story of the Exodus, the institution of sacrifice, the establishment of the priesthood, the promises of God in the covenant were all traced to Moses. Since God's Word through Moses is exemplified in Jesus, their response to Him represents a response to Moses. To reject Jesus is to reject Moses. The phrase *If you believed Moses* suggests that they have not believed Moses even as their ancestors disbelieved him. How so? They do not comprehend the meaning of his leadership and ministry. If they did, they would see that Jesus embodies the deliverance ministry of Moses who was called to establish a new people in a new land for a new life with God.

Prophets Without Honor

The Jews' lack of honor for Jesus closely binds Him to Moses. He alludes to this bond when He asks, "If you do not believe [Moses'] writings, how will you believe My words?" When John reports that Jesus said that "a prophet has no honor in his own country" (4:44), He could have been speaking as much about Moses as about himself.

Many times during the Exodus, Moses contends with the stubbornness and disbelief of the people. Though he speaks the words of God to them and performs signs in their midst, they accuse him of deceit and treachery (Ex. 14:11, 12; 16:2, 3; 17:2, 3). Moses is a prophet without honor among his people. The most blatant example of such dishonor occurs when Aaron and Miriam criticize Moses and wonder, "Does God only speak through His servant Moses?" (Num. 12:2). The answer, of course, is yes. God speaks in a unique way through Moses (Num. 12:6–8). Just as Moses was confronted and doubted by the people, despite the signs he performed, so also the leadership in Jerusalem withstand Jesus and reject His words despite the signs He has given them.

Jesus deserves honor because He does only what He sees God His Father doing. He says, "I do not seek My own will but the will of the Father who sent Me" (5:30). He desires to do what He sees God doing. This is His primary ambition. Yet, He does not receive honor for such ambition. Moses, too, did what God commanded. Even so, he was not honored by his people.

The reason Jesus does not receive the honor due Him is because the Jewish leaders prefer the honor that they have from one another. This honor relates to the tradition of teaching they had received from those before them. The healing of the man by the Pool of Bethesda provokes indignity because it violates that tradition. Moreover, Jesus' ministry among the Samaritans is offensive because of the longstanding enmity between the two peoples. The leaders, in other words, prefer their traditional beliefs, histories, and interpretations to the teaching of Jesus. This is not new. Moses faced similar resistance from his own people during the Exodus. When he fails to come down from the mountain with the commandments of God, the people make a golden calf (Ex. 32). This act represented a return to the religious practice they had learned in Egypt. The people turned away from Moses to the traditions they had received from their ancestors while in slavery. They gave greater honor to their traditions than they did to the words of Moses, through whom God commanded: "Do not make any graven image" (Ex. 20:3, 4). Yet, they did make such an image and, in so doing, gave honor to their Egyptian traditions. Jesus and Moses both spoke the words of God to the people of God. Plus, they both performed signs in their midst. Yet their words and deeds were rejected. This binds their stories together.

Jesus Feeds the People of God (John 6:1–15)

This passage reports the miracle feeding of 5,000 men with five loaves and two fish. It is the only miracle other than the Resurrection that is reported in all four Gospels (Matt. 14:13–21; Mark 6:14–29; Luke 9:10–17). John includes it at this point in his gospel to extend the connection between the new exodus of Jesus leading the people to the new life and the first Exodus of Moses leading the people to the Promised Land. Here Jesus makes the first *I am* statement, asserting that He is the Bread of Life.

After these things Jesus went over the Sea of Galilee, which is the Sea of Tiberias. Then a great multitude followed Him, because they saw His signs which He performed on those who were diseased. And Jesus went up on the mountain, and there He sat with His disciples. Now the Passover, a feast of the Jews, was near (vv. 1–4).

These verses provide the background to the miracle. John reports that Jesus passed over the Sea of Galilee. This body of water was also called the Sea of Tiberias after Tiberias Caesar. Since the other six miracles recorded by John are unique to his depiction of Jesus' ministry, it is significant that he includes this miracle even though each of the other Gospels also recounts it. He wants to show that Jesus is leading the people in a new exodus. Moses led the people through the Red Sea into the wilderness where God provided manna and quail for them to eat. Jesus crosses the Sea of Galilee, followed by a large multitude, and then feeds the 5,000. John reports this event after telling of His time in Jerusalem. In this way he ties the signs Jesus did in Jerusalem and His statement of identification with Moses with the new exodus Jesus is leading. Just as it was with Moses, the feeding miracle is part of this divine work.

Then Jesus lifted up His eyes, and seeing a great multitude coming toward Him, He said to Philip, "Where shall we buy bread, that these may eat?" But this He said to test him, for He Himself knew what He would do. Philip answered Him, "Two hundred denarii worth of bread is not sufficient for them, that every one of them may have a little" (vv. 5–7).

Jesus is conscious of the need of the multitude that is following Him and knows what he will do about it. Yet he asks Philip a question to test him. Remember, Philip initially identified Jesus as "Him of whom Moses in the law and also the prophets wrote" (1:45). Does Philip understand the true meaning of his statement that Jesus is One who is to come after Moses? Jesus' question tests him to discover the extent of his understanding. Philip responds by saying they do not have enough money to buy food for everyone. A denarius was the standard silver coin used throughout the Roman Empire at this time. It had the image of the emperor embossed on it. In His parable of the vineyard, Jesus places the value of a denarius at a day's wages (Matt. 20:2–13). Two hundred denarii, therefore, was a large sum of money but not enough to purchase the food needed to feed so many.

*One of His disciples, Andrew, Simon Peter's brother, said to
Him, "There is a lad here who has five barley loaves and two
small fish, but what are they among so many?" (vv. 8, 9).*

Andrew is once again identified as the brother of Simon Peter, signifying
Peter's special status among the disciples. He says that a boy has five loaves
of barley bread and two fish, not nearly enough for 5,000 men in his opinion. His response is similar to that of Elisha's servant who wonders if the
twenty barley loaves that are available is sufficient for the sons of the
prophets: "What?" he asks. "Shall I set this before one hundred men?" (2 Kin.
4:43). In fact, the feeding of 5,000 is reminiscent of the miracle performed by
Elisha, where a small amount of food is used to feed a large number of people with some left over (2 Kin. 4:42–44).

*Then Jesus said, "Make the people sit down." Now there was
much grass in the place. So the men sat down, in number about
five thousand. And Jesus took the loaves, and when He had given
thanks He distributed them to the disciples, and the disciples to
those sitting down; and likewise of the fish, as much as they
wanted (vv. 10, 11).*

Jesus seats the people, gives thanks for the bread and fish, and distributes the
food through His disciples. By performing these basic duties, Jesus serves as
the host of the meal.

*So when they were filled, He said to His disciples, "Gather up the
fragments that remain, so that nothing is lost." Therefore they
gathered them up, and filled twelve baskets with the fragments
of the five barley loaves which were left over by those who had
eaten (vv. 12, 13).*

The disciples collect the leftovers, not allowing the food to be wasted or
stored for later. In this way, Jesus teaches them that God's provision is available through Him. All they must do is trust Him for their needs. John does
not record the calling of the Twelve and, thus, does not say that there were
twelve disciples, the tradition unquestionably was well known at the time he
composed his gospel (see Matt. 10:1–4; Luke 6:12–16; Mark 3:13–19). The
twelve baskets full of food represent the twelve disciples' stewardship of
God's spiritual provision received through the ministry of Jesus Christ.

THE TWELVE BASKETS OF LEFTOVERS

- Just as with the turning of water into wine, Jesus abundantly provides for the needs of the people. There He created 180 gallons of wine for the wedding guests. Here, He feeds 5,000 people with enough bread fragments leftover to fill twelve baskets. His provision is profuse.
- By collecting the fragments, Jesus reveals a conscientious attitude toward God's creative activity. He also models good stewardship in preserving the fragments of the loaves that God has multiplied.
- Jesus reprises God's command to Israel in the wilderness to collect all the manna needed for the day but not to take so much that it would be wasted. "He who gathered much had nothing left over, and he who gathered little had no lack. Every man had gathered according to each one's need. And Moses said, 'Let no one leave any of it till morning'" (Ex. 16:18). This admonition was given so that each person could show their trust in God by only taking what they needed for one day. This exercise of trust in God prepared them for life in the land of Canaan where they would again be dependent on God for provision.

Then those men, when they had seen the sign that Jesus did, said, "This is truly the Prophet who is to come into the world." Therefore when Jesus perceived that they were about to come and take Him by force to make Him king, He departed again to the mountain by Himself alone (vv. 14, 15).

"Those men" are the 5,000 who were fed by Jesus. They echo Philip's earlier declaration that Jesus is "Him of whom Moses in the law, and also the prophets wrote" (1:45) by saying that Jesus is "the Prophet who is to come into the world." Moses spoke about a prophet who would follow Him and continue to lead the people and teach them God's Word. "The Lord your God will raise up for you a Prophet like me from among your brethren. Him you shall hear . . . [I] will put My words in His mouth, and He shall speak to them all that I command Him" (Deut. 18:15–18). The men recognize their miracle meal as a reprise of the feeding miracle of manna in the wilderness.

In their excitement, the people want to compel Jesus to rule over them. He knows of their plans and dismisses them to diffuse this sentiment. The people are thinking of kingship in political-revolutionary terms, whereas John has already revealed that kingship should be regarded in terms of God's peaceable kingdom that will come in the future. This is indicated by Nathanael's confession of Jesus as the King of Israel.

Jesus Calms the Disciples' Fears John (6:16–25)

John places this story of danger on the Sea of Galilee after the feeding miracle and before Jesus' declaration that He is the Bread of Life. Though he does not identify it as a sign, John says the disciples willingly receive Him into their boat, signifying their faith in Him.

> *Now when evening came, His disciples went down to the sea, got into the boat, and went over the sea toward Capernaum. And it was already dark, and Jesus had not come to them (vv. 16, 17).*

The disciples get into their boat and cross to Capernaum, a town located on the northwest shore of the Sea of Galilee.

John began his gospel by observing that light shines in the darkness but cannot extinguish it. Darkness was the setting for Nicodemus' meeting with Jesus (3:1–21) and will be the setting for Judas' betrayal of Jesus when he goes out into the night (13:30). Here, the disciples cross the Sea of Galilee in the dark. Since darkness signifies ignorance, the fact that the disciples go over the water in darkness suggests that they do not fully understand what Jesus has done or who He is.

> *Then the sea arose because a great wind was blowing. So when they had rowed about three or four miles, they saw Jesus walking on the sea and drawing near the boat; and they were afraid. But He said to them, "It is I; do not be afraid." Then they willingly received Him into the boat, and immediately the boat was at the land where they were going (vv. 18–21).*

The disciples not only cross Galilee at night, but they do so in a storm. John notes that the disciples had rowed three or four miles. This authentic detail indicates that this is an eyewitness account. The disciples are afraid. The source of this fear is usually assigned to the appearance of Jesus on the water in the midst of a storm at night. He is an apparition; a ghost! Alternatively, some of the disciples are fisherman and used to inclement weather. The ferocity of the storm may frighten even these seasoned sailors. Jesus' statement to them may point in this direction. When the disciples see Him, He says, "It is I; do not be afraid." The Greek for "It is I" is *ego eimi* (ἐγώ εἰμι);

often translated "I am." This phrase is used throughout John's gospel by Jesus to signify His inextricable relationship with God His Father, who identified Himself to Moses and the Hebrew people as "I am who I am" (Ex. 3:14). If John intends this phrase to mean "I am [here]," then Jesus is identifying Himself with the God of deliverance who led the Hebrew people from Egypt. He calms their fears in the midst of the storm by saying that He is present to deliver them.

> *On the following day, when the people who were standing on the other side of the sea saw that there was no other boat there, except that one which His disciples had entered, and that Jesus had not entered the boat with His disciples, but His disciples had gone away alone—however, other boats came from Tiberias, near the place where they ate bread after the Lord had given thanks—when the people therefore saw that Jesus was not there, nor His disciples, they also got into boats and came to Capernaum, seeking Jesus. And when they found Him on the other side of the sea, they said to Him, "Rabbi, when did You come here?" (vv. 22–25).*

Jesus' appearance with His disciples the following day near Capernaum arouses wonder by many of the people who were with Him near Tiberias where the feeding occurred. They know He did not cross with His disciples and He was not in any of their boats, so they ask, "How did He get to the other side of the sea?" Not only so, why does John report this unusual event? Given its narrative location between the feeding miracle and Jesus' declaration that He is the Bread of Life, both of which should be understood against the background of the Exodus, Jesus' walk upon the water relates to this momentous event as well.

The feeding miracle and the discourse that follows occur during the season of Passover (6:4). A prominent Scripture read at this time was Isaiah 51. In this prophecy (vv. 1–16) God promises to bless His people with righteousness and salvation (vv. 1–8). God is recognized by the prophet as "the One who dried up the sea, the waters of the great deep; that made the depths of the sea a road for the redeemed to cross over" (v. 10). He reminds the people that their "bread should not fail" because He is "the Lord your God, who divided the sea whose waves roared" (vv. 14, 15). The prophet draws upon the story of the Exodus for the words of hope expressed here. John is certainly familiar with this passage and sees the phenomenal walk of Jesus upon the water as symbolic of the passing of Moses through the Red Sea.

In the midst of the storm, the disciples are afraid so Jesus must assure them: "Do not be afraid." This recalls the fear of the people in their flight from Pharaoh. They cry to Moses, "Why have you so dealt with us, to bring us up out of Egypt . . . For it would have been better for us to serve the Egyptians than that we should die in the wilderness" (Ex. 14:11, 12). Moses responds by saying, "Do not be afraid" (Ex. 14:13). Isaiah picks up on this theme saying the righteous should not fear others because their God will save them: "Listen to Me, you who know righteousness . . . do not fear the reproach of men, nor be afraid of their insults . . . But My righteousness will be forever, and My salvation from generation to generation" (Is. 51:7, 8). He goes on to describe God as the One who dried up the waters of the Red Sea to deliver His people and records God's words, "Who are you that you should be afraid . . . You have feared continually every day because of the fury of the oppressor" (Is. 51:10–13).

Jesus is not the only one who crosses the sea. His disciples go before Him and many come after Him: "Other boats came from Tiberias . . . When the people therefore saw that Jesus was not there . . . they also got into boats and came to Capernaum" (6:23, 24). John's presentation of this miracle does not focus on Jesus' authority over the winds and waves. Rather, he highlights Jesus' words and actions: He walks on the waters and says, "Do not be afraid." Just as Moses is the key figure in God's deliverance of the people through the Red Sea, so also Jesus is central in this story. He provides for the needs of the people and delivers them despite their fears.

Dissention, Desertion, and Disbelief (John 6:26–7:9)

Despite His miraculous signs and marvelous teachings, Jesus encounters dissention from the Jews, desertion by certain disciples, and disbelief from His own family. In other words, people from every type of relationship to Jesus oppose Him. This opposition mimics the resistance to Moses as he led the people through the wilderness. John continues to present Jesus and His ministry in the light of the story of Moses.

In this section we see Jesus using the feeding miracle as an opportunity to reveal that He is the Bread of Life. He has already told Nicodemus, a ruler of the Jews, that He is the Son of Man who will be lifted up on the cross. The Samaritan woman and her people have seen that He is the Messiah who gives living water. Now, He speaks about the True Bread with those who ate the loaves and fish.

Jesus answered them and said, "Most assuredly, I say to you, you seek Me, not because you saw the signs, but because you ate of

the loaves and were filled. Do not labor for the food which per-
ishes, but for the food which endures to everlasting life, which
the Son of Man will give you, because God the Father has set His
seal on Him" (vv. 26, 27).

This section may be divided into two parts, each beginning with the assertion, "Most assuredly, I say to you" (6:26, 32). The people do not follow Him
because of what the miracle means, but because they ate and were satisfied.
Jesus does not condemn them for this. However, He does attempt to draw
their attention to the significance of His ministry. He wants to shift their
focus from the temporary, perishable food to Himself, the eternal Bread of
Life. Jesus' reference to perishable food recalls the manna that God provided
the Hebrew people in the wilderness. That food lasted only a day before it
became wormy and spoiled (Ex. 16:20). God prohibited the people from
storing it to teach them dependency for His provision.

The eternal life that the Son of Man gives recalls Jesus' words to Nicodemus (3:13–17). Only someone who shares the privilege and authority of
God, such as the Son of Man, can be lifted up on a cross and give His life for
the sins of the world. Furthermore, God has set His seal upon His Son;
meaning God has attested or confirmed the Son's ability and right to offer
eternal life to His people. But how is Jesus attested? Given that He enters into
His public ministry and provides signs of God's new creative work among
the people only after He has received the Holy Spirit, the attestation to which
He refers is the presence of the Spirit in His life (1:32, 33). (See Paul's use of
the word *seal* in Ephesians 1:13 and 4:30.)

Then they said to Him, "What shall we do, that we may work the
works of God?" Jesus answered and said to them, "This is the
work of God, that you believe in Him whom He sent" (vv. 28, 29).

This exchange is at first difficult to understand. The key to its understanding
is found in John's use of the noun and verb for the word *work* (*ergon,* ἔργον;
ergazomai, ἐργάζομαι).

Jesus has informed the Jews that "My Father has been working (*erga-*
zomai) until now, and I have been working (*ergazomai*)" (5:17). This means
that God has been active in Jesus' ministry. In these verses, Jesus exhorts the
people not to "labor" (*ergazomai*) for perishable food but for that which
results in eternal life (v. 27). The people respond by asking how they may
"work (*ergazomai*) the works (*ergon*) of God." In other words, they ask how

they can live the life of the Spirit that is modeled by Jesus. The answer: Believe in Jesus Christ, the One whom God sent.

> *Therefore they said to Him, "What sign will You perform then, that we may see it and believe You? What work will You do? Our fathers ate the manna in the desert; as it is written, 'He gave them bread from heaven to eat'" (vv. 30, 31).*

The people's request for a sign shows they do not understand the meaning of the sign of the multiplying of the loaves and fish. This request proves two of Jesus' earlier statements: People require signs in order to believe (4:48) and these people only follow Him because He fed them. They did not discern the meaning of the feeding miracle (v. 26). Yes, they know He has performed a miracle because they refer to the miracle of the manna in the wilderness and quote Exodus 16:15. At the same time, they do not understand the significance of the sign they witnessed.

> *Then Jesus said to them, "Most assuredly, I say to you, Moses did not give you the bread from heaven, but My Father gives you the true bread from heaven. For the bread of God is He who comes down from heaven and gives life to the world." Then they said to Him, "Lord, give us this bread always." And Jesus said to them, "I am the bread of life. He who comes to Me shall never hunger, and he who believes in Me shall never thirst. But I said to you that you have seen Me and yet do not believe. All that the Father gives Me will come to Me, and the one who comes to Me I will by no means cast out" (vv. 32–37).*

Again, Jesus prefaces these remarks by saying, "Most assuredly, I say to you." Then He builds on their quote from Exodus, "He gave them bread from heaven to eat." His Father, not Moses, gave the bread from heaven in the wilderness and gives bread from heaven now. But the present bread from heaven is not something to eat but Someone in whom to believe. It is "He who comes down from heaven and gives life to the world." This recalls Jesus' words to Nicodemus: The Son of Man came down from heaven so the world can be saved through Him (3:13–17).

The people's desire for the bread of which Jesus speaks resembles the desire of the Samaritan woman: "Sir, give me this water, that I may not thirst, or come here to draw" (4:15). Note that both responses are preceded by a title of honor. The people refer to Jesus as "Lord" while the woman addresses

THE BREAD OF LIFE

Jesus says He is the Bread of Life. John quotes this claim of Jesus three times (vv. 35, 48, 51). In addition to this, Jesus three times states He is the bread that has come down from heaven (vv. 33, 50, 58). As the Bread of Life, Jesus gives life to the people of Israel just as God provided new life for their ancestors when He brought them out of Egypt. As the bread that has come down from heaven, Jesus is the very life of God on the earth. In the ancient world bread was the staple food. Individuals and entire societies were dependent upon it for their survival. By identifying Himself as the Bread of Life, Jesus reveals that God has sent Him to provide eternal nourishment and strength. Though the people were satisfied after eating the bread and fish in the grassy place near Tiberius–they had as much as they wanted (6:11)–they can have their hunger and thirst eternally satisfied in Him: "He who comes to Me shall never hunger, and he who believes in Me shall never thirst."

Him as "Sir". This indicates that they recognize His authority and greatly desire what He offers.

> "For I have come down from heaven, not to do My own will, but the will of Him who sent Me. This is the will of the Father who sent Me, that of all He has given Me I should lose nothing, but should raise it up at the last day. And this is the will of Him who sent Me, that everyone who sees the Son and believes in Him may have everlasting life; and I will raise him up at the last day" (vv. 38–40).

Jesus says that He has come to do His Father's will; that is, give eternal life to everyone who believes. Remember, eternal life is not just life that goes on and on forever; it is life that is lived in the presence of God as it was in Eden in the beginning. Jesus has already informed the Jews that He does not do His own will. He does the will of the Father (5:30). In this and the above passage Jesus speaks of the will of God in relation to the act of resurrection. The Jews learn that all will experience resurrection but only some will be resurrected to life (5:29). In chapter 6, Jesus tells the people that on the last day He will raise up the believers to eternal life. God's will is that the people who believe in Jesus Christ, who eat the bread from heaven, will be restored to life in resurrection.

In verses forty-one through fifty-nine the temple leadership murmurs about Jesus' claim to be the Bread of Life. In so doing, they respond to Him in the same way that the Hebrew people responded to Moses as He led them out of Egypt with signs.

THE SEVEN *I AM* SAYINGS IN THE GOSPEL OF JOHN

In John's gospel Jesus identifies Himself with the God of Moses who sees the suffering of His people and determines to deliver them from their affliction into a land of bounty where they will enjoy His presence. In Exodus 3, after God has informed Moses that he is the means by which this deliverance will be accomplished, Moses asks, "Who will I say sent me?" God answers, "I am who I am has sent you." God is the "I am." Yet, seven times in John's gospel Jesus uses the expression *I am* with different predicate names to identify Himself. Who then is Jesus? He is the One who gives new life to the people of God by delivering them from their bondage. Each of the following *I am* statements reveals that Jesus is the means by which life with God may be known. These are also evidence that the new creation of God can only be experienced through Jesus Christ.

Passage	Key Texts	I Am Statements	Significances
6:22–59	6:34, 48, 51	Bread of Life	Jesus offers the life of God in His new exodus.
8:1–12; 9:1–12	8:12; 9:5	Light of the World	Jesus reveals the life of God to the people of His creation.
8:48–59	8:58	Before Abraham	Jesus is the foundation of life with God which comes through faith and righteousness.
10:1–30	10:7, 9, 11, 12–14	Good Shepherd	Jesus delivers the people of God from danger and gives them new life.
11:17–27	11:25	Resurrection and Life	Jesus gives life in the midst of death.
14:1–6	14:6	The Way, the Truth, and the Life	Jesus is the means by which people experience eternal life.
15:1–8	15:1, 5	The Vine	Eternal life flows through Jesus to God's people.

Murmuring against Jesus and Moses

The Greek word used by John to describe the murmuring of the Jewish leaders (*gonguzō*, γογγύζω) is related to the word used in the Septuagint (the Greek translation of the Hebrew Bible) to describe the cynical attitude of the people toward Moses (*diagonguzō*, διαγογγύζω). In fact, *diagonguzō* translates the Hebrew word *lun* (/לוּן) that is exclusively found in passages that describe the Exodus of the people from Egypt (Ex. 15–17; Num. 14–17; also Josh. 9:18). The subject of the verb is the Hebrew people and the object of their unhappiness either Moses or God.

The word *murmur* describes the common and uniform response of the people to Moses as he leads them from Egypt through the wilderness. After passing through the Red Sea the people murmur or complain to Moses because they do not have any water (Ex. 15:24). Then they complain because they do not have any food (16:2). The Lord hears their complaints and provides quail and manna for them (16:7, 8, 12). Though God provides for their hunger, the people continue to thirst and complain at the lack of water in the wilderness of Sin (17:2, 3). He provides water for them as a result, though they have "tested" Him (17:7).

In addition to the people's murmuring at the lack of food and water, they again murmur when they hear the report of the twelve spies whom Moses sends into Canaan. Though Joshua and Caleb remain confident in their ability to conquer the land, the remaining ten spies express pessimism at their chances to do so. Upon hearing their negative report, the people complain and say, "If only we had died in the land of Egypt! Or if only we had died in this wilderness!" (Num. 14:2). The ten spies' report causes the people to murmur and complain (Num. 14:36). God responds with exasperation, "How long shall I bear this evil congregation who complain against Me? I have heard the complaints which the children of Israel make against Me" (Num. 16:27). Because of their attitude, God declares, "The carcasses of you who have complained against Me shall fall in this wilderness" (Num. 16:29).

Yet another wilderness account describes specific leaders among the people gathering to complain against Aaron (Num. 16:11). As a result of this, God causes Aaron's rod to blossom as a sign of His approval and to counter the complaints of those who have gathered against him (Num. 17:1–10).

The result of all this complaining is that Israel is prevented from entering the land of promise. Instead, that generation experiences their greatest fear—death in the wilderness due to their inability to believe in the goodness of God as seen in His promises. Their doubting response to God's promises brings death in the desert rather than life in the land of milk and honey.

The stories of the Exodus liberally use the word *diagonguzō* "murmur." John's use of a similar word to describe the response of the temple leadership to Jesus draws attention to the importance of the ancient story in understanding John's account. Jesus has come to lead Israel in a new exodus, yet they murmur and complain against Him. Despite seven miraculous signs, they doubt that Jesus has come from God to give them a new beginning.

The Jews then complained about Him, because He said, "I am the
bread which came down from heaven." And they said, "Is not this
Jesus, the son of Joseph, whose father and mother we know? How
is it then that He says, "I have come down from heaven?'" Jesus
therefore answered and said to them, "Do not murmur among
yourselves. No one can come to Me unless the Father who sent Me
draws him; and I will raise him up at the last day" (vv. 41–44).

By identifying Jesus as the son of Joseph, the leaders point to his humanity
and subtly question the exalted status implied in His claim, "I have come
down from heaven" (v. 38). Jesus' response to their doubt is emphatic. He
commands them "not to murmur." In other words, "Do not act and speak
like your ancestors in the wilderness!"

Just as God has sent Jesus so also God draws people to Him. Jesus asserts
that God is proactive in His desire to have a relationship with His people.
The goal is that Jesus will in the last day raise up those who are drawn to Him
(v. 40).

"It is written in the prophets, 'And they shall all be taught by
God.' Therefore everyone who has heard and learned from the
Father comes to Me. Not that anyone has seen the Father, except
He who is from God; He has seen the Father" (vv. 45, 46).

Here, Jesus quotes from Isaiah (54:13) where God promises future blessing to
Israel (vv. 11–17). This blessing involves personal instruction from the Lord
and describes a time of protection, peace, and personal relationship with
God. To be taught by God means to hear from God Himself. In John 6:45,
46, Jesus says that those who have heard from God will come to Him. Why?
They will come because His teaching is that of God His Father. They will recognize that His teaching is God's teaching. Thus, the verse from Isaiah that
Jesus quotes indicates that the day of protection, peace, and personal relationship with God has arrived.

"Most assuredly, I say to you, he who believes in Me has everlast-
ing life. I am the bread of life. Your fathers ate the manna in the
wilderness, and are dead. This is the bread which comes down
from heaven, that one may eat of it and not die. I am the living
bread which came down from heaven. If anyone eats of this
bread, he will live forever; and the bread that I shall give is My
flesh, which I shall give for the life of the world." The Jews there-

fore quarreled among themselves, saying, "How can this Man give us His flesh to eat?" (vv. 47–52).

Jesus emphatically declares ("Most assuredly I say to you") that a person who believes in Him has eternal life. Israel's ancestors ate the manna in the wilderness but eventually died there because they murmured against Moses and did not believe God's promises. However, those who eat the Bread of Life will not die because they believe Jesus' teaching. Plus, Jesus makes numerous remarks about the Bread of Life. These remarks converge when He speaks about His flesh. Jesus Christ is this Bread. His humanity is the tangible proof of God's provision for the life of all mankind. Thus, when Jesus says, "The bread that I shall give is My flesh, which I shall give for the life of the world," He means that life comes through the gift of His birth, life, suffering, death, and resurrection.

> *Then Jesus said to them, "Most assuredly, I say to you, unless you eat the flesh of the Son of Man and drink His blood, you have no life in you. Whoever eats My flesh and drinks My blood has eternal life, and I will raise him up at the last day. For My flesh is food indeed, and My blood is drink indeed. He who eats My flesh and drinks My blood abides in Me, and I in him" (vv. 53–56).*

These remarks provoke dissension among the Jewish leadership: "The Jews quarreled among themselves." John uses the Greek word *machomai* (μάχομαι) suggesting a strong verbal dispute. Their dispute, however, is not with one another. They are not disagreeing about how to interpret Jesus' remarks. Rather, their dispute is concerned with what Jesus has said.

Jesus makes an emphatic response to their dissension. He begins by saying they must eat the flesh and drink the blood of the Son of Man to have eternal life. He continues by saying that they must eat His flesh and drink His blood if they are to be raised up on the last day.

To say that His flesh is food and His blood is drink, Jesus means that His humanity is the life of God for His people. To eat and drink of Him is a figurative expression that means one finds his or her life in Jesus. To abide in Jesus Christ is to live in Him. His remarks at this point anticipate what He says to the disciples the night before His crucifixion (15:1–6).

> *"As the living Father sent Me, and I live because of the Father, so he who feeds on Me will live because of Me. This is the bread*

which came down from heaven—not as your fathers ate the
manna, and are dead. He who eats this bread will live forever."
These things He said in the synagogue as He taught in
Capernaum (vv. 57–59).

Life comes from the God whom Jesus describes as "the living Father." Those
who feed on the bread He has sent will live. Their experience can be greater
than that of their ancestors in the wilderness if they respond to Jesus' words
with belief.

Therefore many of His disciples, when they heard this, said,
"This is a hard saying; who can understand it?" When Jesus
knew in Himself that His disciples complained about this, He
said to them, "Does this offend you?" (vv. 60, 61).

The murmuring of the leadership is replaced by the murmuring of some of
Jesus' own disciples. The question behind the dissension of the Jewish leadership and the defection of some disciples has to do with Jesus' teaching.
Many disciples describe it as a "hard word" (*skleros logos*, σκληρὸς λόγος).
A large number are upset. They say, "Who can listen to it?" The problem is
not one of interpretation; it is one of acceptance. Will they accept what Jesus
says about Himself? Jesus knows they murmur and are unhappy. He asks if
they are offended. The word used by John is *skandalizō* (σκανδαλίζω), generally meaning to fall away. Jesus asks the disciples if His teaching is an obsta-
cle to their continued relationship with Him. Having come to Him, will they
remain with Him?

"What then if you should see the Son of Man ascend where He
was before? It is the Spirit who gives life; the flesh profits noth-
ing. The words that I speak to you are spirit, and they are life.
But there are some of you who do not believe." For Jesus knew
from the beginning who they were who did not believe, and who
would betray Him. And He said, "Therefore I have said to you
that no one can come to Me unless it has been granted to him by
My Father." From that time many of His disciples went back and
walked with Him no more. Then Jesus said to the twelve, "Do
you also want to go away?" (vv. 62–67).

Jesus consistently uses the expression Son of Man to refer not only to His
humanity but also His return to His place above with the Father. (See also 1:51;

3:13, 14). This is due to His interpretation of Daniel 7 in reference to His own life. He asks if they would believe in Him if they saw Him ascend. The Greek form of the question indicates that it is not likely they would believe even then.

The Spirit that came upon Jesus at the Jordan (1:32, 33) gives life. Thus, the words He speaks are Spirit-words—words of life. But why does Jesus make this remark? It is because His disciples have complained about the hard word He has spoken. He has said that everyone who desires to experience eternal life must eat His flesh and drink His blood. Of course, those who hear this would be repelled by such figurative speech. The Levitical code specifically prohibited the consumption of any kind of blood: "For the life of the flesh is in the blood . . . No one among you shall eat blood" (Lev. 17:11, 12). Yet, this hard word is a word of life. If the Spirit gives life and Jesus' words are life, then Jesus speaks by the Spirit. Later, after many disciples leave Jesus and He asks if they will leave as well, Peter answers by saying, "Lord, to whom shall we go? You have the words of eternal life" (v. 68).

Just as Jesus knows that some of His disciples are murmuring about His teaching, so also He knows who will not believe and even who will betray Him. He will tell the Twelve that one among them is a devil.

> But Simon Peter answered Him, "Lord, to whom shall we go? You have the words of eternal life. Also we have come to believe and know that You are the Christ, the Son of the living God" (vv. 68–69).

Jesus rephrases the question He asked the disciples who have now left, "Are you offended by this teaching?" Peter recognizes His teaching as possessing eternal life and responds by saying the Twelve have come to believe He is the Anointed One of the living God who shares the very nature of God. The confession that Peter makes at this moment resembles that which is recorded by Matthew: "You are the Christ, the Son of the living God" (16:16). Only the living God can give eternal life; Jesus as His Son possesses the words of such life.

> Jesus answered them, "Did I not choose you, the twelve, and one of you is a devil?" He spoke of Judas Iscariot, the son of Simon, for it was he who would betray Him, being one of the twelve (vv. 70, 71).

In the synoptic Gospels, Peter is the first disciple to declare Jesus to be the Messiah (Matt. 16:13–20; Mark 8:27–30; Luke 9:18–20). Jesus accepts this confession and says that God revealed this to Peter. Jesus then says that He will be handed over to others, put to death, and raised to life. Peter does not understand this and says that it must not happen. For this, Jesus rebukes him saying, "Get behind Me, Satan! You are an offense to Me" (Matt. 16:23). The confession recorded in John 6:67–71 resembles that recorded by Matthew and Mark in that Peter's recognition of Jesus as Messiah is followed by a reference to the devil/Satan. This is another example of John's use of irony in that it refers to Satan's use of Judas to betray Jesus. This, however, is in line with God's plan to have Jesus put to death. John shows that Jesus has full knowledge of the devil's actions and knows the one who will put it into action. On one hand, Peter unwittingly voices opposition to God's plan for the Messiah and so supports Satan's plan. On the other hand, Judas acts in accordance with it.

> *After these things Jesus walked in Galilee; for He did not want to walk in Judea, because the Jews sought to kill Him. Now the Jews' Feast of Tabernacles was at hand. His brothers therefore said to Him, "Depart from here and go into Judea, that Your disciples also may see the works that You are doing. For no one does anything in secret while he himself seeks to be known openly. If You do these things, show Yourself to the world." For even His brothers did not believe in Him. Then Jesus said to them, "My time has not yet come, but your time is always ready. The world cannot hate you, but it hates Me because I testify of it that its works are evil. You go up to this feast. I am not yet going up to this feast, for My time has not yet fully come." When He had said these things to them, He remained in Galilee (vv. 1–9).*

Here, Jesus refrains from going to Jerusalem for the Feast of Tabernacles because the temple leaders want to kill Him. This threat is so real and credible that it keeps Him from celebrating the feast, as is His custom. According to John's chronology, the last time Jesus was in Jerusalem these leaders sought to kill Him because He healed a man on the Sabbath and claimed that God the Father was working in His ministry (5:16–18).

Still, Jesus' brothers urge Him to go to Jerusalem and prove Himself there "so that Your disciples may see the works that You are doing." They think He must promote Himself in Judea in order to become well known to the world. But here, "the world" represents the sphere of unbelief in Jesus and His teaching. Thus, according to John, their advice is ironic. Jesus has already made Himself known to the leaders there and this has caused them to conspire against Him.

John's remark that "even His brothers did not believe in Him" expands the number of people who do not accept Jesus' claims. The Jews who represent temple leadership in Jerusalem murmur against Him; many of His disciples have left Him because of His teaching concerning His flesh and blood; and now His brothers want Him to prove Himself in Judea, dissatisfied with His actions and His teaching thus far.

The world does not hate Jesus' brothers. After all, they do not believe in Jesus; thus they remain a part of the world. The world hates Jesus because He condemns its works by doing the will of God His Father. Since the world does not accept Jesus, it does not accept His works as those of God. This shows that the world's works are evil—the antithesis of the good that Jesus does (3:19–21).

Jesus Teaches at the Feast of Tabernacles (John 7:10–36)

In this passage Jesus speaks about His teaching. The murmuring about it has not reached to the common people. He tells them that they do not really know His origin (vv. 28, 29), nor do they know His destination (vv. 33, 34, 36). Because He comes from God and will return to God, He cannot be known apart from God. This teaching is thematically meaningful in that it is given during the Feast of Tabernacles, eight days during which Israel remembers its sojourn in the wilderness as God led them out of Egypt. Jesus speaks about His origin and His destination at the very time the people celebrate their historic origins under Moses and look forward to their future.

The Feast of Tabernacles (Lev. 23:33–35; Num. 29:12–40; and Deut. 16:13–16) was one of the three primary festivals of the Jewish year and was known for its spirit of rejoicing. It occurred at the beginning of the New Year as the people participated in all the events of the festival except the libation offerings.

> But when His brothers had gone up, then He also went up to the feast, not openly, but as it were in secret. Then the Jews sought Him at the feast, and said, "Where is He?" And there was much complaining among the people concerning Him. Some said, "He is good"; others said, "No, on the contrary, He deceives the people." However, no one spoke openly of Him for fear of the Jews (vv. 10–13).

Jesus goes by Himself to the feast. John reports that there is "much complaining" about Him. The people follow their leaders, the disciples, and even

Jesus' own brothers in murmuring about His teaching. Some say that He deceives the people. They claim that He leads them astray from the way that they should go. The fear of "the Jews" suggests that they possessed authority and the means to impose punishment upon the people.

> *Now about the middle of the feast Jesus went up into the temple*
> *and taught. And the Jews marveled, saying, "How does this Man*
> *know letters, having never studied? Jesus answered them and*
> *said, "My doctrine is not Mine, but His who sent Me. If anyone*
> *wills to do His will, he shall know concerning the doctrine,*
> *whether it is from God or whether I speak on My own authority.*
> *He who speaks from himself seeks his own glory; but He who*
> *seeks the glory of the One who sent Him is true, and no unright-*
> *eousness is in Him" (vv. 14, 18).*

The Feast of Tabernacles lasted for eight days. Though John does not give a full account of Jesus' teaching at this time, the fact that the temple leaders wonder about His knowledge of "letters" indicates that Jesus expounds upon the Scriptures.

The word translated *doctrine* means "teaching." Jesus says that this teaching originates with "the One who sent Me." Numerous times Jesus has said, "Most assuredly, I say to you." By this He means that His teaching does not originate with others, but is unique to Him. He expands on this notion by saying that the ultimate source of His teaching is God His Father.

> *"Did not Moses give you the law, yet none of you keeps the law?*
> *Why do you seek to kill Me?" The people answered and said,*
> *"You have a demon. Who is seeking to kill You?" (vv. 19, 20).*

The people should know that what He teaches is true because they have the Law of Moses which speaks of a prophet like Moses who will come for God's people. They should see that His ministry gives evidence of that prophet. Still, they want to put Him put to death just as Jesus anticipated.

The people even declare that He is demon-possessed. At first, this accusation is unexpected and seems out of place since it is not the Jewish leaders who say this but the people. Why would they accuse Jesus of having a demon? What has He said to be worthy of this? The people say this because He claims that He is righteous and that they are unrighteous. He stands in relation to God while the people do not because they do not keep the law. Moreover, He makes this claim after saying that people, if they are to enjoy such relationship with God, must eat His flesh and drink His blood. Many were repulsed by such an idea.

> *Jesus answered and said to them, "I did one work, and you all marvel. Moses therefore gave you circumcision (not that it is from Moses, but from the fathers), and you circumcise a man on the Sabbath. If a man receives circumcision on the Sabbath, so that the law of Moses should not be broken, are you angry with Me because I made a man completely well on the Sabbath? Do not judge according to appearance, but judge with righteous judgment" (vv. 21–24).*

Much of the controversy about Jesus can be traced back to the healing of the man by the Pool of Bethesda on the Sabbath. The Jews believed that circumcision could be performed on the Sabbath because it is a sign of their covenant with God (Gen. 17:10). By making the man well, Jesus restores him to the covenant community and, in essence, does what the people themselves do when they circumcise infant boys or proselytes so that they can be accepted before God.

This is why Jesus exhorts the people to discern what is right, not on the basis of tradition, but in accordance with God's righteous desires. He admonishes them to judge His work according to the claims made about God in Psalms 113–118 (the *Hallel*). These psalms were sung throughout the feast as the people praised God for His humility and care for the needy (Ps. 113:6, 7), His mighty acts in delivering them from Egypt (Ps. 114), His desire to bless His people (Ps. 115:12, 13) and save them from death (Ps. 116:5–8), and His eternal mercy (Ps. 118). Psalm 118, along with the other psalms of the *Hallel*, describe God as merciful, loving, able and willing to help His people. Thus, Jesus indicates that they should be thankful for and receptive to His ministry because it represents a fulfillment of these psalms and points to God's presence with Him.

> *Now some of them from Jerusalem said, "Is this not He whom they seek to kill? But look! He speaks boldly, and they say nothing to Him. Do the rulers know indeed that this is truly the Christ? However, we know where this Man is from; but when the Christ comes, no one knows where He is from" (vv. 25–27).*

That certain people from Jerusalem observe that Jesus speaks "boldly" is important. The word used by John is *parrēsia* (παρρησία) and means "openness." The people describe Jesus as speaking with openness or candor in public. Thus, Jesus' brothers are mistaken when they claim He conducts His ministry in secret while seeking "to be known openly" (7:3–5). He simply does not conduct it in the way that they desire. According to the testimony of these unnamed people, Jesus openly declares His identity and His mission to the people. Later He will assert before the high priest that He openly taught in synagogues and in the temple during the course of His ministry (18:19–21). Jesus conducts His ministry in the open but many do not respond in belief to it.

> *Then Jesus cried out, as He taught in the temple, saying, "You both know Me, and you know where I am from; and I have not come of Myself, but He who sent Me is true, whom you do not know. But I know Him, for I am from Him, and He sent Me." Therefore they sought to take Him; but no one laid a hand on Him, because His hour had not yet come. And many of the people believed in Him, and said, "When the Christ comes, will He do more signs than these which this Man has done?" (vv. 28–31).*

The fact that they know Jesus' human origins disqualifies Him as the Messiah in the minds of many. He is from Galilee, after all! Jesus cries out in the temple that they know and they also do not know His origins. John uses the Greek *krazō* (κράζω), suggesting that Jesus forcefully declares that they do not know His true origin and that they do not know the One who has sent Him. "The One who sent Me" is a circumlocution (an indirect manner of speech) for God. Jesus knows God, but they do not. For this brazen statement, the people attempt to grab hold (*piazō*, πιάζω) of Him. John uses this word several times to describe the intention of others to arrest Him because of His teaching (7:32, 44; 8:20; 10:39; 11:57).

In the previous passage (6:60–66) many disciples depart because of Jesus' teaching about His flesh and blood. Here many believe in Him because of the signs He has performed.

> *The Pharisees heard the crowd murmuring these things concerning Him, and the Pharisees and the chief priests sent officers to take Him. Then Jesus said to them, "I shall be with you a little while longer, and then I go to Him who sent Me. You will seek Me and not find Me, and where I am you cannot come." Then the Jews said among themselves, "Where does He intend to go that we shall not find Him? Does He intend to go to the*

*Dispersion among the Greeks and teach the Greeks? What is this
thing that He said, 'You will seek Me and not find Me, and
where I am you cannot come'?" (vv. 32–36).*

The Pharisees were observant Jews who carefully followed the Mosaic Law
and Jewish traditions as they anticipated the coming of the Messiah. They
were identified by shared beliefs and common aspirations. The Pharisees and
the high priests hear the murmuring of the crowd and attempt to grab hold
of Jesus. The Pharisees would have been concerned with any disruption in
the celebration of Tabernacles at this time, while the high priests, who controlled the events of the week, would have been alarmed at any dissension
among the crowds.

John uses irony in this passage to show that many do not recognize the
new exodus of God in Jesus' ministry. When Jesus says that they will seek
Him but not be able to follow Him, He is speaking of His return to God His
Father from whom He has come. They cannot follow because they have not
received His teaching and accepted His ministry as from God. Their ignorance is revealed when they wonder if He plans to go to the Gentiles. They
act as their ancestors in the wilderness, who did not receive the promise of
God through Moses and, because of their complaints, did not enter into the
land of promise. The leadership's misinterpretation of Jesus' mission that He
will go among the Gentiles prepares for its eventual declaration among the
Gentiles.

The Offering of the Spirit as a Libation (John 7:37–39)

On the last day of the feast, Jesus repeats the promise given to the woman at
the well (4:14) when He says, "If anyone thirsts, let him come to Me and
drink." Then He says that belief in Him will cause rivers of living water to
flow out of one's heart. John says this refers to the Holy Spirit (vv. 38, 39).
This remarkable declaration should be understood against the background
of the Feast of Tabernacles. Just as libation or drink offerings were poured
out upon the altar during the feast by the high priest in celebration of the
blessings of God, so also the Spirit will flow out of the lives of all who receive
the refreshing life that Jesus offers. Such people will be empowered to daily
worship as priests and bring blessing to others.

The Feast of Tabernacles was an enthusiastic time during which large
lights burned in the temple and men would dance throughout the night to
music. This was followed by processionals and the pouring of libations
on the altar by the high priest after sunrise. Because the feast specifically

celebrated the harvest of olives and grapes, these offerings had a two-fold significance. First, they represented God's provision in the produce of the land. Second, they recalled the flow of water from the rock in the wilderness by which God sustained His people and proved His faithfulness to them. Thus, the offerings declared God to be the Provider, Sustainer, and Faithful Deliverer of His people.

> On the last day, that great day of the feast, Jesus stood and cried out, saying, "If anyone thirsts, let him come to Me and drink" (v. 37).

The last day of the Feast of Tabernacles was a special Sabbath in which a sacred assembly occurred with the giving of animal, grain, and drink offerings (Lev. 23:33–38; Num. 29:35–38). On this day Jesus makes the bold proclamation, "If anyone thirsts, let him come to Me and drink." As the people and their priests give offerings in celebration of God's provision for them, Jesus says that He is God's provision who can satisfy their need for a relationship with Him.

> "He who believes in Me, as the Scripture has said, out of his heart will flow rivers of living water." But this He spoke concerning the Spirit, whom those believing in Him would receive; for the Holy Spirit was not yet given, because Jesus was not yet glorified (vv. 38, 39).

There are many Old Testament passages that link water and the Spirit (such as Isaiah 44:3 noted above). Since the Feast of Tabernacles celebrates God's

JESUS' OFFER OF SALVATION

The offer in John 7:37 recalls both the historical act of deliverance in the Exodus and a prophetic promise of salvation for a people in exile. The promise of salvation is found in God's Word through Isaiah: "I will pour water on Him who is thirsty, and floods on the dry ground; I will pour My Spirit on your descendents, and My blessing on your offspring" (Is. 44:3). By claiming He can satisfy the needs of the people, Jesus identifies with the One who pours out His Spirit upon them (1:32, 33). The historical act of deliverance occurred when God provided water for the Hebrew people in the wilderness from the rock (Ex. 17; Num. 20). When Jesus says that He can satisfy the thirst of the people, He means that He can provide the deliverance that they seek (see 1 Cor. 10:4).

provision for the people in the wilderness, Jesus likely is referring to the narratives in Exodus and Numbers that describe a rock from which water flows for the people. When they complain at Horeb that they have nothing to drink, God directs Moses to strike the rock there for a flow of water (Ex. 17:6). And, when the people again complain at Kadesh, Moses strikes the rock there releasing an abundant rush of water for them (Num. 20:1–11). Both passages depict God's life-giving provision for the people during the Exodus. Jesus recalls the story of water from the rock to claim that He provides the life-giving Spirit by which the people may experience God's eternal life.

John depicts Jesus as the Word of God who receives the Spirit at the Jordan River in order to manifest the new creative work of God in Israel. It is significant that as the Word of God, Jesus Christ does not begin this work apart from the Spirit. Word and Spirit work together to accomplish the creative activity of God. John reveals that those who believe in Jesus will experience the flow of living water in their lives. Since this flow of living water refers to the Holy Spirit, John shows that acceptance of the Word of God results in the reception of the Spirit of God. In this way God's new creative work continues to manifest itself.

The Prophet Foretold by Moses (John 7:40–52)

John's gospel describes an on-going debate about Jesus' identity. Some people believe He is the prophet Moses pointed to, others wonder if He is the Messiah, while others reject both views. Though there is division of opinion about His identity, the Jewish leadership uniformly dismisses the possibility that Jesus is the prophet foretold by Moses. They judge by appearance and not with the righteous judgment urged by Jesus earlier.

> Therefore many from the crowd, when they heard this saying, said, "Truly this is the Prophet." Others said, "This is the Christ." But some said, "Will the Christ come out of Galilee? Has not the Scripture said that the Christ comes from the seed of David and from the town of Bethlehem, where David was?" So there was a division among the people because of Him. Now some of them wanted to take Him, but no one laid hands on Him (vv. 40–44).

Some identify Jesus as the prophet predicted by Moses (Deut. 18:15). This is not surprising since Philip has already made this claim (1:43–46). Moreover, it is not surprising that others regard Him to be the Messiah since the

Samaritan woman and her townspeople came to this conclusion after meeting Jesus (4:39–42). Not everyone holds Jesus in such high esteem, however. Their doubts may be traced to the fact that He comes from Galilee and not Bethlehem. Others want to arrest Jesus with the intention of keeping Him silent.

> Then the officers came to the chief priests and Pharisees, who said to them, "Why have you not brought Him?" The officers answered, "No man ever spoke like this Man!" Then the Pharisees answered them, "Are you also deceived? Have any of the rulers or the Pharisees believed in Him? But this crowd that does not know the law is accursed" (vv. 45–49).

Here the officers of the temple authorities return without Jesus (see 7:32). Having heard Him speak, they cannot bring themselves to arrest Him. Such officers are prominent in John's passion account. There they arrest Jesus and take Him to the High Priest (18:3, 12) at which time one of them strikes Jesus for His alleged irreverent remarks (18:22). Later they join the high priests in calling for Jesus' crucifixion (19:6).

By asking their officers if they, too, have been deceived by Jesus' words the Pharisees reveal their suspicion that Jesus is a false prophet. He performed signs and yet disregarded traditional teachings on such important matters as the Sabbath. So, Jesus qualified as a false prophet who was deceiving the peo-

WORD STUDY: DECEIVED

The Pharisees wonder if the officers have been deceived (*planaō*) by Jesus' teaching as have many of the people (7:12). John's choice of words here is important. Throughout the Septuagint the verb *planaō* describes the activity of foreign gods, false prophets, and evil kings who lead the people away from God to idolatry (Amos 2:4; Jer. 23:13, 22; 2 Kin. 21:9). In particular, the book of Deuteronomy warns the people to beware a prophet who gives signs that come to pass and who urges them to follow other gods: "If there arises among you a prophet or a dreamer of dreams, and he gives you a sign or a wonder, and the sign or the wonder comes to pass, of which he spoke to you, saying 'Let us go after other gods'—which you have not known—'and let us serve them,' you shall not listen to the words of that prophet or that dreamer of dreams" (13:1–3). They are not to listen to the prophet because God is testing them. The prophet should be put to death because he is leading the people away (*planaō*) from the Lord God (13:1–5).

ple. The leadership is of one mind concerning Jesus—He deserved to die. Their question, "Have any of the rulers of the Pharisees believed in Him?" points to the conspiracy of those responsible for the maintenance of worship at the temple (the Jewish leadership) and those motivated to preserve the traditions by which the people lived (the Pharisees).

The crowd is accursed because it is led astray by Jesus. The book of Deuteronomy (28, 29) teaches that there were two ways in life, the way of obedience to God's Law and the way of disobedience. The way of obedience, of course, was the way of blessing; that of disobedience, the way of cursing. In fact, the people are admonished: "If you do not obey the voice of the Lord your God, to observe carefully all His commandments and His statutes which I command you today, that all these curses will come upon you and overtake you" (28:15; see vv. 15–68 for a list of the curses that will befall the people for their disobedience). In the view of the Jerusalem leaders, the people are cursed for following the false prophet Jesus.

> *Nicodemus (he who came to Jesus by night, being one of them) said to them, "Does our law judge a man before it hears him and knows what he is doing?" They answered and said to him, "Are you also from Galilee? Search and look, for no prophet has arisen out of Galilee." And everyone went to his own house (vv. 50–53).*

Nicodemus defends Jesus before his colleagues. John notes that Nicodemus has become "one of them," meaning he believes in Jesus and has accepted His teaching. Nicodemus says that they should not be quick to judge Jesus according to laws such as that found in Deuteronomy until they know what He is doing. In other words, rather than assume He is leading the people away to other gods, they should consider carefully His ministry. His advice is dismissed with the remark, "No prophet has arisen out of Galilee." Nathanael was not impressed that Jesus came from Nazareth and the religious leaders are similarly unaffected. In their view, the only type of prophet that Jesus may be is a false one. But in this section of his gospel (4:43–7:52) John depicts Jesus as a prophet like Moses who leads the people in a new exodus through His words and works. Like Moses Jesus gives signs of God's presence in His life and ministry: He miraculously feeds the people and promises living water for their thirst. Also like Moses He experiences complaints and resistance and does not receive the honor due to One who serves them on behalf of God. Ironically, the religious leaders do not see Jesus as a type of Moses. Rather, they see Him as a false prophet about whom Moses warned them.

QUESTIONS FOR PERSONAL REFLECTION AND GROUP DISCUSSION

1. How does Jesus' ministry resemble that of Moses during the Exodus?
2. Compare the healing accounts of the royal official's son and the lame man at the Pool of Bethesda. How are they different? What common recognition do they make about Jesus?
3. Why does opposition form against Jesus' teaching and miracles during the course of His ministry?
4. How are Jesus and Moses prophets without honor among their own people?
5. What are the seven *I am* statements Jesus makes that are recorded in John's gospel?
6. To what Old Testament passages is Jesus' declaration, "If anyone is thirsty, let him come to Me and drink," related?
7. Why do the Pharisees view Jesus as a false prophet?

CHAPTER 4

A Woman Caught in Sin, a Man Born in Sin, and an Accusation of Sin

John 8:1–9:41

During their deliverance and before they entered Canaan, God taught the Hebrew people how to live with Him and with one another. Through Moses He established a covenant by giving Ten Commandments along with numerous statutes that were to guide the religious and communal life of Israel. These are enumerated in the books of Exodus, Leviticus, and Deuteronomy and outline how the people were to worship God through the system of sacrifice at the tabernacle and special festivals as well as how they were to live together and manage the circumstances of everyday life. However, God's words and statutes were only the framework of His covenant relationship with them. The essence of His covenant was His love for them. "For you are a holy people to the Lord your God; the Lord your God has chosen you to be a people for Himself, a special treasure above all peoples on the face of the earth. The Lord did not set His love on you nor choose you because you were more in number than any other people . . . but because the Lord loves you, and because He would keep the oath which He swore to your fathers" (Deut. 7:6–8).

Since the covenant placed a requirement on the people, they could live in one of two ways in relation to it. They could keep its laws and enjoy the blessing that comes from a covenantal relationship with God, or they could ignore its laws and experience the judgment that comes from being apart from God. In this way the words and statutes of God provided the guidelines by which the people were able to judge their standing before Him. This theology prevailed in the thinking of the people at the time of Jesus and provides the background against which the stories reported in this section of John's gospel are to be read. Simply stated, failure to keep the laws of the covenant was sin while faithfulness to the laws was righteousness.

In this section of his gospel, John shows that the nature of the covenant is addressed by Jesus in His ministry. Jesus first speaks to scribes and Pharisees who want to apply the law to a woman who has committed adultery. He says, in essence, that no one completely keeps the law and fully upholds the covenant. Later, when answering a question from His disciples, He dismisses the notion that a man's blindness is due to his sin or his failure to keep the covenant. In both cases, Jesus takes up issues related to the theology of the Law of Moses. He draws attention to the love and covenantal intention of God behind the law and challenges its strict application. Even though the law of the covenant delineated acceptable and unacceptable behavior and, in doing so, provided the means for viewing and judging the people's standing before God in the community, it was designed primarily to enable them to worship God and live together. Thus, Jesus shifts the focus from the penal use of the law to its original intention as an instrument of God's love and mercy.

A Woman Caught in Adultery (John 8:1–12)

Most biblical scholars doubt that the story of the woman caught in adultery (8:1–12) is original to the gospel since it is not found in the earliest Greek manuscripts of the New Testament. Not only is it missing in these documents, but it is also absent in most of the various Greek textual families or editions. Thus, there is much uncertainty about this passage. Even so, the story does appear in one ancient manuscript tradition and is found later among some church fathers (such as Jerome) and in numerous medieval texts of the gospel, indicating that it was known by some in the early church. The fact that it may not have been original to the gospel, however, does not mean that the story is fiction. Its content and message strongly speak of its authenticity.

The story fits closely with the previous verses in which Nicodemus urges the leaders to listen to Jesus before judging Him. It is a suggestion that brings a rebuke from them (7:45–52). Yet, by bringing the woman to Jesus the scribes and Pharisees do so to judge Him: "Now Moses . . . commanded us that such should be stoned. But what do you say?" (8:5). They set Jesus' words alongside those of Moses. They ask Jesus a difficult question in order to judge His teaching for themselves and He responds by giving them a word of God. Thus, John (or a later writer) has adeptly joined this story to what has already transpired and, at the same time, has used it to show that Jesus' words are equivalent to those of Moses. Jesus' actions, furthermore, clearly express the intention of the covenant for which the law was given in the first place.

But Jesus went to the Mount of Olives. Now early in the morning
He came again into the temple, and all the people came to Him;
and He sat down and taught them (vv. 1, 2).

John's remark that Jesus went to the Mount of Olives is significant because it
is the place where the Messiah was expected to return. Since the Feast of
Tabernacles looked forward to the coming of the Messiah, this note subtly
reveals Jesus to be this person. The Messiah returns to the temple in the
morning and teaches the people. Jesus takes up the conventional posture of
a rabbi when He sits down to teach.

Then the scribes and Pharisees brought to Him a woman caught
in adultery. And when they had set her in the midst, they said to
Him, "Teacher, this woman was caught in adultery, in the very
act. Now Moses, in the law, commanded us that such should be
stoned. But what do You say?" This they said, testing Him, that
they might have something of which to accuse Him. But Jesus
stooped down and wrote on the ground with His finger, as
though He did not hear. So when they continued asking Him, He
raised Himself up and said to them, "He who is without sin
among you, let him throw a stone at her first." And again He
stooped down and wrote on the ground. Then those who heard
it, being convicted by their conscience, went out one by one,
beginning with the oldest even to the last. And Jesus was left
alone, and the woman standing in the midst (vv. 3–9).

John reports that Jesus is teaching in the temple at dawn when a woman
guilty of adultery is brought to Him. The timing is important. She is placed
before Him shortly after being seized in the sexual encounter that night.
According to the Law of Moses (Lev. 20:10), she is a sinner and liable to
stoning. Such a punishment, however, usually was reserved for someone
who had been warned previously yet continued in the behavior. Here is
Jesus' response to the Pharisees' accusation against her: "He who is without
sin among you, let him throw a stone at her first." This should be seen as a
continuation of His earlier remark that "none of you keeps the law" (7:19).
Since no one is perfect before the law, all should exercise "righteous judgment" (7:24). The issue of sin should always be addressed with sensitivity
to the weakness of the human condition and understanding of God's
loving purpose in giving the law. Jesus' behavior during the question is
somewhat peculiar. He writes in the dirt before and after He answers their

question. Is Jesus indifferent to the question? Is He irritated? This is not
likely. By writing in the dirt with His finger, Jesus dramatizes the popular
tradition that the divine commandment was written by the finger of God.
All have sinned against God, He says. No one is innocent. For this reason,
everyone should act with understanding and mercy when confronting the
problem of sin. This is His "writing" of the law. Jesus' answer is not simply
clever. It recalls Deuteronomy 17:2–7, a passage that describes the conditions by which those who break the covenant should be punished. Those
who bring the accusation, according to this passage, must be the first to
cast stones at the accused. They must take responsibility for their accusation. By allowing those without sin to begin the punishment, Jesus places
responsibility upon them for doing so while He reminds them that they
actually do have sin.

> *When Jesus had raised Himself up and saw no one but the*
> *woman, He said to her, "Woman, where are those accusers of*
> *yours? Has no one condemned you?" She said, "No one, Lord."*
> *And Jesus said to her, "Neither do I condemn you; go and sin no*
> *more" (vv. 10, 11).*

By refusing to condemn (*katakrinō*, κατακρίνω) the woman, Jesus puts into
practice what He has taught others. He has already told Nicodemus that He
has not come to condemn (*krinō*, κρίνω) but to save (3:16–21) and He has
spoken to the Jews about the judgment given by God the Father to the Son
(5:22, 27), admonishing them to exercise righteous judgment (*krinō*) with
one another (7:24).

Jesus holds the woman responsible for the mercy she has been granted.
The imperatives used here, "Go and sin no longer," represent His command
to the woman. Even as the men who would stone her are held accountable
for their standing before the law, so also she is accountable for her behavior.

JESUS DOESN'T CONDEMN

When Jesus told the woman, "I do not condemn you" (8:11), He affirmed His previous assertion that He did not come into the world to condemn it (3:17). According to Deuteronomy 19,
the testimony of two or three witnesses is necessary for a judgment to be carried out (v. 15).
In keeping with this, Jesus said that His witness is true because it is also the witness of the
Father (8:13–17). In other words, His response to the woman is also God's response to her. It
should be the Pharisees response as well.

Though she is guilty, Jesus does not condemn her. He exemplifies the love of God that is at the heart of the covenant.

> *Then Jesus spoke to them again, saying, "I am the light of the world. He who follows Me shall not walk in darkness, but have the light of life" (v. 12).*

Jesus declares that He is the Light of the World. This is the second *I am* statement recorded by John. These words were spoken on the day following the Feast of Tabernacles. They reveal that people must be held responsible for their behavior yet be shown compassion by others. To live in this way is to live in the Light.

Jesus Teaches on Judgment and Sin (John 8:13–36)

Jesus' teaching on sin continues when he warns the Pharisees that if they refuse to believe in Him they will die in their sins (8:24). The consequences are severe because Jesus speaks what He has heard God say. Those who believe and abide in His word will be His disciples and they will know the truth and be set free (vv. 31, 32). Jesus' remarks recall the Hebrew experience in the wilderness. The people died in the wilderness because they did not trust the God's promise given by Moses.

When some Jews say that they are Abraham's descendents, it seems as though they have turned the conversation away from the topic of sin. This is not so. Jesus reminds them that if they commit sin they are slaves to sin regardless of their lineage (vv. 33–36).

> *The Pharisees therefore said to Him, "You bear witness of Yourself; Your witness is not true" (v. 13).*

Despite Jesus' emphasis on the intention of the law, the Pharisees return to their precise interpretation of it to say that Jesus may speak for Himself ("I am the Light of the World") but such testimony is inadequate according to the guidelines laid down by Moses. Their criticism is harsh. They say that Jesus gives false testimony about Himself, "Your witness is not true," meaning He is a false prophet.

> *Jesus answered and said to them, "Even if I bear witness of Myself, My witness is true, for I know where I came from and where I am going; but you do not know where I come from and*

where I am going. You judge according to the flesh; I judge no
one. And yet if I do judge, My judgment is true; for I am not
alone, but I am with the Father who sent Me. It is also written
in your law that the testimony of two men is true. I am One who
bears witness of Myself, and the Father who sent Me bears wit-
ness of Me." Then they said to Him, "Where is Your Father?"
Jesus answered, "You know neither Me nor My Father. If you
had known Me, you would have known My Father also." These
words Jesus spoke in the treasury, as He taught in the temple;
and no one laid hands on Him, for His hour had not yet come
(vv. 14–20).

Jesus says the Pharisees judge according to the flesh. In other words, they judge by their own understanding and tradition. Concerning Himself, He says, "I judge no one." What does this mean? It means that Jesus, filled with the Spirit of God, is dependent on the Father for the judgment that is exercised in His ministry. It is not Jesus who judges, therefore, but God who performs such necessary activity through Jesus. In fact, God is a witness to the truth of what Jesus says about Himself. Because the Pharisees do not know who Jesus is, even though He has declared to them that He is the Light of the World, they do not know God His Father.

This intense discussion occurs in the temple at Jerusalem, revealing that the Pharisees are either officially or unofficially related to that holy place. They participate in its activities either as members of the Sanhedrin or as devout worshipers. John's observation that the encounter takes place in the treasury, indicates that this is an eyewitness report.

Then Jesus said to them again, "I am going away, and you will
seek Me, and will die in your sin. Where I go you cannot come."
So the Jews said, "Will He kill Himself, because He says, 'Where
I go you cannot come'?" And He said to them, "You are from
beneath; I am from above. You are of this world; I am not of this
world. Therefore I said to you that you will die in your sins; for
if you do not believe that I am He, you will die in your sins" (vv.
21–24).

Jesus repeats what He has said before: He will depart and the people will not be able to follow (see 7:33–36). They will die in their sin because in rejecting Him they will have demonstrated that they do not know God the Father.

The Pharisees response, "Will He kill Himself?" says much about their view of Jesus. Since they regard suicide as an unpardonable sin, the notion that Jesus would entertain such a thought means that they see Him as a sinner already.

The thrust of Jesus' declaration, "You are from beneath; I am from above. You are of this world; I am not of this world," recalls the words of God through the prophet Isaiah: "My thoughts are not your thoughts, nor are your ways My ways . . . For as the heavens are higher than the earth, so are my ways higher than your ways, and My thoughts than your thoughts" (55:8, 9). The context of Isaiah's prophecy is the wonderful intention of God to bless His people who have experienced the hardship of the Exile. He will provide abundantly for their physical needs as well as for their souls. Thus, Isaiah urges the people to "seek the Lord while He may be found" and to "call upon Him while He is near" (v. 6). Anyone who will return to God will experience His mercy and forgiveness (v. 7). The truth of the promise in Isaiah is linked to the fact that God's Word goes out and does not return void; it accomplishes God's purposes (v. 11). Thus, Jesus' response to the Pharisees is an exhortation to receive the blessing of God in His ministry. He provides for body and soul and offers the mercy and forgiveness of God to those who believe that He is the One sent from God.

Jesus' sober declaration, "If you do not believe that I am He, you will die in your sins," is not an angry threat but a profound observation that the mercy and forgiveness of God is not an indefinite or indiscriminate offer. It is found in His life and ministry and the time is coming when they will seek for it—they will desire to know the mercy and forgiveness of God of which Jesus has spoken—but they will not find it.

> Then they said to Him, "Who are You?" And Jesus said to them, "Just what I have been saying to you from the beginning. I have many things to say and to judge concerning you, but He who sent Me is true; and I speak to the world those things which I heard from Him." They did not understand that He spoke to them of the Father. Then Jesus said to them, "When you lift up the Son of Man, then you will know that I am He, and that I do nothing of Myself; but as My Father taught Me, I speak these things. And He who sent Me is with Me. The Father has not left Me alone, for I always do those things that please Him." As He spoke these words, many believed in Him (vv. 25–30).

Jesus alludes to the Holy Spirit when He says, "He who sent Me is with Me. The Father has not left Me alone." The presence of God's Spirit enables Jesus to know what His Father is saying and doing. The fact that Jesus "always [does] those things that please Him," shows His obedience to the Spirit of God.

> *Then Jesus said to those Jews who believed Him, "If you abide in My word, you are My disciples indeed. And you shall know the truth, and the truth shall make you free." They answered Him, "We are Abraham's descendants, and have never been in bondage to anyone. How can You say, 'You will be made free'?" Jesus answered them, "Most assuredly, I say to you, whoever commits sin is a slave of sin. And a slave does not abide in the house forever, but a son abides forever. Therefore if the Son makes you free, you shall be free indeed" (vv. 31–36).*

Here Jesus links truth with knowledge of His Word. What is the nature of truth? It is that which does not change. As such, it is eternal. Jesus says that His unchanging Word brings freedom to those who will live their in obedience to it. His promise is not unlike that made by God to His people during the course of their deliverance from Egypt. Before the people enter the land of Canaan, Moses promises abundant blessing to the people as they remain faithful to God's commandments (Deut. 28:1–14).

Some Jewish leaders, like Nicodemus, accept what Jesus says about Himself and become His disciples. Such a disciple remains in the logos—Jesus' words that liberate them from their traditions and theology. The conditional statement, "If you remain," indicates that they may choose to not live in such a way. Discipleship requires an affirmative response to this revelation.

Though these Jews may believe what Jesus says about Himself, they do not believe what He says about them. They are not in bondage! Such language reveals that they are constrained by sin. They point to their ancestry as proof they are not bound by sin; after all, they are children of the covenant that God made with Abraham—the very covenant that the Law of Moses upholds. Jesus says that every person who commits sin is a slave to sin. He challenges their belief that they are free of sin because they have the covenant of Abraham. This is not a new observation. Jesus made this point to the men who brought the adulterous woman before Him in the temple: "He who is without sin among you, let him throw a stone at her first" (v. 7).

Jesus says that a slave is one who commits sin and thereby transgresses the Law of Moses and fractures the covenant with God. Since they do not keep the covenant in its entirety, their desire for eternal life with God cannot be achieved apart from Him. Sin tears apart the relationship the people have with God. Freedom from sin and the restoration of a relationship with God results from believing God's Son who remains with God forever.

The Lineage of the People and the Lineage of Jesus (John 8:37–59)

The covenant remains the principal subject in this passage. In the previous two sections (8:1–36) Jesus interprets the law through the prism of God's love. Though the woman found in sin was liable to the extreme punishment

---

THE QUESTION OF ANCESTRY IN JOHN 8:31–59

The exchange between Jesus and the Jewish leaders about their relationship to Abraham begins with their acclamation, "We are Abraham's descendents." It continues with Jesus' renunciation, "You are of your father the devil," and concludes with His declaration, "Before Abraham was, I am." The contentious discussion between Jesus and the religious leaders is given in the following table.

Claims	Counter Claims
The leaders assert, "We are Abraham's descendents, and have never been in bondage to anyone" (v. 33).	Jesus says that everyone is in bondage to sin. They may be descendents of Abraham, but they reject the Son (vv. 34, 37).
The leaders say that Abraham is their father (v. 39).	Jesus disputes this claim and says they would act like Abraham if they were his children. That is, they would believe (vv. 39, 40).
The leaders say that God is their father (v. 41).	If this were true, Jesus says, they would accept Him because He is God's Son (v. 42).
Jesus says that the devil is their father (v. 44).	The leaders counter that Jesus is a Samaritan and possessed by a demon (vv. 48, 52).
The leaders ask if Jesus is greater than Abraham (v. 53).	Jesus says, "Before Abraham was, I AM" (v. 58).

The exchange between Jesus and the Jews begins with the leaders' positive affirmation of their identity with Abraham (v. 33). It concludes with a similar, though different, affirmation by Jesus (v. 58). Whereas the leaders claim to be the descendents of Abraham, Jesus claims a prior relationship to the patriarch. He trumps their ancestral status to Abraham by claiming a greater one.

of stoning according to a strict reading of the Law of Moses, Jesus points out that everyone is guilty of sin and of violating the law. He responds to the woman with mercy even as He urges her to turn away from her sin. Furthermore, those who refuse to accept His teaching will die in sin. That is, they will die outside the covenantal relationship with God because they will have rejected God's offer of salvation through Him. In this passage, Jesus sees the covenantal relationship with God rooted not in physical ancestry but in the word He speaks. He says that everyone is bound by sin. All are slaves to sin. Claiming relationship with Abraham does not answer the question of sin, nor does it guarantee covenantal standing before God. Only relationship with the One who has been sent by God provides such a relationship.

> *"I know that you are Abraham's descendants, but you seek to kill Me, because My word has no place in you. I speak what I have seen with My Father, and you do what you have seen with your father" (vv. 37, 38).*

Jesus does not question the ancestry of the people. Their rejection of His Word, however, reveals that their spiritual lineage is different from His. He speaks what He has seen God doing while they model what they have seen their father do.

> *They answered and said to Him, "Abraham is our father." Jesus said to them, "If you were Abraham's children, you would do the works of Abraham. But now you seek to kill Me, a Man who has told you the truth which I heard from God. Abraham did not do this. You do the deeds of your father." Then they said to Him, "We were not born of fornication; we have one Father—God" (vv. 39–41).*

The leaders again claim that Abraham is their father. They have already said they are Abraham's descendents, a fact that Jesus does not deny. However, Jesus challenges their claim to be his children. Physical ancestry is not the same as spiritual heritage. If this were so, they would follow the example of their father Abraham. What is this example? It is belief in the Word of God. Abraham responded to the command of God to leave his nation, his community, and his family (Gen. 12:1–3). He left every sphere of social relationship that formed his identity. His act of obedience resulted in a new identity centered in God and expressed in a new name (Gen. 17:5). Jesus says that if the leaders were sons of Abraham they would be willing to set aside their interpretations of the law which forms their identity, trust in the words that He speaks concerning God, and receive a new identity.

Yet the Jews claim not only Abraham as their father; God is their father as well. They then cast ridicule upon Jesus when they say, "We were not born of fornication." It is likely that they are aware of the unusual circumstances surrounding His birth and accuse of Him of being illegitimate. If Jesus is illegitimate, then He was born in sin and stands outside the law and covenant as a sinner. This implies the question, "Who are you to speak of God as your Father?"

> *Jesus said to them, "If God were your Father, you would love Me, for I proceeded forth and came from God; nor have I come of Myself, but He sent Me. Why do you not understand My speech? Because you are not able to listen to My word. You are of your father the devil, and the desires of your father you want to do. He was a murderer from the beginning, and does not stand in the truth, because there is no truth in him. When he speaks a lie, he speaks from his own resources, for he is a liar and the father of it. But because I tell the truth, you do not believe Me. Which of you convicts Me of sin? And if I tell the truth, why do you not believe Me? He who is of God hears God's words; therefore you do not hear, because you are not of God" (vv. 42–47).*

The conditional statement, "If God were your Father," shows that Jesus does not believe this to be true. God loves Jesus and the fact that the leaders reject Him means that they have another father. Jesus says the devil is both their father and a man-killer who rejects the truth of God and speaks lies. In other words, the devil is the antithesis of Jesus who offers eternal life, embodies the truth, and speaks God's words. Their rejection of Jesus reveals their acceptance of the devil. This acceptance is manifest in their desire to kill Him.

The devil was a man-killer from the beginning in that his lies persuaded Adam and Eve to renounce God's commandment not to eat from the tree of the knowledge of good and evil (Gen. 2:17) and exposed them to death (Gen. 2:16, 17; 3:1–5). By misunderstanding Jesus' speech and rejecting His teaching, the leaders show they are accepting the lies of the devil in the same way that the man and woman did in the beginning. Such lies lead to death. If they belonged to God they would understand Jesus' words because He only

speaks the words He hears God speak. Just as Jesus is the Word of God from
the beginning (1:1–3) so also the devil is a liar from the beginning and "the
father of lies."

The fact that some of these people attempt to convict Jesus of sin is further evidence that they do not know God. Rather they are motivated by the
devil. They believe that not only was Jesus conceived in sin (v. 41) but His
words and actions speak of sin as well.

> *Then the Jews answered and said to Him, "Do we not say rightly*
> *that You are a Samaritan and have a demon?" Jesus answered,*
> *"I do not have a demon; but I honor My Father, and you dishon-*
> *or Me. And I do not seek My own glory; there is One who seeks*
> *and judges" (vv. 48–50).*

The leaders renew their accusation that Jesus is possessed by a demon (7:20).
In so doing, they accuse Him of being a Samaritan. This accusation refers to
the journey Jesus made through Samaria and the positive reception He
received from the people there (4:4–42). The Samaritans accepted an edited
form of the Pentateuch so the name *Samaritan* is a slur that asserts Jesus is
outside the covenant. He, not they, belongs to the devil. Jesus defends
Himself by saying that He does not have a demon and the proof is in the fact
that He seeks to honor God rather than bring glory to Himself.

> *"Most assuredly, I say to you, if anyone keeps My word he shall*
> *never see death." Then the Jews said to Him, "Now we know that*
> *You have a demon! Abraham is dead, and the prophets; and You*
> *say, 'If anyone keeps My word he shall never taste death.' Are*
> *You greater than our father Abraham, who is dead? And the*
> *prophets are dead. Who do You make Yourself out to be?" Jesus*
> *answered, "If I honor Myself, My honor is nothing. It is My*
> *Father who honors Me, of whom you say that He is your God.*
> *Yet you have not known Him, but I know Him. And if I say, 'I do*
> *not know Him,' I shall be a liar like you; but I do know Him and*
> *keep His word. Your father Abraham rejoiced to see My day, and*
> *he saw it and was glad." Then the Jews said to Him, "You are not*
> *yet fifty years old, and have You seen Abraham?" Jesus said to*
> *them, "Most assuredly, I say to you, before Abraham was, I AM"*
> *(vv. 51–58).*

Jesus' statement, "Most assuredly, I say to you, if anyone keeps My word he shall never see death," is covenant language. Several points support this. First, "most assuredly," indicates the importance and unique nature of what Jesus is about to say. Second, the word *keep* (*tēreō*, τηρέω) often connotes the act of obeying commandments or laws. For example, the Pharisees will soon accuse Jesus of not keeping the Sabbath (9:16). Third, the singular form of the noun *word* (not *words*), encompasses the entirety of His message (8:31, 37, 43). By speaking of His teaching in this way, Jesus places it on the level of God's word in the covenant as expressed in the Law of Moses. Fourth, Jesus promises a benefit to all those who enter this covenant with Him. His assertion that those who keep His word will not see death is another way of saying that they shall experience eternal life. It is comparable to the promise of blessing for those who keep God's covenant (Deut. 28:1–14).

The force of Jesus' statement, "If anyone keeps My word he shall never taste death," is not lost on the leaders and elicits an angry and indignant response. John draws attention to its significance by having the Jews repeat it. They ask, "Are You greater than our father Abraham . . . and the prophets who are dead?" echoing the woman at the well who wonders, "Are You greater than our father Jacob?" (4:12).

John has recorded the discourse so that the Jews' question "Who do You make Yourself out to be?" leads to Jesus' astounding claim, "Before Abraham was, I AM." His initial response to the question, however, is that He is One who keeps God's word. He does not say that He keeps the commandments or the traditions though He was not indifferent to these. In fact, He honored the commandments and observed the practices of His people. Nonetheless, Jesus says that He keeps God's word, which, as John has already indicated, means that He does the will of the Father.

Keeping God's word explains Jesus' claim that Abraham rejoiced and was glad to see His "day." In a world where men were determined to make a name for themselves (Gen. 11:1–9, see v. 4), Abraham was the one man willing to trust the word of God and find his name in Him (Gen. 12:2). When God commands Abram, "Get out of your country, from your family and from your father's house, to a land that I will show you," he obeys: "So Abram departed as the Lord had spoken to him" (v. 4). He does so because he believes the promise attached to the command: "I will make you a great nation; I will bless you and make your name great; and you shall be a blessing . . . And in you all the families of the earth shall be blessed." The story of Abraham tells of an on-going response to God's word. Though Abraham equivocates at times—he is not perfect—at the critical moment, he shows unequivocal trust in God's word concerning Isaac. He is willing to sacrifice His son because of his trust in God's promise that "one who will come from your own body shall be your heir" (Gen. 15:4). Abraham's example of trust in God's promises of a name and a heritage opens the way for all people to find their identity and future in God as he did.

As God's Son, Jesus keeps God's word. He shows complete confidence in this word in that He speaks only what He hears God speak and He does only what He sees God do. His desire is to honor God and to perform His will. In this way, Jesus demonstrates the type of commitment to God His Father that Abraham displayed.

Jesus says that Abraham not only anticipated a day in which commitment to God's word would be lived out as it is in Jesus' life and ministry, but He saw it and rejoiced in it. What does Jesus mean? Though He does not elaborate on this remarkable statement, a clue to its meaning may be found in the account of Abraham and Isaac. Abraham's willingness to give God his son (the embodiment of God's promise and the living treasure of all of his hopes for the future) elicits a strong reaffirmation of the promise by God Himself. "Because you have done this thing, and have not withheld your son, your only son" (Gen. 22:16), He will abundantly bless Abraham. This promise of abundant blessing reveals to Abraham that God will not act with less commitment to the covenant than he himself has shown and is certainly cause for rejoicing. Abraham's willingness to give his son to God prepares for the greatest of blessings—the giving of God's Son to Abraham and all of his descendents.

Not surprisingly, the leaders are dubious of Jesus' assertion. How does He know this? He was not alive then! He is not even fifty years old! Jesus responds by saying, "Before Abraham was, I AM." With this claim, He identifies with God who revealed Himself to Moses as *I AM* (Ex. 3:14). The importance of this assertion cannot be overstated. God told Moses the name by which He will forever be known to Israel. *I AM* is the basis for the covenant name Yahweh (יהוה), a name so holy that the people would not pronounce it. Rather, they would speak the word "lord" or "master" (*adonai*, אֲדֹרֹנָי) in place of it. Thus, Jesus identifies Himself with the God who delivered the people from servitude in Egypt and who gave them the covenant by which they could live in His presence and in harmony with one another.

When God called to Abraham to give his son as a sacrifice, Abraham responded by saying, "Here I am" (Gen. 22:1), standing before God in his full humanity. His response was humble and reverent as he waited upon God's word. Jesus stands before the Jewish leaders as the Word of God who speaks God's words. His claim to the Jews that "before Abraham was, I AM," reveals that He is the Word and deserves the same obedience from them that Abraham gave to God's word.

Then they took up stones to throw at Him; but Jesus hid Himself
and went out of the temple, going through the midst of them,
and so passed by (v. 59).

The first day after the Feast of Tabernacles began with certain men prepared to stone a woman who had been caught in adultery. The Law of Moses allowed for such punishment. Jesus reminds the men that no one is without sin and that all should act with mercy toward one another, which is the essence of the covenant. The day concludes, according to the narrative, with men prepared to stone Jesus because *He* is a sinner and because of His claim to be God's Son whose words are as important as the covenant.

A Man Born in Sin and an Accusation of Sin (John 9:1–41)

In this chapter, Jesus heals a blind man whose condition is believed to be caused by sin. But this act of grace only brings rebuff from the Pharisees. The disciples voice the popular view that human infirmity or weakness such as blindness is divine judgment for sin. Meanwhile, while the Pharisees voice their view that Jesus is a sinner outside the covenant relationship with God because He does not honor the laws and traditions that comprise the covenant.

Now as Jesus passed by, He saw a man who was blind from
birth. And His disciples asked Him, saying, "Rabbi, who sinned,
this man or his parents, that he was born blind?" Jesus
answered, "Neither this man nor his parents sinned, but that the
works of God should be revealed in him. I must work the works
of Him who sent Me while it is day; the night is coming when no
one can work. As long as I am in the world, I am the light of the
world" (vv. 1–5).

This man did not lose his sight in an accident of some kind but was born blind. The disciples wonder about the actual cause of his blindness. The man could not have sinned prior to his birth, so the disciples are confused. Their confusion stems from their theology. Most people of their time believed that faithfulness to God's covenant would consistently result in blessing while disobedience would result in curses (see Deut. 28). Blindness represents such a curse. So, the disciples ask in effect, "Who transgressed the law of the covenant and brought about this condition upon this man?"

Jesus challenges their theology. No one transgressed the covenant. In fact, violation of the covenant is not the issue. But if the covenant is not the issue, then what is? Jesus says the man's condition presents an opportunity for God to reveal His creative work in his life. This new creative work already is being accomplished through Jesus' ministry. This is why Jesus says that He must do the works of God while He has the opportunity. Jesus shifts their focus from sin that destroys to God who renews and creates.

Jesus earlier exhorted the people to work for food that does not spoil. When the people ask how they may work the works of God, He says that they should believe in Him (6:27–29). The renewal and creative work of God begins with belief in Jesus who does God's works.

For the second time Jesus here announces that He is the light of the world (see also 8:12). It is significant that he makes this declaration at the time of the Feast of Tabernacles when the people gathered together and lit up the temple with lights in order to celebrate God's goodness and mercy. The God celebrated at the Feast of Tabernacles is the God of light and mercy. Likewise, Jesus is the light of the world in that He exemplifies the mercy of God to the woman caught in adultery and prepares to show similar mercy to the man born blind. While the adulterous woman was guilty of sin, this man is innocent of any wrongdoing in relation to his blindness. Yet both benefit from the mercy Jesus gives.

> *When He had said these things, He spat on the ground and made clay with the saliva; and He anointed the eyes of the blind man with the clay. And He said to him, "Go, wash in the pool of Siloam" (which is translated, Sent). So he went and washed, and came back seeing (vv. 6, 7).*

Jesus' action here is a dramatic representation of God's creative activity. By making a paste out of the dirt with His own saliva, Jesus is not following some kind of magical practice; rather He is providing a symbol by which people will think of God the Creator. The miracle is not the restoration of something lost. It is the creation of something that never existed. Jesus identifies Himself with the God of creation as He gives sight to a man who has never seen before.

Jesus commands the man to wash the paste from his eyes in the Pool of Siloam. The Greek word for wash (*niptō*, νίπτω) is used thirteen times in the four Gospels: here and later in the description of Jesus' ministry to His disciples during their last evening together. It is found only four other times in the New Testament. For John, the word does not merely mean "wash" but signifies preparation for service in Jesus' ministry.

> *Therefore the neighbors and those who previously had seen that*
> *he was blind said, "Is not this he who sat and begged?" Some*
> *said, "This is he." Others said, "He is like him." He said, "I am*
> *he." Therefore they said to him, "How were your eyes opened?"*
> *He answered and said, "A Man called Jesus made clay and*
> *anointed my eyes and said to me, 'Go to the pool of Siloam and*
> *wash.' So I went and washed, and I received sight." Then they*
> *said to him, "Where is He?" He said, "I do not know" (vv. 8–12).*

The response of the people speaks to the extraordinary nature of the miracle. The man was blind from birth. Now he can see. Some recognize the man while others doubt that he is the one who was blind. They cannot fathom how a man whose eyes have never seen now sees with those eyes.

So, the man proclaims that he is indeed the one who was blind and now sees and gives a clear and unambiguous account of his healing. Even as Jesus has proclaimed "I am the Bread of Life" and "I am the Light of the World," so also the man who was blind proclaims that he is the man who now sees. In answer to the question of the people, "Are you the man who was blind and begged?" he says, "I am." He has a new identity as a result of his encounter with the Light of the World.

> *They brought him who formerly was blind to the Pharisees. Now*
> *it was a Sabbath when Jesus made the clay and opened his eyes.*
> *Then the Pharisees also asked him again how he had received*
> *his sight. He said to them, "He put clay on my eyes, and I*
> *washed, and I see." Therefore some of the Pharisees said, "This*
> *Man is not from God, because He does not keep the Sabbath."*
> *Others said, "How can a man who is a sinner do such signs?"*
> *And there was a division among them. They said to the blind*
> *man again, "What do you say about Him because He opened*
> *your eyes?" He said, "He is a prophet" (vv. 13–17).*

Before the Pharisees, the man repeats the report of his healing. But because the healing occurred on the Sabbath, some of the Pharisees decry Jesus' claims of relationship with God. As discussed above, this is due to their view that a violation of the tradition (performing work on the Sabbath) represented a violation of the Law of Moses. Anyone who transgressed the Law of Moses and, yet, also performed signs among the people was identified by the law as a false prophet (Deut. 13:1–5). It is evident from the ensuing dispute that some have this view while others are not so sure because of the goodness of the miracle. The opinion of the man, however, is unambiguous. He says that Jesus is a prophet. Since a prophet is a person who speaks the words of God, the man has surmised from his healing that what Jesus says is true and He, indeed, speaks on behalf of God Himself.

> *But the Jews did not believe concerning him, that he had been blind and received his sight, until they called the parents of him who had received his sight. And they asked them, saying, "Is this your son, who you say was born blind? How then does he now see?" His parents answered them and said, "We know that this is our son, and that he was born blind; but by what means he now sees we do not know, or who opened his eyes we do not know. He is of age; ask him. He will speak for himself." His parents said these things because they feared the Jews, for the Jews had agreed already that if anyone confessed that He was Christ, he would be put out of the synagogue. Therefore his parents said, "He is of age; ask him" (vv. 18–23).*

Next, the parents of the man are interviewed. They confirm that their son was blind and now sees. The Pharisees therefore have the testimony of the

CONTROVERSY CONCERNING JESUS DURING HIS LIFE

Many scholars point to passages such as John chapter 9 as evidence that the evangelist transferred the later conditions and realities of the church into the story of Jesus. Their view is that, because of the widening division between the church and the synagogue in the latter years of the first century, the author of the Gospel of John inserted this story into the narrative to depict Jewish hostility toward the church long after Jesus was gone from the scene. Though it is true that tensions existed between the church and the synagogue in the latter part of the first century, the story recounted here speaks of conflicting views about Jesus that arose within the Jewish community during His ministry in response to the claims He made about Himself as God's Son. Thus, it is as legitimate to see this story as descriptive of the ambivalence of Jewish leadership toward Jesus during His public ministry as it is to see it descriptive of the rejection of the gospel message by certain Jewish people several decades later.

man as well as that of his parents. This should be sufficient evidence for belief. John reports that the parents feared the Jews. This means that the Jews are men who possessed authority within the community to pronounce judgment and enforce punishment.

> *So they again called the man who was blind, and said to him, "Give God the glory! We know that this Man is a sinner." He answered and said, "Whether He is a sinner or not I do not know. One thing I know: that though I was blind, now I see." Then they said to him again, "What did He do to you? How did He open your eyes?" He answered them, "I told you already, and you did not listen. Why do you want to hear it again? Do you also want to become His disciples?" Then they reviled him and said, "You are His disciple, but we are Moses' disciples. We know that God spoke to Moses; as for this fellow, we do not know where He is from." The man answered and said to them, "Why, this is a marvelous thing, that you do not know where He is from; yet He has opened my eyes! Now we know that God does not hear sinners; but if anyone is a worshiper of God and does His will, He hears him. Since the world began it has been unheard of that anyone opened the eyes of one who was born blind. If this Man were not from God, He could do nothing." They answered and said to him, "You were completely born in sins, and are you teaching us?" And they cast him out* (vv. 24–34).

The Pharisees again accuse Jesus of being a sinner. Their admonition to the man, "Give God the glory!" is not praise, but a warning to the man who was formerly blind. He has received his healing from a false prophet and so should be very careful not to give him glory. Jesus is a sinner; outside the covenant. The man responds by saying he can only judge Jesus by what He has done. And Jesus has given him his sight.

Do the Jewish leaders want to be Jesus' disciples? Certainly not! They are already disciples of Moses. They follow the Law of Moses and attempt to put it into practice through their various interpretations. They follow Moses because God spoke to Moses. In their view, God does not speak to Jesus. The man's response is actually a rebuke of the leaders. They should know that Jesus is from God since He heals; God does not empower sinners to do such works. God hears Jesus, the man says, because Jesus does God's will. In saying this, he repeats what Jesus has asserted throughout His ministry (4:34;

5:30; 6:38–40; 7:16–18). Mark records a similar event when he reports the accusation that Jesus heals by the power of Beelzebub. Jesus rejects this notion by saying, "If a kingdom is divided against itself, that kingdom cannot stand" (see Mark 3:20–27).

The healed man points out that a healing such as his has never occurred since the world began. This tells of the unique nature of his healing. Jesus does not merely restore his sight, but He gives him sight when he never possessed sight. The miracle is not restorative, it is creative. This is another example of irony in John's gospel. It links Jesus' ministry to the work of God in the beginning, the very thing the Pharisees deny.

Because he defends Jesus, the man is accused of being born in sin, even as Jesus was similarly accused (8:41). The man is thrown out of the temple—out of the Jewish religion. The Pharisees declare that both the healed man and the One who healed him are outside the covenant of God and do not know God.

> *Jesus heard that they had cast him out; and when He had found him, He said to him, "Do you believe in the Son of God?" He answered and said, "Who is He, Lord, that I may believe in Him?" And Jesus said to him, "You have both seen Him and it is He who is talking with you." Then he said, "Lord, I believe!" And he worshiped Him. And Jesus said, "For judgment I have come into this world, that those who do not see may see, and that those who see may be made blind." Then some of the Pharisees who were with Him heard these words, and said to Him, "Are we blind also?" Jesus said to them, "If you were blind, you would have no sin; but now you say, 'We see.' Therefore your sin remains" (vv. 35–41).*

As the finale of this drama, Jesus asks the man if he believes in the Son of Man. (The earliest Greek texts read "Son of Man" rather than "Son of God." This is preferred since Jesus has used this expression for Himself earlier in the passage.) Though the man does not know Jesus in this way, he is prepared to believe Jesus because of the miracle he has received. Jesus says that the Son of Man is the One he has seen. In other words, the Son of Man is the One who has given the man his sight. According to Daniel 7, the Son of Man receives the power and glory of God. And so the man worships Jesus as the Son of Man.

Jesus' words about judgment are a summary of what He has said and done at the Feast of Tabernacles. His judgment is that those who are blind, that is do not know God, will see, that is know Him, through Jesus Christ. Those who see, that is those who think they know God—Pharisees and the like, will become blind. Thus, they too will become dependent upon Jesus for their knowledge of God. Jesus' judgment is that all will eventually know God.

The Pharisees wonder if Jesus thinks they are blind. They ask, in so many words, "Do we need your help to know God?" If they were really blind and did not know God they would not be responsible for their status before God. Yet, because they say that they see, meaning that they know God apart from Jesus, they remain apart from God which is to remain in sin.

In the previous sections of his gospel, John presents Jesus as the one through whom creation came into being and through whom the covenantal promise of many descendents to Abraham and Jacob begins to find fulfillment. He shows Jesus to be like Moses who leads the people in a new exodus through His miracles and teaching. He manifests a new way of life. In this section (8:1–9:41) John shows Jesus to be the one who exemplifies the intention and essence of the covenant by acting with mercy and responding to others with righteous judgment. The centuries-old problem of sin is given an answer in the acts and teaching of Jesus. Thus, John continues to portray Jesus as the Old Testament exemplar of God's redemptive and recreative love for all people.

QUESTIONS FOR PERSONAL REFLECTION AND GROUP DISCUSSION

1. What is the Old Testament background to this section of John's gospel?
2. What type of judgment does Jesus exercise toward the woman caught in adultery?
3. How should Jesus' remark that "Abraham rejoiced to see My day, and he saw it and was glad" be understood?
4. Why was Jesus viewed as a sinner by certain leaders of the people?
5. What theological view informs the disciples' understanding of the blind man's condition?

CHAPTER 5

THE GOOD SHEPHERD
AND THE RETURN FROM EXILE

John 10:1–11:57

In the previous section of his gospel John portrays Jesus as the one who interprets the covenant according to its original foundation in God's mercy and love. His teaching represents a new word or commandment of God and His actions, forgiving the woman found in adultery and healing the man born blind, reestablish love as the basis for the law. Though He is accused of being a sinner—someone outside the covenant of God—in reality Jesus is the embodiment of God's covenant with Israel. Thus, John shows Jesus as the one through whom a relationship with God is attained and who gives an example of how Israel should live as a nation. He presents Jesus as the basis for life with God even as the Old Testament presented the covenant as the basis for life in community.

However, the ancient people of faith struggled to maintain the covenant after they settled in the land of Canaan. Due to the influence of surrounding tribes, the Israelites violated the covenant by engaging in idolatry. This problem continued throughout their history in the land until the time of the Babylonian Exile in the early sixth century B.C. During this time, God sent prophets to warn of the jeopardy such practices posed to their relationship with Him under the covenant. The language used by the prophets to decry this situation is often figurative and draws on many sources. One of the most common metaphors used to describe the relationship of God to His people as well as the nature of the people themselves is that of shepherds and sheep. On several different occasions God's prophets describe the leaders as false shepherds who fail to fulfill their duties to the people. They describe the people as scattered sheep that have no shepherd to care for them. Even so, this is not their ultimate fate. The prophets promise that God will send His own shepherd to care for the people and provide for their needs (Jer. 23; Ez. 34).

The abundant provision that will come through this shepherd speaks of life in God's presence as a result of a renewed relationship with Him. John builds upon such prophetic passages to describe Jesus as the shepherd of the people. He has depicted the Jerusalem leadership as those who reject Jesus' word, accuse Him of sin, and lead the people astray. According to Jesus, however, they have sin and, thus, do not keep the covenant. They are the modern-day false shepherds described in the Old Testament who scatter the people, while He is God's true Shepherd who provides a new way for them. As God's shepherd, Jesus offers abundant life to Israel. By raising Lazarus from the dead, Jesus shows that He can make good on this claim and return them from exile into life with God.

Shepherds and False Shepherds in the Old Testament

The imagery of shepherds is used throughout the Old Testament to speak of God and the leaders of Israel. It is an important metaphor that speaks of the need that people have for leaders who are committed to their protection, provision, and well-being as well as the responsibility given to leaders to provide such benefits to the people. Not only this, but it speaks of the need of people to be led in the ways of God as outlined in the covenant and the responsibility of leaders to so lead them.

One of the first occurrences of this image is found in the book of Numbers. Since Moses cannot lead the people into Canaan, he asks that God appoint a new leader for them: "Let the God of the spirits of all flesh, set a

THE GOSPEL OF JOHN AND THE OLD TESTAMENT NARRATIVE

John presents Jesus in the light of the Old Testament narrative of God's redemptive work among His people. Here is how we have thus far seen Jesus in John's gospel:

- He was in the beginning with God as God's Word.
- He embodies the promise that God made to Abraham, Isaac, and Jacob.
- He leads a new exodus of the people into relationship with God.
- He speaks God's Word or command while representing the New Covenant that God makes with them.

In John chapters 10 and 11, John continues in the Old Testament theme by showing that Jesus is the promised Shepherd of the people who will lead them in a return from exile.

man over the congregation, who may go out before them and go in before them, who may lead them out and bring them in, that the congregation of the Lord may not be like sheep which have no shepherd" (27:16, 17). As a one-time shepherd who tended his father-in-law's flock, Moses uses shepherd language to ask for a new leader for the people (Ex. 3:1). He knows that the people need a leader who will lead them out and bring them in even as a shepherd leads the sheep out in the morning to water and graze and brings them back in the evening to rest. God answers by having Moses lay his hands upon Joshua, "a man in whom is the Spirit" (Num. 27:18). By Joshua's word the people will go out and by his word they will come in (v. 21). That is, he will care for the people and provide for them even as he enables them to live as God's flock.

The prophet Jeremiah draws upon the imagery of shepherds to describe the behavior of the Jerusalem leaders in the late seventh and early sixth centuries B.C. They fail to act as shepherds who take care of the sheep and protect them. How have they failed? The prophet laments, "Woe to the shepherds who destroy and scatter the sheep of My pasture . . . You have scattered My flock, driven them away, and not attended to them" (23:1, 2). The leaders have scattered the flock—they have driven the people into exile—by not leading them in the way of the covenant. Time and again Jeremiah, along with other prophets, calls for a return to God's covenant (3:11; 11:1–10). God's response is to be a shepherd to the people. He will bring them back to their folds where they will be fruitful and increase (v. 3).

Jeremiah's later contemporary, Ezekiel, gives an extended commentary on the leaders of the people at the time of the Babylonian Exile who not only have failed to take care of the people but have abused them (Ezek. 37). They have not fed the flock, strengthened the weak, healed the sick, bound up the injured, or brought back the lost. They are false shepherds who are indifferent to the needs of the people because of their preoccupation with their own concerns. They have not led the people in the way of the covenant and so the people have practiced idolatry (5:6; 6:1–14; 8:1–18; 11:1–13; 14:1–11; 16:15; 22:1–16). For this reason the people of Israel were scattered because there was no shepherd "and they became food for all the beasts of the field when they were scattered" (34:5). Ezekiel, like Jeremiah, warns that God will judge the shepherds and promises that He will be a shepherd to the people Himself. "Indeed, I myself will search for My sheep and seek them out . . . And I will bring them out from the peoples and gather them from the countries, and will bring them to their own land; I will feed them on the mountains of Israel . . . I will feed My flock and I will make them lie down" (34:11–15).

According to Jeremiah and Ezekiel the Babylonian Exile is judgment for the idolatry of the people. Responsibility for this idolatry, however, is placed at the feet of the leaders. Since a primary duty of the king and religious leadership was to model faithfulness to the covenant, their failure to keep the covenant and provide an example for the people results in the Exile—the scattering of the sheep. Without an example of fidelity to the covenant, Israel practiced idol worship and fell out of their relationship with God. They were destroyed and became "food for wild beasts." They no longer exist as God's people. It was as though they were dead. Despite the dire consequences of idolatry, the prophets are not without hope. They say that God will bring Israel back and provide a Shepherd who will renew their relationship with Him. In other words, God will give them life again.

John draws on this imagery to depict Jesus as Israel's Shepherd. Even as the promised Shepherd of God would provide for the people and enable them to enjoy His abundance (Jer. 23:4; Ezek. 34:23–31), so also Jesus promises abundant life. The people who went into exile because of their idolatry due to the failure of their leaders were dead, figuratively speaking. They had been devoured by wild beasts (Ezek. 34:8). Yet, God brought them back from exile. Likewise, when Jesus brings Lazarus back to life, He demonstrates that as the Good Shepherd He has come to gather God's people together and to offer them abundant life in place of death.

The Shepherd Who Gives Abundant Life (John 10:1–39)

When Jesus says that He is the Good Shepherd, He draws upon one of the most common images in the Old Testament to describe Himself and the nature of His ministry. He does so knowing that the people would be intimately familiar with this particular image and keenly aware of its literary usage in a number of prophetic texts having to do with exile.

> *"Most assuredly, I say to you, he who does not enter the sheepfold by the door, but climbs up some other way, the same is a thief and a robber. But he who enters by the door is the shepherd of the sheep. To him the doorkeeper opens, and the sheep hear his voice; and he calls his own sheep by name and leads them out. And when he brings out his own sheep, he goes before them; and the sheep follow him, for they know his voice. Yet they will by no means follow a stranger, but will flee from him, for they do not know the voice of strangers." Jesus used this illustration, but they did not understand the things which He spoke to them (vv. 1–6).*

Jesus once again begins His teaching by saying, "Most assuredly, I say to you." In these verses He contrasts two kinds of shepherds: false shepherds who do not enter the sheepfold by the gate and the true shepherd who enters the sheepfold by the gate. The true shepherd calls the sheep by name and leads them out. One of the primary duties of a shepherd was to lead his sheep out. Each day he would lead the sheep to fresh grass and water, calling them to follow. Even as sheep will follow the shepherd because they recognize his voice, so also the sheep of God's fold will follow Jesus and recognize in His teaching and healing ministry the work of God.

The term *voice of strangers* refers to the criticism of His teaching and healing ministry by others. Those who reject His words, which are God's words, speak another message with another voice. People who do not speak with the voice of the shepherd are strangers and described as thieves and robbers who take from others and do harm to them. By rejecting Jesus' teaching, the leaders take sheep away from Jesus the Shepherd and do harm to them.

John remarks that the Jewish leaders do not understand Jesus' words. They do not understand the metaphor. This is because Jesus has modified the traditional shepherd metaphor by speaking of the gate of the sheepfold. It was not uncommon for shepherds to lie down to sleep in the opening of a sheepfold and act as a living gate that protected the sheep from animals outside the fold and kept the sheep inside. Still, what is the gate to which Jesus refers here? It is the means by which the sheep are led out and led in; it is how the people are governed. To the leaders the gate would be the authority of the law of the covenant that God had given to them. Since they led by showing precise fidelity to the law, they would think of themselves as shepherds to the people. However, the preceding exchanges between Jesus and the leaders indicate that they are not true shepherds. They do not keep the covenant. They do not fulfill it according to its original intention. Thus, they do not lead the people by means of the gate. Jesus, however, fulfills the covenant and acts in conformity with its foundation of love. He opens the gate of the covenant to provide for the needs of the people.

> *Then Jesus said to them again, "Most assuredly, I say to you, I am the door of the sheep. All who ever came before Me are thieves and robbers, but the sheep did not hear them. I am the door. If anyone enters by Me, he will be saved, and will go in and out and find pasture. The thief does not come except to steal, and to kill, and to destroy. I have come that they may have life, and that they may have it more abundantly" (vv. 7–10).*

Jesus elaborates on what He has said about the gate of the sheepfold. He is not only the One who leads them, but He is the very One who makes it possible for them to live as God's sheep. False shepherds attempt to enter the fold in ways other than the gate. Not only does Jesus enter through the gate—meaning He fulfills the covenant as He ministers what He receives from His Father—but He is the gate. He is the embodiment of the covenant and is not only the example of the way to live by the covenant, He enables the people to do so. All who reject Him—His teaching, His miracles— are thieves and robbers. They steal the covenantal relationship with God that Israel is given through Jesus.

Jesus contrasts His ministry as the gate to the sheepfold to that of the thief by identifying the threefold blessing for those who believe Him: They will be saved, they will go in and go out, and they will find pasture. Through Jesus, Israel will find life with God and enjoy His provision as was promised so long ago. This experience is contrasted with the threefold plan of the thief who wants to steal, kill, and destroy. Such behavior is antithetical to the work of Jesus, of course. Its goal is a reprise and continuation of the serpent's work in the garden in the beginning who sought to steal Adam's innocence, bring death to his human experience, and destroy his relationship with God (Gen. 3). For this reason, Jesus has come to offer abundant life. Such life recalls that given to Adam when he was made a living being and enjoyed the provision of God, the privilege of serving God in His creation, and knowing the presence of God (Gen. 2). By describing the life He offers as "abundant," Jesus says that He has come to provide for the needs of God's people, to restore them to their place of service, and to escort them into the presence of God.

> "I am the good shepherd. The good shepherd gives His life for the sheep. But a hireling, he who is not the shepherd, one who does not own the sheep, sees the wolf coming and leaves the sheep and flees; and the wolf catches the sheep and scatters them. The hireling flees because he is a hireling and does not care about the sheep. I am the good shepherd; and I know My sheep, and am known by My own. As the Father knows Me, even so I know the Father; and I lay down My life for the sheep. And other sheep I have which are not of this fold; them also I must bring, and they will hear My voice; and there will be one flock and one shepherd. "Therefore My Father loves Me, because I lay down My life that I may take it again. No one takes it from Me, but I lay it down of Myself. I have power to lay it down, and I have power to take it again. This command I have received from My Father" (vv. 11–18).

Twice Jesus says that He is the Good Shepherd and He defines such a shepherd as one who gives his life for the sheep. He is unlike those who are paid by the owners to watch the sheep but who will not risk their lives because they do not have an investment in the sheep. It was common for sheep owners to hire men to watch their sheep. At the time of Jesus such men were not regarded as trustworthy and had low reputations.

Jesus is willing to give His life for the sheep. In fact, John records this affirmation four times in these verses (vv. 11, 15, 17, 18). His willingness is based in His relationship with God His Father as well as with His sheep. He knows God and is known by God. He knows His sheep and is known by them. Jesus is prepared to give His life with full knowledge of the will of God and the need of the people. His death will not be a tragic accident. It will be the culmination of God's plan to give eternal life to His people.

This is not the first time that Jesus has spoken of His death. He alluded to it in His conversation with Nicodemus (3:13–15) as well as in His remarks to the Jewish leaders (8:21, 28).

Eternal life is not limited to those within the Jewish community. The "other sheep . . . not of this fold" is a reference to those outside the ancient people of faith. Though Jesus focuses His public ministry on His own people, He observes that others will hear His voice. In fact, His voice has already been heard by the Samaritans when He spoke His word to them (4:39–42).

> *Therefore there was a division again among the Jews because of these sayings. And many of them said, "He has a demon and is mad. Why do you listen to Him?" Others said, "These are not the words of one who has a demon. Can a demon open the eyes of the blind?" (vv. 19–21).*

This teaching, like that which Jesus has already given, causes dissension among those who hear Him. The leaders view Him in one of two ways: He either performs His ministry by demonic power or He does miracles because God is His Father.

> *Now it was the Feast of Dedication in Jerusalem, and it was winter. And Jesus walked in the temple, in Solomon's porch. Then the Jews surrounded Him and said to Him, "How long do You keep us in doubt? If You are the Christ, tell us plainly." Jesus answered them, "I told you, and you do not believe. The works that I do in My Father's name, they bear witness of Me. But you do not believe, because you are not of My sheep, as I said to you.*

*My sheep hear My voice, and I know them, and they follow Me.
And I give them eternal life, and they shall never perish; neither
shall anyone snatch them out of My hand. My Father, who has
given them to Me, is greater than all; and no one is able to
snatch them out of My Father's hand. I and My Father are one"
(vv. 22–30).*

The Feast of Dedication is also known as Hanukkah, an eight-day celebration of the recovery of the temple by Judas Maccabeus and the restoration of worship in it. The feast occurred in December and was noted for the lights that were lit in the temple. John's chronology suggests that Jesus remained in Jerusalem after the Feast of Tabernacles which was celebrated a couple of months earlier (7:10). At that time Jesus described Himself as the Good Shepherd. Here Jesus repeats that the sheep hear His voice and follow Him. He will give them eternal life and none shall be destroyed (vv. 3, 4, 10). This teaching is given in Solomon's Portico, a public area on the east side of the temple mount that was surrounded by colonnades. It was so named because it was believed to include part of the original temple built by Solomon. The details given by John in this passage again indicate it is an eye-witness report. Jesus teaches in a specific location in the temple during the early winter Feast of Dedication.

The Jews will not be satisfied until Jesus pronounces Himself to be the Messiah. But will they believe Jesus if He will admit to this? It is not probable. Such an admission by Jesus will not change their view of Him since He is redefining the popular conception of the Messiah. His definition includes the observation that He has come to give His life for the people. Most people at this time believed that the Messiah would come in victory over enemies such as the Romans and establish a new government in Jerusalem. They did not conceive of the Messiah as One who would die at the hands of the Romans.

The miracles that Jesus has performed are signs of His identity as God's Son. Yet, the Jewish leaders do not believe. In this they show that they are not His sheep. Jesus gives eternal life to His sheep. They will not be destroyed or stolen away by the thief.

*Then the Jews took up stones again to stone Him. Jesus answered
them, "Many good works I have shown you from My Father. For
which of those works do you stone Me?" The Jews answered
Him, saying, "For a good work we do not stone You, but for blasphemy, and because You, being a Man, make Yourself God."*

Jesus answered them, "Is it not written in your law, 'I said, "You are gods"'? If He called them gods, to whom the word of God came (and the Scripture cannot be broken), do you say of Him whom the Father sanctified and sent into the world, 'You are blaspheming,' because I said, 'I am the Son of God'? If I do not do the works of My Father, do not believe Me; but if I do, though you do not believe Me, believe the works, that you may know and believe that the Father is in Me, and I in Him." Therefore they sought again to seize Him, but He escaped out of their hand (vv. 31–39).

The Jews threaten to stone Jesus a second time. As before, they do so because Jesus identifies Himself with God the Father. Earlier He claimed, "Before Abraham was, I AM" (8:29); here He says, "I and My Father are one."

Jesus quotes from Psalm 82 to defend Himself. He does not refute their assertion that He identifies Himself with God, but He reminds them of the psalmist's astounding remark that the people are gods (v. 6).

The psalm begins with the psalmist claiming that God judges among the mighty ones and gods in the congregation of the people. He describes the people with exalted language though they are the poor and needy who require God's justice and deliverance. They do not know God or understand His ways. It is with this background that the psalmist declares to the people, "You are gods and all of you are children of the Most High." Still, though they are gods they are also mortal and will experience death. Nevertheless, the psalmist describes the very human people of God's congregation as gods. Jesus picks up on this description and asks why the psalmist can make such a statement yet He cannot identify Himself as the Son of God. He exhorts the people to believe what He says about Himself by considering the works that He does—His miracles signify His identity. But once again the authorities attempt to seize Jesus (7:32, 44).

The Good Works of Jesus in the Gospel of John

Jesus exhorts the Jewish leaders to believe the works He does even if they cannot believe Him (10:37, 38). He urges them to trust in the goodness of the works they see (10:32). Throughout John's gospel Jesus describes the miracles that He performs as works that the Father does through Him.

Jesus alludes to the healing of the lame man on the Sabbath when He says that just as God His Father is working so also He is working (5:17, 7:21). Jesus does what He sees the Father do (5:19) and will do even greater works (v. 20).

Later He says that His works testify to God's presence in His life and ministry and that He has come from God (5:36, 37).

Jesus says that He must do the works of the One who sent Him (9:4). He says this in view of the miracle that He is about to perform for the man who is born blind "so that the works of God should be revealed in him" (v. 3). The works of God to which Jesus refers speak of the goodness of God. Jesus here says that the goodness of God will be revealed in the healing of the blind man. The God who created light and eyes with which to see the light will show His goodness in the miracle Jesus is about to perform.

All the works or miracles that Jesus does are done in the name of God and testify of Jesus' relationship with God (10:25). In fact, He does many good works (v. 32). The miracles that Jesus performs are not neutral acts. They are good works, not evil works done by the power of the Evil One (Matt. 9:34, 12:24; Mark 3:22; Luke 11:15), and not of the world (7:7). In fact, His works overthrow the ruler of this world (12:31; 16:11).

By working miracles Jesus fulfills the work of God His Father. He tells His disciples that His food is to do the will of the One who sent Him and to finish His work (*ton ergon*). What is this work? It is the harvest of fruit for eternal life. It is the gathering of people to God to enjoy life in His presence (4:34).

So why does Jesus urge the leaders to believe His works if they cannot believe Him? The miracles declare that God is in Him and He is in God! They are one. The miracles reveal that the eternal God from the beginning of time who always does good is present in the life and ministry of Jesus. For this same reason Jesus urges Philip and the disciples to believe He is in the Father and the Father is in Him as a result of the works He has done (14:11). Those who believe this astounding truth will do even greater works (vv. 12, 13).

The works of Jesus show that God continues to do His good work from the beginning. It will be recalled that throughout the creation account in Genesis 1 God declares the works completed by His word to be "good" (vv. 10, 12, 18, 21, 25, 31). Of course, the good works that God does reveals a truth about God Himself. He is good and what He does is good. Since Jesus does what He sees His Father doing and claims that the works He does are the works of God Himself, then the miracles He does are good works that speak of God's continued creative activity and gift of eternal life in His ministry. God continues to do good works through His Word that has become flesh.

Belief in the Gospel of John

Belief is a foundational theme in John's gospel. This is apparent from John's climactic statement that he recorded Jesus' miraculous signs so that his readers "may believe that Jesus is the Christ, the Son of God, and that believing [they] may have life in His name" (20:31). What does John mean by belief? He means a personal response to Jesus' claim of being from God (5:24, 38; 6:29; 12:44; 17:8, 21; 16:27, 50; and 17:8) and one with God (14:10; 11:27); it is acceptance of His assertion that He is the Son of God (3:18; 11:27) who has come into the world (11:27; 12:46). To believe that Jesus is from God as God's Son is to believe that His teaching is the word of God and that His miracles are the works of God.

Interestingly, John does not use the noun "faith" or "trust" (*pistis*, ἡ πίστις) anywhere in his gospel. Rather, he uses the verb "believe," "trust," or "obey" (*pisteuō*, πιστεύω) almost 100 times. The related Hebrew verb (/אמן) in its causal mood means to make stable or firm or to become dependent on someone or something. This means that belief is not a mere act of the mind but it is a conviction that results in specific behavior and action. John often describes such action with figurative language. It is coming to Jesus (5:40; 6:35, 37, 44, 65; 7:37), receiving Jesus (1:12; 5:43), and following Jesus (8:12). It is to love Jesus (14:15, 21, 23; 16:27).

Signs inspire belief. Nathanael believes in Jesus because of a sign (1:50) as do other disciples because of the miracle He performs at Cana (2:11). Moreover, the royal official believes in Jesus because of the sign of His word (4:48) and the man who was blind believes in Jesus as the Son of God because he sees (9:35–38). People believe after the raising of Lazarus (11:45). Yet, even before Lazarus is raised to life, Jesus challenges Martha to believe and she responds by saying that He is "the Christ, the Son of God, who is to come into the world" (11:25–27). Not only do signs issue in belief, but so do Jesus' words (4:39, 41, 50; 5:24, 27; 8:30, 17:20; also 10:3, 16, 27; 18:37).

Jesus speaks about belief throughout His ministry. At the beginning He tells Nicodemus that whoever believes in God's Son will experience eternal life (3:16–18). This includes the hard teaching that the Son of Man will be put to death. In His last discourse with the disciples, Jesus speaks to them about belief (13:19; 14:10–12, 28, 29). And in Gethsemane He declares that the disciples have believed He is from God and He prays for those who will believe He is from God as a result of their testimony (17:8, 20, 21). After His resurrection, Jesus tells Thomas that those who believe in Him without having experienced His earthly ministry are blessed (20:8). Clearly, belief is a key theme throughout Jesus' teaching. He continuously challenges people to respond with belief to His claim that He has come from God and does the work of God in their midst.

All of this reveals that Jesus' ministry does not allow for indifference. One must decide if He has come from God, spoken the words of God, and performed the works of God. Unbelief is to deny that the words and works of Jesus are the very words and works of God. Such denial results in condemnation because it exposes one to the wrath that comes from being separated from God (3: 18, 36).

Lazarus' Sickness and the Glory of God (John 10:40–11:16)

The abundant life that the Good Shepherd offers is spectacularly manifested in the last miraculous sign performed by Jesus when He raises Lazarus to life from death. John shows Jesus as the Shepherd of Israel who has come to lead them out of a state of exile from God into a familial relationship with Him. He pointedly contrasts Jesus with the thief who comes to destroy. In addition, he places special stress on the fact that Lazarus is sick. Though sickness is common to the human physical condition, it is particularly descriptive of God's people at this time. Lazarus is representative of those loved by God and, yet, are sick because they are away from Him. They need to be healed and restored by Jesus.

> *And He went away again beyond the Jordan to the place where John was baptizing at first, and there He stayed. Then many came to Him and said, "John performed no sign, but all the things that John spoke about this Man were true." And many believed in Him there (vv. 40–42).*

Jesus returns to the place of His baptism where the Spirit came upon Him as He began His ministry. There, many people declare that the Baptist's testimony about Jesus is true. That is, they agree that Jesus is the Lamb of God who takes away the sin of the world, who baptizes with the Holy Spirit, and is the Son of God (1:29–34).

> *Now a certain man was sick, Lazarus of Bethany, the town of Mary and her sister Martha. It was that Mary who anointed the Lord with fragrant oil and wiped His feet with her hair, whose brother Lazarus was sick (vv. 1, 2).*

Here, John establishes the background to the last miracle of Jesus. Bethany is the name of a town near Jerusalem. Its name means "House of Affliction." This name is appropriate for this story since Lazarus is sick and indeed afflicted. Mary, Lazarus' sister, is well-known by her ministry to Jesus when she anoints His feet with oil and wipes them with her hair. That story is described later in the gospel (12:1–8) and is also reported by Matthew (26:6–13).

> *Therefore the sisters sent to Him, saying, "Lord, behold, he*
> *whom You love is sick." When Jesus heard that, He said, "This*
> *sickness is not unto death, but for the glory of God, that the Son*
> *of God may be glorified through it." Now Jesus loved Martha*
> *and her sister and Lazarus. So, when He heard that he was sick,*
> *He stayed two more days in the place where He was. Then after*
> *this He said to the disciples, "Let us go to Judea again" (vv. 3–7).*

John draws attention to Lazarus' sick condition by noting the fact five times. He describes Lazarus as sick (v. 1), identifies Mary as the sister to Lazarus who was sick (v. 2), has Mary and Martha send a message to Jesus saying that "he whom You love is sick" (v. 3), reports Jesus as saying "this sickness is not unto death" (v. 4), and then observes that Jesus did not go immediately to him when He received the news of his sickness (v. 6). The word for sickness (*astheneia*) used by John and its verbal form "to be sick" (*astheneō*, ἀσθενέω) is a general term that is descriptive of human weakness and frailty.

John also portrays Lazarus' family as having a special relationship with Jesus. First, he describes Mary as the woman who anointed Jesus' feet with oil and wiped them with her hair (v. 2). Then he reports that Mary and Martha describe their brother as "he whom You love" (v. 3). Finally, he writes that Jesus loved them (v. 5).

Still, despite the fact that Lazarus is sick and Jesus loves him and his family, He does not immediately go to him. In fact, He remains two more days where He is. Is Jesus too busy to go to Lazarus? This cannot be the reason since He has already said that the sickness is "for the glory of God, that the Son of Man may be glorified through it." His statement here is much like the one He makes to His disciples prior to giving sight to the man born blind (9:3). There, Jesus says that the blindness is so that the works of God might be performed in him. Here, it is for God's glory, which, as was noted earlier, speaks of the present life-giving work of God. God creates out of nothing and Jesus raises Lazarus from the nothingness of death. The powerlessness of the human condition to sickness and death will be matched by the power of God's glory. God is glorified in the giving of life.

> *The disciples said to Him, "Rabbi, lately the Jews sought to stone*
> *You, and are You going there again?" Jesus answered, "Are there*

not twelve hours in the day? If anyone walks in the day, he does
not stumble, because he sees the light of this world. But if one
walks in the night, he stumbles, because the light is not in him"
(vv. 8–10).

Once Jesus decides to go to Judea, His disciples remind Him of the danger
there. When He was last in Jerusalem the Jews picked up stones with the
intention of stoning Him (8:59; 10:31–33).

Jesus responds to the disciples' fears with a proverb that means He must
perform His ministry while He has the opportunity. He begins by asking,
"Are there not twelve hours in the day?" Everyone understands this observation since the Jewish day was divided into two twelve-hour periods. While
Jesus is with them, the light of the world is present—it is daylight, the time
for Jesus to do the works of God.

These things He said, and after that He said to them, "Our friend
Lazarus sleeps, but I go that I may wake him up." Then His disci-
ples said, "Lord, if he sleeps he will get well." However, Jesus
spoke of his death, but they thought that He was speaking about
taking rest in sleep. Then Jesus said to them plainly, "Lazarus is
dead. And I am glad for your sakes that I was not there, that you
may believe. Nevertheless let us go to him" (vv. 11–15).

When Jesus says that Lazarus sleeps, He speaks figuratively of His friend's
death. The inability of the disciples to understand His meaning is indicative
of the dullness of most people toward His teaching. The Jewish leaders, for
example, wonder where Jesus plans to go when He says, "I shall be with you
a little while longer, and then I go to Him who sent Me. You will seek Me and
not find Me, and where I am you cannot come." They remark to themselves,
"Where does He intend to go that we shall not find Him? Does He intend to
go to the Dispersion among the Greeks and teach the Greeks?" (7:32–36).
They do not understand that Jesus refers to His return to God His Father
from whom He has come.

Then Thomas, who is called the Twin, said to his fellow disciples,
"Let us also go, that we may die with Him" (v. 16).

Thomas is introduced by John as he gives voice to the real concern among
the disciples about a return to Jerusalem since the last time they were in
Jerusalem, certain leaders attempted to stone Jesus (10:31–39).

Martha's Confession (John 11:17–37)

In this passage the Good Shepherd who gives abundant life to the sheep identifies Himself as the Resurrection and the Life. He not only offers life, but He *is* Life. The promise of resurrection is found in several Old Testament passages. Two of the most significant are Daniel 12:2, 3 and Ezekiel 37:1–14. The Daniel passage is especially important in that it reveals that those who sleep will be awakened to everlasting life. By telling Martha that He is the Resurrection and the Life, Jesus identifies Himself with the future work of resurrection envisioned by Daniel. The raising of Lazarus anticipates that final resurrection.

> *So when Jesus came, He found that he had already been in the tomb four days. Now Bethany was near Jerusalem, about two miles away. And many of the Jews had joined the women around Martha and Mary, to comfort them concerning their brother (vv. 17–19).*

John reports that by the time Jesus arrives Lazarus had been dead four days and mourners have gathered with Mary and Martha to console them. Since popular belief held that a person's spirit remained with the body three days before departing, the fact that Lazarus had been dead for four days removes all doubt that the miracle was not simply a resuscitation from unconsciousness.

In this passage the term *the Jews* refers to community members who know the family and have come to share in their grief.

> *Now Martha, as soon as she heard that Jesus was coming, went and met Him, but Mary was sitting in the house (v. 20).*

Martha is depicted in Luke as a woman preoccupied with household matters and inattentive to Jesus' teaching. Mary listens to Jesus and is complimented for choosing the "good part" (10:38–42). Here, Martha goes to Jesus as He draws near to them while Mary remains at home.

> *Now Martha said to Jesus, "Lord, if You had been here, my brother would not have died. But even now I know that whatever You ask of God, God will give You." Jesus said to her, "Your brother will rise again." Martha said to Him, "I know that he will rise again in the resurrection at the last day." Jesus said to her, "I am the resurrection and the life. He who believes in Me,*

though he may die, he shall live. And whoever lives and believes
in Me shall never die. Do you believe this?" She said to Him,
"Yes, Lord, I believe that You are the Christ, the Son of God, who
is to come into the world" (vv. 21–27).

Martha expresses belief in what Jesus could have done as well as in what He can do. "Whatever you ask of God, God will do." Moreover, she accepts Jesus' promise that Lazarus will live. Yet, her understanding of His prophetic word is that it will occur in the end time (Dan. 12:2, 3). Jesus responds by saying that the promise of the end time is a present reality in His very life: "I am the Resurrection and the Life." The last day has arrived with Jesus. Physical death is a reality, He says, but so is the eternal life of God. Judging by her response, Martha does not seem to understand the idea that Jesus is the Resurrection and the Life. So, she confesses what she does understand, "You are the Christ, the Son of God, who is to come into the world."

And when she had said these things, she went her way and
secretly called Mary her sister, saying, "The Teacher has come
and is calling for you." As soon as she heard that, she arose
quickly and came to Him. Now Jesus had not yet come into the
town, but was in the place where Martha met Him. Then the

THE REVELATION OF THE CHRIST

Martha's confession of Jesus' identity is comparable to Peter's revelatory pronouncement that Jesus is "the Christ, the Son of the living God" (Matt. 16:16). It also resembles John's own declaration that Jesus is the Light "that was coming into the world" (1:9).

Martha's Confession	Peter's Confession
You are the Christ	You are the Christ
The Son of God who is come into the world	The Son of the living God

Both Martha and Peter declare Jesus to be God's Anointed One (Christ / Messiah) in response to a question from Jesus. Jesus asks Martha if she believes He is the Resurrection and the Life even as He asks Peter, "Who do you say I am?" (Matt. 16:15). Both declare Jesus to be the Son of God. According to Peter, He is related to the living God, while Mary observes that Jesus is related to the world as God's Son who has come to offer eternal life.

Jews who were with her in the house, and comforting her, when they saw that Mary rose up quickly and went out, followed her, saying, "She is going to the tomb to weep there." Then, when Mary came where Jesus was, and saw Him, she fell down at His feet, saying to Him, "Lord, if You had been here, my brother would not have died" (vv. 28–32).

Mary's behavior reveals both her grief and her humility; it reveals her nature. Her grief is indicated by her words, "If You had been here, my brother would not have died." She repeats what her sister has already said. Lazarus would be alive if Jesus had been present. Her humility is indicated by her actions. First, she addresses Jesus as Lord. She does not presume to speak His name, rather she gives Him a title of honor. Second, by falling before Jesus, Mary behaves in a manner that is consistent with her earlier actions. John has already identified her as the woman who anointed Jesus' feet with oil and wiped them with her hair (11:2). Thus, her action here can be seen as a continuation of her worship. In addition, John will shortly describe this act of worship on the eve of Jesus' entry into Jerusalem. In this way, John clearly depicts Mary as a woman who worships Jesus.

Therefore, when Jesus saw her weeping, and the Jews who came with her weeping, He groaned in the spirit and was troubled. And He said, "Where have you laid him?" They said to Him, "Lord, come and see." Jesus wept. Then the Jews said, "See how He loved him!" (vv. 33–36).

Jesus groans out loud (*embrimaomai*, ἐμβριμάομαι) by His spirit and is troubled (*tarassō*, ταράσσω). The Greek words express agitation or deep anger on the one hand and intense distress on the other hand. The word *tarassō* is used several times in the Gospel of John to speak of distress in relation to Jesus (11:38; 13:21; 14:1, 27). Jesus is disturbed when confronted with the death of Lazarus and when He speaks of the one who will betray him (13:21). He tells His disciples not to be distressed that He must leave them because the Father will send the Spirit in His name (14:27). Here, the Spirit-anointed Son who has ministered eternal life to the people reacts with impassioned feeling to the grief and suffering brought about by death. Jesus weeps because He is so moved by the loss of his friend and the effect that death has on the people who are close to Him.

John emphasizes the love that Jesus has for Lazarus and his sisters by noting the remarks made by the people present. As mentioned above, John draws attention to Jesus' love for Lazarus by identifying Lazarus as "he whom You love" (11:3) and by explicitly stating, "Now Jesus loved Martha and her sister and Lazarus" (11:5). By describing Lazarus in this way, John makes it clear that Jesus' actions are prompted by love. Even as God searched, gathered, and brought back His people from exile out of His love for them (Jer. 23:3; Ezek. 34:11–16), so also Jesus acts in love toward His friend who is afflicted.

> *And some of them said, "Could not this Man, who opened the eyes of the blind, also have kept this man from dying?" (v. 37).*

For the third time, people express regret that Jesus was not present while Lazarus was sick. The fact that people remember the healing of the man born blind speaks of its lasting impact on them.

The Word of Resurrection and Life (John 11:38–44)

Jesus has given six signs to enable people to believe that He has come from God. These climax in the raising of Lazarus. As the Resurrection and the Life, Jesus speaks the word of resurrection and calls Lazarus from death to life. The Word who from the beginning by which all things came into existence now speaks to one who no longer lives and restores him to life. This shows that Jesus is the One who has come to bring the people back into a right relationship with God—to lead them out of the darkness of death into the light of God's salvation by His word and by His works.

> *Then Jesus, again groaning in Himself, came to the tomb. It was a cave, and a stone lay against it. Jesus said, "Take away the stone." Martha, the sister of him who was dead, said to Him, "Lord, by this time there is a stench, for he has been dead four days" (vv. 38, 39).*

Jesus remains agitated and angered by the death of Lazarus as He approaches the tomb. Martha's remark that Lazarus has been dead four days underscores the fact that he is, indeed, dead.

> *Jesus said to her, "Did I not say to you that if you would believe you would see the glory of God?" (v. 40).*

Jesus reminds Martha of His earlier promise. Before going to Bethany, Jesus told the disciples that Lazarus' sickness and death would result in the glory of God (v. 4). And upon arriving there He told Martha that whoever believes in Him "though he may die, he shall live" (v. 26). God's glory is a manifestation of the eternal life of the One who gives life where there is no life.

> *Then they took away the stone from the place where the dead man was lying. And Jesus lifted up His eyes and said, "Father, I thank You that You have heard Me. And I know that You always hear Me, but because of the people who are standing by I said this, that they may believe that You sent Me." Now when He had said these things, He cried with a loud voice, "Lazarus, come forth!" And he who had died came out bound hand and foot with graveclothes, and his face was wrapped with a cloth. Jesus said to them, "Loose him, and let him go" (vv. 41–44).*

Here we see Jesus offering thanksgiving to God for hearing Him. At what time did God hear Jesus? Though John does not elaborate, it is likely the voicing of deep emotion by the Spirit in Jesus. God hears the passion of the Spirit-anointed Jesus in response to the death of Lazarus and the grief of his family and friends.

Jesus prays out loud for the benefit of those who have gathered at the grave so they will know that what He does is accomplished because He has come from God. He does not seek His will but that of His Father. Jesus loudly proclaims, "Lazarus, come forth!" He speaks the command of life and the one who was dead returns from the grave alive. Just as in the beginning God speaks His Word and brings into existence heaven and earth culminating in the creation of Adam, so also at the conclusion to His ministry Jesus speaks His word, knowing that His Father hears Him, bringing Lazarus to life from the nothingness of death.

The First and Last Miracles of Jesus

The first and last miracles performed by Jesus during His public ministry complement each other and reveal that He has brought life to the people of God.

The beginning of Jesus' public ministry begins when He goes to Bethany "beyond the Jordan" to be baptized. The Baptist proclaims that He is the "lamb of God who takes away the sin of the world." He says that Jesus has the Spirit and is the very Son of God (1:28–36). As soon as Jesus is identified in this way, men begin to follow Him (vv. 35–42) and He goes to Cana where He performs His first miracle. There, Jesus turns the water in six stone jars into wine (2:1–12).

Jesus goes "beyond the Jordan" a second time (10:40) where many believe in Him. This is the staging area for the final miraculous sign. When He hears that Lazarus is sick, He says that it is for the glory of God and His Son (11:4). He performs His last miracle when He goes to the gravesite, has the stone removed from before the tomb, and commands Lazarus to come out of it (11:38–41).

After performing the first sign in Cana, Jesus goes to Jerusalem where He overturns the tables of the vendors in the temple (2:13–22). He is challenged, "What sign do You show to us, since You do these things?" to which He responds, "Destroy this temple, and in three days I will raise it up."

After Jesus' last sign, a temple council gathers in fear the Romans will forcibly respond to the excitement He has generated. They fear that the Romans will take away the holy place (11:47–48). Caiaphas the high priest says that Jesus should die for the nation (v. 52).

Both miracles affirm the truth of the Baptist's teaching about Jesus given before the first miracle: The Lamb of God who takes away the sin of the world (of which death is the most grievous effect) is the One through whom the relationship of God and Israel is preserved as well as the One through

The Miracle of the Wine	The Miracle of Lazarus
Jesus goes "beyond the Jordan" where John baptizes Him (1:29).	Jesus goes "beyond the Jordan" where many believe in Him (10:40).
The Baptist announces that Jesus is the Lamb of God who takes away the sin of the world (1:29).	Mary announces that Jesus is the Christ the Son of God who is to come into the world (11:27).
Jesus performs His first miracle by turning water into wine (2:1–12). Jesus draws wine out of stone water pots.	Jesus performs His last miracle by raising Lazarus from the dead (11:38–44). Jesus draws life out of the stone tomb of death.
Jesus overturns the tables of the money-changers in the temple. The leaders are indignant: "What sign do You give to do these things?" (2:1–12).	The religious leaders are worried about the Roman response to Jesus and ask, "What shall we do?" (11:47–48).
Jesus prophesies His death and resurrection (2:19).	The high priest prophesies that Jesus will die for the nation (11:51–52).

whom life is reclaimed in the midst of death. Both miracles reveal that such life may be gained only through Jesus' death and resurrection.

The Death of One Man and the Return of the Nation (John 11:45–57)

The news of Lazarus' resurrection is reported to the leadership in Jerusalem and certain Pharisees and chief priests plot Jesus' death. At that time the chief priest utters a prophecy about Jesus' death that indicates that, as its result, the nation will be saved and the scattered people of Israel returned to the land. Though the prophecy is based on an erroneous perception of Jesus, the ironic truth of its message is that Jesus the Good Shepherd has come to give His life for His sheep so that they will experience abundant life.

> *Then many of the Jews who had come to Mary, and had seen the things Jesus did, believed in Him. But some of them went away to the Pharisees and told them the things Jesus did. Then the chief priests and the Pharisees gathered a council and said, "What shall we do? For this Man works many signs. If we let Him alone like this, everyone will believe in Him, and the Romans will come and take away both our place and nation"* (vv. 45–48).

Many people believe as a result of the raising of Lazarus, but others go to the Pharisees and chief priests to report that the false prophet continues to cause havoc among the crowds. They recognize His signs and see that many are following Him. Such a movement could arouse the Romans and result in harsh repressive measures. In the words of the high priest, "They [the Romans] will take away the nation." The word for nation is *ethnos* (ἔθνος). It is used in these verses (vv. 48, 50, 51) by the high priests in reference to the special identity they have as Jewish people.

The term *high priests* refers to the high priest and others responsible for the religious worship and administration of the temple. They include the captain of the temple who supervised its daily activities, the overseers or custodians of the temple who maintained the buildings and facilities of the temple, the temple treasurers who managed the finances of the temple, as well as the leaders over the twenty-four weekly and daily groups of priests that periodically served at the temple.

> *And one of them, Caiaphas, being high priest that year, said to them, "You know nothing at all, nor do you consider that it is*

expedient for us that one man should die for the people, and not
that the whole nation should perish." Now this he did not say on
his own authority; but being high priest that year he prophesied
that Jesus would die for the nation, and not for that nation only,
but also that He would gather together in one the children of
God who were scattered abroad. Then, from that day on, they
plotted to put Him to death. Therefore Jesus no longer walked
openly among the Jews, but went from there into the country
near the wilderness, to a city called Ephraim, and there
remained with His disciples (vv. 49–54).

Ominously, Caiaphas states that the nation can be spared Roman reprisal against the popular excitement over Jesus (6:14, 15) by putting Him to death. The high priest is both right and wrong about this. He is right to say that Jesus' death will preserve the people of God. He is wrong on two counts: He believes that such death is justified because Jesus is a false prophet and he thinks that Jesus' death will appease the Romans. (See discussion 7:40–52— Jesus as a false prophet.)

John reports that Caiaphas prophesied that the death of Jesus would result in the return of those scattered abroad. In this way, the high priest predicts that Jews will return from exile as a result of Jesus' death. His prophecy is true! Jesus is the Shepherd who leads His people in a return from exile to God. He fulfills the hope of the prophets for a Shepherd who will restore the people in their relationship with Him (Jer. 23:3, 4; Ezek. 34:11–16). This will occur when Christ comes again and people "come from the east and the west, from the north and the south, and sit down in the kingdom of God" (Luke 13:29).

Since the temple leadership is formally discussing Jesus' death, He withdraws to a place near the wilderness.

And the Passover of the Jews was near, and many went from the
country up to Jerusalem before the Passover, to purify them-
selves. Then they sought Jesus, and spoke among themselves as
they stood in the temple, "What do you think—that He will not
come to the feast?" Now both the chief priests and the Pharisees
had given a command, that if anyone knew where He was, he
should report it, that they might seize Him (vv. 55–57).

The excitement over Jesus is fueled in part by the order that news about Him is to be reported to the Jerusalem leadership so they can seize Him. Jesus is a wanted man.

Lazarus' resurrection reveals Jesus as the Good Shepherd who brings abundant life to the people. He is not like the thieves and false shepherds who steal, kill, and destroy. Rather, He does the opposite. As the Good Shepherd who is also the Resurrection and the Life, Jesus is the One who will lead the people back into life with God. Just as the Old Testament prophets spoke of a return from exile through the ministry of God's Shepherd, Jesus initiates a return from exile in His ministry as symbolized in the raising of Lazarus from the dead. Remarkably, the chief priest prophesies this when he says that Jesus should be put to death for the advantage of the nation. His death will bring many who have been scattered abroad back to their land. Though Caiaphas' presupposition for his action is wrong—he is convinced that Jesus is a false prophet who is leading many people astray from the covenant of God with His teaching and miracles and who is risking the wrath of the Romans because of the excitement His miracles are generating—he is correct when he says that Jesus' death will bring many to God. Thus, it is ironic that the chief priest thinks that the death of Jesus is the means by which the nation may be saved. In reality, the chief priest is the false shepherd who does not lead the people in the ways of God but strikes against God's true Shepherd.

QUESTIONS FOR PERSONAL REFLECTION AND GROUP DISCUSSION

1. How does the imagery of shepherd and sheep in Jeremiah and Ezekiel inform John's depiction of Jesus as the Good Shepherd? How is the raising of Lazarus related to this imagery?
2. What do the good works of Jesus reveal about God His Father?
3. Compare Martha's confession of Jesus to that of Peter.
4. What people would be included under the title "high priests"?
5. In what way is Caiaphas' prophecy about Jesus true?

CHAPTER 6

The Hour of the King

John 12:1–13:35

John has portrayed Jesus as the Word of God in the beginning, the One who fulfills the promise to the patriarchs, and the One who, like Moses, both leads the people in a new exodus and, like God's Shepherd, in a return from exile. In addition, John has depicted Jesus as the One who exemplifies the covenant of love that enables the people to live free from sin in the presence of God. In this section, John presents Jesus as the anticipated King of the people who would rule over them.

During the long history of Israel and Judah, psalmists and prophets looked forward to a day when God's rule over His faithful people would be personal and permanent. Both before and after the Assyrian (722 B.C.) and Babylonian (598–587 B.C.) Exiles, these spokesmen anticipated a king who would rule with justice and righteousness.

In the Old Testament psalmists, sing that God is the King of His people and over all the earth. He is the King of Glory who will be welcomed by the gates of His kingdom (Ps. 24:7–10), who rules forever in behalf of the lowly and humble (Ps. 10:16–18), and who gives His people victory in battle (Ps. 44:4–8). More importantly, the psalmist declares that God's Son will be His King who receives the nations as an inheritance and the earth as a possession (Ps. 2:6–8). Yet, the psalmists are not the only ones who anticipate the appearance of God's King. The prophets also declare that God will one day return and His King will rule over all the earth (Zech. 14:9). He will appoint a king who will bring judgment and righteousness to Israel so that they may live in security (Jer. 23:5, 6; 33:14–17; Is. 11:1).

This day of God's anticipated King is related to the future Day of the Lord, which is a time of judgment and salvation for Israel and all the nations. It is a day of judgment for Israel because of the nation's pride and idolatry (Is.

2:5–21; Amos 5:18–20) that results in darkness (Is. 12:10; Amos 5:18–20, 8:9; Joel 3:15; Zeph. 1:15) and sorrow (Amos 8:10–11; Zeph. 1:10). Judgment comes to the nations as well (Is. 12:11; Joel 3:1–13; Zeph. 2:4–15; Zech. 14:3). This day is not only about judgment, however. It is also a day of healing (Mic. 4:6–7; Zeph. 3:19), peace, and prosperity (Amos 9:11–15) as Israel's king defeats the nation's enemies (Zeph. 3). The nations, too, will experience salvation (Is. 2:2–4; Mic. 4:1–4; Zeph. 3:8, 9; Zech. 14:16).

John reports that after Jesus raised Lazarus from the dead, He went into the wilderness. He is careful to show that when Jesus returns before Passover, He returns as God's King. Mary anoints His feet, He enters Jerusalem to the songs of the people, and He speaks on the solemn matter of His death to His disciples. The night before His crucifixion Jesus washes the disciples' feet as their Teacher and Lord and prepares them for future service under His authority. At this time He gives them a new commandment by which to pattern their lives.

At this time Jesus informs the disciples His hour has arrived (12:23, 27). This "hour" is His passion, death, and resurrection. It is the moment for which He has come into the world. John's gospel points to this hour. All that he records about the teaching and miracles of Jesus anticipates the moment when the gift of eternal life is realized in Jesus' death and resurrection.

John draws from the longstanding scriptural traditions briefly noted above to show that Jesus is this anticipated King whose "hour" is the beginning of a new day for Israel. Yet, as God's King He does not come to exercise political or military power; He comes to exemplify the power of humility and sacrifice.

The Anointing of the King (John 12:1–11)

Now, Mary anoints the feet of Jesus so that He may lead the people as their King. This unusual act—she anoints His feet and not His head—reveals that Jesus will not lead in the common manner of earthly kings. He will lead by giving His life for the people. The Good Shepherd of the previous section is now welcomed by the people as the King of Israel as He enters the city of Jerusalem.

> *Then, six days before the Passover, Jesus came to Bethany, where Lazarus was who had been dead, whom He had raised from the dead. There they made Him a supper; and Martha served, but Lazarus was one of those who sat at the table with Him (vv. 1, 2).*

Jesus returns to Bethany and eats a meal with Mary, Martha, and Lazarus. Once again, John sets the background for the narrative by giving time and place information. Six days before Passover Jesus is in Bethany.

> *Then Mary took a pound of very costly oil of spikenard, anointed the feet of Jesus, and wiped His feet with her hair. And the house was filled with the fragrance of the oil. But one of His disciples, Judas Iscariot, Simon's son, who would betray Him, said, "Why was this fragrant oil not sold for three hundred denarii and given to the poor?" This he said, not that he cared for the poor, but because he was a thief, and had the money box; and he used to take what was put in it. But Jesus said, "Let her alone; she has kept this for the day of My burial. For the poor you have with you always, but Me you do not have always" (vv. 3–8).*

John says that Mary anointed Jesus' feet with expensive oil and wipes them with her hair. "A pound of very costly oil of spikenard" refers to an ointment made from the nard plant cultivated in India. The ointment is genuine and not an imitation. John says that Mary uses it to anoint Jesus' feet. The word "anoint" (*aleiphō*, ἀλείφω) is used in the Gospels to signify ministry for the sick or preparation of the dead (Mark 6:13; 16:1) as well as ministry to oneself when one fasts (Matt. 6:17). Mary's act is similar to that performed by the sinful woman who anoints Jesus' feet with her tears and dries them with her hair (Luke 7:36–50; vv. 38, 46). She shows reverence for the One who raised her brother from death through her extravagance (the ointment is valued by Judas at 300 denarii, the equivalent of one year's wages for a laborer) and humility (wiping His feet with her hair). Thus, Mary's act has twofold significance: it recognizes Jesus as Israel's King, and it anticipates the death of this King. John's description of the meal along with his comment that "the whole house was filled with the fragrance of the oil" speaks of an eyewitness account.

Throughout the Old Testament, individuals are anointed and set apart from others for a special service to God. To anoint a king of Israel was not only to set him apart from other people, however; It was to confer power upon him to accomplish the specific tasks he was to perform as their leader. For this reason, the kings Saul (1 Sam. 10:1), David (1 Sam. 16:3), and Solomon (1 Kin. 1:39) are anointed to rule over God's people. In each case, oil is poured over his head and he is empowered to carry out his responsibilities. Jesus' anointing is unusual in that it is not His head but His feet that are anointed. This is because His task is unusual. Jesus is anointed King to perform the task of giving His life for the world.

Judas is introduced into the story when he complains about the waste of money in Mary's use of the ointment. John says that Judas is the one who betrayed Jesus and was a thief who took money from the money box entrusted to him. In addition, John remarks that Judas' question is not asked out of concern for the poor. His words are disingenuous. This description links him with the devil who is described as a "thief and a liar" (8:44).

Jesus rebukes Judas. He says, "Leave her," a command to not interfere with her ministry to Him. He says that Mary has prepared Him for burial. Thus, He prophesies about His death nearly a week before the Crucifixion. Up to this time He has spoken of His death in an elliptical manner—the Son of Man who is lifted up (3:14; 6:53, 54; 8:28), the One who is going away (7:33, 34; 8:21), the Good Shepherd who lays down His life (10:15, 17, 18)—now He speaks plainly.

The proverbial remark Jesus makes about the poor is not an indication of His indifference to the poor, of course. He simply speaks of the impoverishment of the human condition, which should be contrasted with the abundant life that He provides (10:10).

> *Now a great many of the Jews knew that He was there; and they came, not for Jesus' sake only, but that they might also see Lazarus, whom He had raised from the dead. But the chief priests plotted to put Lazarus to death also, because on account of him many of the Jews went away and believed in Jesus (vv. 9–11).*

PERSISTENT OPPOSITION TO JESUS

Opposition to Jesus is behind the plot against Lazarus. This will result in Jesus' crucifixion. But such opposition is not new. Jesus has encountered resistance throughout His ministry. John establishes this conflict as a primary theme of his gospel, saying, "The Light shines in the darkness, and the darkness did not contain it" (1:5). Several passages describe this conflict:

- John states that the Jews wanted to kill Jesus (6:16–18).
- Many of Jesus' disciples leave Him over His remarks about His body and blood (6:66).
- People claim that Jesus has a demon (7:20; 9:52; 10:20).
- Others pick up stones to kill Him (9:59; 10:31) and attempt to seize Him (10:39).
- The leaders plan to kill Jesus (11:45–57).
- The Jews scheme to kill Lazarus because of his testimony about Jesus (12:9–11).

Unsurprisingly, Lazarus is the center of attention. A large number of the people gather to see Jesus and the man whom He raised from the dead. At the same time, the temple leadership reaches the conclusion that Lazarus should die. He is living testimony of the life-giving power of Jesus and is the reason many believe in Jesus.

The Coming of the King (John 12:12–19)

Jesus enters Jerusalem as the Good Shepherd who has been anointed King— the Shepherd-King of Israel. Such a depiction of Jesus draws upon Jeremiah's prophecy about a future shepherd-king of Israel who would bring the people back from exile and rule over them with justice and righteousness (Jer. 23:1–8).

> *The next day a great multitude that had come to the feast, when they heard that Jesus was coming to Jerusalem, took branches of palm trees and went out to meet Him, and cried out: "Hosanna! Blessed is He who comes in the name of the LORD! The King of Israel!" Then Jesus, when He had found a young donkey, sat on it; as it is written: "Fear not, daughter of Zion; Behold, your King is coming, Sitting on a donkey's colt" (vv. 12–15).*

The public response to Jesus swells after the miracle of Lazarus. John reports that a great multitude welcomes Him as He enters Jerusalem. Many Jews believed in Jesus after the miracle (11:45) and many go to the Passover expecting to see Him (11:57). "A great many of the Jews" went to see Jesus when He visited Lazarus (12:9) and many believed in Him because of Lazarus (12:11).

The people shout a welcome as Jesus draws near to the city: "Blessed is He who comes in the name of the LORD" (Ps. 118:26). At the same time they add the title, "The King of Israel," to their acclamation. The psalm from which they speak rejoices in the mercy of God. The enduring mercy of God (vv. 1–4, 29) is manifest in the One who saves Israel from the surrounding nations (vv. 5–14) with His right hand (vv. 15, 16). The psalmist asks that the gates of the Lord be opened to the righteous ones and that prosperity will be granted to the people (vv. 19, 20, 25). The psalm concludes with a rousing expression of trust and expectancy in God. The people call upon God to save and three times they declare the Lord to be God: "God is the LORD," "You are my God," "You are my God" (vv. 27, 28).

By proclaiming Psalm 118 as Jesus comes to Jerusalem, the people are expressing their view of Jesus. He is God's King who has come to give His righteous people victory over the surrounding nations—the Romans—as well as prosperity in their lives. They are aroused by the raising of Lazarus and certainly recall the feeding of the 5,000. Many people wanted to make Him their King at that time (6:15).

Psalm 118 proclaims that "the stone which the builders rejected has become the chief cornerstone" (v. 22). By identifying Jesus with this psalm, the people unknowingly prophesy about His death. According to the synoptic Gospels, Jesus uses it to refer to His passion (Matt. 21:42). And early Christians drew upon this text in a similar way, remembering that the people recited it when Jesus entered Jerusalem (Eph. 2:20; 1 Pet. 2:7, 8).

Not only do the people proclaim Jesus as God's King and, unwittingly, prophesy His death, but Jesus fulfills the arrival of the King anticipated by Zechariah when He rides a donkey into the city (9:9). Zechariah, a visionary post-exilic prophet, announced the arrival of a King who would bring peace to the nations and who would exercise universal rule (9:10). Whereas the people's use of the psalms indicates that they longed for a king who would expel their enemies and bring prosperity to them, John's use of Zechariah's prophecy shows that Jesus comes for a different purpose. He comes to establish peace for all people and to extend His rule over all.

> *His disciples did not understand these things at first; but when Jesus was glorified, then they remembered that these things were written about Him and that they had done these things to Him (v. 16).*

John reports that the disciples do not understand the significance of these events until after Jesus' resurrection. Nor have they understood other teachings or acts of Jesus. For example, early in His ministry when He overturned the tables in the temple, Jesus said, "Destroy this temple and I will raise it in three days." John reports that it was not until after His resurrection that the disciples understood His meaning (2:22). Their vision of Jesus' teaching and miracles is sharpened because of His resurrection.

> *Therefore the people, who were with Him when He called Lazarus out of his tomb and raised him from the dead, bore witness. For this reason the people also met Him, because they heard that He had done this sign. The Pharisees therefore said among themselves, "You see that you are accomplishing nothing. Look, the world has gone after Him!" (vv. 17–19).*

The Pharisees are divided about how they should respond to Jesus and to the growing excitement of the people. By saying that "the world has gone after Him," the Pharisees speak ironically. John has already said that the Light came into the world but the world did not accept it. It seems that the world is following Jesus when, in fact, they are following their own conception of the King of Israel.

JESUS AND THE WORLD

John uses the word *world* in his gospel almost eighty times. This word generally indicates two things: the ways and means of human experience and the universal nature of Jesus' ministry. It speaks of the world that is in need of God's recreative work and the fact that Jesus came for all people. John's use of "world" may seem surprising given that he sets the public ministry of Jesus against the background of the Old Testament story of God's redemption of Israel. Why would John speak of Jesus in terms of the world and record Jesus telling of the world and at the same time depict His ministry as resembling God's redemptive work as recounted in the Law, Prophets, and Writings? John intends to show that the God who first called Israel is now present in Jesus Christ to call all people. For Jews, this is good news for two reasons. First, it reveals that the God of their ancestors, who demonstrated His love for them in the covenant, is present in Christ—the continuation of God's love to them. Second, it shows that the purpose of God for calling Israel is achieved. They were chosen to lead the other nations in worship of God (Ex. 19:5, 6). This is done through Israel's Messiah, Jesus Christ, as He gives His life so that the nations apart from Israel might be saved. For this reason, it is good news for Gentiles. The God who was faithful to His covenant people throughout the Old Testament has now come to make a covenant of life with all.

For this reason, the world is the focus of Jesus' ministry. John records a series of events that verify this truth: (1) Jesus teaches Nicodemus (a Jewish leader) that God loves the whole world; (2) He tells a non-Jewish (Samaritan) woman that worship of God will no longer be limited to a place or a tradition but will occur anywhere the Spirit of God is found; and (3) He heals the son of a Hellenistic official even though he likely embraced the countervailing attitudes of the Greco-Roman culture at that time. Jesus ministers to the world through these people. But these are not the only ones who experience His ministry. Many Jews and non-Jews came into contact with Jesus during the major festivals of Passover, Pentecost, and Tabernacles. (See Acts 2:5–11.) Thus, when He says to Nicodemus during Passover that "God so loved the world that He gave His only begotten Son . . . He did not send His Son into the world to condemn the world but that the world through Him might be saved" (3:16, 17), He does so with a mind to those from various countries who were in Jerusalem for the festival at this time. In fact, many people (the whole world) seek out Jesus at a later Passover because of the miracle of Lazarus (12:19).

JESUS AND THE WORLD (CONTINUED)

Likewise, during the Feast of Tabernacles Jesus says that He is the Light of the world. He says this first to the woman caught in adultery (8:12) and then to His disciples before He heals the man born blind (9:5). His ministry to these two people is proof that He gives life to all since both of them stand outside the covenant community. The woman has no status among the people because of her sin and the man because of his infirmity (9:30–35). Jesus reaches beyond the covenant community to bring restoration to them.

The world is not only on Jesus' mind during the festivals but also during the night of His passion. According to John, at this most urgent moment of His life, Jesus refers to the world nearly twenty times to describe the compromised realm of human ambition, endeavor, and valuation (vv. 6, 9, 11, 13–18, 25). It is from this realm that Jesus leads out those who believe in Him and it is within this realm that His followers will continue to live. By experiencing the life of the new creation in Jesus they are no longer part of this human realm, yet even as He entered into it to manifest the creative life of God, so also they live within it for the same purpose.

In addition to this, "the world" describes the antithesis of God's recreated realm from the beginning resisting the establishment of that realm through Jesus. The world through its leaders hates Jesus (7:7) and is represented by the thief who has come to steal, kill, and destroy (10:10). In God's realm, Adam enjoyed the presence and provision of God even as he served God. The world does not know God's presence—it is ignorant of His Son and rejects His teaching and ministry—and suffers with great physical need. For this reason, the people live in darkness. Jesus has entered into that realm in order to redeem it; He has come to establish God's new creation.

Not all understand Jesus or believe in Him and because of their unbelief they remain in the world. The negative reaction to His teaching mostly comes from the temple leadership, who represent all people who reject Him as the Son of God. Yet, Jesus has overcome the world (16:33). He has triumphed over human and non-human resistance to His ministry. The fact that many believe in Him at a time that He is proclaimed the King of Israel (12:13–15) shows that Jesus is, indeed, the King of the whole world.

The Hour of the King (John 12:20–50)

Jesus announces that His hour has come. Up to this time His hour has been in the future (2:4; 4:21, 22; 7:6, 8, 30; 8:20). Here, Jesus speaks of His hour in terms of judgment and darkness. He says, "Now is the judgment of this world" (v. 31), and urges, "A little while longer the light is with you. Walk while you have the light, lest darkness overtake you; he who walks in darkness does not know where he is going" (v. 35). With these words, John indicates that Jesus' "hour" is related to the future day of the Lord declared by the prophets. That day is one of judgment in which the world is darkened (Zech. 14:6, 7; Joel 2:2, 10; 3:15; Is. 60:2) and, yet, the Gentiles will come to Israel to bless them (Zech. 14:16; Is. 60:4) and to be judged by God (Zech. 14:17–19; Joel 3:1–17). This future time of judgment and salvation has its origin, according to John, in Jesus' hour. Already, Gentiles are coming to Jesus as the servant-king (12:20, 21) who draws all nations to God as declared by the prophets (Is. 60:1–3; see Ps. 2:6–12). The future day of God's judgment and salvation is telescoped into the time Jesus calls His "hour" for it is with His death and resurrection that a new day begins.

> *Now there were certain Greeks among those who came up to worship at the feast. Then they came to Philip, who was from Bethsaida of Galilee, and asked him, saying, "Sir, we wish to see Jesus" (vv. 20, 21).*

Greeks approach the disciples to see Jesus. These are probably God-fearers who have traveled to Jerusalem for Passover. God-fearers were those who practiced Judaism but did not undergo circumcision. They were welcomed to participate in the festivals and the religious life of Israel.

> *Philip came and told Andrew, and in turn Andrew and Philip told Jesus (v. 22).*

The fact that Philip reports to Andrew and Andrew asks Jesus if He will meet with the God-fearing Greeks indicates that the disciples observed some protocol with respect to each other and to Jesus. Andrew is close to Jesus and passes Philip's request on to Him.

> *But Jesus answered them, saying, "The hour has come that the Son of Man should be glorified" (v. 23).*

Jesus informs the Greeks that His hour has arrived. The Greeks' request indicates that people outside the Jewish community are seeking Him out. Sheep not of "this" fold are gathering to Jesus (10:16). This is a sign to Jesus that God's purpose is being fulfilled and will be completed as the Son of Man is glorified. As previously mentioned, Jesus' use of the phrase *Son of Man* is not merely a self-description. It speaks of His mission on behalf of all people. John shows that Jesus usually uses the term in reference to His passion and death (3:13, 14; 6:53; 8:28; 12:34; 13:31). In His death Jesus will be revealed as the One who gives life to the people. This is what Jesus means when He says that the Son will be glorified.

> "Most assuredly, I say to you, unless a grain of wheat falls into the ground and dies, it remains alone; but if it dies, it produces much grain. He who loves his life will lose it, and he who hates his life in this world will keep it for eternal life" (vv. 24, 25).

Here, Jesus explains what His "hour" entails: death, resurrection, and life-giving. He remarks on a basic principle of life—the planting of a seed—and simultaneously prophesies about His death, which is like a grain of wheat that is planted in the ground and results in a harvest.

Jesus also relates death and resurrection to the believer. However, He does not mean that a person should despise or loathe his or her life. His statement contrasts two views of life, highlighting one over the other. He stresses eternal life over life defined by the human condition—the world. "This world" refers to the disaffected condition of humanity; it is not God's ultimate intention for people. Eternal life is God's desire for humankind. It should be our desire as well.

> "If anyone serves Me, let him follow Me; and where I am, there My servant will be also. If anyone serves Me, him My Father will honor" (v. 26).

In this verse, Jesus speaks as a King. Anyone who would serve Him must follow Him. This means that he or she must accept His teaching and obey His commands. God will honor such disciples. Even as Jesus will be given glory in His death—His service to His Father—so those who will follow and serve Him will be honored by God.

> "Now My soul is troubled, and what shall I say? 'Father, save Me from this hour'? But for this purpose I came to this hour" (v. 27).

Jesus is troubled in His soul. Even as He was distressed by the death of Lazarus (11:33), He is distressed now at the thought of His own impending death. Jesus says that His death will give glory to His Father for the purpose of eternal life.

Should Jesus ask His Father to save Him from His hour? The question resembles His ambivalence in the Garden of Gethsemane when He implores His Father, "If it is possible, let this cup pass from Me; nevertheless, not as I will, but as You will" (Matt. 26:39, 42; Mark 14:36; Luke 22:42). The answer is "No." Jesus has come from the Father for this reason. He has come to give His life so others might live.

> *"Father, glorify Your name." Then a voice came from heaven, saying, "I have both glorified it and will glorify it again." Therefore the people who stood by and heard it said that it had thundered. Others said, "An angel has spoken to Him" (vv. 28, 29).*

The synoptic Gospels record a voice from heaven at the beginning of Jesus' ministry with His baptism (Matt. 3:17; Mark 1:11; Luke 3:22) as well as a voice from the cloud at the Transfiguration of Jesus on the mountain (Matt. 17:5; Mark 9:7; Luke 9:35). John records a voice from heaven at the conclusion of

THE VOICE FROM HEAVEN

The voice from heaven recorded in John 12:28, 29 is not a general or non-specific endorsement of Jesus. It has three-fold significance:

- It affirms Jesus as God's divine Son.
- It implicitly declares that the death of Jesus is the plan of God for Him.
- It binds the glory of God to Jesus' death.

In John, the voice is heard after Jesus compares His approaching death to a grain of wheat that is planted in the ground. Thus, the voice endorses Jesus as God's Son who will die a human death. This affirmation is supported by the synoptic Gospels. In the account of the Transfiguration, Jesus is identified as God's beloved Son who is glorified before the disciples (Matt. 17:2) and who begins to speak about His death to them (Matt. 17:9, 12; Mark 9:12, 10:31, 33, 34; compare Luke 9:22, 23–26). God's glory is tied to Jesus as God's Son who will die at the hands of men. Also, the accounts of Jesus' baptism at the Jordan report that the voice expresses pleasure in the beloved Son after which time Jesus is led by the Spirit into the wilderness (Mark 1:12) where He is tempted by the devil to abandon the way of the Cross (Matt. 4:1–11; Luke 4:1–13). Matthew's account makes this clear. If Jesus will worship the devil, he will give Jesus the nations of the world—the very thing that Jesus has entered the world to gain! (Matt. 4:8–10). Yet, the nations are not to be won in this way. They will be gained through Jesus' death. The voice from heaven thus approves of Jesus as the Son who will give His life for the people. Jesus will be glorified in His death by giving His life so that others may live.

His public ministry. The Gospels in this way show God's divine approval of the entirety of Jesus' ministry.

The "voice from heaven" is a circumlocution or indirect manner of referring to God. Some scholars understand this voice as the Bath Qol ("daughter of the voice") of God. Early rabbis referred to the prophetic word of God given through men as the Bath Qol and many believe this is the manner in which this event should be understood. Thus, John is not necessarily referring to an audible voice when he records this speech from heaven. Despite this scholarly viewpoint, John's report that a sound like thunder was heard by the people indicates that he intends to say God spoke audibly but only Jesus was able to interpret His speech.

Though it is uncertain if the voice from heaven at Jesus' baptism is heard by anyone other than Jesus and possibly John the Baptist, it is certain that only Peter, James, and John hear the voice from the cloud on the mountain when Jesus is transfigured. Here in John, it is heard as thunder by all the people who are present with Him. It is a sign that what Jesus says about Himself is true.

> Jesus answered and said, "This voice did not come because of
> Me, but for your sake. Now is the judgment of this world; now
> the ruler of this world will be cast out. And I, if I am lifted up
> from the earth, will draw all peoples to Myself." This He said,
> signifying by what death He would die (vv. 30–33).

Jesus says that the judgment of the world has begun and the ruler of the world cast out. The ruler of the world will be dethroned through the death of Israel's King. A new era begins with the death and resurrection of Jesus.

The grammar in this passage asserts that Jesus indeed will be lifted up (3:14; 8:28) and because of this all people will come to Him. The anticipated King of the prophets who would bring all nations to Israel inaugurates the Day of the Lord by His exaltation on the cross. John reports that Jesus is aware not only that He will die but that He will die the shameful death of crucifixion.

> The people answered Him, "We have heard from the law that
> the Christ remains forever; and how can You say, "The Son of
> Man must be lifted up'? Who is this Son of Man?" Then Jesus
> said to them, "A little while longer the light is with you. Walk
> while you have the light, lest darkness overtake you; he who
> walks in darkness does not know where he is going. While you
> have the light, believe in the light, that you may become sons of

light." These things Jesus spoke, and departed, and was hidden
from them (vv. 34–36).

The people are confused. If Jesus is the messianic King that God has sent to deliver them, then why does He speak of His death? After all, the prophet Micah proclaimed that the Messiah, the One who would heal the people and restore them, would rule forever (Mic. 4:7).

When the people ask, "Who is the Son of Man?" they are actually asking, "Who are You?" Jesus answers that He is the Light of the World that enables people to make their way to God. He urges them to become sons of light and to identify with Him as the Light of God. The term *sons of light* would have been familiar to many of the people. The community at Qumran, for example, identified the sons of light as those who would enter battle alongside God's Messiah at the end of the age and fight against the sons of darkness. The Qumran War Scroll states, "The first attack by the sons of light will be launched against the lot of the sons of darkness." Ultimately, victory will be won and "in the time of God, his exalted greatness will shine for all the [eternal] times, for peace and blessing, glory and joy, and long days for all the sons of light" (The War Scroll, 1QM I 1f; also see The Rule of the Community,1QS III, 17–26). Again, Jesus challenges their notions because He is Israel's King and Messiah—the Son of Man who possesses the authority of the Ancient of Days—yet He does not wield authority in the manner that the people anticipate.

> *But although He had done so many signs before them, they did*
> *not believe in Him, that the word of Isaiah the prophet might be*
> *fulfilled, which he spoke: "Lord, who has believed our report?*
> *And to whom has the arm of the LORD been revealed?"*
> *Therefore they could not believe, because Isaiah said again: "He*
> *has blinded their eyes and hardened their hearts, Lest they*
> *should see with their eyes, Lest they should understand with*
> *their hearts and turn, So that I should heal them." These things*
> *Isaiah said when he saw His glory and spoke of Him (vv. 37–41).*

The fact that many fail to believe Jesus' words about Himself is a fulfillment of two passages in the book of Isaiah. Israel does not believe Jesus' teaching about the Son of Man any more than the people of Isaiah's time believed the prophet's report about the Man who is beaten and disfigured for the benefit of many (Is. 52:13–53:12). John subtly identifies Jesus with the Suffering Servant described by Isaiah. This Servant will be lifted up, disfigured, and seen by the nations (vv. 13–15). No one will believe Isaiah's report that the

Servant, a man of sorrows rejected by the people, will take their sorrow, transgression, iniquity, and affliction upon Himself (53:1–6) and please God by becoming an offering for sin and the righteousness of many (vv. 10, 11).

In addition, John attributes the disbelief of the people to the plan of God. He quotes Isaiah who says that the Jews are not able to understand God's ways in Christ because God prevents them from understanding (6:9, 10). It is not God's intention that they should be healed at that time. Why does God prevent them from understanding and being healed? It is necessary for the people to first experience His judgment for their infidelity to God's covenant (6:11, 12). As the prophet observes in a later passage, God's thoughts and ways are different from the thoughts and ways of His people (55:8, 9). Just so, the people do not believe what Jesus says about the Son of Man being lifted up because it is God's inscrutable plan that He die on the cross so that all may be saved.

> *Nevertheless even among the rulers many believed in Him, but*
> *because of the Pharisees they did not confess Him, lest they*
> *should be put out of the synagogue; for they loved the praise of*
> *men more than the praise of God (vv. 42, 43).*

Many of the rulers believe in Jesus but do not confess or give public acknowledgment to Jesus. Why? Because they are afraid that they will be barred from the synagogue and they prefer the praise (*doxa*) of men to that of God.

WORD STUDY: PRAISE OF MEN

The word praise (*doxa*) is used throughout John's gospel to describe the life-giving nature of God (see discussion in chapter 2). But here, John says that certain leaders prefer the *doxa* of men to that of God; they prefer the status they have with their fellow men to the new status they might have with God through His Son. Moreover, in John 12:42, the tense of the word "confess" (*homologeō*, ὁμολογέω) is imperfect and indicates that they are retreating from a view that they once held. That is, they are being influenced by the pressure brought to bear by others and abandoning their acceptance of Jesus and His teaching.

The fact that those who had believed in Jesus are turning away from belief in Him for the *doxa* of men should be read in view of what John says in the previous verses (vv. 41, 42). There, he quotes from Isaiah to explain this behavior. It was as Isaiah beheld the *doxa* of God in the temple that God proclaimed the people should remain in their present state until they had been judged. This truth is reported by John as descriptive of the inconsistent response to Jesus by many rulers. He says that the *doxa* of men prevents many from receiving the revelation (*doxa*) of God in Jesus Christ.

*Then Jesus cried out and said, "He who believes in Me, believes
not in Me but in Him who sent Me. And he who sees Me sees
Him who sent Me. I have come as a light into the world, that
whoever believes in Me should not abide in darkness. And if
anyone hears My words and does not believe, I do not judge him;
for I did not come to judge the world but to save the world. He
who rejects Me, and does not receive My words, has that which
judges him—the word that I have spoken will judge him in the
last day. For I have not spoken on My own authority; but the
Father who sent Me gave Me a command, what I should say and
what I should speak. And I know that His command is everlasting life. Therefore, whatever I speak, just as the Father has told
Me, so I speak" (vv. 44–50).*

One's response to Jesus is a response to God. The last public words Jesus
speaks to Israel resemble the first words He spoke to Nicodemus: "The light
has come into the world, and men loved darkness rather than light . . . But
he who does the truth comes to the light, that his deeds may be clearly seen,
that they have been done in God" (3:19, 21). His words also reflect His declaration to the woman caught in adultery (8:12).

In addition, Jesus repeats that He did not come to judge the world but to
save the world (3:17, 18). People judge themselves by their response to Jesus'
words. By refusing to accept His words, they choose to live in darkness and
not the light.

Jesus has obeyed the command that God His Father gave Him by speaking His words. By speaking God's words Jesus has offered the eternal life that
comes from them to the people.

The Service of the King (John 13:1–17)

In this passage Jesus is presented as God's King who has come to serve; with
humility that the King washes the feet of those who are His followers. This
fulfills the prophetic anticipation of a King who comes to Jerusalem for His
installation in meekness and humility (Zech. 9:9).

*Now before the Feast of the Passover, when Jesus knew that His
hour had come that He should depart from this world to the
Father, having loved His own who were in the world, He loved
them to the end. And supper being ended, the devil having
already put it into the heart of Judas Iscariot, Simon's son, to*

> *betray Him, Jesus, knowing that the Father had given all things*
> *into His hands, and that He had come from God and was going*
> *to God, rose from supper and laid aside His garments, took a*
> *towel and girded Himself. After that, He poured water into a*
> *basin and began to wash the disciples' feet, and to wipe them*
> *with the towel with which He was girded (vv. 1–5).*

Jesus prepares to wash the feet of His disciples with full knowledge that His hour has arrived and that He will soon return to His Father. John says that Jesus' act of humility occurs after supper, meaning that Jesus has eaten the Passover meal with them and washes their feet as an expression of His love for them.

Even as Mary anointed Jesus' feet for His death, which is the reason He has come into the world (12:27), so also Jesus washes the disciples' feet in preparation for their service to Him. He does not wash their feet simply as an example of humility; He does so to prepare them for their future ministry. The verb "wash" (*niptō*) is used thirteen times by John—in this account and in the healing of the blind man—to signify preparation for service. After the blind man washes his face he can see and begins to testify to his healing (9:13–34). So also the disciples will testify to the Kingship of Jesus after they have been washed and Jesus has fulfilled His hour.

> *Then He came to Simon Peter. And Peter said to Him, "Lord are*
> *You washing my feet?" Jesus answered and said to him, "What I*
> *am doing you do not understand now, but you will know after*
> *this." Peter said to Him, "You shall never wash my feet!" Jesus*
> *answered him, "If I do not wash you, you have no part with Me."*
> *Simon Peter said to Him, "Lord, not my feet only, but also my*
> *hands and my head!" Jesus said to him, "He who is bathed needs*
> *only to wash his feet, but is completely clean; and you are clean,*
> *but not all of you." For He knew who would betray Him; there-*
> *fore He said, "You are not all clean" (vv. 6–11).*

Peter expresses the confusion of all the disciples: he wonders what Jesus is doing as He washes their feet. Not even Jewish servants were required to wash the feet of their masters. Peter says, "You shall never wash my feet." This recalls his reaction to Jesus' prediction that He would suffer at the hands of the leaders of the people and be killed: "Far be it from You, Lord; this shall not happen to You" (Matt. 16:22; see Mark 8:31–33). Peter no more understands the nature of Jesus' Kingship now than he did then. Likewise, Jesus' response to

Peter is as strong as His earlier one. Then He said, "Get behind Me, Satan! You are an offense to Me, for you are not mindful of the things of God, but the things of men" (Matt. 16:23; see Mark 8:33). Now, He says, "If I do not wash you, you have no part of Me." Peter is reminded that he must trust Jesus. If he cannot accept this ministry, he cannot have a place in His work.

> *So when He had washed their feet, taken His garments, and sat down again, He said to them, "Do you know what I have done to you? You call Me Teacher and Lord, and you say well, for so I am. If I then, your Lord and Teacher, have washed your feet, you also ought to wash one another's feet. For I have given you an example, that you should do as I have done to you. Most assuredly, I say to you, a servant is not greater than his master; nor is he who is sent greater than he who sent him. If you know these things, blessed are you if you do them" (vv. 12–17).*

Here, Jesus interprets His actions for the disciples. As their Teacher and Lord, He has served them and loved them. John has already noted that He "loved them to the end." In the same way they should serve and love one another.

THE MEANING OF FOOT WASHING

If having a part in Jesus' ministry requires the washing of his feet, then Peter wants his whole body washed so he can either have a full part or at least more than the other disciples. At first, Jesus' response appears curious. What does He mean, "He who is bathed needs only to wash his feet, but is completely clean"?

The word "bathe" (*louō*, λούω) is uncommon in the New Testament; it occurs only five times. John's use of the word here is its only occurrence in the Gospels. It suggests a total cleansing. Peter is totally cleansed in the sense that he has heard and received Jesus' word and experienced His ministry. In addition, the word "clean" (*katharos*, καθαρός) conveys the theological notion of purity according to the Law of Moses. For the ancient community of faith, purity was the secure status of the individual and community before God that came through observance of the law; impurity indicated an uncertain relationship because of a trespass of the law in some way. Peter and the disciples have been made pure by the teaching and ministry of Jesus. By washing His disciples' feet, Jesus declares that they are clean, not through the Law of Moses, but through His word and act of humility. Thus they are prepared to serve others in His name. Not all are clean or pure, however. John reports that Jesus knows who will betray Him. Judas is not pure because he has not accepted Jesus' word. So, he will betray Jesus Christ to His enemies.

Jesus prefaces three statements with the customary statement "most assuredly I say to you." Jesus affirms His status as their Master and identifies them as those who are sent. The Greek for "one who is sent" is *apostolos* (ὁ ἀπόστολος), which is often translated in English as "apostle." Thus, the language here became the standard description in the early church for Jesus and those He called to continue His ministry.

Even as Jesus has been sent, so also He sends. Throughout John's gospel, Jesus describes Himself being sent by the Father (3:17; 5:43; 7:16, 28, 29; 8:29, 42; 12:44) and from heaven as bread (6:33, 38, 41, 42, 50, 51, 58). For this reason He is not greater than His Father, but He does what His Father desires (4:34; 5:19, 30; 7:16–18; 8:29; 10:25, 32, 37, 38; 12:49). In the same way, the disciples will be sent by Jesus. They are not greater than Jesus and should do what He desires. So, Jesus pronounces a blessing upon those who hear and do what He says. These verses record a beatitude Jesus speaks to the disciples about their service to Him. He says, in essence, "Blessed are you when you recognize that I am your Lord and do what I desire."

The word *Lord* is an exalted title. Even though it usually means "master," it is used throughout the Septuagint to translate the covenant name for God. Due to His intimate, unparalleled relationship with God the Father, Jesus accepts the title as an appropriate description of His standing and relationship with the disciples.

Abandoning the King (John 13:18–30)

Jesus predicts His betrayal by Judas. He quotes from a psalm of David to show that this is in accordance with God's plan. According to John, even as the first great king of Israel was betrayed during his kingship (in the revolt of Absalom), so also the King who has entered Jerusalem at Passover will be betrayed by one of His own disciples.

> "I do not speak concerning all of you. I know whom I have chosen; but that the Scripture may be fulfilled, 'He who eats bread with Me has lifted up his heel against Me.' Now I tell you before it comes, that when it does come to pass, you may believe that I am He" (vv. 18, 19).

John has already identified Judas as a thief (12:6) and the one who would betray Jesus (6:71; 12:4). By calling him a thief, John links Judas to the thief that comes to steal, kill, and destroy (10:10).

Earlier, after He had fed the 5000, Jesus indicated that one of His disciples would betray Him: "Did I not choose you, the twelve, and one of you is a devil?" (6:70). But now, He says, "You are clean, but not all of you" (13:10). Jesus knows Judas and knows what he will do. The betrayal does not shock Him.

Not only does Judas' betrayal not shock Jesus, it is God's plan for Him. Jesus quotes a psalm of David to describe this situation (Ps. 41). In the psalm,

PSALM 41

To the Chief Musician. A Psalm of David.

1 Blessed is he who considers the poor;
    The LORD will deliver him in time of trouble.
2 The LORD will preserve him and keep him alive,
    And he will be blessed on the earth;
    You will not deliver him to the will of his enemies.
3 The LORD will strengthen him on his bed of illness;
    You will sustain him on his sickbed.
4 I said, "LORD, be merciful to me;
    Heal my soul, for I have sinned against You."
5 My enemies speak evil of me:
    "When will he die, and his name perish?"
6 And if he comes to see me, he speaks lies;
    His heart gathers iniquity to itself;
    When he goes out, he tells it.
7 All who hate me whisper together against me;
    Against me they devise my hurt.
8 "An evil disease," they say, "clings to him.
    And now that he lies down, he will rise up no more."
9 Even my own familiar friend in whom I trusted,
    Who ate my bread,
    Has lifted up his heel against me.
10 But You, O LORD, be merciful to me, and raise me up,
    That I may repay them.
11 By this I know that You are well pleased with me,
    Because my enemy does not triumph over me.
12 As for me, You uphold me in my integrity,
    And set me before Your face forever.
13 Blessed be the LORD God of Israel
    From everlasting to everlasting!
    Amen and Amen.

the king laments over his feeling of abandonment by those who are close to him. Yet, he continues to espouse God's pleasure with him and confirms that his enemies will be defeated (v. 11). Likewise, Jesus enjoys the pleasure of God, yet has people speak against Him and even accuse Him of being a sinner. Psalm 41 describes this particular act and Jesus' Kingship overall.

> *"Most assuredly, I say to you, he who receives whomever I send receives Me; and he who receives Me receives Him who sent Me"* *(v. 20).*

The second statement in this section that begins with the phrase *most assuredly I say to you* concerns everyone who receives Jesus' words through the disciples. Just as the first statement was a beatitude for the disciples— they will be blessed if they follow Jesus' example and do as He commands,— this is a beatitude for all believers. He will be present with everyone who receives the words of the apostles.

> *When Jesus had said these things, He was troubled in spirit, and testified and said, "Most assuredly, I say to you, one of you will betray Me." Then the disciples looked at one another, perplexed about whom He spoke. Now there was leaning on Jesus' bosom one of His disciples, whom Jesus loved. Simon Peter therefore motioned to him to ask who it was of whom He spoke. Then, leaning back on Jesus' breast, he said to Him, "Lord, who is it?" Jesus answered, "It is he to whom I shall give a piece of bread when I have dipped it." And having dipped the bread, He gave it to Judas Iscariot, the son of Simon. Now after the piece of bread, Satan entered him. Then Jesus said to him, "What you do, do quickly." But no one at the table knew for what reason He said this to him. For some thought, because Judas had the money box, that Jesus had said to him, "Buy those things we need for the feast," or that he should give something to the poor. Having received the piece of bread, he then went out immediately. And it was night (vv. 21–30).*

For the third time Jesus is described as being troubled. The first time was when He approached the tomb of Lazarus (11:33). The second was after His entry into Jerusalem when the Greeks wanted to see Him (12:27). Now Jesus is troubled by the fact that one of His disciples will betray Him. The period

WORD STUDY: BETRAY

In John's gospel, the word *betray* (*paradidōmi*, παραδίδωμι) speaks not only of Judas' action, the temple leadership betray Jesus when they bring Him to Pilate (18:30, 35). The word suggests a transfer from one sphere of authority to another and stands in contrast to God's act of giving (*didōmi*, δίδωμι) His Son to the world: "For God so loved the world that He gave His only begotten Son" (3:16). In John, *paradidōmi* (betray) is the act of those who do not believe Jesus. It means to reject or throw away. *Didōmi* (give), however, refers to God's gracious act of love in giving the Son as a gift to the world. God gives His Son but Judas and the Jewish leadership reject Him.

leading up to Passover has been distressful for Jesus because He is anticipating His death—not an easy thing for anyone, even Jesus Christ.

Who will betray Jesus? This is the one who receives the bread from Him. John says that Satan enters Judas at this time. This is his first use of the proper name *Satan*. Previously, the term *devil* described Jesus' betrayer (6:70). Jesus used this term to describe the father of those who reject His word (8:44). But now John uses the name, Satan, to show that Judas comes under the control of an authority other than Jesus. The giving of Bread to Judas is ironic. Earlier in His ministry, Jesus described Himself as the bread that had come down out of heaven given (6:32–40, 48–51) whose body and blood results in eternal life. Some of the disciples left Jesus over this, prompting Jesus to say that one among them is a devil (6:60–71). Here Jesus gives Judas a piece of bread before he departs under the power of Satan. John emphasizes the giving of bread by repeating the fact (vv. 27, 30). With this act, Jesus symbolically offers Himself to Judas a final time. However, "Satan" enters Judas and he not only rejects Jesus, he betrays Him to death.

A formal translation of the Greek in this passage reads, "After the small piece of bread, then Satan entered that one." In the view of John, Judas loses his sense of self and personal identity and becomes "that one." He now is under the authority not of evil spirits or demons, but of the very Satan. In other words, God allowed His personal adversary to carry out the crucifixion of Christ. A lesser authority could not accomplish this profound act. So, Judas goes out into the night, leaving the Light of God; entering the world of darkness (3:19, 20).

Though there has been much debate about the identity of the "beloved disciple," the most likely candidate is the apostle John himself. (See the *Introduction* for a brief discussion of this question.)

The Commandment of the King (John 13:31–35)

John concludes this section of his gospel by recording the King of Israel's new commandment. Jesus has been anointed, He has been hailed by the people of Jerusalem, He has spoken about the nature of His Kingship, and He has prepared the disciples for their future service to Him. For the plan of God to be fulfilled, however, Jesus will be betrayed to others. This betrayal has begun. Now Jesus gives a final commandment to His disciples. It constitutes the standard rule for their life.

> *So, when he had gone out, Jesus said, "Now the Son of Man is glorified, and God is glorified in Him. If God is glorified in Him, God will also glorify Him in Himself, and glorify Him immediately" (vv. 31, 32).*

Jesus' hour is not only the time of death but also the hour of glory when both the Son of Man and the God of all things receive glory for the life that They give for the world.

> *"Little children, I shall be with you a little while longer. You will seek Me; and as I said to the Jews, 'Where I am going, you cannot come,' so now I say to you. A new commandment I give to you, that you love one another; as I have loved you, that you also love one another. By this all will know that you are My disciples, if you have love for one another" (vv. 33–35).*

Jesus' hour is also the hour of His departure. So, Jesus speaks with comfort to the disciples, calling them children. The Greek word for *children* (*teknon*, τέκνον) generally describes "little ones."

The new commandment resembles the greatest commandment. When a scribe asked Jesus which commandment is the greatest, He responded by reciting the Deuteronomy 6:4, 5: "Hear, O Israel, the LORD our God, the Lord is one. And you shall love the LORD your God with all your heart, with all your soul, with all your mind, and with all your strength." To this He adds, "You shall love your neighbor as yourself," a quote from Leviticus 19 (vv. 18, 34) that elaborates several of the Ten Commandments (see Mark 12:28–34).

THE NEW COMMANDMENT

As Jesus prepares to leave the disciples, He gives them a new commandment: They are to love each other as He has loved them. This command comes from the exalted King of Israel who loved His disciples to the end (13:1). It may be outlined in the following manner:

  I. A new commandment I give to you
    A. Love one another
       1. As I have loved you
       2. So also, you love one another.

This brief mandate reveals that His love for them is the basis for their love of one another.

In other words, the love of God will find expression in love for others. Here Jesus tells His disciples that they should love each other in the same way that He has loved them.

QUESTIONS FOR PERSONAL REFLECTION AND GROUP DISCUSSION

1. What events does John record to show that Jesus is the King of the people in His final return to Jerusalem?
2. Why does John declare that Jesus came for the world when he presents Jesus' ministry in terms of the Old Testament story of redemption?
3. The "hour" of Jesus is related to what other biblical and temporal period? How is it related?
4. Why does Jesus wash the feet of His disciples?
5. The new commandment that Jesus gives His disciples resembles what other commandment?

CHAPTER 7

The Promise of the Spirit

John 13:36–17:26

Here begins Jesus' work of preparing the disciples for life after His death, resurrection, and ascension:

- He gives them the commandment by which they are to live together as His disciples—They are to love one another as He has loved them.
- He promises to send the Holy Spirit to them so that they may live together as He has lived among them. The Spirit will bring them into the knowledge and understanding of Christ just as Jesus revealed the Father to them.
- He warns that all this will not be easy and the world will reject them. Still, His victory over the world guarantees their victory as well.

Jesus' final teaching involves His word and the Spirit. For the disciples to live as God's new creation in a darkened world, they must have the Lord's word and the Spirit. In the beginning, God brought all creation into being by His word and Spirit. So it is with the new beginning depicted in the Gospel of John; All that the disciples experience and minister springs from the convergence of the Spirit and the word in their lives.

Jesus says that the Spirit will come and be with the disciples to recall for them what He has taught them so they may live in unity with one another and in affinity with His word. John's record of Jesus' extensive teaching on the Spirit prior to His passion shows that the prophet's anticipation of a day of the Spirit is inaugurated by Jesus when He departs from the disciples.

THE PROPHETS AND THE PROMISE OF THE HOLY SPIRIT

Jesus' promise of the Holy Spirit recalls the promise of the Spirit by the prophet Joel. Little is known of this prophet. Some scholars think he may have lived during the reign of Josiah, the king of Judah (640–609 B.C.). He prophesied that God would send His Spirit in order to make Himself known to His people (Joel 2). He said that the sons and daughters of Israel will prophesy, the old men will have dreams, and the young men will see visions (vv. 28, 29). In other words, they will know what God is saying and what He is doing. This knowledge of God's purposes will not be limited to priests or wise men, but will be unveiled to all of His people, young and old, men and women.

The description of the Spirit that Jesus gives to the disciples also recalls that of Ezekiel. This prophet lived among the Jewish captives in Babylonia and began to write in about 570 B.C.. Ezekiel prophesied that God will give the people a new spirit in place of their hard hearts (11:19; 18:31). God's Spirit will be given so that they may walk in His statutes and live in the land with His blessing (36:27–30). Joel says the Spirit, through prophecy, dream, and vision, will reveal the will of God for Israel. Ezekiel says the Spirit will remind the people of God's word so they may live together in the land. Jesus attributes both of these activities to the Spirit in this section of John's gospel.

Peter's Promise (John 13:36–38)

After Judas abandons his fellow disciples and goes out into the night, Jesus announces that He, too, will leave them (v. 33). Peter asks where Jesus is going and pledges to follow Him and lay his life down for Him (vv. 36, 37). Jesus both affirms and denies Peter's promise: Peter will follow Him but not presently; sadly, rather than lay down his life Peter will deny Jesus three times before the rooster crows (18:15–18, 25–27).

Peter's promise initiates Jesus' extended discourse in which He speaks about the Holy Spirit and promises the disciples that they will not be left alone. Peter cannot keep his promise; he will deny Jesus in order to save his own life. Yet, what is important is not what Peter can or cannot do. It is what Jesus has done and what He will do after He leaves them. Jesus will give His life for the disciples and, as a result, He will give them the Holy Spirit.

Simon Peter said to Him, "Lord, where are You going?" Jesus answered him, "Where I am going you cannot follow Me now, but you shall follow Me afterward." Peter said to Him, "Lord why can I not follow You now? I will lay down my life for Your

sake." Jesus answered him, "Will you lay down your life for My
sake? Most assuredly, I say to you, the rooster shall not crow till
you have denied Me three times." (vv. 36–38)

By asking where Jesus is going, Peter repeats the question asked by the Jews earlier (7:35). From the beginning of His public ministry Jesus has talked about going where others cannot go (3:13; 7:33, 34; 8:21). According to the synoptic Gospels, Peter boasts that he will die with Jesus if necessary (Matt. 26:3; Mark 14:31; Luke 22:33). He is moved by what Jesus has done in washing his feet and reacts by asserting his faithfulness to the death. But Jesus emphatically says that Peter will not keep his promise: "Most certainly, I say to you . . . the rooster will not crow until you have denied me three times." To deny Jesus means to disavow any knowledge of Him. This is the world's response to the Light that has come into it (1:5; 3:19). Jesus has come so that the people might be delivered from their ignorance of God and come to know Him. He prophesies that Peter will respond like the world and choose to remain in ignorance.

The Way to the Father's House (John 14:1–14)

Jesus has told His disciples He will leave them for the specific purpose of preparing a place for them in the presence of God. So, now He speaks words of comfort to them. No one can go where Jesus goes until He has made it possible to do so (3:13; 7:33, 34; 8:21). For this reason, He is God's Way, Truth, and Life. Jesus does not merely point in the direction of God, but He is the very Way to God. His words and works represent the truth of God to the world, and He exemplifies the life of God who, according to the Old Testament story of redemption, has worked ceaselessly to have a relationship with His people.

By saying that He is "the Way, the Truth, and the Life" Jesus identifies Himself with the Holy God of Israel proclaimed by the prophet Isaiah. In the first of several messages to the people in exile, this prophet is commanded to give consolation to Israel: "Comfort, yes, comfort My people!" And again, "Speak comfort to Jerusalem . . . that her warfare is ended, that her iniquity is pardoned" (40:1, 2). In the verses that follow these, a voice calls for a highway to be built for God in which His glory will be revealed (vv. 3–5), the eternal nature of His word is proclaimed (vv. 6–8), and His rule is compared to a shepherd who feeds, gathers, and leads His sheep (vv. 9–11). Thus, the prophet speaks of a way made for God whose truth is present in His eternal word and who gives life to His people as a shepherd does the sheep.

Here in John, Jesus speaks comfort to the disciples by drawing from Isaiah's promise to the people in exile. Jesus does not promise to lead the disciples out of exile, however. He promises to lead them into the Father's house.

> *"Let not your heart be troubled; you believe in God, believe also in Me" (v. 1).*

Jesus urges the disciples not to be troubled (ταρασσω). The third person imperative used by John indicates that Jesus exhorts the disciples to overcome the fear they may feel by placing confidence in His words. Even though He has experienced trouble since the death of Lazarus (11:33; 12:27), Jesus moves to calm their fears by speaking of His continuing ministry on their behalf.

> *"In My Father's house are many mansions; if it were not so, I would have told you. I go to prepare a place for you. And if I go and prepare a place for you, I will come again and receive you to Myself; that where I am, there you may be also" (vv. 2, 3).*

Jesus leaves the disciples to continue the work that He has begun among them. He goes to prepare a place for them in the presence of God—figuratively speaking, in the Father's house. Once their place is ready, He will return for them so that they can be with Him there.

Jesus' new work of creation will culminate in the disciples' life with the Father. Throughout this gospel, John has recorded Jesus' words about eternal life (3:15, 16; 4:14; 5:24, 39, 40; 6:27, 35, 40, 47, 51, 54, 58; 11:25, 26; 12:24, 25,

FIGURATIVE LANGUAGE IN THE BIBLE

The figurative language of "My Father's house" speaks of a place in God's presence and, like any father's house, of provision and protection. It follows a biblical tradition of describing such places of divine presence and provision with imaginative language. For example, in Genesis, Adam and Eve are placed in a "garden" where they enjoy God's presence and have access to the abundant provision of the trees that grow there. The Hebrew people are led by Moses to a "land of milk and honey" (Ex. 3:8, 17) in which they will worship God and live with Him through the words that He gives to them. And Ezekiel has a vision of a new temple and new city in which fresh water flows and the people experience the healing grace of God (Ezek. 40–48; especially 47:1–12).

49, 50). This life is lived in God's presence. The eternal life that Jesus has announced to the disciples will be realized as they go to where Jesus is in the presence of the Father.

This is not Jesus' first reference to His Father's house. Earlier in His ministry Jesus overturned tables in the temple and lamented that His Father's house had become a place of business: "Take these things away! Do not make My Father's house a house of merchandise!" (2:16). He is apoplectic that the holy place of worship has become preoccupied with business matters. Jesus' remarks in the present passage, however, reveal that He does not see the Jerusalem temple as God's exclusive residence. God cannot and will not be confined to the 100 square cubits of the Most Holy Place in the temple! His true house is the place wherever His presence may be experienced. This is not a new notion for Jesus. He said as much to the woman at the well when He observed that the day had arrived when worship of God would no longer be restricted to temples in Samaria or Jerusalem but experienced wherever people worship in Spirit and truth (4:21–24). Jesus prepares to go into the presence of His Father (His Father's house) to make a place for those who will worship God in this way.

> *"And where I go you know, and the way you know." Thomas said to Him, "Lord, we do not know where You are going, and how can we know the way?" Jesus said to him, "I am the way, the truth, and the life. No one comes to the Father except through Me. "If you had known Me, you would have known My Father also; and from now on you know Him and have seen Him" (vv. 4–7).*

Though Jesus says that the disciples know the way to the Father's house, Thomas voices Peter's concern (13:36) when He says, "Lord, we do not know where You are going and how can we know the way?" Jesus responds by saying that He Himself is the way. By knowing Him the disciples know the way to the Father because He is the Truth of God as well as the Life of God. Jesus is the human manifestation of the divine truth and life of God that has come into the world.

John the Baptist prepared the way for Jesus (1:23) who is Himself the way to the Father. Earlier Jesus said that He is the gate of the sheepfold that leads to salvation (10:7–9). Entry into the presence of God is through Jesus who has manifested the life of God before them. Jesus says that by knowing Him they have come to know His Father and they will continue to grow in their knowledge as a result of His passion, death, and resurrection.

> *Philip said to Him, "Lord, show us the Father, and it is sufficient*
> *for us" (v. 8).*

Philip follows Peter and Thomas in asking Jesus what He means. The disciples are disturbed by Jesus' announcement that He will leave them. Philip wants to see the Father. No Jew at this time conceived of God as having a corporeal body. In fact, Jesus has said to the woman at the well that God is Spirit and must be worshiped in spirit (4:24). He has also observed that no one has seen God the Father except the Son (6:46). Thus, Philip is not so much asking for a distinct manifestation of the Father as he is asking for clarification about what Jesus is saying.

> *Jesus said to him, "Have I been with you so long, and yet you*
> *have not known Me, Philip? He who has seen Me has seen the*
> *Father; so how can you say, 'Show us the Father'? Do you not*
> *believe that I am in the Father, and the Father in Me? The words*
> *that I speak to you I do not speak on My own authority; but the*
> *Father who dwells in Me does the works. Believe Me that I am in*
> *the Father and the Father in Me, or else believe Me for the sake*
> *of the works themselves" (vv. 9–11).*

Jesus says plainly that they have seen God the Father by seeing Him. He and His Father are one. They are inextricably related to one another. Not only so, the Son is the unique expression of the Father. John established this truth in the first few verses of his gospel (John 1:1–3). If the disciples cannot believe this marvelous truth, then He points them to the miracles He has done since He only speaks what the Father speaks and does what He sees His Father doing (5:19, 30; 6:16; 10:32).

Just as God spoke words to Moses for the life of the people and to give them direction, so also Jesus speaks words (*rhēmata*, ῥήματα) that give the life of God to His disciples. In fact, the word *rhēmata* is used here to describe Jesus' words as God's words (3:34). His words are not simply descriptive of God, but they comprise and convey God's truth.

> *"Most assuredly, I say to you, he who believes in Me, the works*
> *that I do he will do also; and greater works than these he will do,*
> *because I go to My Father. And whatever you ask in My name,*
> *that I will do, that the Father may be glorified in the Son. If you*
> *ask anything in My name, I will do it" (vv. 12–14).*

The ministry that Jesus has inaugurated will continue among His disciples and will actually increase among them as they call upon His name. They will do greater works than He has done! But how is this possible? Just as Jesus came in the name of His Father to do His works (5:43), so also He will continue to perform His works through those who believe in Him. His departure is not the end of His ministry; rather, it is the beginning of the disciples' involvement and the collective extension of His ministry to others.

The name of Jesus is not a verbal talisman by which the disciples will wield divine power. It signifies Jesus Himself. As discussed in chapter 2, names denote the identity and essence of an individual. The name Jesus, which is *Yeshua* (Joshua) in Hebrew, is derived from the root word for salvation. By calling upon this name, the disciples identify themselves with the One who saves and, because of their relationship with Him, are enabled to invoke His authority for the benefit of others. Just as God gave His name to Moses as He prepared to lead the Hebrew people out of Egypt to signify His personal relationship with them, so also Jesus gives His name to the disciples so that they may continue His ministry and know that He will do whatever they ask. As they call upon the name of Jesus who is the Bread of Life, the Light of the World, the Good Shepherd, the Resurrection and the Life, the Way, the Truth, and the Life, and the Vine of the branches, the disciples are calling upon the name of the One who is the very expression of God. All of these titles point to Jesus as the One who brings the new creation of God into existence from a dark and deadened world. The disciples participate in this new creation as they identify with the name and, in essence, with the One who possesses God's authority. This means that the work of new creation is not a distant eschatological event. It is an event that has its beginning in the ministry of Jesus Christ and continues through all those who believe in Him and call upon His name.

Will Jesus really do whatever the disciples ask? Jesus here compares the relationship the disciples will have with Him after He has gone to the Father with the relationship He has with the Father. That is, Jesus speaks what He hears the Father speak and does what He sees the Father doing. Everything that He has done has been done for the purpose of manifesting God among the people. As the disciples serve in the manner that Jesus has served and seek to do the will of God—that is, speak His words and perform His works—they will ask what they need and it will be granted to them. The grammar underscores the reality of the promise: If they ask, Jesus will grant their request. The result is that God will be glorified by the works they do in the name of His Son. This is because the witness that God receives from the works they do under the authority of Christ reveals Him to be a loving and life-giving God.

The two criteria that Jesus establishes for doing "greater works" are first, that the disciples believe He and the Father are one and second, that they ask for Him to continue to show signs in His name. By asking in Jesus' name, the disciples not only recognize His authority to do the works of God but they also recognize His will and purpose. To call upon the name of Jesus is to invoke His authority and to submit to His purposes.

The New Commandment and the Promise of the Spirit (John 14:15–15:17)

In this section Jesus elaborates on the new commandment He has given to His disciples and anticipates the arrival of the Spirit in their lives. In the same way that Jesus' ministry represents the convergence of God's Word and God's Spirit, the ministry of the disciples will be grounded in both the commandment of Jesus and the gift of the Spirit sent by the Father at the request of Jesus Christ.

"If you love Me, keep My commandments" (v. 15).

Jesus expects that the disciples who love Him will keep His commandments. Adherence to the words of Jesus is a sign of love for Him and of being His disciple (vv. 15, 21, 23).

The commandments that the disciples are to keep are grounded in the new commandment that He has already given to them. The teachings of Jesus may be summarized in His admonition to love each other as He has loved them (13:34). This is reminiscent of His answer to the scribe who asks which of the commandments is the greatest (Mark 12:28–34). Jesus responds by quoting the Shema (the name given to Deuteronomy 6:4, 5 from the Hebrew word meaning "Listen!"): "Hear, O Israel, the LORD our God is one. And you shall love the LORD your God with all of your heart, and all your soul and all your strength." He then adds, "And you shall love your neighbor as yourself" (Lev. 19:18, 34). To the scribe Jesus says that love of God and of one's neighbor is the greatest commandment. It is incongruent to say that one loves God without also loving those with whom one lives. The love of God finds expression in the love that one shows to family, friends, and neighbors. Thus, Christ's new commandment only makes sense if there is an appreciation for the old commandment. The new commandment is the old commandment exemplified in Jesus' life with the disciples. The disciples will fulfill it by loving each other in the way that Jesus has shown them.

The result of this love is that everyone will know that the disciples are related to Jesus (13:35). Such testimony recalls the divine intention to deliver the Hebrew people out of Egypt and give them the Law of Moses. God's great act of deliverance provided an example to the nations of His love and power

(Deut. 4:6–8). By living according to the law, Israel provided a testimony to all nations of the goodness and faithfulness of their God.

> *"And I will pray the Father, and He will give you another Helper, that He may abide with you forever—the Spirit of truth, whom the world cannot receive, because it neither sees Him nor knows Him; but you know Him, for He dwells with you and will be in you. I will not leave you orphans; I will come to you" (vv. 16–18).*

How is all this possible if Jesus is absent? The resurrected Christ will send the Holy Spirit to help the disciples. It is important to note that the promise of the Holy Spirit is made in the context of keeping Jesus' commandments (14:15). Jesus says to His disciples, "If you love Me, keep My commandments," and follows with a promise that He will ask His Father to send the Spirit of Truth to be with them. The words of Jesus together with the Spirit will enable the disciples to continue His ministry once He has left them.

Jesus promises the disciples that His Father will send a paraclete, the Spirit of Truth, in His absence. Though the world does not know the Spirit, the disciples do. How do the disciples know the Spirit? They know the Spirit through the ministry of Jesus because Jesus conducts His ministry by the Spirit.

Jesus' statement recalls the world's ignorance of the Word described by John in chapter 1. There, the true Light is described as entering the world and giving those who believe in Him the right to become children of God. Still, He remains unknown to the world (vv. 6–13). Here, the Spirit of Truth comes in the place of the true Light to be with the disciples despite the fact the world does not receive Him.

In fact, this relation between Jesus and the Spirit has been anticipated in Jesus' proclamation that He is the Way, the Truth and the Life (14:6). The Spirit of Truth who will come in place of Jesus is indeed related to Jesus who is the truth of God. Jesus will come to the disciples in the person of the Spirit of Truth.

> *"A little while longer and the world will see Me no more, but you will see Me. Because I live, you will live also. At that day you will know that I am in My Father, and you in Me, and I in you. He who has My commandments and keeps them, it is he who loves Me. And he who loves Me will be loved by My Father, and I will love him and manifest Myself to him" (vv. 19–21).*

Jesus again says that He will not be with the disciples much longer (13:33). The term *at that day* refers to the time of fulfillment—the Crucifixion, Resurrection, and Ascension.

Jesus is the Mediator of the believer's relationship with the Father. He is both in the Father and in them. Their relationship with God comes through Jesus as the Way, the Truth, and the Life. Jesus repeats, love for Him will manifest itself in love for one another. In turn, the love of Jesus and the Father will be revealed to them.

Judas (not Iscariot) said to Him, "Lord, how is it that You will manifest Yourself to us, and not to the world?" (v. 22).

PERPLEXITY AND PROMISE

Four of Jesus' disciples ask how Jesus will show Himself to the world. Like Philip, Thomas, and Peter before him, Judas, not the son of Iscariot, cannot make out Jesus' teaching. These four disciples ask the Lord what He means when He says that He is going away, has shown them the Father, and will show Himself to them even after He is gone. They are perplexed. Jesus' answers represent the essential promises that He leaves with them at this time. The following chart outlines the disciples' perplexity and the Lord's promise.

Perplexity and Promise

Peter	"Lord, where are You going— Why can I not follow You?" (13:36, 37)	Jesus	"In My Father's house are many dwelling places—I go to prepare a place for you" (14:2).
Thomas	"Lord, we do not know where You are going, and how can we know the way?" (14:5)	Jesus	"I am the way, the truth, and the life" (v. 6)
Philip	"Lord, show us the Father, and it is sufficient for us" (14:8).	Jesus	"I am in the Father and the Father is in Me" (vv. 10, 11)
Judas	"Lord, how is it that You will manifest Yourself to us, and not to the world?" (14:22)	Jesus	"If anyone loves Me . . . and My Father will love him, and we will come to him and make Our home with him" (v. 23)

What does Jesus promise? Not only that He prepares a place for them in the presence of His Father but that He is the Way to that place. They cannot get there apart from Him. To love Jesus is to prepare a place for the Father in one's own life even as Jesus prepares a place in the Father's presence for those who love Him.

Jesus answered and said to him, "If anyone loves Me, he will
keep My word; and My Father will love him, and We will come
to him and make Our home with him. He who does not love Me
does not keep My words; and the word which you hear is not
Mine but the Father's who sent Me (vv. 23, 24).

For the third time since Jesus washed the feet of His disciples, He links their love for Him with their response to His words (14:15, 21). They will manifest their love not by what they say but what they do with the words that He has given to them. And what has Jesus said? He has given them a new commandment and said that they are to love one another (13:34, 35). This means that the reality of loving Jesus is both personal and communal. It is personal in that it involves the reception of His words and, thus, Him; it is communal in that it involves the reception of others who follow Him. Jesus teaches the disciples that their relationship with Him will affect their relationship with one another.

The Ten Commandments given by God to Israel at Sinai (Ex. 20:1–17; Deut. 5:6–21) contain this same truth. Love for God is not limited to the program of offerings and sacrifices at the tabernacle (and later at the temple). As important as this was to the worship of God, it was meaningless if the dignity of others within the faith community was ignored. First, the people were to devote themselves exclusively to God and eschew idolatry, honor His name, and set aside one day to worship Him (Ex. 20:1–8). Second, they were to honor parents and abide by a code of behavior that honored others within the community (Ex. 20:9–17).

"These things I have spoken to you while being present with you.
But the Helper, the Holy Spirit, whom the Father will send in
My name, He will teach you all things, and bring to your
remembrance all things that I said to you" (vv. 25, 26).

The instruction that Jesus gives to the disciples will not cease with His departure. God His Father will send the *Helper* (Paraclete) to teach the disciples all things and remind them of what Jesus has already made known to them (see 15:26). This promise is reminiscent of that recounted by Ezekiel when he tells the people that God will give His Spirit to them in order that they will walk in His ordinances and keep His judgments (36:27–30). Just as God promises to give His Spirit to help the people live according to the covenant that He had made with them, so also Jesus promises the Paraclete to help the disciples recall and live by what He has taught them.

THE PARACLETE

The term *Paraclete* (paracletos) is unique to John. In the gospel it is used in four passages (14:16, 14:26; 15:26; 16:7–11) and in John's first epistles it is used once (1 John 2:1). As a title for the Holy Spirit, it speaks of the role of the Spirit in the disciples' lives in the physical absence of Jesus. In fact, the Spirit is "another" *paracletos* (14:16), indicating that Jesus is also a *paracletos*. The Paraclete continues the revelatory teachings regarding God's purpose until, at last, the apostle Paul completes the word of God (Col. 1:25).

The Father sent the Son into the world to save the world (3:16, 17) and He will send the Spirit to the disciples to enable them to live in the world and testify to the love of God in the Son (13:34, 35). Throughout the gospel Jesus describes God as "the One who sent me" and so implicitly describes Himself as the One who is sent. (See 4:34; 5:24, 30, 37; 6:38, 39, 44; 7:16, 28, 33; 8:16, 18, 26, 29; 9:4; 12:44, 45, 49; 13:20; 14:24; 15:21; 16:5.) The sending activity of God the Father continues with the Holy Spirit even as the ministry of Jesus continues through the disciples.

> *"Peace I leave with you, My peace I give to you; not as the world gives do I give to you. Let not your heart be troubled, neither let it be afraid" (v. 27).*

Jesus urges the disciples not to be troubled (*tarassō*) or timid (*deiliaō*, δειλ-ιάω). These terms are found in the LXX version of Isaiah to describe the experience of the people of Judah and Jerusalem during the day of God's judgment at the hand of the Babylonians (Is. 13). The hour of judgment may be upon Jesus, but it is a day of promise for the disciples who are to hold onto the word of peace that He speaks to them.

The word translated "peace" (*eirēnē*, ἡ εἰρήνη) is related to the Hebrew *shalom* (שָׁלוֹם) that speaks of God's blessing. Here it is linked with the Spirit. Jesus encourages the disciples with the promise of God's welfare, provision, and presence through the Holy Spirit who will abide with them in Jesus' absence. It is the same word that Jesus will speak when He appears to them after His resurrection (20:19, 21).

> *"You have heard Me say to you, 'I am going away and coming back to you.' If you loved Me, you would rejoice because I said, 'I am going to the Father,' for My Father is greater than I. And now I*

have told you before it comes, that when it does come to pass, you
may believe. I will no longer talk much with you, for the ruler of
this world is coming, and he has nothing in Me. But that the
world may know that I love the Father, and as the Father gave Me
commandment, so I do. Arise, let us go from here" (vv. 28–31).

Jesus speaks of His impending passion as an encounter with "the ruler of this world." Not only is the world ignorant of Jesus, but its ruler has no claim upon Him.

Then, Jesus and the disciples leave the place where He has washed their feet and they have eaten a meal together. Though John does not describe the meal, it is likely a Passover meal. The teaching of the vine and branches that

---

PSALM 80:8–19

8 You have brought a vine out of Egypt;
   You have cast out the nations, and planted it.
9 You prepared room for it,
   And caused it to take deep root,
   And it filled the land.
10 The hills were covered with its shadow,
   And the mighty cedars with its boughs.
11 She sent out her boughs to the Sea,
   And her branches to the River.

12 Why have You broken down her hedges,
   So that all who pass by the way pluck her fruit?
13 The boar out of the woods uproots it,
   And the wild beast of the field devours it.
14 Return, we beseech You, O God of hosts;
   Look down from heaven and see,
   And visit this vine
15 And the vineyard which Your right hand has planted,
   And the branch that You made strong for Yourself.
16 It is burned with fire, it is cut down;
   They perish at the rebuke of Your countenance.
17 Let Your hand be upon the man of Your right hand,
   Upon the son of man whom You made strong for Yourself.
18 Then we will not turn back from You;
   Revive us, and we will call upon Your name.
19 Restore us, O LORD God of hosts;
   Cause Your face to shine,
   And we shall be saved!

John records at this point in his narrative is best understood within the context of such a meal—rich with symbolic meaning.

> *"I am the true vine, and My Father is the vinedresser" (v. 1).*

This is the last of Jesus' seven "I am" statements. Having shared a Passover meal with His disciples in which the wine symbolized life and renewal, Jesus describes Himself here as the Vine and His disciples as branches of the Vine. Moreover, God His Father is the farmer or vineyard worker. Jesus may have Psalm 80 in mind in this self-description. The psalm describes Israel as a vine that was once brought out of Egypt, but is now burned and broken and in need of cultivation. The psalmist calls upon God to be with the "son of man" who will revive the people (vv. 9–17). By describing Himself as the Vine of God, Jesus identifies with the Son of Man spoken of by the psalmist who will enjoy God's blessing as He revives the vineyard of His people.

> *"Every branch in Me that does not bear fruit He takes away; and every branch that bears fruit He prunes, that it may bear more fruit. You are already clean because of the word which I have spoken to you" (vv. 2, 3).*

God the vineyard worker will prune (*kathairō*, καθαίρω) the branches so that fruit will grow in their lives. The basic meaning of the Greek verb is "cleanse" and its figurative use here connects God's work among the disciples with Jesus' work with them. The disciples have been made "clean" (*katharos*) by the word He has spoken and His ministry to them. In fact, Jesus has just washed their feet and prepared them for ministry in His name by doing so (13:1–17). God the Vineyard Worker will continue the work of Jesus by sending the Spirit to remind them what Jesus has taught.

> *"Abide in Me, and I in you. As the branch cannot bear fruit of itself, unless it abides in the vine, neither can you, unless you abide in Me. I am the vine, you are the branches. He who abides in Me, and I in him, bears much fruit; for without Me you can do nothing. If anyone does not abide in Me, he is cast out as a branch and is withered; and they gather them and throw them into the fire, and they are burned. If you abide in Me, and My words abide in you, you will ask what you desire, and it shall be done for you. By this My Father is glorified, that you bear much fruit; so you will be My disciples" (vv. 4–8).*

THE BREAD AND THE VINE

This *I am* statement recalls what Jesus told the Jews earlier when He identified Himself as the Bread of Life: "He who eats My flesh and drinks My blood abides in Me, and I in him" (6:56). The two discourses share several points in common:

- Both titles are linked closely with Jesus' actions. Jesus says He is the Bread of Life after feeding the 5,000 and He says He is the Vine of the Branches after eating the Passover meal with His disciples.
- Jesus tells the Jews that eternal life may be experienced in His flesh and blood, even as He tells the disciples that they are to bear the fruit of His life themselves. In both cases, the people must abide in Him. The Jews must abide in His flesh and blood to have eternal life and the disciples must abide in Him as a Vine in order to bear fruit.
- Conversely, not to abide in the flesh and blood of Jesus means the Jews will not have eternal life and the disciples will be cast away as useless branches.
- In both discourses, Jesus says that this is a divine work of God. He tells the Jews that no one comes to Him unless the Father draws him. And He instructs the disciples that they did not choose Him; rather, He chose them (see 6:65).
- In each discourse, Jesus makes a profound promise to those who hear Him. To the Jews He says that they will have eternal life and be raised up on the last day. To the disciples He says that they will have whatever they ask Him.

Thus, in His teaching to the Jews Jesus says that they will live with God if they abide in Him and take strength and nourishment from His flesh and blood (meaning His death and resurrection). In His remarks to the disciples Jesus says that they will bear fruit and manifest the life of God to one another as they remain in Him.

Bread of Life (6:35–58)	Vine of the Branches (15:1–17)
Jesus tells the Jews that He is the Bread of Life after feeding 5,000 men.	Jesus says He is the Vine of the Branches after eating the Passover with His disciples.
The Jews must abide in His flesh and blood. They must accept and take strength from His death and resurrection.	The disciples must abide in His commandments. His commandments include love for one another as well as acceptance of His teaching.
To abide in Jesus' flesh and blood results in eternal life.	To abide in Jesus' commandments results in the cultivation of much fruit.
Jesus promises that they will have eternal life and be resurrected on the last day.	Jesus promises that the disciples will have whatever they ask.
Only the Father can draw them to Jesus.	Jesus chose the disciples, they did not choose Him.

The verb *abide* is recorded seven times in these verses. Jesus challenges the disciples to remain in Him so that they can produce fruit. The production of fruit is important because it is the way that they will be nourished. Moreover, Jesus promises that they will have what they desire if His words (*rhēmata*) remain in them. Of course, this does not mean that they will have all of their personal gratifications satisfied; rather, as they seek to produce fruit for the benefit of others they will find that they have the capacity to do so as they live in accordance with Jesus' command by the Spirit.

Those who do not remain in Jesus will be cast away and destroyed. Dead, dried out grapevines had no use among ancient peoples except as kindling for fires. Such wood could not be used for construction nor could it be carved into tools or implements. Any branches that are not attached to Jesus Christ as the vine of God have little usefulness except as fuel for burning. Such branches cannot produce fruit for others. Though Jesus has insisted throughout His ministry that He has not come to judge or condemn (*krinō, katakrinō*, 3:17; 5:30; 8:11), He has not denied God's judgment. He alludes to such judgment here. If branches are not *pruned* (cleansed) by God to bear fruit, then they will be burned in the fire of God and destroyed.

> *"As the Father loved Me, I also have loved you; abide in My love. If you keep My commandments, you will abide in My love, just as I have kept My Father's commandments and abide in His love" (vv. 9, 10).*

Even as Jesus abides in the love of God by keeping His commandments, so also the disciples are to abide in the love of Jesus by keeping His commandments to them. Thus, what Jesus exhorts the disciples to do is nothing more than what He already has done Himself (14:31).

Keeping the commandments of Jesus is closely related to the reception of the Spirit. Jesus' first reference to the Spirit comes after He has urged the disciples to keep His commandments (14:15). If they love Him and keep His commandments, He will have His Father send the Spirit to them so that they will not be left alone as orphans. They have already come to know the Spirit through His ministry and will enjoy the Spirit's direct presence in their lives after He has left them. Jesus' second reference comes after He observes, "If anyone loves Me, he will keep My *word* (logos); and My Father will love him, and We will come to him and make Our home with him" (14:23).

*"These things I have spoken to you, that My joy may remain in
you, and that your joy may be full. This is My commandment,
that you love one another as I have loved you" (vv. 11, 12).*

The disciples will experience the joy of Jesus when they honor His commandments and welcome His Spirit. Since the word of Jesus is really that of His Father and the Spirit comes at the behest of the Father, the joy that Jesus speaks of is the presence of the Father in the life of the disciples.

Jesus repeats the new commandment that He has given to the disciples (13:34) and calls it "My commandment" when He exhorts them to love each other as He has shown. To follow this command is to show friendship toward Jesus. The grammar is emphatic: "You are My friends if you do whatever I

KEEPING JESUS' COMMANDMENTS

It is interesting to note that love, peace, and joy are experienced when the word of Jesus is honored and the Spirit is present. Such gifts of love, peace, and joy will be part of the disciples' experience after Jesus has gone. Love, in particular, is the indeclinable expression of word and Spirit in their lives as His disciples. He commands them to love one another as He has loved them (13:34; 15:12, 17) and says that by loving each other they demonstrate their love for Him (14:15, 21, 23, 24), remain in His love (15:10), and show that they are His friends (15:14) and disciples (13:35).

The table shows how these gifts, which resemble the first fruits of the Spirit described by Paul in Galatians 5 (vv. 22, 23), are given when Jesus' word is received along with the Spirit.

Keeping Jesus' Commandments	The Promise of the Spirit	The Gifts Jesus Gives
"If you love Me, keep My commandments" (14:15).	The Father will send another Helper who will abide with the disciples (14:16).	Jesus gives His love to those who keep His commandments (14:21).
"If anyone loves Me, he will keep My word" (14:23).	The Father will send the Helper who will teach the disciples all things (14:26).	Jesus gives His peace to the disciples (14:27).
"Abide in My love. If you keep My commandments, you will abide in My love" (15:9, 10).		Jesus gives His joy to the disciples (15:11).

command you." The disciples must do what Jesus says—He has commanded them to love each other.

> *"Greater love has no one than this, than to lay down one's life*
> *for his friends. You are My friends if you do whatever I com-*
> *mand you. No longer do I call you servants, for a servant does*
> *not know what his master is doing; but I have called you friends,*
> *for all things that I heard from My Father I have made known to*
> *you. You did not choose Me, but I chose you and appointed you*
> *that you should go and bear fruit, and that your fruit should*
> *remain, that whatever you ask the Father in My name He may*
> *give you" (vv. 13–16).*

In one breath Jesus speaks of His joy being fulfilled in the faithful acceptance
of His teaching by the disciples, and in the next He alludes to His death and
urges them to keep His words. The joy of Jesus is not unrelated to His death.
For His joy to be complete, the disciples must enter into a relationship with
God through His words and by the Spirit. This is only possible through His
death.

Only those who keep His commandment, however, will benefit from the
"laying down" of His life. Jesus repeats what He said when He identified
Himself as the Good Shepherd earlier and asserted five times that He lays
down His life for the sheep (10:11, 15, 17, 18). Jesus does not say that He will
lay down His life but that He lays it down. The present tense is important.
Jesus is in the process of laying down His life for the disciples. The Word that
was in the beginning has conformed to the dimension of human limitation
and reality and, in doing so, has begun to give His life to them by serving
them. Here Jesus says that by laying His life down as an example for the disciples, He shows they are no longer servants but friends who know what God
is doing through Him. They are no longer in the dark but have knowledge of
God through the Light that He has sent into the world.

The disciples are chosen by Jesus to bear fruit, not to simply enjoy God's
blessing. Thus, the selection of the disciples is for the same reason God chose
Israel to be His people. Deuteronomy chapter four suggests that Israel was
selected so that God might manifest His love to them and have them serve
as a witness to the nations.

For the third time in this discourse Jesus tells the disciples that they may
ask His Father what they need and He will provide it for them. Again, the
promise is conditional. As with the previous pronouncements, such requests
must be made in the name of Jesus and for the purpose of good works. (See
14:13, 14; 15:7.)

"These things I command you, that you love one another" (v. 17).

For the third time, Jesus commands the disciples to love one another. They are to keep His word even as they receive the Spirit. They are to be people of word and Spirit who express the joy of Jesus in their lives.

Father and Spirit-Anointed Son

In John's gospel, Jesus refers to God as His Father more than 130 times. He also describes Himself as God's Son. While this familial manner of referring to God is not without biblical precedent, Jesus' frequent use of *father* to describe His relationship with God is unique. It is one reason scholars have written extensively on the Sonship Christology of the Gospel of John. Jesus' self-identity is that of a Son whose role is to carry out His Father's plans. This is right. The emphasis given to the relationship between Jesus and God as Son and Father, however, has deflected attention away from Jesus' relation with the Spirit even though John clearly portrays Jesus as having a close relationship with the Spirit in his gospel.

In the Old Testament the people of God occasionally are described as God's son or firstborn. For example, God refers to Israel as "My son, My firstborn" when giving Moses the words he will speak to pharaoh (Ex. 4:22, 23), and the prophet Hosea describes the people delivered from Egypt as God's child and son (11:1). Not only are the people depicted as God's son, but the king of the people is called the son or firstborn of God as well. Nathan the prophet says to David that God will be a father to one of his descendents (2 Sam. 7:14). This one, according to the psalmist, will call God father and be His firstborn (Ps. 89:26, 27). Thus, the Old Testament refers to the people of Israel as God's son that has been delivered from bondage by their father at the same time it refers to the Davidic king of Israel as a son who will lead the people in future deliverance.

In addition to this, Jeremiah announces that God is a father to those who survive the Babylonian Exile. He will lead them back to the land where He will give them joy, mercy, and provision (31:7–34; see v. 9) even as He is praised as the father to the people for bringing them out of Egypt (Deut. 32:6). God is Father because He delivers His people.

This Old Testament background reveals the two-fold nature of Jesus' understanding of His relationship to God. On the one hand, Jesus' recognition of God as His Father suggests that He saw Himself as the King of Israel who had come to bring liberty to the people of God. He was the future King anticipated by the prophets. On the other hand, it reveals the close and intimate relationship He had with God. Since it was not altogether common to refer to God as father except in relation to the community or the community's special anticipated leader, Jesus' references should be viewed as a fresh and revelatory understanding of His familial relationship to God and the purpose for which He came. Jesus has come to lead others into a similar type of relationship. By providing a way for His followers to have a close and intimate relationship with God as their Father (17:21), Jesus leads them to the place of relationship with God that He enjoys and that God intended them to have from the beginning.

For John, Jesus is not simply God's Son who is close to Him, however. He is the Spirit-anointed Son of God who fulfills the will of the Father. John reports the Baptist as saying he saw the Spirit descend and remain on Jesus (1:32, 33). The Spirit does not come upon Jesus in a flash of inspiration or momentary revelation. But the Spirit comes upon Jesus to remain with Him in an exultation of divinity and humanity. The Greek word μεῦ and the tense used by John (imperfect, v. 32) suggest that the Spirit was a permanent partner with Jesus in His ministry.

The implications of this are profound. How is Jesus able to say that He only does what He sees the Father doing? "The Son can do nothing of Himself, but what He sees the Father do; for whatever He does, the Son also does in like manner" (5:19). How can He claim to speak only what He hears the Father speaking?

"My doctrine is not Mine, but His who sent Me," says Jesus Christ (7:16). Not only so, "I speak to the world those things which I heard from Him" (8:26). As God's Son Jesus knows the heart and will of God as God's Spirit reveals the intention of God to Him. The Spirit makes known to Jesus what the Father is saying and doing and enables Him to speak His Father's words and perform His works. Jesus does not teach or perform miracles simply because He is God's Son. He does not draw upon His infinite knowledge to teach the people about eternal life nor does He tap into His boundless power to perform miraculous signs. He teaches and gives signs by means of the Spirit who remains with Him. It is not the divine Son of God who manifests the new creation of God among the people; it is the Spirit-anointed divine Son of God who does this.

When Jesus first tells the Jews that He will soon leave them, He affirms that "He who sent Me is with Me. The Father has not left Me alone, for I always do those things that please Him" (8:29). With this statement, Jesus alludes to the presence of the Spirit in His life as well as the means by which He is able to please God. He is not alone because the Spirit is with Him and has been with Him since His baptism. This fact helps explain what Jesus means when He says, "I always do those things that please Him." Of course Jesus pleases God. After all, He does what He sees the Father doing. But how does Jesus see what His Father is doing? The Spirit reveals the things the Father is doing to Him. This also explains His previous statement, "I do nothing of Myself; but as My Father taught Me, I speak these things" (8:28). Jesus is taught by the Father through the Spirit who has come upon Him from heaven and remains with Him.

Each time Jesus asserts that He does what He sees God doing and speaks the words of God He not only alludes to His close relationship with God His Father but He also implicitly speaks of His relationship with the Spirit. John presents the testimony of the Baptist about Jesus' baptism with the Spirit at the beginning of His gospel because he wants his readers to understand that Jesus knows God as His Father and does the will of His Father through the ever-present fellowship of the Spirit. John presents Jesus as the Spirit-anointed Son who does the will of His Father. His Christology is not only that of Sonship, it is one of Spirit-anointed Sonship.

The Rejection of Jesus in the World (John 15:18–16:4)

In this passage Jesus describes the prevailing attitude of the world toward Him and those who identify with Him. The world hates Jesus. It does not know Him and has rejected His works. As much as Jesus has spoken to the

LOVE AND HATE

The opposition that Jesus has faced during His ministry will continue as the disciples keep His word and receive the Spirit that the Father will send. The verity of love and the reality of hate in chapters 13–15 is outlined in the following table:

Jesus Speaks about Love	Jesus Warns about Hate
The disciples are exhorted to love each other as He has loved them (13:34, 35; 15:12, 17).	The world will hate the disciples because they have been delivered by Jesus and they are no longer a part of it (15:19).
Whoever keeps Jesus' commandments shows his or her love for Him (14:21, 23) and Jesus loves them (14:21).	The world first hated Jesus (15:18).
Jesus manifests His love for His Father by keeping His commandments (14:31; 15:10).	The one who hates Jesus hates His Father as well (15:23, 24).
Jesus has demonstrated His love for the disciples (13:34) by loving them as the Father has loved Him (15:9) and laying down His life for them (15:13).	The world has hated Jesus despite the works He has done. For this reason the world hates without a reason (15:24, 25).

disciples about God's love, their need to love each other, and His love for them, He now speaks of the hate that He has experienced and they will experience as well. Just as they have experienced God's love in Him, so also they will experience the antipathy of the world because of Him.

> "If the world hates you, you know that it hated Me before it hated you" (v. 18).

Half of the forty occurrences of the word *hate* (*miseō*) in the New Testament occur in the Johannine literature—the gospel, the letters, and Revelation. Jesus tells Nicodemus that there are those who hate the Light because the Light exposes their evil works (3:20) and He tells His brothers that though the world does not hate them it hates Him because He testifies that its works are evil (7:7). Thus, Jesus is the true object of the world's hatred because He reveals the true nature of its deeds.

> "If you were of the world, the world would love its own. Yet because you are not of the world, but I chose you out of the world, therefore the world hates you. Remember the word that I said to you, 'A servant is not greater than his master.' If they persecuted Me, they will also persecute you. If they kept My word, they will keep yours also. But all these things they will do to you for My name's sake, because they do not know Him who sent Me" (vv. 19–21).

Here, Jesus repeats that He has chosen the disciples (v. 16). The world will respond to the disciples in the same way that it responded to Jesus. Because of the name of Jesus, the disciples will experience persecution (see Matt. 5:11, 12). Jesus gives special emphasis to His name in this last discourse. He tells the disciples that anything they ask in His name will be given to them (14:13, 14); He asks the Father to send the Holy Spirit to them in His name (14:25); and He says that the persecution the disciples will experience will be due to His name. That is, because they have the Spirit and minister in His name they will encounter rejection on account of His name.

In the introductory section of his gospel, John asserts that "as many as received Him, to them He gave the right to become children of God, to those who believe in His name" (1:12). And Jesus says to Nicodemus that belief in the name of the Son of God results in eternal life (3:18). Thus, the name of Jesus brings persecution at the same time it brings the Spirit, the right to be called children of God, and the blessed gift of eternal life.

"If I had not come and spoken to them, they would have no sin,
but now they have no excuse for their sin. He who hates Me
hates My Father also. If I had not done among them the works
which no one else did, they would have no sin; but now they
have seen and also hated both Me and My Father" (vv. 22–24).

The works that Jesus has performed are miracles that represent the new creation. By rejecting His works, the world is convicted of sin. Thus, in one
sense Jesus does not convict or judge the world. The world judges itself by
rejecting the new creation of God in Him. In this, the world shows that it
hates the Father as well as the Son.

But this happened that the word might be fulfilled which is writ-
ten in their law, "They hated Me without a cause" (v. 25).

Jesus prophesies that the hatred He has experienced is a fulfillment of
Scripture. Though He says this fulfillment is found in the law, it is in fact
found in Psalms 35 and 109. Jesus refers to these Scriptures as law since all of
God's written word represents God's instruction.

These two Davidic poems accurately describe the reality of Jesus' experience. In both, the psalmist cries out to God to help him against his enemies.
He calls upon God to fight, rescue, vindicate (Ps. 35), and save him (Ps. 109).
Of those who hate him without a cause, the psalmist says that they do not
speak peaceably but plan against "the quiet ones in the land" (35:19, 20). That
is, the enemies of the psalmist turn on others as well. Moreover, they "have
surrounded me with words of hatred" and "have rewarded me evil for good
and hatred for my love" (109:3–5). Jesus draws on these psalms to refer to His
opponents as people who hate Him without a cause because they attempt to
do harm to others even while they respond to His good works with evil. This
closely describes the response of many to Him. Those whom John calls the
Jews (and Jesus refers to as the world) have responded to the good works of
Jesus with negative criticism and rejection. By planning His death, they
return His good with evil.

"But when the Helper comes, whom I shall send to you from the
Father, the Spirit of truth who proceeds from the Father, He will
testify of Me. And you also will bear witness, because you have
been with Me from the beginning" (vv. 26, 27).

For the third time Jesus refers to the Holy Spirit as the Paraclete and, for the
third time, He says that the Spirit will come from His Father. How does Jesus

THE PARACLETE PASSAGES

A comparison of the three Paraclete passages reveals the complete nature of the Spirit's work among the disciples.

The Spiritual Aspect	14:15–18	14:26	15:26, 27
The promise of the Spirit	"I will pray the Father, and He will give"	"the Holy Spirit, whom the Father will send in My name"	"When the Helper comes, whom I shall send to you from the Father?"
The work of the Spirit	The Helper is the Spirit of Truth who will abide with the disciples forever.	The Helper will remind the disciples of what Jesus has said to them.	The Helper is the Spirit of Truth who testifies of Jesus.
The result of the Spirit's work	The disciples will not be left as orphans.	The disciples will recall what Jesus taught.	The disciples will testify about Jesus.

The disciples will not be left alone without guidance. Rather, the Paraclete will be given to them and will recall for them all that they have learned from Him. This is so that they might tell others about Him. Though the disciples will experience the same rejection that Jesus experienced, they will have the same Spirit to continue His irrepressible ministry of new creation. The Spirit of Truth will continue to testify to the world of the new creative work of God in Jesus through the disciples.

send the Spirit, then? He sends the Spirit in the sense that He will request that the Spirit be given to the disciples. The Father sends the Spirit but only at the volition of the Son.

> "These things I have spoken to you, that you should not be made to stumble. They will put you out of the synagogues; yes, the time is coming that whoever kills you will think that he offers God service. And these things they will do to you because they have not known the Father nor Me. But these things I have told you, that when the time comes, you may remember that I told you of them. And these things I did not say to you at the beginning, because I was with you" (vv. 1–4).

Jesus has spoken of the hatred of the world and the promise of the Spirit so that the disciples will have knowledge of the things that will happen to them once He has left them. He does not want them to stumble or fall from faith because the persecution they will experience will be very real. They will be shunned and they will be put to death.

Jesus says that those who persecute the disciples will think that they are doing God's service. How is this possible? The simple reason is that they do not know God. They have been deceived by the devil who has been a deceiver from the beginning. Earlier in His ministry Jesus confronted the disbelief of certain Jews by identifying them as children of the devil—the antithesis of truth and the one who "when he speaks a lie, he speaks from his own sources, for he is a liar and the father of it" (8:44). Even as those who seek His death do so because they see Him as a false prophet who leads the people astray, so also they will attempt to stop those who continue His ministry in His name because they will see them as false prophets as well.

Darkness and the Devil in the Gospel of John

According to John, Jesus encounters adamant and persistent opposition to His teaching and miracles. In particular, the temple leadership in Jerusalem rejects His claims and moves to silence Him. This is not the only opposition Jesus faces, however. John suggests that Jesus faces spiritual resistance as well. He does this by presenting the ministry of Jesus in terms of light and darkness and by recording Jesus' own remarks about the devil, the thief, and the ruler of this world.

Before Jesus speaks one word or performs a single sign, John set His ministry within the context of darkness. The light shines in the darkness, but the darkness was not able to overcome it (1:5). The best translation for the Greek *katalambanō* in this passage is "overcome." The darkness was not able to resist or suppress the coming of the light of God. The backdrop for Jesus' ministry, therefore, is that of conflict and struggle. As an introductory remark, it defines John's subsequent testimony concerning Jesus.

John develops the imagery of darkness and light throughout the gospel. Nicodemus, for example, approaches Jesus at night (3:2). Even though he is a teacher of Israel, he does not understand Jesus' teaching and wants to know more about Him. The darkness represents ignorance and lack of understanding. In addition, Judas leaves Jesus and the disciples after he has dipped his bread into the dish and goes into the night. The night represents his rejection of Jesus as well as his own demise. The night is the domain where Jesus is not known and not believed.

For this reason, Jesus cautions Nicodemus (and through him others) away from the darkness. He says that some people love darkness rather than light and show their preference for it through their works (3:19, 20). At another time, He exhorts the people to turn to the Light before the darkness overcomes them (12:35). These remarks indicate that Jesus regards darkness as a realm or sphere of power that must be resisted.

Not only does Jesus speak of darkness in impersonal terms like *realm* or *power*, He also refers to that realm or power in the personal terms of *devil*, *thief*, and *ruler of this world*. Jesus has known from the beginning that one of His disciples will reject Him and calls him a devil (see 6:70, 71). He later accuses certain leaders among the people of having the devil for their father because they reject the word He has spoken to them. This is true to form because the devil is a liar (8:44). But this is not the only way Jesus describes his opposition. When He identifies Himself as the Good Shepherd, Jesus says that there is one who desires to steal, kill, and destroy them (10:1, 8–10). The illegitimate and violent work of this thief stands in sharp contrast to that of Jesus Himself. In fact, according to the brief description of his activities, the thief wants to take away and even eradicate the new creative work of God in Him. Finally, Jesus' passion represents a direct confrontation with "the ruler of this world" who has no claim upon Him (14:30) and will be cast out and judged by Him (12:31; 16:11). Yet, his presence indicates that he possesses some authority within the world of darkness that Jesus has entered as the light of God. His rule is temporary and is in the process of being dismantled.

Thus, throughout John's gospel Jesus speaks of supra human opposition to His ministry in personal terms. For Jesus, the opposition He faced was not merely human, it was not a personification of myth, nor was it a general, ambiguous force of evil. It was personal; based on His understanding of the biblical story of the Fall. The terms *devil*, *thief*, and *ruler of this world* all plausibly identify the one who attempted to undermine God's good work in the beginning (Gen. 3:1–15). Jesus comes as the truth of God to restore the original relationship between God and mankind.

John's depiction of Jesus' confrontation with impersonal darkness as well as the personal devil, thief, and ruler may explain why he does not record any of Jesus' exorcisms. Whereas the synoptic Gospels record numerous confrontations with unclean spirits (Mark 1:21–28, Luke 4:31–35; Matt. 8:28–34, Mark 5:1–20, Luke 8:26–39; Matt. 9:32–34), John does not record even one. Is John ignorant of these stories? Does he wish to avoid a discussion of this tradition because he rejects it or is somehow embarrassed by it? Another answer may be given. The synoptic evangelists record these accounts to show the supremacy of the kingdom of God over every dimension of life and over all powers including the spiritual. John, on the other hand, shows that Jesus is the light of God who, in all that He does, represents a confrontation and overthrow of the realm of darkness and the one who reigns in that realm. Jesus establishes a new creation in the midst of this darkness and chaos. The seven miracles He performs represent the total life-giving work of God through Him. John does not record any exorcisms because he views the entire ministry of Jesus as the exorcism of the darkness in the world. In Him, light has come and a new beginning has started.

The Work of the Spirit in the World (John 16:5–15)

Jesus repeats that He is going away and says that He will send the Paraclete to the disciples. There are three dimensions to the Spirit's role and work described in this passage. First, the Spirit will bring evidence to refute or challenge (*elenchō*, ἐλέγχω) the world's understanding of sin, righteousness, and judgment (vv. 8–11). Second, the Spirit will lead (*hodēgeō*, ὁδηγέω) the disciples in all truth as He communicates to them what He hears from Jesus (vv. 13, 14). The Spirit does not provide new teaching, rather He continues the teaching that has already been given. Nonetheless, there is much that Jesus cannot teach His disciples (v. 12), so the Spirit will continue their instruction. Third, the Spirit will glorify Jesus. He will give attention to Jesus Christ in His work just as Jesus has glorified the Father.

> *"But now I go away to Him who sent Me, and none of you asks Me, 'Where are You going?' But because I have said these things to you, sorrow has filled your heart" (vv. 5, 6).*

Peter and Thomas have previously asked Jesus where He is going (13:36; 14:5) as have others (8:21; see also 7:33, 34; 8:14). Is Jesus being forgetful? Has John clumsily reported this exchange? No. Jesus' remarks make sense in the context of the narrative. He has just told the disciples that He must leave them and that they will experience the same kind of rejection and persecution that He has experienced. They no longer ask about His departure because they are bewildered by His words.

The disciples' response is one of sorrow or heaviness. Jesus has already exhorted them, "Let not your heart be troubled" (14:1). Yet, the disciples are disturbed at the news of His departure and His dark forecast concerning the world's hatred of them. Though the meaning of the Greek connotes pain and sadness, here the word suggests the feeling of abandonment. The disciples are afraid at the thought of continuing without Jesus to guide them and teach them. They will be alone in a hostile world. Jesus understands their feelings and has already promised to send the Holy Spirit to them so they will not be orphans (14:18).

> "Nevertheless I tell you the truth. It is to your advantage that I go away; for if I do not go away, the Helper will not come to you; but if I depart, I will send Him to you. And when He has come, He will convict the world of sin, and of righteousness, and of judgment: of sin, because they do not believe in Me; of right-eousness, because I go to My Father and you see Me no more; of judgment, because the ruler of this world is judged. I still have many things to say to you, but you cannot bear them now" (vv. 7–12).

Jesus must leave in order that the Spirit may come. As the Word-become-flesh, Jesus cannot remain with the disciples indefinitely. Again, Jesus identifies the Spirit as the Paraclete (14:16, 26; 15:26) and, in this way, He compares the role of the Spirit to His own work among the disciples. In His most extensive remarks on the Spirit recorded by John, Jesus begins by describing the Spirit's work in the world before He describes the Spirit's work with the disciples. He does this for at least two reasons. First, having already foretold the world's attitude and behavior toward the disciples (15:18–16:4), Jesus now describes the Spirit's activity in relation to that world. Even as the world judges the disciples with hostility because of their association with Jesus, so also the Spirit will reprove the world of sin, righteousness, and judgment at the instigation of Jesus. Second, the Spirit who was present in the beginning of creation (1:1) will continue to be present in God's new work of creation both in the world as well as in Israel.

- His presence brings evidence of the world's present condition. The world is removed from God and in a state of sin.
- The Spirit not only exposes the sin of the world but will also give positive proof to the world that a righteous relationship with God is possible through Christ (6:62; 7:33; 14:28).
- The presence of the Spirit is a sign that Jesus has achieved God's pur-pose in the world and has returned to His Father according to His words.
- The exposure of sin and the revelation of God's righteousness in Jesus by the Spirit will occur through the work of the Spirit in the lives of the disciples. Their works will refute the works of the ruler of

the world and show that judgment has already been placed upon him as the new creation of God comes into being.

What does Jesus mean when He says that the Paraclete will convict the world of sin, righteousness, and judgment? Such activity may be clarified by John's use of the verb *convict* in his gospel. Throughout His ministry Jesus countered the prevailing condition of sin by living in conformity to the will of God. He spoke what He heard God speak and He does what He sees God doing (9:4, 38; 10:32, 37, 38; 12:49; 14:10, 24). Jesus exemplified righteousness in all that He said and did. His intimate relationship with God was an example for all to see. Still, certain people rejected His words and suspected His works. In this context He asked the Jews, "Which of you convicts (*elenchō*) Me of sin?" (8:46). In other words, who could bring evidence of sin given the things He has done.

Also, Jesus was public about nearly all He did. He did not fear the light. This is in contrast to those who hate the light and avoid it for fear that their works will be revealed and censured as wrong. Early in His ministry Jesus told Nicodemus that though God's Son entered the world to save the world, the world continued to love darkness and do evil works. "For everyone practicing evil hates the light and does not come to the light, lest his deed should be exposed" (3:20). These two passages indicate that the Paraclete sent by Jesus will bring evidence against and censure to the world's view of sin, righteousness, and judgment.

The Spirit and the World

What is the world's view of sin, righteousness, and judgment? The world views Jesus as a sinner who does not maintain the traditions of Israel. For this reason He is judged unrighteous. The Spirit will confront and confound this view when He comes.

The Spirit and Sin

Jesus says that He has come from His Father above, spoken His words, and performed His works. Those who reject His ministry reject the fact that He is from God and reject God Himself (8:13–19, 47). This is sin (8:21–25). When the Spirit comes He will remind the disciples of the things Jesus taught. They will continue to live according to the words of Jesus as they recall them by the Spirit. By giving the words of Jesus to the disciples, the Spirit will continue to confront the world with His message and expose the sin of unbelief.

The Spirit and Righteousness

The only use of the word *righteousness* (*dikaiosunē*, ἡ δικαιόσυνη) in John's gospel occurs here. Jesus would have understood righteousness in terms of relationship with God. What was once possible only through the Mosaic covenant is now possible in Christ. By speaking and acting according to what the Father says and does, Jesus submits Himself to His will (5:30; 6:38; 7:17, 18). The fullest expression of His acceptance of God's plan is His acceptance of death (10:11–18; 12:23–25, 27, 32–36; 14:2, 3). This results in the permanent presence of the Spirit among the disciples—proof that Jesus came from God His Father and has returned to Him. The Spirit reveals that Jesus indeed is the means by which covenantal relationship with God may be experienced and people may have righteous standing before Him.

The Spirit and Judgment

Just as the darkness could not prevent the light from entering into the world (1:5), so also the ruler of the world cannot bar the Spirit from working within the world for its redemption. Concerning judgment, the Spirit will provide further proof about Jesus in the works He will perform through the disciples. These works will refute the death dealing, thievery, and destruction of this ruler with the very life of God. Such works by the Spirit reveal that the new creation of God is coming into existence, inexorably moving toward a day of final consummation and completion.

The Spirit makes the case before the world that one may have a relationship with God in Christ. Jesus' words are the standard by which belief or disbelief (sin) may be measured. His return to the Father reveals the accomplishment of God's purposes and represents the opportunity for God's new creative work to continue through the disciples The work that they will do by the Spirit declares that judgment already has come to the ruler of the world and the new beginning has begun.

> *"However, when He, the Spirit of truth, has come, He will guide you into all truth; for He will not speak on His own authority, but whatever He hears He will speak; and He will tell you things to come" (v. 13).*

Jesus continues His remarks on the Holy Spirit by observing the Paraclete's work among the disciples. Here Jesus identifies Him as the Spirit of Truth (14:17; 15:26). Just as Jesus is the truth to the disciples so the Spirit will be the truth to them as well. Even as Jesus spoke the truth to them, the Spirit will

THE NATURE OF TRUTH

What is truth? It is the word that God speaks. Jesus is the truth of God in that He is the very Word of God. And the Spirit is described by Jesus as the Spirit of Truth because He conveys the word of God to the disciples. The correlation between the truth of God and His word is seen in four progressive steps:

1. God the Father manifests His truth through His Word (1:14).
2. Jesus: the Way, the Truth, and the Life (14:6) reveals the will of His Father through His words.
3. The Spirit of Truth testifies about Jesus (15:26) and speaks what He hears (16:13).
4. The people of truth are guided by the Word of God through the Spirit.

guide them into all truth. He will speak what He hears, just as Jesus spoke what He heard His Father say. The Spirit reprises the role that Jesus has had with the disciples.

> *"He will glorify Me, for He will take of what is Mine and declare it to you. All things that the Father has are Mine. Therefore I said that He will take of Mine and declare it to you" (vv. 14, 15).*

Jesus concludes His remarks about the Spirit by noting the Spirit's work in relation to His own. The Spirit will bring glory to Jesus even as Jesus has brought glory to His Father (7:17, 18; 8:49, 50; 13:31, 32; 17:4). The Spirit does this by manifesting the life-giving nature of Jesus' ministry as Jesus has manifested the life-giving nature of God the Father.

The Disciples' Joy and Jesus' Victory (John 16:16–33)

Jesus concludes His teaching to the disciples by speaking of their joy and His victory over the world. Their joy will emerge out of sorrow even as His victory will be won in His death.

> *"A little while, and you will not see Me; and again a little while, and you will see Me, because I go to the Father" (v. 16).*

In a little while the disciples will no longer see (*theoreō*, θεωρέω) Jesus. A little while after this, they will see (*horaō*, ὁράω) Him again. The use of these two Greek verbs in other passages in the gospel (for example, 6:35–40) gives meaning to this portion of Scripture (vv. 16–19). It suggests that Jesus distinguishes two different acts of seeing. What might these be? The verbs indicate that though the disciples will no longer be able to observe (*theoreō*) Jesus in the manner that they have, yet they will once again see (*horaō*) in the ministry of the Holy Spirit. This means that they will cease being observers of Jesus' ministry and become participants in it through the Spirit. Their experience will be far different from that of those who do not believe Jesus and, thus, see but do not see (*blepō*, βλέπω, 9:39–41).

> *Then some of His disciples said among themselves, "What is this that He says to us, 'A little while, and you will not see Me; and again a little while, and you will see Me'; and, 'because I go to the Father'?" They said therefore, "What is this that He says, 'A little while'? We do not know what He is saying" (vv. 17, 18).*

Again, the disciples are confused by Jesus' remarks. Though He has spoken about His departure, He now speaks of leaving soon. The Greek reads "a little" and means that Jesus' departure is imminent. The time of His passion and death is almost present.

> *Now Jesus knew that they desired to ask Him, and He said to them, "Are you inquiring among yourselves about what I said, 'A little while, and you will not see Me; and again a little while, and you will see Me'? Most assuredly, I say to you that you will weep and lament, but the world will rejoice; and you will be sorrowful, but your sorrow will be turned into joy. A woman, when she is in labor, has sorrow because her hour has come; but as soon as she has given birth to the child, she no longer remembers the anguish, for joy that a human being has been born into the world. Therefore you now have sorrow; but I will see you again and your heart will rejoice, and your joy no one will take from you" (vv. 19–22).*

The disciples will respond to Jesus' departure with weeping and lamentation. The Greek verb *mourn* (*thrēneō*, θρηνέω) occurs only here in John's gospel while the verb *weep* (*klaiō*, κλαίω) is more frequent (it occurs eight times in the gospel) and is often used to describe human anguish in the face of death (20:11–15). Their grief is temporary and will be replaced with joy. Jesus' remarks follow the biblical tradition that depicts those who laugh as members of the world and those who weep as related to God. (See Is. 35:10; 65:17–25; Ps. 126.)

Jesus uses the analogy of a pregnant woman to describe the experience of the disciples. Just as she will have sorrow or distress in labor only to experience joy in the birth of a child, so also the disciples will have sorrow in the departure of Jesus only to experience joy in His resurrection and the new birth that it presages.

Their experience at this time recalls that of God's people in the Day of New Creation described by Isaiah (65:17–25). It is in this day that the people will rejoice in a new heaven and new earth. Not only will they rejoice, but they become a source of joy to God Himself. Weeping and crying will cease and the people will enjoy long life and peace in His new creation. God declares, "The wolf and the lamb shall feed together, the lion shall eat straw like the ox" (v. 25). The sorrow and joy of the disciples, then, anticipates that of all of God's people in the future.

What is this joy that Jesus speaks about? He gives a full description of it in these verses:

- It is the opposite of sorrow. Sorrow in these verses is distress and fear at the absence of Jesus. Joy is the assurance and acceptance found in relationship with Him.
- It is the hopeful response to birth and new life. Joy is the sense of anticipation that issues out of the beauty and mystery of God's creation.
- Joy is participation in the new creative life of God that comes from asking and receiving in Jesus' name. As noted above, asking and receiving has nothing to do with one's own gratification. Rather, it is to participate in God's new creative work; it is to be dependent on Jesus' word and to have knowledge of God's purposes as one serves others.

"And in that day you will ask Me nothing. Most assuredly, I say to you, whatever you ask the Father in My name He will give you. Until now you have asked nothing in My name. Ask, and you will receive, that your joy may be full" (vv. 23, 24).

The disciples will not need to ask where Jesus is going or what He is doing "in that day" when He is absent from them. They will know where He is and what He is doing by the Spirit. This helps to explain the apparent contradiction in the statement: "In that day you will ask Me nothing . . . Until now you have asked nothing in My name. Ask, and you will receive." The Spirit will come in the name of Jesus (14:26) and the disciples will ask in that same name. They have not asked because they have not been given the responsibility for continuing Jesus' ministry. They will ask once they have such responsibility. They will have access to Jesus by the Spirit and receive what they need to serve others. His name will bind the disciples to the Spirit and enable them to continue in relationship with Him.

Joy comes from knowing God through Jesus and experiencing His will in one's life as one serves others. Jesus says that one can know the will of God in one's life and have everything that is needed to live according to His will. This is complete joy.

> *"These things I have spoken to you in figurative language; but the time is coming when I will no longer speak to you in figurative language, but I will tell you plainly about the Father" (v. 25).*

Jesus acknowledges that He has spoken with figurative language to the disciples. This means that His manner of teaching in this discourse has been analogical. But why has Jesus spoken in this way? Certainly not to confuse or frustrate them! He has used figures and images to force them to think about His teaching and wrestle with it. He wants them to make connections. He wants the disciples to engage the revelation that He has given to them from His Father about the Spirit.

> *"In that day you will ask in My name, and I do not say to you that I shall pray the Father for you; for the Father Himself loves you, because you have loved Me, and have believed that I came forth from God. I came forth from the Father and have come into the world. Again, I leave the world and go to the Father" (vv. 26–28).*

In His concluding remarks to the disciples Jesus speaks plainly. He says that the Father loves them because they have believed He has come from God. Thus, Jesus concludes His last discourse much as He did His first discourse with Nicodemus—He speaks about the love of God. To Nicodemus He said that God loves the world and whoever believes in the Son will have eternal life. To the disciples He says the Father loves them because they believe that He has come from God.

> *His disciples said to Him, "See, now You are speaking plainly, and using no figure of speech! Now we are sure that You know all things, and have no need that anyone should question You. By this we believe that You came forth from God" (vv. 29–30).*

The disciples reveal their belief and understanding by declaring that Jesus knows all things. Since only God possesses such knowledge, to exclaim that Jesus has this type of knowledge is to endorse the teaching that He has given to them as divinely inspired.

> *Jesus answered them, "Do you now believe? Indeed the hour is coming, yes, has now come, that you will be scattered, each to his own, and will leave Me alone. And yet I am not alone, because the Father is with Me. These things I have spoken to you, that in Me you may have peace. In the world you will have tribulation; but be of good cheer, I have overcome the world" (vv. 31–33).*

The hour of Jesus' passion is the hour of the disciples' dispersion. His prediction recalls the prophecy of Zechariah 13 that the synoptic writers quote: "Strike the shepherd and the sheep will be scattered" (v. 7; see Matt. 26:31; Mark 14:27). As the Good Shepherd, Jesus will be abandoned by His flock during His arrest, beating, and crucifixion. This passing remark is recorded by John to show that everything Jesus says and does is in accord with the plan of God as registered in Scripture.

Like the prophets of the Old Testament, however, Jesus does not let judgment be the last word that He speaks. He asserts to the disciples that despite their tribulation He has won a victory over the world. The perfect tense of the Greek *nikaō*, νικάω indicates that the victory has already been accomplished and continues to be won. He will not win it in the future; He has already won it by entering the world. Now He will consummate His victory through His death. Jesus has already said that a seed of wheat that falls into the ground produces much grain and the person who disregards the desires of life in this world will find eternal life (12:24, 25); He has said that the greatest love a friend can show another is to lay down his life for him (15:13); and He has told Nicodemus that the Son of Man must be lifted up so the love of God may be manifest and people believe in Him (3:14–17). Thus, what Jesus says about victory at this time (on the verge of apparent defeat) is not a platitude to pacify the disciples in a moment of duress. It is the boast of truth by One who has lived in obedience to His Father's will from the beginning of His ministry and has been consistently depicted by John as One who knows all things.

The Lord's Prayer (John 17:1–26)

Jesus turns from the disciples and now addresses His Father. This marks a dramatic movement in the narrative as Jesus shifts from instructing His followers and giving them encouragement to facing His death. In the Gospel of John, this prayer takes the place of the Gethsemane Prayer recorded in the synoptic Gospels (Matt. 26:36–46; Mark 14:32–42; Luke 22:39–46).

> *Jesus spoke these words, lifted up His eyes to heaven, and said:*
> *"Father, the hour has come. Glorify Your Son, that Your Son also*
> *may glorify You, as You have given Him authority over all flesh,*
> *that He should give eternal life to as many as You have given Him.*
> *And this is eternal life, that they may know You, the only true*
> *God, and Jesus Christ whom You have sent. I have glorified You on*
> *the earth. I have finished the work which You have given Me to do.*
> *And now, O Father, glorify Me together with Yourself, with the*
> *glory which I had with You before the world was" (vv. 1–5).*

Jesus begins His prayer by looking to heaven, an action that John records in order to highlight the divine-human union in Jesus. He is indeed in the world while not being of the world. He has become part of the created world of His Father while refusing to be conformed to its principles, systems, or ways of living. These verses can be organized in a short chiasmus—a literary device in which the words of parallel lines are reversed:

A. Jesus asks the Father to glorify Him now that the hour has come (v. 1).
   B. Jesus has authority from the Father over all flesh to give eternal life (v. 2).
   B1. Eternal life is to know God and His Son Jesus (v. 3).
   A1. Jesus has finished the Father's work and glorified Him (v. 4).
      Jesus asks the Father to glorify Him with the glory He had in the beginning (v. 5).

This chiasmus reveals that the initial focus of Jesus' prayer is the truth that eternal life is knowledge of God and Jesus His Son. Jesus is aware of His place in the salvation plan of His Father. He asks, therefore, that the Father impress His glory upon Him at this time as at the beginning. Jesus wants the life-giving power of God to be released in His suffering and death for a new creation in a distressed world even as it was released in the beginning in the fashioning of the world.

When Jesus says that God has given Him authority over all flesh, He evokes the concluding prophecy of the book of Isaiah where God promises to make priests from all nations and declares that all flesh will worship Him in His new creation (Is. 66:18–24). In the Old Testament, the term *all flesh* usually signifies all humanity or all nations (Gen. 6:12, 13, 17; Is. 49:26; Joel 2:28). In Isaiah's pronouncement, God will gather the nations to see His glory and disperse them to tell others about it (vv. 18, 19). As a result, the nations will bring offerings to God (v. 20) and some will serve as priests (v. 21). God then declares that "all flesh" will worship Him (v. 23). Thus, according to this climactic prophecy, the nations will see God's glory, give offerings to God, serve as priests, and worship Him. Jesus' prayer reveals His knowledge of these words and His belief that their realization is found in Him. He urges His Father to glorify Him at this time through His passion so that the nations will see God's glory in the most gruesome of spectacles and come to worship Him.

> *"I have manifested Your name to the men whom You have given Me out of the world. They were Yours, You gave them to Me, and they have kept Your word. Now they have known that all things which You have given Me are from You. For I have given to them the words which You have given Me; and they have received them, and have known surely that I came forth from You; and they have believed that You sent Me. I pray for them. I do not pray for the world but for those whom You have given Me, for they are Yours. And all Mine are Yours, and Yours are Mine, and I am glorified in them. Now I am no longer in the world, but these are in the world, and I come to You. Holy Father, keep through Your name those whom You have given Me, that they may be one as We are. While I was with them in the world, I kept them in Your name. Those whom You gave Me I have kept; and none of them is lost except the son of perdition, that the Scripture might be fulfilled. But now I come to You, and these things I speak in the world, that they may have My joy fulfilled in themselves. I have given them Your word; and the world has hated them because they are not of the world, just as I am not of the world. I do not pray that You should take them out of the world, but that You should keep them from the evil one. They are not of the world, just as I am not of the world. Sanctify them by Your truth. Your word is truth. As You sent Me into the world, I also have sent them into the world. And for their sakes I sanctify Myself, that they also may be sanctified by the truth" (vv. 6–19).*

These verses record Jesus' intercessory prayer for His disciples. In them He recalls what He has done and what He continues to do in their lives. First,

Jesus has manifested God's name to them and given God's words to them (vv. 8, 26). This resembles God's activity among the Hebrew people when He delivered them from Egypt: God first gave His name to them (Ex. 3:15; Deut. 6:2–9) and then He entrusted them with His words (Ex. 20; Deut. 5). However, Jesus did more than make God's name known to the disciples. He has preserved them through the name that God gave to Him (v. 12). The name of God identifies the disciples as those who belong to God.

Second, Jesus asks His Father to keep them so they may be one (vv. 9–10), protect them from the evil one who would deceive them with his words (8:44), and sanctify them by His word (vv. 15–19). As those sanctified by God's word, Jesus sends the disciples into the world (v. 18). The ancient people of faith belonged to God and testified to the nations of God by their adherence to His covenantal word (Ex. 19:4–6). Likewise, the disciples will testify to the world of God's love by keeping the word of Jesus Christ. They belong to God and, yet, live in the world.

Third, Jesus prays that those who will follow the disciples will be unified and will experience the revelation of God's glory in Jesus Christ. Unity is a primary feature of the ancient Israelites in their mission to the nations. They were to be holy. That is, set apart to God in both their lives and in their service as a unified nation in the midst of the Gentile nations. (See Ex. 19:6; Deut. 7:6–11; 26:16–19.)

> "I do not pray for these alone, but also for those who will believe in Me through their word; that they all may be one, as You, Father, are in Me, and I in You; that they also may be one in Us, that the world may believe that You sent Me. And the glory which You gave Me I have given them, that they may be one just as We are one: I in them, and You in Me; that they may be made perfect in one, and that the world may know that You have sent Me, and have loved them as You have loved Me. Father, I desire that they also whom You gave Me may be with Me where I am, that they may behold My glory which You have given Me; for You loved Me before the foundation of the world. O righteous Father! The world has not known You, but I have known You; and these have known that You sent Me. And I have declared to them Your name, and will declare it, that the love with which You loved Me may be in them, and I in them" (vv. 20–26).

Jesus prays for the unity of those who will believe in Him through the word of His disciples. His ambition is that they may experience unity of relationship in two dimensions: unity with one another like Jesus has with His Father as well as unity in their own relationship with God. Such relationships with each other and with God reflect the very glory of God. They serve as a testimony to the world so that it may believe Jesus is from God and experience the love of God. The unity of which Jesus speaks means more than "togetherness." It is singularity of purpose as they testify to the world about God's love.

Jesus draws upon the Shema (Deut. 6:4, 5) to reveal His deepest desire for the disciples. Even as the Shema declares the unity of God ("Hear Israel, the Lord our God, the Lord is One") it also establishes love as the basis of relationship with God. God first loved Israel and chose the people to be the means of His redemptive work among the nations (Deut. 7:7, 8), and He expects His people to respond to Him in kind: "You shall love the Lord your God with all of your heart, and all of your mind, and all of your strength" (6:5). Love and unity mark the disciples of Jesus. By them the world will know the disciples belong to Him and He is from God.

In summary, Jesus prays for God's glory to be revealed so the nations may worship Him (vv. 1–5). He has already manifested God's name to the disciples and spoken His revelatory words to them. He prays for their sanctification so they may continue the ministry He has begun in them (vv. 6–19). This is why Jesus asks that those who believe in Him through the ministry of the disciples be bound together in unity. They, too, are to participate in His ministry (vv. 20–26). Jesus' prayer is an appropriate conclusion to this section of John's gospel in that it is about the continuation of God's work among the disciples and those who will follow them. His concern is that the new creation that has begun with His ministry among the disciples would continue by the Spirit. Jesus is not consumed with misgivings or doubt at this penultimate moment. Rather, His prayer reveals that He is already looking ahead to the continued creative work of God.

The Disciples' Prayer and the Lord's Prayer

The prayer Jesus offers at this crucial moment includes aspects of the prayer He earlier taught the disciples in the Sermon on the Mount (Matt. 6:9–13). That prayer is known as The Lord's Prayer but, in fact, is better understood as The Disciples' Prayer since Jesus teaches it to the disciples to follow in their devotion to God. The prayer Jesus prays here before His passion is the true Lord's Prayer since it is the one He Himself prays to His Father.

The prayer reveals that Jesus practices what He teaches. The following table outlines these two prayers and shows how the prayer Jesus prays resembles the prayer He taught His disciples.

The Disciples' Prayer—Matthew 6:9–15	The Lord's Prayer—John 17:1–26
"Our Father in heaven, Hallowed be Your name" (v. 9). The disciples are to address God as Father and sanctify His name in their lives.	Throughout His prayer Jesus identifies God as His Father (vv. 1, 5, 11, 21, 24, 25). He addresses God as Holy Father (v. 11) and Righteous Father (v. 25). Jesus speaks to God in the very way that He instructs the disciples. Jesus also asks the Father to sanctify the disciples in His name or by His authority (vv. 17–19).
"Your kingdom come, Your will be done on earth as it is in heaven" (v. 10). The disciples are to ask that God's purposes be accomplished.	Jesus has finished the work that God gave Him to do (v. 4). He has accomplished God's will by manifesting and declaring God's name to the disciples (vv. 6, 12, 26) and by keeping all of those who were given to Him (vv. 6, 12).
"Give us this day our daily bread. And forgive us our debts as we forgive our debtors" (vv. 11, 12). The disciples confess their dependence on God for all that they need and are to respond to others with the same love and grace He has shown to them.	Jesus asks that the disciples be sanctified by God's truth and made perfect together (vv. 17–19, 23). The disciples are to live in unity with one another and with God (vv. 21–23). This is only possible as they love and forgive each other.
"And do not lead us into temptation, but deliver us from the evil one" (v. 13)	Jesus asks that God guard the disciples from the evil one (v. 15). Though they are not of the world they are in the world and need God's protection.
"For Yours is the kingdom and the power and the glory forever" (v. 13). The disciples are to declare that all things belong to God for all time.	God has given Jesus authority over "all flesh" and made eternal life dependent upon belief that He has come from God Himself (vv. 8, 21, 25).

QUESTIONS FOR PERSONAL REFLECTION AND GROUP DISCUSSION

1. What Old Testament texts does Jesus' promise of the Spirit recall?
2. Jesus' claim to be "the Way, the Truth, and the Life" is drawn from what Old Testament passage?
3. How does Jesus' last *I am* statement resemble His first one?
4. What gifts are given when the word of Jesus is honored and the Spirit is present?
5. What type of "Son" does John portray Jesus to be?
6. John does not recount Jesus performing any exorcisms in his gospel? Why not?
7. What does Jesus mean when He says that the Spirit will convict the world of sin, righteousness, and judgment?
8. What is truth, according to John's presentation of Jesus?
9. How does Jesus' prayer to the Father resemble the prayer He teaches His disciples (Matt. 6:9–13)?

CHAPTER 8

BETRAYAL, DENIAL, AND PUBLIC TRIAL

John 18:1–19:16

Jesus has reenacted the Old Testament history of redemption in His life and ministry and now enters the hour for which He has come. All that Jesus has said, all that He has done, has led Him to this moment. The new creation of God begins with the betrayal by Judas, the rejection by Peter, and the interrogation by Pilate. It begins in the chaos and darkness of human unfaithfulness, self-preservation, and misunderstanding.

Jesus has time and again identified Himself to His disciples, the people, and the Jews. Plus, He has identified Himself to the world. Whereas John says that He is the Light that has entered the world, Jesus says that He is the One sent by the Father to bring eternal life to the world. Unequivocally, Jesus has said that He is the *I am* of eternal life. John's account of Jesus' passion records a sequence of unequivocal responses to the One who gives eternal life. These responses reveal the truth of John's initial statement that "He was in the world, and the world was made through Him, and the world did not know Him. He came to His own, and His own did not receive Him" (1:10, 11).

Betraying the I Am of Nazareth (John 18:1–11)

Judas leaves Jesus after the foot washing and prior to His teaching about the Holy Spirit. He is the son of perdition (17:12). The Greek word translated *perdition* (*apōleia*, ἡ ἀπώλεια) includes the notion of destruction. By leaving Jesus, Judas aligns himself with the one who opposes God's creative, life-giving work. Jesus is the Son of God who brings eternal life into the world while Judas is the son of destruction whose betrayal represents a rejection of that life and acceptance of the status quo. Judas has become a disciple of destruction who, in ignorance, has chosen the death of the world to the life of God.

When Jesus had spoken these words, He went out with His disciples over the Brook Kidron, where there was a garden, which He and His disciples entered. And Judas, who betrayed Him, also knew the place; for Jesus often met there with His disciples. Then Judas, having received a detachment of troops, and officers from the chief priests and Pharisees, came there with lanterns, torches, and weapons (vv. 1–3).

Jesus leaves the city and leads His disciples to a garden where they often gathered together. The garden is descriptive of a place where vegetables and flowers were planted and grown. At the same time, Judas leads a cohort of soldiers and officials to the same place. In the Roman army a cohort was generally a tenth of a legion or about 500 men. Here John uses the term to describe a non-specific number of soldiers. The assemblage that arrives to arrest Jesus is comprised of several groups—a detachment of Roman soldiers and servants or officials of the chief priests and of the Pharisees. Jesus

THE CHIEF PRIESTS

Who were the chief priests (*hoi archiereis*, οἱ ἀρχιερεῖς) who sent the officials to arrest Jesus? They were permanent members of the temple who comprised a court of law and ruled on matters related to the priesthood as well as the giving of offerings and sacrifices. They included the captain of the temple, the leaders of the weekly and daily courses (groups of priests assigned regular temple functions for short periods of time), supervisors of the temple, and the treasurers of the temple.

- The captain of the temple assisted the high priest with certain ceremonial duties and sometimes substituted for the high priest. He supervised the system of sacrifice and served as the chief of police. Often, the captain of the temple succeeded the high priest in office.
- The leaders of the courses were priests who directed those who came from around the country to serve at the temple once every twenty-four weeks.
- Seven priests served as supervisors and gave daily assignments to priests, oversaw the music and worship, and who maintained the baths for purification.
- Three treasurers received the monetary gifts to the temple, administered the temple tax, approved expenditures for the sacrifices and maintenance of the temple, and kept inventory of the temple possessions.

All of these men enjoyed high rank not only among the people but also among the lower classes of priests and exercised considerable authority on all matters related to the temple.

and His closest followers converge upon the garden about the same time as Judas and those charged with Jesus' arrest. These soldiers and officials wield weapons; they regard Jesus as a potentially dangerous criminal.

> *Jesus therefore, knowing all things that would come upon Him, went forward and said to them, "Whom are you seeking?" They answered Him, "Jesus of Nazareth." Jesus said to them, "I am He." And Judas, who betrayed Him, also stood with them. Now when He said to them, "I am He," they drew back and fell to the ground. Then He asked them again, "Whom are you seeking?" And they said, "Jesus of Nazareth." Jesus answered, "I have told you that I am He. Therefore, if you seek Me, let these go their way," that the saying might be fulfilled which He spoke, "Of those whom You gave Me I have lost none" (vv. 4–9).*

These verses reveal John's eye for irony: Jesus is found by a detail of soldiers, officials, Pharisees, and one unfaithful disciple yet none of them seem to recognize Him. John emphasizes Judas' complicity in the arrest by twice describing him as the one who betrayed Him (vv. 2, 5) and observing that he stands with the detail rather than with Jesus.

Jesus twice acknowledges He is the One they seek by saying, "I am" (vv. 5, 7). In so doing, He gives binding testimony about Himself. He is the One who has identified Himself with the God of Moses—the *I am* who will deliv-

---

THE SEVEN *I AM* STATEMENTS

The Gospel of John reveals Jesus to be:

1. The Bread of Life (6:35)
2. The Light of the World (8:12)
3. Before Abraham (8:58)
4. The Good Shepherd (10:11)
5. The Resurrection and the Life (11:25)
6. The Way, Truth, and Life (14:6)
7. The Vine of the Branches (15:5)

Together, these *I am* statements reveal Jesus Christ as the *I am* of eternal life. As such He is handed over to the high priest and the Roman governor to be put to death with thieves.

er the people from their bondage in Egypt (Ex. 3:14). The *I am* will be bound and delivered to the high priest, the successor to Moses (vv. 12, 13).

The collapse of the detail upon the ground is viewed by some as an inadvertent act of worship; it is certainly a reflex of uncertainty and fear. The men misunderstand Jesus and, as a result, they fear Him. The Jewish officials and representatives who are present likely have heard that Jesus is a sinner who has a demon and performs His miracles by such power (8:37–59, see vv. 48–52). This causes them to fear Him.

The saying to which John refers is Jesus' own prayerful assertion to the Father that He has kept all those given to Him except the son of destruction (17:12).

> *Then Simon Peter, having a sword, drew it and struck the high priest's servant, and cut off his right ear. The servant's name was Malchus. So Jesus said to Peter, "Put your sword into the sheath. Shall I not drink the cup which My Father has given Me?" (vv. 10, 11).*

The members of the detail are not the only ones who fear. Peter reacts with fear to the soldiers by striking out with a sword at a servant of the high priest. Being a fisherman, it is not surprising that he carries a knife-like tool with him. The servant of the high priest was a man of high position who possessed considerable authority in his own right given his relation to the religious leader of the people. By assaulting this man, Peter places himself in jeopardy of official reprisal. Jesus rebukes him for his action: "Shall I not drink the cup which My Father has given Me?" If Jesus is the *I am* who has come to deliver God's people, He will do so through suffering and death. If a person is to drink the blood of Jesus—the figure of speech depicting faith in Christ's death and resurrection (6:53–55)—Jesus must first drink from the cup His Father gives Him. This cup is a figure of Jesus' suffering and death.

The specific details of this passage strongly indicate an eyewitness report. The description of the place, the different people present, the cohort's questions and Jesus' responses, and the precise description of Peter's action as he draws out the knife, thrusts it, and severs the right ear of a man named Malchus, all point to the recollection of one who was present at the time. This is true for John's full account of the arrest, execution, and resurrection of Jesus. His description of time and place, dialogue, and attention to detail in the passion narrative suggest that he recalled from his own memory what happened.

THE PATTERN OF JESUS CHRIST'S BETRAYAL

John 18:1–11 can be outlined as a chiasmus that depicts Jesus as the *I am* who possesses all authority as well as the man from Nazareth who is about to be arrested (v. 12). As the *I am*, Jesus leads the disciples to the garden and commands Peter to put away his sword; the cohort falls to the ground in His presence even as He commands the release of the disciples. Despite being the *I am*, Jesus is also the man from Nazareth (1:45) who will be led away to the high priest. In addition to this, Judas and Peter represent the two prevailing responses to Jesus at this time. Judas rejects Jesus and leads others against Him while Peter is afraid and acts upon his fear.

A. Jesus leads His disciples to the garden (v. 1).
  A1. Judas leads the soldiers, officials and Pharisees to the garden (vv. 2, 3).
B. Jesus knows all things and asks, "Whom do you seek?" (v. 4).
  The detail responds, "Jesus of Nazareth" (v. 5).
  "I am" (v. 5).
  The *I am* causes the detail to fall to the ground (v. 6).
B1. Jesus asks, "Whom do you seek?" (v. 7).
  The detail responds, "Jesus of Nazareth" (v. 7).
  "I am" (v. 8)
  The *I am* releases the disciples (vv. 8, 9).
C. Peter draws his sword and attacks Malchus (v. 10).
  C1. Jesus commands Peter to return his sword to its sheath and submits to arrest (v. 11).

Peter Denies Jesus (John 18:12–27)

Jesus is taken first to Annas the former high priest and the patriarch of the high priesthood at this time. Later He is taken to Caiaphas, who has already prophesied that Jesus should die (11:45–53). Peter and an unnamed disciple follow and gain access to the high priest's court because that disciple is known to the high priest. Peter follows Jesus yet denies knowing Him. When a girl-servant of the high priest asks if he is a disciple of Jesus, he says, "I am not," thus denying his relationship to Jesus and contradicting what Jesus has said about Himself. Though Jesus answers the armed detail with a positive affirmation of His identity ("I am"), Peter dissembles before the girl who watches the gate ("I am not").

Peter's cold denial matches the cold conditions of the night. Peter stands with the servants and officers around a fire (v. 18) just as Judas stood with the armed detail when Jesus was arrested (v. 5). John's description of these two scenes shows that Jesus experiences rejection not only from the most distant of His disciples but also from the closest.

> *Then the detachment of troops and the captain and the officers*
> *of the Jews arrested Jesus and bound Him (v. 12).*

The cohort of soldiers and their commander along with officials of the Sanhedrin seize and bind Jesus. These people are acting on behalf of the temple leadership. Thus, according to John, the leaders of the temple—those whom John identifies as "the Jews"—are responsible for the arrest of Jesus.

> *And they led Him away to Annas first, for he was the father-in-*
> *law of Caiaphas who was high priest that year. Now it was*
> *Caiaphas who advised the Jews that it was expedient that one*
> *man should die for the people (vv. 13, 14).*

As the high priest, Caiaphas was the reigning member of the nation in the absence of a king. By virtue of his divine authorization to make atonement for the nation (Ex. 30:10; Lev. 16) and the vestments he wore on special occasions, he was unique among the people and was granted several privileges that no other man possessed. For instance, only he could enter the Most Holy Place and only he could participate in temple sacrifices any time he chose. In addition, he served as the president of the Sanhedrin, the most important court among the people. Along with these privileges, however, came strict responsibilities, the most important being unequivocal adherence to special purity regulations.

Jesus is first taken to Annas, the father-in-law of Caiaphas. This would not be unusual since Annas was a former high priest (A.D. 6–15) who, like all former high priests, retained the title and authority of the office even after leaving it. One of the qualifications for the high priesthood was marriage to a daughter of a priest. The fact that Caiaphas had married Annas' daughter reveals the ensconced power and elevated status of this ruling family.

Caiaphas has already advised the high priests that the death of one man benefits the people and has prophesied that Jesus should die on their behalf (11:49–53). John repeats this fact since it shows Caiaphas has prophesied greater truth than he knows.

> *And Simon Peter followed Jesus, and so did another disciple.*
> *Now that disciple was known to the high priest, and went with*
> *Jesus into the courtyard of the high priest. But Peter stood at the*

door outside. Then the other disciple, who was known to the
high priest, went out and spoke to her who kept the door, and
brought Peter in (vv. 15, 16).

The unnamed disciple gains access for himself and Peter in the courtyard of
the high priest. The fact that he is known indicates there is a personal, professional, or familial relationship between them.

> *Then the servant girl who kept the door said to Peter, "You are*
> *not also one of this Man's disciples, are you?" He said, "I am*
> *not." Now the servants and officers who had made a fire of coals*
> *stood there, for it was cold, and they warmed themselves. And*
> *Peter stood with them and warmed himself (vv. 17, 18).*

The girl who watches the gate to the courtyard asks Peter if he is with Jesus.
He gives his first denial by exclaiming, "I am not." John reports that Peter
stands with the girl and others around a charcoal fire when he denies a relationship with Jesus. He follows Judas' example in standing with others while
denying Jesus (18:5).

> *The high priest then asked Jesus about His disciples and His doc-*
> *trine. Jesus answered him, "I spoke openly to the world. I always*
> *taught in synagogues and in the temple, where the Jews always*
> *meet, and in secret I have said nothing. Why do you ask Me? Ask*
> *those who have heard Me what I said to them. Indeed they know*
> *what I said." And when He had said these things, one of the offi-*
> *cers who stood by struck Jesus with the palm of his hand, saying,*
> *"Do You answer the high priest like that?" Jesus answered him,*
> *"If I have spoken evil, bear witness of the evil; but if well, why*
> *do you strike Me?" Then Annas sent Him bound to Caiaphas the*
> *high priest (vv. 19–24).*

Caiaphas wants to know about Jesus' disciples and teaching. How large is His
following? What is the content of His teaching? Jesus says that His teaching is
common knowledge: "I have spoken openly to the world . . . in secret I have
said nothing." Since His testimony has not been accepted by the leadership up
to this point, why should it be accepted now? (8:13–18). Jesus points the high
priest to those who have heard Him teach and have seen His miracles.

Jesus is slapped by an official for His remark and then asks how He has
spoken wrongly. Because Annas is a former high priest and still one of the

highest ranking men among the Jewish people, Jesus' response is interpreted as contemptible. By asking the question, however, He simply places responsibility upon Annas to bring his own evidence in support of the arrest and calls the official to account for his action. Earlier, when confronted by certain Jews who wanted to stone Him, Jesus said, "Many good works I have shown you from My Father. For which of those works do you stone Me?" (10:32). Jesus has done good works that support His teaching about His relation to His Father. The burden of proof for any wrong that He has spoken or done rests with His accusers.

> *Now Simon Peter stood and warmed himself. Therefore they said to him, "You are not also one of His disciples, are you?" He denied it and said, "I am not!" One of the servants of the high priest, a relative of him whose ear Peter cut off, said, "Did I not see you in the garden with Him?" Peter then denied again; and immediately a rooster crowed (vv. 25–27).*

Jesus will not testify about Himself; He testifies to God His Father and will leave it to others to give testimony about Him and His teaching. Will others testify? While Jesus points Annas to the testimony of those who have heard Him, John shows such testimony is mute in the mouth of one of His closest disciples. Peter repeats his denial, "I am not", when asked if he is one of Jesus' disciples (v. 25). A disciple is a learner, one who learns from his teacher or master, yet Peter says that he is not a disciple of Jesus. Unwilling to identify himself as a disciple, Peter is unwilling to testify to what he learned from Jesus. This denial is followed by a third one when a relative of the man Peter attacked in the garden asks if he had been there with Jesus. In his three denials, Peter claims ignorance of Jesus. In doing so, he claims the status he had in life before He met Jesus and was given a new name. Peter chooses to be Simon again. John reports that a rooster crowed at that moment, bringing to an end a sequence of events in which Jesus experiences betrayal and denial by those closest to Him. John leaves the reader with an implied question, "Who will testify for Jesus?"

The Roman Governor and the King of the Jews (John 18:28–19:16)

John's passion narrative has moved from a garden outside the city to the courtyard of the high priest to the residence of the Roman governor. The account of Jesus before the Roman governor—His interrogation, flogging and deliverance to crucifixion—is advanced by seven questions that he poses to Jesus. Though Jesus refused to give testimony concerning Himself to the high priest, He acknowledges His Kingship to Pilate.

> *Then they led Jesus from Caiaphas to the Praetorium, and it was early morning. But they themselves did not go into the Praetorium, lest they should be defiled, but that they might eat the Passover. Pilate then went out to them and said, "What accusation do you bring against this Man?" They answered and said to him, "If He were not an evildoer, we would not have delivered Him up to you." Then Pilate said to them, "You take Him and judge Him according to your law." Therefore the Jews said to him, "It is not lawful for us to put anyone to death," that the saying of Jesus might be fulfilled which He spoke, signifying by what death He would die (vv. 28–32).*

Jesus is led from Caiaphas' house to the governor's residence to be judged by Pontius Pilate. Though his permanent residence and headquarters were located in Caesarea Maritima on the Mediterranean coast, Pilate traveled to Jerusalem for the high festivals to personally oversee security. The Praetorium in Jerusalem was likely located in Herod's palace on the west side of the city.

The Jewish leaders will not enter the Praetorium. To enter the residence of a Gentile, which they consider an impure place, would result in ritual impurity through transference and prevent them from participating in the Passover. More generally, any man or woman who was ritually impure was excluded from participating in the services and ceremonies of the temple.

Before Pilate asks Jesus any questions, however, he wants to know the nature of the specific charge made against Him. He is told that Jesus is an evildoer. Jesus has earlier defended Himself against this charge before Annas. When He is struck by one of his officials, He asks, "If I have spoken evil, bear witness of the evil, but if well, why do you strike Me?" (v. 23). The charge stems from their view that Jesus is a false prophet who performs miracles by the power of the devil. Even though His works are good, the Jews want to stone Him for blasphemy (10:31–33). Their assertion that He does evil contradicts the evidence of the signs which reveal Jesus doing good for others. The leaders have rejected His testimony that He has come from God and God is His Father and thus misunderstand His miracles. In their eyes Jesus does evil. This charge carries no weight with Pilate.

Since the charge that Jesus is an evildoer appears to be an intra-faith issue, having to do with their understanding of His ministry, Pilate initially refuses

THE ROMAN GOVERNOR

The word for governor can signify one of three types of Roman officials: a military ruler over an imperial province (Quirinius in Syria; Luke 2:2), a combination civil and military ruler called a proconsul who administered a senatorial province (Gallio in Achaia; Acts 18:12), or a procurator, which is a military ruler over a provincial district and who commanded an auxiliary of troops there (Felix and Festus; Acts 23:24, 24:27). The governor was responsible for enforcing Roman law in a province or district, collecting taxes, and maintaining stability among the people.

to take it up. When they suggest that Jesus has committed a capital offense by observing that they cannot put Him to death, Pilate apparently reconsiders. John views their argument as prophetic. First, the Jews could not carry out executions under Roman governance. Second, if they could, such an execution would be by stoning. This would not support Jesus' claims that in death, He would be lifted up (3:14; 8:28; 12:32–33). Thus, their release of Jesus to the Romans made possible the fulfillment of His words since only Romans could perform the torture of crucifixion. Crucifixion was reserved for traitors to the state and those guilty of violent crimes. Only the government could carry out its brutal penalty.

John introduces the Roman governor simply as "Pilate." He does not give his title or any background information. He assumes that his readers know about this man. So, who is he? Pilate was the Roman procurator (A.D. 26–36) who the synoptic Gospels depict quelling unrest among the people by relenting to their demands for Jesus' death (Matt. 27:24; Mark 5:15; Luke 23:1–2, 18–25) though he believes Jesus is innocent of the accusations they make. He attempts to shift responsibility to others by symbolically washing his hands of the matter at the insistence of his wife (Matt. 27:19–25) and by sending Jesus to Herod to be tried (Luke 23:6–12). In the writings of the Jewish historian Josephus, Pilate is depicted as a harsh and brutal official who was antagonistic to the faith and customs of the Jewish people. He writes that Pilate one time had banners bearing the image of the emperor brought into the Jerusalem in direct violation of Jewish law and another time incited a riot by using money from the temple to build an aqueduct in the city (*Antiquities of the Jews* 18.3.1–2; *The Jewish War* 2.9.2–4; see Philo's *De legatione ad Gaium* 299–305). He eventually was recalled to Rome when he approved a massacre of Samaritans who were on their way to worship at Mount Gerizim (*Antiquities of the Jews* 18.4.1–2).

Then Pilate entered the Praetorium again, called Jesus, and said to Him, "Are You the King of the Jews?" Jesus answered him, "Are you speaking for yourself about this, or did others tell you this concerning Me?" Pilate answered, "Am I a Jew? Your own nation and the chief priests have delivered You to me. What have You done?" Jesus answered, "My kingdom is not of this world. If My kingdom were of this world, My servants would fight, so that I should not be delivered to the Jews; but now My kingdom is not from here" (vv. 33–36).

Inside the Praetorium, away from the high priest's officials, Pilate first asks Jesus, "Are you the King of the Jews?" The popular view of Jesus has reached his ears (12:13, 15). He certainly would not have been deaf to the chants of the people during His entry into Jerusalem. When Jesus counters, "Are you speaking for yourself?" the governor responds with indignation, "Am I a Jew?" Jesus typically responds to a question with a question as He does here with Pilate. Pilate's response reveals that He does not identify with Jesus or with His people. He points to their essential difference. Jesus is a Jew and He is not. Why have the religious leaders brought these charges against Him?

Pilate then asks, "What have You done?" likely referring to the charge that Jesus does evil. Speaking the language that Pilate understands, Jesus addresses Pilate's initial question and says that His kingdom is not an earthly kingdom. If Pilate has nothing in common with Jesus, as implied in his previous question, then Jesus' kingdom resembles nothing that is familiar to Pilate. The things He has done and now does represent an economy of works different from that of Rome or any other human system or authority. Jesus has done the work of His Father (8:29; 10:32; 14:10; 17:4). This means that He is not the kind of king that the people anticipate (6:15) and He is not a threat to Pilate. If His kingdom were like Caesar's, His servants would already be fighting on His behalf.

What is the kingdom of which Jesus speaks? It is not the exercise of military or political power nor is it the rule of human law. It is the conjunction of God's Word and Spirit in the lives of all who identify with Jesus and keep His teaching. The kingdom transcends generation and place and historical situation. Whenever and wherever the Word and Spirit join in the lives of those who believe in Jesus and call God Father the kingdom is manifested in proclamation and miracles. Though Jesus' disciples will remain in the world they will have His words and the Spirit the Father sends at His urging (14:15–18, 26; 15:26, 27; 16:13, 14) so they can continue the works of the king (14:12–14).

Pilate therefore said to Him, "Are You a king then?" Jesus
answered, "You say rightly that I am a king. For this cause I was
born, and for this cause I have come into the world, that I should
bear witness to the truth. Everyone who is of the truth hears My
voice" (v. 37).

Pilate asks Jesus a second time, "Are you a king then?" And for a second time
Jesus affirms His kingship to Pilate. As with Nicodemus and the woman at
the well the conversation with Pilate results with insight into His identity.
Jesus says that He has come into the world to bear witness to the truth. He
reveals that the purpose of His life and ministry is to serve the cause of the
One who has sent Him into the world. Again, Pilate would not feel threatened by this kind of king.

Pilate said to Him, "What is truth?" And when he had said this,
he went out again to the Jews, and said to them, "I find no fault
in Him at all" (v. 38).

Pilate responds to Jesus by asking, "What is truth?" (v. 38). Though the question appears to be rhetorical—Pilate leaves without waiting for Jesus'
answer—it is the gospel's quintessential question. Jesus, who is the Word of
God that has come into the world and has described Himself as the Way,
Truth, and Life of God, stands before Pilate but is not recognized by him. He
is God's Word through which His disciples have life and He will send the
Spirit of Truth to them once He has left them. The world to which Pilate
belongs does not recognize the One who has come to bring light into it. John
reveals that truth is not a philosophical concept or even a virtue but the very
word of God exemplified in Jesus. So far, Pilate does not find reason to condemn Jesus. The grammar is emphatic and the Greek could be translated: "I
find no trace of a crime in Him."

As a king, Jesus has entered the world not to condemn it or rule with raw
authority and power but to provide a witness to the intention of God. What
is His intention? It is God's desire to be known as the Father to Israel and all
the world. Jesus has completely manifested this truth.

"But you have a custom that I should release someone to you at
the Passover. Do you therefore want me to release to you the
King of the Jews?" Then they all cried again, saying, "Not this
Man, but Barabbas!" Now Barabbas was a robber (vv. 39, 40).

Pilate uses this occasion to provoke the officials of the high priest. He asks them if they would rather Jesus, the "King of the Jews," be released or the robber Barabbas. The Greek word translated *robber* (*lēstēs*) indicates that Barabbas was a violent man. They respond by asking for Barabbas and not "this man." Though Jesus has just asserted that He is a king to Pilate (v. 37), He is regarded as a common man by the temple leadership. The leaders loudly shout for Barabbas to be released rather than Jesus. The Greek word *kraugazō* (κραυγάζω) is here translated "cried." This is a relatively uncommon word in the New Testament. It describes the leaders' response in this passage (also 19:6, 12). John has already used *kraugazō* to describe the people's response to Jesus when He entered Jerusalem (11:43; 12:13). Thus, the welcome acclamation of "King of Israel" that Jesus received upon entering the city prior to Passover has turned to denunciation. John's use of this verb sharply highlights the change in public response to Jesus in the span of a few days.

The custom of releasing a prisoner at the Passover, mentioned here, is attested in extra-biblical Jewish literature. The Greek word for *custom* used by John (*synētheia*, ἡ συνήθεια) is uncommon in the New Testament and simply suggests a practice. It does not indicate how permanent or longstanding the practice was or anything about its nature. Such practices are known to have occurred during festivals in other cultures of the period, as well.

> *So then Pilate took Jesus and scourged Him. And the soldiers twisted a crown of thorns and put it on His head, and they put on Him a purple robe. Then they said, "Hail, King of the Jews!" And they struck Him with their hands. Pilate then went out again, and said to them, "Behold, I am bringing Him out to you, that you may know that I find no fault in Him" (vv. 1–4).*

The Romans dress Jesus in purple like a king. Since purple dye was expensive to manufacture, it was used to color clothing only worn by the wealthy and powerful. The crown and purple robe would have been part of the ceremonial dress for a Roman general or proconsul during a public celebration of a successful military campaign. Such a man would have exulted in the adulation of the people. Jesus appears to be anything but a victorious king at this moment. He is dressed up, derided, and slapped by the soldiers. Yet John includes this description to show that Jesus' victory is won with awful humility.

> *Then Jesus came out, wearing the crown of thorns and the purple robe. And Pilate said to them, "Behold the Man!" Therefore,*

when the chief priests and officers saw Him, they cried out, say-
ing, "Crucify Him, crucify Him!" Pilate said to them, "You take
Him and crucify Him, for I find no fault in Him." The Jews
answered him, "We have a law, and according to our law He
ought to die, because He made Himself the Son of God" (vv. 5–7).

Pilate presents Jesus as a beaten mock king to the leaders. Though he finds Jesus innocent of any crime, he uses the occasion to display the talon-like grip of power that Rome possessed over the Jews. This is how Rome honors their king.

To emphasize Pilate's callous attitude to Jesus, John reports that he has Jesus whipped (*mastigoō*, μαστιγόω) at this time. The verb *mastigoō* describes the Roman act of scourging, a form of severe punishment that usually preceded crucifixion and often resulted in death. Why does Pilate subject Jesus to this tortuous experience if he has detected no crime in Him? He may have done so to appease the Jewish leaders or he may have attempted to elicit confession of a crime. In any case, such punishment reveals that the possibility of crucifixion is already in Pilate's mind since it usually preceded crucifixion. After having Jesus whipped inside the Praetorium, Pilate brings Jesus outside where he pronounces, "See, the Man." Like the temple leadership, Pilate deduces nothing extraordinary about Jesus.

Early in his gospel, John observes that Jesus knew all men and "knew what was in man" (2:24, 25). This knowledge was grounded in the fact that Jesus was the Word of God that had become flesh to reveal the glory of God to the world (1:14). He knows mankind because he is a fellow human being. John records Pilate's remark to remind his readers that Jesus is indeed a man who reveals God's glory by giving His flesh and blood so that all men and women might experience eternal life (6:51–57). Thus, Pilate's presentation of the beaten Jesus to the leaders is a counterpoise to John the Baptist's declaration of Jesus at the beginning of His ministry. At the Jordan River the Baptist proclaims, "See, the Lamb of God who takes away the sin of the world" (1:29). He makes a knowing and revelatory confession of Jesus as God's offering for sin. Pilate makes an unknowing and, yet, revelatory confession of Jesus when he says, "See, the Man." This beaten man is God's prepared Lamb given for lost humanity.

The perverse parody of Jesus by the Roman soldiers gives way to loud shouts (*kraugazō*) for His crucifixion. Pilate refuses to act without greater cause. (Though he possesses the power to order crucifixion, he can do so only under certain conditions.) By now, however, the reason given for His execution has sharpened: Jesus must die not because He is "an evildoer" but

JESUS CHRIST, THE DIVINE KING

Pilate cannot casually dismiss Jesus' claim to be both a king and the Son of God. It is one thing for Jesus to claim to be a king since there were a number of rulers throughout the empire like Herod Antipas who were permitted to use this title. It is altogether another thing to claim to be God's Son.

The Romans first began to assign an exalted status to their emperors with Julius Caesar in 42 B.C. when they posthumously proclaimed him to be *divus Iulius* "Deified Julius." At the same time his son Augustus became known as *divi filius* "the son of the Deified One." Tiberius Caesar made emperor worship permanent when he declared Augustus a god like his father Julius. This meant that Tiberius became *divi filius* like his father since he, too, was the son of the Deified One. Though the presumption and belief of the people regarding the divinity of their emperors is difficult to measure, without question they gave formal and public reverence to them. Pilate cannot ignore someone who acknowledges a kingdom, is adulated as a king by the people, and professes to be the Son of God—that is, a deity. Such a person was a rival to Caesar.

because He has made Himself to be the Son of God. The leaders refer to Leviticus (24:16) and argue that Jesus should die for blasphemy. This is not a new charge. In fact, they have accused Him of blasphemy before by saying "You, being a Man, make Yourself God" (10:33; also 5:18). Blasphemy may be thought of as impudent speech or action toward God that degrades His holiness. In their view, the fact that Jesus identifies Himself with God, claims that the words He speaks are God's words and the miracles He performs are God's works, He impugns God's holiness because He is only a man.

> *Therefore, when Pilate heard that saying, he was the more*
> *afraid, and went again into the Praetorium, and said to Jesus,*
> *"Where are You from?" But Jesus gave him no answer (vv. 8, 9).*

As Caesar's designated representative in Judea Pilate is responsible for enforcing public allegiance to the emperor. Recalling Jesus' earlier comment that His kingdom is not one of this world, he immediately acts by asking Jesus, "Where are you from?" Of course, the question is ironic since throughout the gospel John has recorded Jesus as saying that He has come from His Father and will return to His Father. Indeed, His return to His Father is inevitable—with Pilate's assistance.

> *Then Pilate said to Him, "Are You not speaking to me? Do You*
> *not know that I have power to crucify You, and power to release*
> *You?" Jesus answered, "You could have no power at all against*
> *Me unless it had been given you from above. Therefore the one*
> *who delivered Me to you has the greater sin" (vv. 10, 11).*

When Jesus refuses to answer, he asks, "Do you not know that I have the power to crucify You, and the power to release You?" Pilate believes that he has the power of life and death. Jesus corrects him and says that he does not possess any power over Him except that given from above, that is, from God the Father (3:7). Pilate's authority is delegated authority. Jesus, however, knows all things (16:30), possesses authority over all flesh (17:2; also 16:37, 38; 17:6, 9), holds all things in His hands (3:35), and by the Spirit exercises divine authority over all creation (6:15–21). And it is Jesus, not Pilate, who has the authority to give eternal life (3:14–16, 36; 4:14; 5:21, 24, 26; 6:27, 40; 47; 8:12; 10:10, 28; 11:25; 12:49, 50; 14:6) and to execute judgment (5:22, 27; 8:16; 9:39; 12:47, 48).

Jesus does not say that Pilate is without sin; He says that the one who ordered Jesus brought to Pilate has the greater sin in that he has acted with knowledge. The high priest and temple leadership have rejected Jesus' words and works and, in this, they have rejected the testimony that He gives of God His Father. Jesus has already accused them of having sin because they claim to know God and His purposes, yet they reject Jesus' teaching and miracles (9:41). Why do they have greater sin? Because they have been given signs in which to believe. Pilate, however, has not been given any sign except that of Jesus the Man who stands before him.

> *From then on Pilate sought to release Him, but the Jews cried*
> *out, saying, "If you let this Man go, you are not Caesar's friend.*
> *Whoever makes himself a king speaks against Caesar" (v. 12).*

The imperfect tense of the verb *seek* (*zēteō*, ζητέω) indicates that Pilate tried time and again to release Jesus. He does not do so, however, because of the ominous shouts and the implied threat from the temple leaders. He cannot risk reports or rumors of treason to be broadcast abroad.

Though Pilate is not threatened by someone whose kingship is not of this earth, the temple leadership is threatened. They are the indigenous ruling body among the people due to their governance of the temple and the daily worship life of the people and they are not prepared to risk their position nor the institution in which they are entrenched for this pretender. This is why they voice support for Caesar. Caesar will maintain the status quo, but Jesus threatens life as usual. Though they have no formal right to appeal to Caesar, as Paul does when he is accused by the high priest leadership (Acts 25:1–12), their warning to Pilate is effective.

> *When Pilate therefore heard that saying, he brought Jesus out and sat down in the judgment seat in a place that is called The Pavement, but in Hebrew, Gabbatha (v. 13).*

Pilate responds to the implied threat of the Jewish leaders by bringing Jesus out to the judgment seat (*bēma*, βῆμα). The *bēma* was a raised platform located on the pavement (*lithostrōton*, λιθόστρωτον) upon which speakers and judges would speak or rule on matters concerning the state. It is a place of judgment. It is terribly ironic that Jesus who has declared that He does not judge or condemn (3:17; 8:15; 12:47) now stands in the place of condemnation.

> *Now it was the Preparation Day of the Passover, and about the sixth hour. And he said to the Jews, "Behold your King!" But they cried out, "Away with Him, away with Him! Crucify Him!" Pilate said to them, "Shall I crucify your King?" The chief priests answered, "We have no king but Caesar!" (vv. 14, 15).*

Jesus stands before the temple leaders at the time when the lambs are being slaughtered in the temple—about noon. As noted in the introduction, because thousands of people brought lambs for the Passover, sometimes not all were prepared in one day. Some were prepared on following days. Even though Jesus has eaten Passover with the disciples, the sacrifice and preparing of lambs seems to have continued during the week.[14] John makes note of this in order to show that the Lamb of God who takes away the sin of the world (1:29, 36) declared by the Baptist is being prepared as a sacrifice. He will be sacrificed to the shouts of crucifixion.

Pilate presents Jesus to the leaders as "Your King" (v. 14). He spites them by asking, "Shall I crucify your King?" and he gets the answer he wants. Rather than say, "Yes, crucify our king," they declare, "We have no king but Caesar" (v. 15). Pilate deftly has manipulated the events surrounding Jesus so that the high priest leadership makes a public confession of Caesar as their king. He has turned the veiled accusation of disloyalty to the emperor into a public declaration of the high priest's own loyalty. For this oath, Pilate gives the order for Jesus to be crucified. The Man who has acknowledged His Kingship to Pilate will die on a cross.

Once again, it is ironic that the temple leaders proclaim allegiance to the emperor who is considered the son of a god and reject the Son of God who as the Son of Man has predicted that He would be lifted up before the world (3:14–16; 8:28; 12:34). Upon hearing their pledge of loyalty, Pilate hands Jesus to his execution squad.

Then he delivered Him to them to be crucified. Then they took Jesus and led Him away (v. 16).

Verse	The Kingship Question or Statement	Verse	The Response
18:33	Pilate asks Jesus, "Are You the King of the Jews?"	18:36	Jesus answers, "My kingdom is not of this world . . . My kingdom is not from here."
18:37	Pilate wants confirmation, "Are You a king then?"	18:37	Jesus confirms that He is a king, "I am a king . . . I have come into the world that I should bear witness to the truth."
18:39	Pilate asks the high priests, "Do you want me to release the King of the Jews?"	18:40	"Not this Man." The high priests do not recognize Jesus as their king.
19:3	Roman soldiers mock Jesus, "Hail, King of the Jews."	19:3	Jesus is struck. The soldiers do not recognize Jesus as their king.
19:5	Pilate presents Jesus to the chief priests, "Behold, the Man."	19:6	The high priests cry, "Crucify Him." Pilate does not recognize Jesus as a true king.
19:12	The high priests threaten, "If you let this Man go you are not Caesar's friend. Whoever makes himself a king speaks against Caesar."	19:13	Pilate evaluates the implications of Jesus' claim to be a divine king.
19:14	Pilate presents Jesus to the chief priests, "Behold your King."	19:15	The high priests cry, "Crucify Him." Again, they reject Jesus as their king.
19:15	Pilate provokes, "Shall I crucify your King?"	19:15	The high priests respond, "We have no king but Caesar." They reject Jesus as king and replace Him with the Roman emperor.
19:19	Pilate places a sign on the cross: JESUS OF NAZARETH, THE KING OF THE JEWS	19:21	The high priests complain that Jesus claims to be a king but that they do not recognize Him as such.

Pilate gives Jesus to the detachment of soldiers who have responsibility for crucifixion. This type of execution was performed by those who had been trained for the brutal job.

A Question of Kingship

The primary issue during Jesus' interrogation by Pilate is His kingship. Is Jesus a king? The table shows how important this question is for John and for understanding the verdict ultimately given against Jesus.

The shaded row in the preceding table marks the turning point in this drama. When Pilate comes out of the Praetorium and declares, "Behold, your King" (19:14), his statement represents a shift from what he had said earlier, "Behold, the Man" (v. 5). Pilate is no more convinced that Jesus is a King than he was earlier; however, now he uses the charge of kingship to his advantage and provokes the Jewish leaders into saying that Caesar is their king.

QUESTIONS FOR PERSONAL REFLECTION AND GROUP DISCUSSION

1. What is the significance of Peter's three denials of Jesus?
2. Why would the Jewish leaders not enter Pilate's house?
3. What is central issue in Pilate's interrogation of Jesus?
4. Why can Pilate not ignore the charges made against Jesus?
5. How does Pilate expose the true allegiance of the Jewish leaders?

CHAPTER 9

DEATH, BURIAL, AND RESURRECTION

John 19:17–20:30

Jesus' crucifixion occurs at the time lambs were being sacrificed in the temple for Passover (19:14, 31, 42). These lambs were sacrificed in remembrance of the first Pass over when God protected the Hebrew people in Egypt from judgment. Then, the people killed their lambs, smeared the blood on the doorposts, and ate the meat in obedience to God's command (Ex. 12). The fact that Jesus was crucified at the same time the Passover lambs were being slaughtered means that Jesus is the Lamb of God who takes the judgment of God upon Himself and gives eternal life to His followers through His death. Moreover, what God did for righteous Abraham in providing a ram in the thicket (Gen. 22:9–14) He also does for unrighteous humanity by providing His own Lamb.

This section concludes John's record of Jesus' "hour." This hour, however, does not only include His death; it also includes His resurrection. John describes the resurrection of Jesus by recounting His appearances to a woman with a dubious past, Mary Magdalene; His fearful friends, the disciples; and Thomas, a disbelieving disciple. Just as the Day of the Lord is a temporal event of judgment and salvation, so also the hour of Jesus is one of judgment (crucifixion) and salvation (resurrection).

The Crucified King (John 19:17–24)

Throughout John's account of Jesus' passion, the reader is aware of Jesus' declaration that the Son of Man must be lifted up (3:13, 14; 8:28; 12:32). Jesus shows the majesty of His kingship through the exaltation of the Cross. For Him, there is no other way to receive the glory that He possessed with His Father in the beginning.

And He, bearing His cross, went out to a place called the Place of
a Skull, which is called in Hebrew, Golgotha, where they cruci-
fied Him, and two others with Him, one on either side, and Jesus
in the center (vv. 17, 18).

Jesus carries the crossbar weighing 75–125 pounds to Golgotha where it will
be attached to a fixed post driven into the ground. The Aramaic word for
Golgotha is *gulgaltā* "skull" and is translated into Latin by the word *calvaria*
"calvary."

Now Pilate wrote a title and put it on the cross. And the writing
was: JESUS OF NAZARETH, THE KING OF THE JEWS. Then
many of the Jews read this title, for the place where Jesus was
crucified was near the city; and it was written in Hebrew, Greek,
and Latin. Therefore the chief priests of the Jews said to Pilate,
"Do not write, 'The King of the Jews,' but, 'He said, "I am the
King of the Jews."'" Pilate answered, "What I have written, I
have written" (vv. 19–22).

It was common for a soldier to carry a placard as part of a processional to
the site of crucifixion that declared the name of the condemned man and the
crime for which he was being crucified. Pilate orders that it read "KING OF
THE JEWS," giving the official reason for Jesus' execution. He refuses to alter
the placard at the request of the leaders and, unwittingly, offers the final testimony to Jesus' identity. In fact, for John, Jesus is the rejected King of His
people. The solemn declaration of chapter one, "He came to His own, and
His own did not receive Him" (v. 11), is proven true.

The Jews demand that Pilate cease from declaring Jesus is the King of the
Jews. Pilate's response, however, indicates that his act is official and permanent.

Then the soldiers, when they had crucified Jesus, took His gar-
ments and made four parts, to each soldier a part, and also the
tunic. Now the tunic was without seam, woven from the top in
one piece. They said therefore among themselves, "Let us not
tear it, but cast lots for it, whose it shall be," that the Scripture
might be fulfilled which says: "They divided My garments
among them, And for My clothing they cast lots." Therefore, the
soldiers did these things (vv. 23, 24).

PSALM 22 AND THE CRUCIFIXION OF CHRIST

The first twenty-one verses of Psalm 22 describe the pathos of One who is a reproach to people and despised by them. He is poured out like water and His bones are out of joint (v. 14). He has been brought to the dust of death (v. 15). And, as John recalls, there are those who "divide My garments among them" (v. 17). These verses give a riveting description of Jesus' ordeal. Yet, the psalm does not end in despair. Verses 19–21 record the psalmist's cry for deliverance and conclude, "You have answered Me" (v. 21). This One who is despised by the people, who suffers pain to the point of death, and who has even His clothes taken and divided, calls out to God and is answered. As a result, the poor will be fed (v. 26) and God will be praised among the nations and by generations (vv. 27–31). According to Matthew and Mark, Jesus views His ordeal as a means by which God will be praised among the nations; according to John, Jesus' ordeal fulfills Scripture and happens so that God may be glorified (17:1, 2).

Jesus' death is of no consequence to the soldiers. It was common for soldiers to treat the clothing of condemned persons as spoils. They divide his clothes among themselves, taking care not to tear his tunic since it is made of one piece of cloth and has special value. The tunic was a linen or woolen undergarment that reached to the knees or ankles. Thus, they are far more careful with Jesus' undergarment than they have been in their treatment of Him.

John quotes from Psalm 22, finding fulfillment of this Scripture in the soldiers' self-interested behavior. He is not alone in seeing this psalm as an important passage of Scripture for understanding Jesus' passion. Matthew and Mark find an enactment of this psalm in Jesus' cry, "My God, My God, why have You forsaken Me?" (Matt. 27:46; Mark 15:34) since these are the very words with which it begins. By reciting this verse in the midst of His agony, Jesus reveals His great struggle and suffering as well as His ultimate hope and anticipation of victory. Unable to speak at any length given the delirium of pain He was enduring, Jesus refers to the entire passage through this one line. It is a passage that is not only about rejection and suffering but also is about victory.

The Command from the Cross (John 19:25–27)

Though Jesus' death means little to the soldiers, it is of momentous consequence to others, including three women all of whom are named *Mary* and the beloved disciple who is presumably John himself. These four stand by the cross. The honor of being the first to witness the Resurrection will go to

Mary Magdalene, one of the last to see Him die (20:11–18). As these who are closest to Jesus look upon Him on the cross, He charges them to look upon one another and care for each another. His words put into effect the new commandment He gave to His disciples to love one another (13:34, 35). People will know that they are related to Him by the love that they manifest to each other. That love will begin with the care Jesus' mother will show the beloved disciple and the love the beloved disciple will show His mother.

> *Now there stood by the cross of Jesus His mother, and His moth-*
> *er's sister, Mary the wife of Clopas, and Mary Magdalene (v. 25).*

Crucifixions were public spectacles intended to horrify everyone who looked upon the victims and to deter them from following such behavior. The women have not been deterred and have drawn close to the cross to express their grief.

> *When Jesus therefore saw His mother, and the disciple whom He*
> *loved standing by, He said to His mother, "Woman, behold your*
> *son!" Then He said to the disciple, "Behold your mother!" And*
> *from that hour that disciple took her to his own home (vv. 26, 27).*

At the wedding in Cana Jesus asks Mary why she wants His help: "What does your concern have to do with Me?" He tells her that His hour has not yet come. Jesus wants Mary to think about His identity and His purpose. Now that His hour has come, He tells her to find solace and a home with the disciple He loves. Both passages, one at the beginning of His ministry and one at the end, show His interest in and concern for her and for those who are closest to Him.

Early Christian tradition reports that Mary lived with John in Ephesus and that his burial place became the site of a Christian basilica in that city in the sixth century.

Jesus Thirsts (John 19:28–30)

In the final passage describing Jesus' crucifixion, John picks up the theme that he has developed through his gospel—knowledge versus ignorance. Jesus, "knowing that all things were now accomplished" in fulfillment of Scripture also thirsts. Neither the temple leadership, the Romans, nor the disciples understand the significance of the events that have come upon Jesus. They do not know the One they have put upon the cross and do not understand the meaning of His life and ministry. Jesus, however, in the midst of the agony of the Cross, knows that He has fulfilled God's purpose.

After this, Jesus, knowing that all things were now accomplished, that the Scripture might be fulfilled, said, "I thirst!" (v. 28).

Once again John sees a fulfillment of Psalm 22 in the events of the crucifixion and the words of Jesus. Jesus thirsts even as the psalmist says, "My strength is dried up like a potsherd, and My tongue clings to My jaws; You have brought Me to the dust of death" (v. 15). However, John does not record Jesus' expression of need, "I thirst," simply to underscore His suffering. Rather, His words recall the promise that He made to the woman at the well and the people at the temple during the feast (7:37, 38). To the woman He said, "Whoever drinks of the water that I shall give him will never thirst. But the water that I shall give him will become in him a fountain of water springing up into eternal life" (4:14). To the people at the temple He said, "If anyone thirsts, let him come to Me and drink. He who believes in Me, as the Scripture has said, out of his heart will flow rivers of living water" (7:37, 38). For John, the promise of Jesus is fulfilled only by the thirst that He experiences on their behalf. The fountain of water springing up into eternal life and the rivers of living water have their source in His passion and death.

Now a vessel full of sour wine was sitting there; and they filled a sponge with sour wine, put it on hyssop, and put it to His mouth (v. 29).

In response to Jesus' plea, a sponge is saturated with the wine vinegar that is usually drunk by the soldiers. It is lifted to His mouth. Here, again, John records a seemingly minor action not only because it shows human concern to Jesus' terrible need, but because it speaks of the first sign that Jesus performed at Cana in Galilee. There, He transformed the purification water in six stone jars into wine, revealing that He makes possible the marriage of God and humanity. The miracle signifies that the traditional purification rituals that made relationship between God and His people possible now find new sustaining expression in His life and ministry. The new wine of the relationship between God and humanity comes into existence when Jesus sucks the vinegar of human rejection. It is at this moment that John notes Jesus' final words on the cross, "It is finished," and records that He gave up His spirit.

*So when Jesus had received the sour wine, He said, "It is fin-
ished!" And bowing His head, He gave up His spirit (v. 30).*

It is significant that John does not say that Jesus gave up the Holy Spirit.
Throughout his gospel, John has been careful to specifically identify the Holy
Spirit with God the Father. For example, John the Baptist describes the Spirit
that comes upon Jesus as descending from heaven (1:32) and says later that
the Spirit is given by God (3:34). In addition to this, Jesus links the Spirit to
God's kingdom (3:5, 6) and the worship of God His Father (4:23, 24). In His
Passover discourse, Jesus describes the Spirit as another Paraclete who is sent
by His Father (14:16, 17; 15:16; 16:13). Most importantly, Jesus has served the
Father by doing what the Father does and speaking what the Father speaks.
How is this accomplished? It is accomplished by the Holy Spirit as implied
by Jesus' remarks in 8:29. The Holy Spirit remains with Jesus to enable Him
to accomplish the greatest task of His ministry, which is death on the cross.
Finally, John observes that those who believe in Jesus will receive the Holy
Spirit that Jesus likens to rivers of living water (7:38). To say that Jesus gives
up the spirit, without any further description, simply means that He died.
Jesus died a true death on the cross.

The Sacrificial Lamb and the Spirit of Grace (John 19:31–37)

Throughout his account of Jesus' passion, John emphasizes that Jesus was
crucified on the Day of Preparation (19:14, 31, 42) when the lambs were being
sacrificed in the temple as part of Passover. He does this in order to present
Jesus as God's Lamb who is sacrificed for the sins of the world, as announced
by John the Baptist (1:29). Here John shows that Jesus is unbroken. Just as
lambs and all other sacrificial animals brought to the temple had to be without defect or injury, so Jesus is whole as He is offered to God by the Roman
soldiers. They do not break His legs since He has already died. (John views
the scourging of Jesus as part of His "preparation," and, thus, does not present Him as a defective or injured sacrifice.) This complies with the divine
directive that prohibits the legs of the lambs from being broken (Ex. 12:46;
Num. 9:12).

> *Therefore, because it was the Preparation Day, that the bodies
> should not remain on the cross on the Sabbath (for that Sabbath
> was a high day), the Jews asked Pilate that their legs might be
> broken, and that they might be taken away (v. 31).*

According to the Pentateuch, the body of a person hung from a tree in punishment for "sin deserving of death" had to be removed before nightfall and buried that day (Deut. 21:23). The temple leadership asks Pilate to remove the bodies of the crucified men from the crosses since the Sabbath, which occurs on the holy day of Passover, begins that evening.

> *Then the soldiers came and broke the legs of the first and of the other who was crucified with Him (v. 32).*

It was common practice for soldiers to break the legs of victims of crucifixion to hasten their death. This was known as crucifracture. A man who could not push up with his legs to breathe in air would quickly die by asphyxiation. The Roman soldiers break the legs of the two men crucified alongside Jesus to hurry their deaths, but they do not break Jesus' legs since He is already dead.

> *But when they came to Jesus and saw that He was already dead, they did not break His legs. But one of the soldiers pierced His side with a spear, and immediately blood and water came out. And he who has seen has testified, and his testimony is true; and he knows that he is telling the truth, so that you may believe. For these things were done that the Scripture should be fulfilled, "Not one of His bones shall be broken." And again another Scripture says, "They shall look on Him whom they pierced" (vv. 33–37).*

A spear is thrust into His ribs to make sure Jesus is dead. John confirms the reality of His death by saying that he saw it happen. Writing in the deferential third person, he says, "He who has seen has testified, and his testimony is true; and he knows that he is telling the truth, so that you may believe." Throughout John's gospel Jesus urges the people to believe the truth of His teaching and, if not the teaching, the signs that He performs. John now urges those who read (or hear) his eyewitness testimony to believe. What are they to believe? That Jesus' death on the cross was not a terrible accident. Jesus died in fulfillment of Scripture according to the purpose of His Father.

In death, as in life, Jesus fulfills Scripture. Like the Passover lambs whose bones were not broken (Ex. 12:46; Num. 9:12), the bones of God's Lamb are not broken by the soldiers. What does this mean? According to Psalm 34 it means that though Jesus is condemned by Pilate and temple leaders, He is not condemned by God. The psalmist declares that God "guards all [the] bones" of the righteous so that "not one of them is broken," and He does not condemn anyone who trusts in Him (vv. 19–22). The unbroken Jesus upon the cross is God's righteous Man who, instead of being condemned, will be glorified by Him (17:2, 5).

The prophet Zechariah declares that God will "pour out" the "Spirit of grace and supplication" upon the House of David and "they will look on Me whom they pierced" (12:10). John sees a fulfillment of this verse in the Roman action at the cross. What John sees is not the simple action of the soldier's jab with his spear, however. In Zechariah's prophecy, God's Spirit of Grace is closely related to the One who is pierced. The people will mourn for this man and at that time "a fountain shall be opened for the house of David . . . for sin and for uncleanness" (13:1). The prophet goes on to say that the One who is pierced will be asked, "What are these wounds between your arms?" And he will say that he was wounded for his friends (v. 6). John recalls this passage in the piercing of Jesus at the cross because it highlights for him the convergence of Jesus' sacrifice and the work of the Spirit of Grace. The Spirit of Grace will be given as a result of the piercing of Jesus so the people may live in relationship with God. The fountain that cleanses sin is the work of the Spirit that restores people into a covenant fellowship with God through Jesus.

THE BLOOD AND WATER

A soldier with a spear draws blood and water from the lifeless body of Jesus. The water probably flowed from the wound first. John lists blood first to recall what Jesus said earlier in His ministry about His blood giving eternal life. The presence of blood and water may indicate acute heart failure. Most victims of crucifixion died of several related factors, including shock, exhaustive asphyxiation, and/or acute heart failure. John records these events to establish that Jesus died; He did not appear to die, but He died. In addition, the blood and water alludes to the life that He offers in His death. After feeding 5,000 men, Jesus declared to the Jews that His blood provides eternal life (6:53–56). And, throughout the gospel, water is related to eternal life and the work of the Spirit as well. To Nicodemus Jesus asserted that one must be born of water and the Spirit to enter the kingdom of God (3:5), and to the woman at the well He said that He offers living water that issues in eternal life (4:9–15). Whoever believes in Him will have "rivers of living water," which John says refers to the Holy Spirit (7:38, 39). By reporting that blood and water issue from Jesus' body, John gives definite testimony to His death as well as affirmation that eternal life comes through His sacrifice and by the Spirit.

Thus, John sees in the soldiers' actions after Jesus' death confirmation that He is the "Lamb of God who takes away the sin of the world." On the one hand, their restraint from breaking Jesus' legs shows Him to be righteous; on the other hand, the spear in His ribs shows that His death results in the release of the Spirit of God's grace to cleanse people of sin.

Burial in a Garden (John 19:38–42)

John describes Jesus' burial in detail. The attention he gives to the efforts of Joseph and Nicodemus is noteworthy. First, John continues to emphasize the death of Jesus. He died on a cross and His body was buried in an unused tomb in a garden. There can be no question on this matter. Any interpretation of Jesus' life and death that contends He did not die or only appeared to die is refuted by these facts. Second, he shows that though the disciples closest to Jesus are not with Him during His crucifixion or burial (except John) these two men of public standing, who would gain no benefit from identifying with a condemned man, come forward to honor Him in death.

> *After this, Joseph of Arimathea, being a disciple of Jesus, but secretly, for fear of the Jews, asked Pilate that he might take away the body of Jesus; and Pilate gave him permission. So he came and took the body of Jesus (v. 38).*

Joseph of Arimathea asks Pilate for possession of Jesus' body so that he may place it in a tomb. Luke describes him as "a council member, a good and just man" (23:50) and it is likely that he is a member of the Sanhedrin. He does so secretly "for fear of the Jews" (see 7:13; 9:22; 12:42). His fear suggests that the Jews are those who exercise unique authority in relation to his own as a member of this ruling body. This again points to the temple leadership. Joseph is afraid of those who have participated in Jesus' death and who could punish him for showing allegiance to Jesus by preparing His body for burial.

John shows his reverence for Jesus in these verses (vv. 38–42) by consistently speaking of the body of Jesus. He carefully avoids using the impersonal pronoun *it* and even refers to Jesus being placed in the tomb even though it was only His body that was placed there.

> *And Nicodemus, who at first came to Jesus by night, also came, bringing a mixture of myrrh and aloes, about a hundred pounds. Then they took the body of Jesus, and bound it in strips of linen with the spices, as the custom of the Jews is to bury (vv. 39–40).*

Nicodemus joins Joseph in preparing Jesus' body for burial by bringing a mixture of myrrh and aloes that would be sprinkled with the linen cloths used to bind the body. Since a Roman pound was twelve ounces, Nicodemus brings about seventy-five pounds. The spices were used to mask the odor of decay.

Nicodemus first approached Jesus at night, due to concern or fear of being identified with Him (3:1, 2), but later urged the temple leadership to listen to His teaching and consider the nature of His ministry (7:50–52). Now he shows honor to Jesus by caring for His body. John depicts Nicodemus as a man who moves from uncertainty to certainty in his identification with Jesus. By reporting his presence with Joseph of Arimathea at the tomb, John shows that the one who once came to Jesus at night (3:1, 2; 8:50; 19:39) now stands by Him in the day of His death.

John notes "the custom of the Jews" for those among his readership who were not familiar with Jewish burial practices.

> *Now in the place where He was crucified there was a garden,*
> *and in the garden a new tomb in which no one had yet been*
> *laid. So there they laid Jesus, because of the Jews' Preparation*
> *Day, for the tomb was nearby (vv. 41, 42).*

Having bound Jesus' body with linen cloths, they place it in a nearby, newly-hewn tomb in a garden. The amount of spices used to prepare Jesus' body and the fact that they place the body in such a tomb in a garden show the honor that these disciples have for Jesus. The rejected King of the Jews receives an honorable burial from them upon His death.

John is the only gospel writer to mention that the tomb in which Jesus is placed is located in a garden. This detail reveals his precise knowledge of the events of Jesus' death and burial. It also locates the place of God's new creation. The reality of eternal life and the beginning of this new creation that reverses the effects of Adam's disobedience in the first garden has an improbable origin in an obscure garden near the place of Jesus' crucifixion.

Resurrection in a Garden (John 20:1–18)

The first sign of the new creation is the resurrection of Jesus. Mary Magdalene, who is one of the last people to see Jesus alive as He suffers upon the cross, is the first to see Him alive after His resurrection. She becomes the first evangelist of the good news when she reports the empty tomb to Peter and the beloved disciple and speaks of the appearance of the Lord to all the disciples.

Now the first day of the week Mary Magdalene went to the tomb
early, while it was still dark, and saw that the stone had been
taken away from the tomb (v. 1).

Sunday morning before daybreak Mary finds Jesus' tomb unsealed. The stone has been rolled away. Many tombs had tracks that ran across the entrance in which large boulders were placed to keep out animals and weather. The boulder seems to have been dislodged from the track altogether.

Then she ran and came to Simon Peter, and to the other disciple,
whom Jesus loved, and said to them, "They have taken away the
Lord out of the tomb, and we do not know where they have laid
Him" (v. 2).

Mary tells Peter and the beloved disciple that "they" have taken the body. She likely refers to the temple leaders who would not want the location of Jesus' body to be known out of concern that the place would become a memorial for His followers.

In this verse John refers to the beloved disciple with the Greek word *philō* (φίλω) though at other times he uses the word *agapaō* (13:23; 19:26; 21:7, 20). Both verbs mean "to love" and John's use of both in reference to the disciple simply suggests that Jesus loved him as a friend like Lazarus (11:3, 36).

Throughout this passage Mary refers to Jesus as Lord (*kyrios*). The word means "master" or "owner" and was a term of honor. By the time that John wrote his gospel, it was common for Christians to refer to Jesus as Lord and understand by this a reference to His exalted status.

Peter therefore went out, and the other disciple, and were going
to the tomb. So they both ran together, and the other disciple
outran Peter and came to the tomb first. And he, stooping down
and looking in, saw the linen cloths lying there; yet he did not go
in. Then Simon Peter came, following him, and went into the
tomb; and he saw the linen cloths lying there, and the handker-
chief that had been around His head, not lying with the linen
cloths, but folded together in a place by itself (vv. 3–7).

The two disciples run to the tomb with the unnamed disciple arriving first but Peter going straight inside only to find the linen cloths lying in the space. The Greek indicates that the unnamed disciple bent over to get a better look inside. The description that John gives of the tomb provides convincing evidence that the body of Jesus had not been surreptitiously moved to another location. Had someone taken the body, the linen cloths would have been removed from the tomb with it. Moreover, the folded face cloth that was set apart from the bandages points to a deliberate act that was not furtive or hurried. The cloths are evidence of a remarkable event.

> *Then the other disciple, who came to the tomb first, went in also; and he saw and believed. For as yet they did not know the Scripture, that He must rise again from the dead. Then the disciples went away again to their own homes (vv. 8–10).*

PSALM 16

¹ Preserve me, O God, for in You I put my trust.
² O my soul, you have said to the LORD,
    "You are my Lord,
    My goodness is nothing apart from You."
³ As for the saints who are on the earth,
    "They are the excellent ones, in whom is all my delight."
⁴ Their sorrows shall be multiplied who hasten after another god;
    Their drink offerings of blood I will not offer,
    Nor take up their names on my lips.
⁵ O LORD, You are the portion of my inheritance and my cup;
    You maintain my lot.
⁶ The lines have fallen to me in pleasant places;
    Yes, I have a good inheritance.
⁷ I will bless the LORD who has given me counsel;
    My heart also instructs me in the night seasons.
⁸ I have set the LORD always before me;
    Because He is at my right hand I shall not be moved.
⁹ Therefore my heart is glad, and my glory rejoices;
    My flesh also will rest in hope.
¹⁰ For You will not leave my soul in Sheol,
    Nor will You allow Your Holy One to see corruption.
¹¹ You will show me the path of life;
    In Your presence is fullness of joy;
    At Your right hand are pleasures forevermore.

The beloved disciple believes that Jesus has resurrected. The evidence of the tomb causes him to recall and trust in the words that Jesus had spoken. Without fully understanding the witness of the Scriptures concerning Jesus' death and resurrection, this disciple understands the evidence of the linen cloths. He trusts the words that Jesus spoke to them about His departure and His return.

The Scripture to which John refers is Psalm 16. The psalmist expresses trust in God who has always been before him and who is at his right hand. He declares, "You will not leave my soul in Sheol, nor will You allow Your Holy One to see corruption" (v. 10). Instead, he will have life, joy, and eternal pleasure with God (v. 11). The disciples do not yet understand that this Scripture is descriptive of Jesus' resurrection. Nonetheless, for John the empty tomb reveals the truth of the psalm that God has delivered His Son and given Him life, joy, and pleasure. The beloved Son who pleases His Father, according to the unanimous testimony of the synoptic Gospels (Matt. 3:17; Mark 1:11; Luke 3:22), now receives pleasure from Him.

> *But Mary stood outside by the tomb weeping, and as she wept she stooped down and looked into the tomb. And she saw two angels in white sitting, one at the head and the other at the feet, where the body of Jesus had lain. Then they said to her, "Woman, why are you weeping?" She said to them, "Because they have taken away my Lord, and I do not know where they have laid Him" (vv. 11–13).*

Mary weeps at the tomb of Jesus just as Jesus wept at the tomb of Lazarus (11:35). She bends over to look inside like the disciple before her, and she sees (*theoreō*, θεωρέω) two angels. The Greek word for *see* indicates that though Mary sees the angels she does not perceive who they are. John uses the same verb to report Jesus' remarks that once He goes away the world and the disciples will not see Him anymore. Yet, with the help of the Holy Spirit, the disciples will indeed see Him (14:17, 19; 16:10, 16–19).

The fact that the angels are dressed in white is significant for John. Since a tomb was an unclean place according to the law, any person who came into contact with such a place was regarded as unclean (Num. 19:11–22). The white garments of the angels, however, represent the purity of these messengers from God. Their presence in the tomb suggests that God has overcome the impurity of death through the resurrection of His Son.

Mary continues to think that the temple leaders have taken the body of Jesus away so that the burial place does not become a shrine for His followers.

Now when she had said this, she turned around and saw Jesus
standing there, and did not know that it was Jesus. Jesus said to
her, "Woman, why are you weeping? Whom are you seeking?"
She, supposing Him to be the gardener, said to Him, "Sir, if You
have carried Him away, tell me where You have laid Him, and I
will take Him away" (vv. 14, 15).

Mary does not recognize Jesus. He asks the same question as the angels, "Woman, why are you weeping?" As He has done so many times before, according to John, Jesus asks a question to stimulate insight in the one with whom He speaks. By addressing Mary as "woman," Jesus uses a familiar and friendly term.

Because the tomb is in the garden, Mary thinks that Jesus is the gardener and he, perhaps, has removed the body.

Jesus said to her, "Mary!" She turned and said to Him,
"Rabboni!" (which is to say, Teacher). Jesus said to her, "Do not
cling to Me, for I have not yet ascended to My Father; but go to
My brethren and say to them, 'I am ascending to My Father and
your Father, and to My God and your God'" (vv. 16, 17).

Mary addresses Jesus as rabboni, a variant form of rabbi meaning "my master" not known to all of John's readers.

Jesus tells Mary to stop holding onto Him because "I have not yet ascended to My Father." What does this mean? Why should Mary release Him? The answer is that His mission is incomplete. Jesus said during His Passover discourse that He came from His Father and would one day return to His Father (13:1, 3; 16:10, 17, 28; 17:11; also 7:33). Jesus must return to the Father from whom He will receive the glory that was His in the beginning (17:5, 24). She is to tell the disciples that He goes up to His Father and, in doing so, fulfills all the words that He spoke to them. Furthermore, He calls them brothers, meaning that their relationship to Him translates into a relationship with God as their Father.

Mary Magdalene came and told the disciples that she had seen
the Lord, and that He had spoken these things to her (v. 18).

Mary is the first evangelist; she is the first person to proclaim the good news that Jesus is alive. The report that Jesus is victorious over the grave and has gone up to His Father as He prophesied is given by a woman who had experienced the disgrace of men but also the cleansing grace of the Son of Man.

Jesus Breathes the Spirit (John 20:19–23)

Jesus as the *I am* of eternal life appears to His disciples and breathes the Spirit of Life upon them. As in the beginning when God breathed the breath of life upon Adam and he became a living being (Gen. 2:7), so also Jesus breathes the Spirit upon these sons of Adam making them alive to God. The reality of death—the expulsion of Man from the immediate presence of God—is now trumped by the reality of the Spirit who brings the divine presence once again to His people.

> *Then, the same day at evening, being the first day of the week, when the doors were shut where the disciples were assembled, for fear of the Jews, Jesus came and stood in the midst, and said to them, "Peace be with you" (v. 19).*

The evening of Resurrection Day the disciples are sequestered together in fear of the Jews. They are afraid that what the temple leaders have done to Jesus will be done to them. They join many others who have been fearful of these men: Nicodemus who first approached Jesus at night (3:2; 7:50; 19:39), the parents of the man who was born blind (9:22), as well as unnamed rulers (12:42) including Joseph of Arimathea (19:38). The disciples have closed the doors to hide from these men. John gives a picture of the disciples hiding in the dark at the dawn of Christ's new creation.

John does not explain how Jesus came into the midst of the disciples. The absence of such an explanation points to a theophany or divine manifestation of God. The first word spoken by the resurrected Jesus to His disciples is "peace" (*eirēnē*). This is more than a simple greeting. Jesus is doing two things. First, He is calming the disciple's fears of the temple leaders as well as His startling appearance. Second, He is describing what He has accomplished in His death and resurrection. He brings peace to them. The enmity between God and mankind that has existed from the beginning due to the disobedience of Adam has come to an end. Yet, this is not all! The word *eirēnē* is related to the Hebrew *shalōm* that speaks of welfare and wholeness. As the subject of God's activity, *shalōm* represents the restoration of fellowship between God and humanity once enjoyed and then lost and the reinstatement of responsibility that was once abrogated. Jesus says to the disciples, "Peace belongs to you once more."

When He had said this, He showed them His hands and His side.
Then the disciples were glad when they saw the Lord (v. 20).

Jesus' initial action, like His initial word ("peace"), has dual significance. First, by showing them His wounds, Jesus proves to the disciples that He is alive. He is not a ghost or an apparition. He is alive and He stands in their midst. Second, He shows Himself as the Lamb who takes away the sins of the world. The marks that His body bears, and will forever bear, reveal the requirement of their peace with God.

The disciples respond with joy. As Jesus promised, they rejoice in the glory of God revealed in His resurrection from death (16:20, 22).

So Jesus said to them again, "Peace to you! As the Father has
sent Me, I also send you" (v. 21).

Jesus speaks "peace" to the disciples once again, affirming their reinstatement in the plans of God as in the beginning when He says that He sends them as He has been sent. To be restored to fellowship with God means to participate in God's work. Just as Adam was given responsibility in the garden (Gen. 2:19, 20), so also the disciples are given responsibility to go into the world as Jesus entered it and to continue His ministry.

Throughout His ministry, Jesus repeatedly asserts that He has been sent by His Father (3:16, 17; 5:30, 36–38; 6:29, 38, 39, 44; 7:16, 28, 29, 33; 8:16; 12:45; 13:20; 17:18) to do His will (4:34; 5:30; 6:38, 39; 9:4). He has come from heaven into the world as the light of God (1:4–9; 3:19; 8:12; 12:46). The Light is to continue to shine in the world through the ministry of the disciples. This is not a new notion for Jesus, however. Early in His ministry Jesus told them that they would be sent to the harvest (4:35–38) and before His crucifixion Jesus prayed for them because they were being sent into world (17: 18) for the purpose of continuing the work of the Father that He had begun.

And when He had said this, He breathed on them, and said to
them, "Receive the Holy Spirit" (v. 22).

Jesus imparts the Holy Spirit to the disciples by breathing on them. John's brief report of this unusual action recalls the life-giving act of God when He breathed the breath of life into Adam (Gen. 2:7): "And [God] breathed into his nostrils the breath of life; and man became a living being." The word used by John to describe Jesus' breathing action (*emphusaō*, ἐμφυσάω) is the same one found in the Septuagint version of Genesis 2 and Ezekiel 37:9. By commanding the disciples to receive or take the Holy Spirit, Jesus exercises the authority that He has from His Father over all flesh to give eternal life (17:2). Jesus' action is life-giving like that of God in the beginning with Adam. It restores the disciples to a state of being antecedent to that of Adam's disobedience (Gen. 3) when he enjoyed the very breath of God in his being. John presents Jesus' exhalation as an act of new creation.

This event is not John's version of Pentecost as suggested by some scholars. The release of the Holy Spirit is not an alternative description of the outpouring of the Spirit recounted in Acts 2:1–4. It describes the initial act of new creation by Jesus among the disciples. For this reason, what Jesus does here should not be interpreted as fulfillment of the promises He made earlier about the Spirit (chs. 14–16). In those passages, John records Jesus saying that His Father will give the Spirit of Truth to the disciples to abide with them (14:16–18), to enable them to testify about Jesus (15:26), and to glorify Jesus through them (16:13–15). He says that the Spirit of Truth will take what belongs to Him and declare it to them. The Spirit not only shares divine information with the disciples, however, He authorizes the disciples to act on what they hear. Just as Jesus spoke what He heard His Father speak and performed His Father's works by the Spirit (8:28, 29; 1:32, 33), so also the same Spirit will announce what belongs to Jesus to the disciples so they can speak His words and perform His works. The authority Jesus exercised in His earthly ministry at the discretion of His Father will be impressed upon them by the Spirit, and He will be glorified by the Spirit in their lives as they continue the works that He did. Simply stated, the Spirit will reprise the ministry of Jesus through the disciples.

When will this Spirited-ministry of Jesus in the disciples begin? When will His promise be realized? John does not say, but he does leave several clues:

- Jesus tells Mary that He is ascending to His Father (20:17), which refers to His resurrection. He says that the Son of Man who comes from heaven will also go up to heaven (3:13; 6:62). By referring to Himself as the Son of Man who descends from and goes up to heaven, Jesus draws attention to Himself as the One who identifies fully with humankind and, yet, will receive the glory and authority that only God possesses (Dan. 7:13, 14). To ascend is to emerge from death in resurrection and to return to His place of glory in His Father's presence. When Jesus appears to Mary, He has yet to enter this place of glory, and it is unclear if He has entered it by the time He appears to the disciples.
- When Jesus promised the people at the temple that rivers of living water would flow from those who believe in Him, John says He

meant the Holy Spirit who had not been given because Jesus was not yet glorified (7:38, 39). John observes that the giving of the Spirit follows the glorification of Jesus. Thus, though the promise Jesus makes to the people then may be viewed as fulfilled in the breathing of the Spirit by Jesus here, this is uncertain unless the glorification of Jesus has already occurred. So when is Jesus glorified?

• Jesus makes it clear that the Spirit will be sent by God the Father (14:16; 15:26) once He has returned to Him (16:7). It appears that John understood the return of Jesus to the Father as the permanent withdrawal of His person from the world. In recording Jesus' passion prayer, John gives the clear impression that Jesus foresees a time when He will be absent from the world though His disciples will remain in it (17:11).

• At the time Jesus breathes the Spirit upon them He is in the process of ascending to His Father. However, he has not made a final return to the Father since He must still give proof of His resurrection to the disciples and instruct them for a time. Jesus remains in contact with the world as He maintains personal contact with His followers. When He finally withdraws from the world, He will return to the Father to ask that the Spirit be given to them. In other words, as long as Jesus continues to appear to the disciples they are not orphans bereft of His presence (14:18) who need the Spirit to testify of Him (15:26). They do not need to be guided by the Spirit into all truth and receive all the things that belong to Jesus from Him (16:13–15) since the risen Lord is still with them.

By breathing on the disciples, Jesus restores them to life with God as their Father as in the beginning. The promise of the Spirit will enable them to carry on the ministry of signs that Jesus began when He was with them. It is not unreasonable, then, to view the exhalation of the Spirit as a separate event from the promise of the Spirit. Just as God's initial creation did not happen in one day, so also the work of new creation is not completed in one discrete act. So, Christ's breathing on the disciples is a step along the way to the fulfillment of the promise of the Spirit.

"If you forgive the sins of any, they are forgiven them; if you retain the sins of any, they are retained" (v. 23).

After breathing upon the disciples, Jesus speaks of the authority they possess as people who have received the life of God and know Him as their Father.

This authority will be displayed in the forgiveness they extend to or withhold from others. Earlier in His ministry Jesus refused to condemn a woman who had been caught committing adultery and, in effect, offers forgiveness to her when He says, "Go and sin no more" (8:11).

Moreover, Jesus said to certain Pharisees in the temple, "[If] you do not believe that I am He, you will die in your sins" (8:24). To refuse Jesus' teaching that He has come from God the Father to offer His life to them is to refuse the relationship with God (and His forgiveness) that comes through Him. Some of the Pharisees remain in their sin because they claim to know God and yet they reject God's Son (9:41). As those who have the Spirit of God due to their relationship with Jesus, the disciples exercise His prerogative when they withhold condemnation or when they identify disbelief and condemnation in others.

The Beatitude of Belief (John 20:24–31)

The importance of belief for receiving the life-giving Spirit of God is outlined by John in these verses. First, Jesus pronounces a blessing upon all who will believe through the testimony of the disciples. Second, John describes belief as the reason he has composed his gospel. Belief in the testimony that John gives, then, leads to the blessing of life promised by Jesus.

> *Now Thomas, called the Twin, one of the twelve, was not with them when Jesus came (v. 24).*

John describes Thomas as the Twin (11:16). It is customary for John to introduce those close to Jesus with descriptive titles or short accounts of their contact with Him. For example Andrew is described as Simon Peter's brother (1:40); Philip is from Bethsaida, the city of Andrew and Peter (1:44); Nicodemus is the one who came to Jesus by night (3:2; 7:50; 19:30); Lazarus, Mary, and Martha are those who were loved by Jesus and live in the town of Bethany (11:1); Joseph of Arimathea is a disciple of Jesus (19:38); and Judas is described as the son of Simon (12:4; 13:26) who would betray Him (12:4; 18:5). Moreover, John introduces Simon and describes how he became Peter (1:42) and how Nathanael is identified as an Israelite in whom there is no deceit (1:47). In this way John reveals an intimate knowledge of those close to Jesus. The personal information he provides about them is in contrast to his description of those who oppose Jesus. Other than Annas and Caiaphas, the high priest patriarch and the sitting high priest, John does not mention by name any opponents and he withholds all personal information about them. They are simply the Jews, certain Pharisees, officers of the high priest, or soldiers. The only other person who is described by name is Pilate and John gives no personal information about him.

> *The other disciples therefore said to him, "We have seen the Lord." So he said to them, "Unless I see in His hands the print of the nails, and put my finger into the print of the nails, and put my hand into His side, I will not believe" (v. 25).*

Thomas was introduced earlier in this gospel. John records him as saying, "Let us also go, that we may die with Him" (11:16). He was not sanguine about the prospects that awaited them in Jerusalem as a result of the violent resistance they had already encountered there (10:31–39). Likewise, he is not convinced now by the reports of Jesus' resurrection from his fellow disciples. He declares that He will not believe unless he puts his finger into the nail-wounds of Jesus' hands.

> *And after eight days His disciples were again inside, and Thomas with them. Jesus came, the doors being shut, and stood in the midst, and said, "Peace to you!" Then He said to Thomas, "Reach your finger here, and look at My hands; and reach your hand here, and put it into My side. Do not be unbelieving, but believing" (vv. 26, 27).*

Eight days pass before Jesus appears to the disciples again. Then He says for the third time, "Peace." He not only reiterates their place in God's plan of new creation but He includes Thomas among those who are called to continue His ministry. As He did for the disciples, so also He does for Thomas. Plus, He presents the marks of His crucifixion to him.

Jesus commands Thomas to see and feel His wounds. He says, "Reach your finger and see the nail-wounds; reach your hand and feel My side." Jesus immediately moves to establish belief in Thomas. The imperatives reveal the authority of the Son of God who shared the glory of God in the beginning as the Word of God and shares it still as the risen Lamb of God: "Reach out! Touch and see! Be of faith!" These commands indicate that Jesus is moved by compassion rather than frustration with Thomas. He exhorts Thomas to move from unbelief to belief: "Be not unbelieving but believing!" He wants Thomas to move from darkness to light. The desire of the risen Jesus is that Thomas and all of His disciples live in a state of being defined by belief.

And Thomas answered and said to Him, "My Lord and my
God!" Jesus said to him, "Thomas, because you have seen Me,
you have believed. Blessed are those who have not seen and yet
have believed" (vv. 28, 29).

Thomas responds with an acclamation of belief: "My Lord and My God!" Though he is the last of the disciples to come to faith, Thomas is the first to declare the exalted divine nature of the risen Jesus. But this is not all. Thomas defines himself as much as he defines Jesus. When he says, "My Lord and my God," he acknowledges that he belongs to Jesus as one belongs to a master and to God. For Thomas, to touch and to see the risen Jesus leads to an exclamation of humility and worship of the living God.

Jesus' response to Thomas is not so much a rebuke as it is a pronouncement of blessing upon those who believe without the bodily manifestation of Jesus that he has been given. They will be blessed. Though the precise nature of this beatitude is not described by Jesus, without a doubt it is life with God. In fact, John has written this gospel for those who will not have the chance to see Jesus and touch Him as Thomas has. Such people will be blessed as they believe in Jesus through such accounts as John's. They are different from the disciples because they believe the message about Jesus apart from His physical presence.

This response is more than quiet acceptance. After Jesus washed the feet of the disciples He said that they would be blessed if they followed His imperative and did the same for each other (13:17). "Blessed" is the state of being in which the disciples will live as they believe the testimony of others like John and follow Jesus' example of love and humility in serving one another. The beatitude of belief is both the reception of eternal life in Jesus Christ by His Spirit and the manifestation of this life in humble regard for one another.

And truly Jesus did many other signs in the presence of His disci-
ples, which are not written in this book; but these are written
that you may believe that Jesus is the Christ, the Son of God, and
that believing you may have life in His name (vv. 30, 31).

John reveals that there is much that Jesus said and did among the disciples that he has not recorded. He has selected certain signs, events, and teachings in order to secure the faith of those who read his book. Jesus did the same as he secured the faith of Thomas by showing him the signs of His crucifixion. John's gospel is a testimony about Jesus Christ. It is personal evidence that Jesus, who was with God in the beginning as His Word, has come into the world and manifested God for all people. Even as Thomas responds to the evidence that Jesus gives in His own body by saying, "My Lord and my God," so it is John's ambition that everyone who reads (or hears) his report will respond by acknowledging Jesus is the Spirit-anointed Son of God through whom they may receive eternal life.

THE ENDING OF JOHN'S GOSPEL

Many biblical scholars believe that the original version of John's Gospel concluded with these verses. There is good reason for this opinion:

- It represents a fitting conclusion to John's introductory statement that the Light entered the world and "as many as received Him, to them He gave the right to become children of God, to those who believe in His name" (1:12). Jesus came to arouse belief and lead people into the eternal life of God. John concludes His gospel by saying he has written it to strengthen belief in his readers in Jesus so they may enjoy eternal life.
- Thomas' declaration that the risen Jesus is Lord and God strongly complements John's declaration that "the Word became flesh and dwelt among us, and we beheld His glory, the glory as of the only begotten of the Father, full of grace and truth" (1:14). John concludes by saying that everyone (plural pronoun "you") may be a son or daughter of God by believing Jesus came from God as His unique divine Son. Everyone may enjoy the life of the new creation by responding with Thomas' declaration: "My Lord and my God."

The following section (21:1–25), however, is likely the authentic ending to the gospel for several reasons:

- The restoration of Peter by Jesus to a place in His ministry correlates well with the initial remarks made by Jesus to him at the beginning of His ministry (1:40–42) and illustrates the nature of the new creation that John has depicted in his gospel. The work of new creation is one of renewal and restoration.
- The depiction of Jesus' miracles as signs throughout this gospel continues with the catch of fish in this passage. The catch is more than a wondrous event proving Jesus still lives; it reveals the ongoing nature of His ministry through the disciples. Whereas the seven miracles recounted in the gospel speak of the new work of creation in Jesus' ministry, the miracle of the fish speaks of the continued manifestation of new creation in the lives of Jesus' disciples.
- Even as the love of God is a central feature of Jesus' teaching throughout John's gospel (3:16), so also love for Jesus is a central feature of this passage. Jesus asks Peter, "Do you love Me?" To which Peter replies, "Yes, Lord, I love You." Together, these thematic features of chapter twenty-one give worthy evidence that it is original to John's gospel.

There are two variant readings of verse 31. A slight preference is given to the ancient manuscripts that read, "These have been written so that you should firmly believe" (aorist subjunctive tense). This would indicate that the gospel was written to found faith in those who do not know Jesus as Lord. Even so, the difference of meaning in the aorist and present subjunctive is subtle and either form may indicate that John wants to establish new faith in those who do not yet know Jesus in this way as well as to secure faith in those who do. (See the Introduction, "John's Ambition," for additional comments.)

Testimony and History in the Gospel of John

As noted in the introduction, John's gospel may be viewed as a testimony to the life and work of Jesus Christ to strengthen and inspire belief in Him. Throughout his gospel John uses the noun *martyria* (ἡ μαρτυρία) to describe the evidence or report given about Jesus and the verb *martyreō* (μαρτυρέω) to describe the act of giving such evidence or report. John sees his gospel as a compilation of incontrovertible evidence in support of Jesus as the Word of God who has entered into human history to give eternal life. This is indicated by the frequency with which he uses these two words.

The verb *martyreō* occurs seventy-six times in the New Testament, with nearly half of these occurrences (thirty-three) found in this gospel; the noun *martyria* occurs thirty-seven times in the New Testament and most of these occurrences are in John (fourteen). John thus presents Jesus before the court of world opinion as the One who begins a new work of creation.

This is particularly evident in the three testimony passages of John 19–21 (19:35; 20:30–31; 21:24, 25). In the first passage John writes that "he who has seen has testified (*martyreō*), and his testimony (*martyria*) is true; and he knows that he is telling the truth, so that you may believe" (19:35). Here he asserts that what he reports about Jesus' crucifixion is true because he saw it happen and he recounts it so that people may believe. This is a remarkable statement since victims of crucifixion were viewed with abhorrence and disgust. What does John want the reader to believe? That Jesus died according to purpose of God as recorded in the Old Testament (Ex. 12:46; Num. 9:12; and Zech. 12:10). John testifies that Jesus' death was not an accident of history.

In the second passage John claims, "Jesus did many other signs in the presence of His disciples . . . but these are written that you may believe Jesus is the Christ, the Son of God, and that believing you may have life in His name" (20:30, 31). Written in view of Jesus' appearances to Mary, the disciples, and Thomas, John wants those who have not seen or touched the risen Jesus to know that the Resurrection and miracles he has recorded (which are only a sample of what He did) are true and they may have eternal life if they believe this. John testifies that the miracles of Jesus and His resurrection are facts of history.

In the third passage John vouches for the veracity of his report about Jesus' appearance to Peter and the disciples and humorously asserts that no number of books could contain all that He did (21:24, 25). In effect, John testifies that the ministry of Jesus continues after His resurrection and not only fulfills but also exceeds the requirements of human history. In these three passages, John testifies to Jesus' crucifixion, resurrection, and activity after His resurrection. Deftly, he concludes his gospel much as he began it by giving testimony to Jesus.

John began in the prologue reporting that Jesus is the Word of God in the beginning through whom all things were made (1:1–3). With this observation he links Jesus to the beginning of creation and universal history. Throughout the rest of the gospel he elaborates on this astounding truth by having numerous people give testimony to Jesus as the Word of God who has become flesh (1:14). In other words, John cites the testimony of others to support his assertion that the Word of God through whom history began also lived in history.

This testimony begins with John the Baptist who appeared before Jesus "for a witness" (*martyria*) to give testimony (*martyreō*) concerning the light of God so that through Him all might believe (1:7, 8). The Baptist proclaims the greatness of Jesus and says He is the Lamb of God who takes away the sin of the world (1:27, 36). This means that God's redemptive work in history as recorded in the Old Testament continues in Jesus. Not only does it continue in Jesus but it will continue after Jesus since the Baptist testifies (*martyreō*, vv. 32, 34) that He will baptize with the Holy Spirit.

Other witnesses include His disciples (6:68, 69; 11:27; 20:28), the people of Jerusalem (7:40–42), and those blessed by His ministry (4:29, 42; 9:17). Though John does not use the words *martyria* or *martyreō* to describe their affirmation of Jesus, their response to Him may be interpreted as testimonials to Him.

The most compelling testimony comes from Jesus Himself. He uses the plural personal pronoun *we* to indicate that the testimony (*martyria*) He gives is also that of God His Father (3:11). Yet, as the Baptist observes, though His testimony is that of His Father, it is rejected (3:31). What is the testimony that is rejected? That Jesus has come from God to complete God's works. This is ironic since the works He does testify (*martyreō*) that God has sent

Him (5:36, 37). Jesus defends His testimony by saying that God also testifies of Him through the works that He does. (See 8:12–20.) This is the same God who throughout the Old Testament is described as doing good works. It is not surprising, then, that Scripture also testifies to Jesus (5:39, 46; 12:37–41; 19:36). Such testimony will continue through the Holy Spirit who will testify (*martyreō*) to Jesus by performing His works through the disciples (15:26, 27; 16:8). Testimony to Jesus will continue in history through those who receive the Holy Spirit from the Father.

Every positive testimony given about Jesus identifies Him with God. He is the Word of God (1:1–5); Lamb of God (1:6–8, 19–36); Son of God (1:49; 6:69; 11:27); Teacher of God (3:1–2); Messiah (4:29, 39–42; 6:67, 68; 7:41; 11:27); Prophet (6:14; 7:40; 9:17); King of Israel (1:49; 12:13); and Lord and God (20:28). The array of testimony brought together by John establishes the truth that God entered history in the person of Jesus to inaugurate a new history for all people.

The reader of John's gospel is confronted with overwhelming testimony to enable him or her to respond with belief. And a response is required. He or she can no more remain indifferent to the testimony that John has given of Jesus than those who were confronted by Jesus in person 2,000 years ago.

QUESTIONS FOR PERSONAL REFLECTION AND GROUP DISCUSSION

1. What is the significance of Jesus' crucifixion on the Day of Preparation?
2. What does Jesus' cry, "My God, My God, why have You forsaken Me?" reveal about His understanding of His death?
3. What meaning does the piercing of Jesus' side have for John?
4. Who is the first evangelist?
5. Does Jesus fulfill the promise He makes of the Spirit when He breathes upon the disciples and says, "Receive the Holy Spirit"?
6. How should Jesus' words to Thomas after His resurrection be interpreted? How should Thomas' response to Jesus be understood?
7. How does John's view of history influence his presentation of Jesus?

CHAPTER 10

FEEDING AND FOLLOWING

John 21:1–25

In chapter one, Jesus is introduced as the Lamb of God who takes away the sin of the world (1:29) and prepares for a new work of creation. Here, God's Lamb calls Peter and the other disciples into this work by giving them responsibility for His lambs.

It is apparent that apart from Jesus, Peter is the focus of this passage: he goes fishing; he throws himself into the water to get to Jesus; he professes his love for Jesus; and he wonders about the future of the beloved disciple. Why does John give such close attention to Peter at the conclusion of his gospel? Several answers may be offered:

- The synoptic Gospels report that Peter is the first to pronounce Jesus to be the Son of God: "You are the Christ, the Son of the living God" (Matt. 16:16; see Mark 8:29; Luke 9:20). For his confession, Jesus gives him the name *Peter* and prophesies that upon the rock (meaning Peter) His church would be built (Matt. 16:17, 18). The restoration story recounted by John would have explained how Jesus' prophecy is fulfilled despite Peter's well-known denial.
- Peter's story features a major principle of the new creation. The judgment of Jesus is restorative; it is not primarily punitive. Earlier in the gospel, Jesus says to the temple leaders, "Do not judge according to appearance, but judge with righteous judgment" (7:24). Here He demonstrates such righteous judgment and gives Peter an opportunity to again resume his place in His ministry.
- This is an appropriate conclusion to the gospel that has portrayed Jesus as the One who lives out the Old Testament story of redemption among God's people and before the world. John shows that

God's historic outreach to bless the nation of Israel and call them to mission now includes individuals. Redemption involves restoration and Peter's restoration reveals that God's redemptive purpose for all people is personal and compassionate.

Jesus Feeds the Seven (John 21:1–14)

Peter and several other disciples go fishing on the Sea of Tiberias (Galilee). Jesus appears on the shore and asks if they have caught any fish. When they reply that they have been unsuccessful, He tells them to try on the other side. The nets fill with fish and the beloved disciple recognizes Jesus. Peter puts on his outer garment and plunges into the water to swim to Him. When they arrive at the shore, they find that Jesus has prepared a fire and is grilling fish and warming bread for them. This is the second meal of fish and bread that Jesus has prepared. Earlier He used five barley loaves and two small fish to feed 5,000 men (6:1–14). That meal revealed Jesus as the One who had come from heaven to sustain the people in their walk with God.

By recording this event, John shows that Jesus will continue to meet the needs of those who follow Him. Just as the feeding of the 5,000 recalled God's provision for the Israelites in the wilderness and served as a sign of God's faithfulness to deliver them, so also the feeding of the seven on the shores of Galilee serves as a sign of God's faithfulness to sustain the disciples and restore Peter.

In earlier times, God blessed the Israelites with manna and quail after they complained about His provision for them. They murmured that He had brought them into the wilderness to kill them, even though He had recently delivered them from Pharaoh's army, drowning the Egyptian soldiers in the Red Sea! (Ex. 16:1–3). Not unlike the Israelites, Peter has denied the truth of God's work in his life by denying any knowledge of Jesus. Not once does he do this, but three times (18:16, 17, 25–27). By preparing a meal for Peter and the others who have followed him back to the former occupation of fishing, Jesus acts with righteous judgment toward them. He does not hold Peter's denial, which resembles the false accusation of the Israelites about God, against him. Instead, He gives Peter an opportunity to affirm his love and fidelity by asking, three times, if Peter loves Him.

After these things Jesus showed Himself again to the disciples at the Sea of Tiberias, and in this way He showed Himself (v. 1).

John describes Jesus' third appearance to the disciples since His resurrection. He says that Jesus revealed Himself to them. His revelation is more than a physical appearance, however. Through this encounter Jesus reveals His self-lessness, His righteousness, and His compassion to Peter and to all of the disciples. This third appearance of Jesus represents Peter's day of restoration.

> *Simon Peter, Thomas called the Twin, Nathanael of Cana in Galilee, the sons of Zebedee, and two others of His disciples were together. Simon Peter said to them, "I am going fishing." They said to him, "We are going with you also." They went out and immediately got into the boat, and that night they caught nothing (vv. 2, 3).*

Since Simon Peter, Nathanael, and the sons of Zebedee are from Galilee, it is logical that they would return there from Jerusalem. Peter's announcement that he is going fishing signifies a return to his former vocation. The other disciples join him. The disciples' quick response shows their identification with Peter: "We, too, are going with you." John's account of the night before Jesus' crucifixion shows Peter taking a leading role among the disciples. He exclaims that He wants Jesus to wash his whole body and not only his feet (13:6–10) and he is the first among the disciples to question Jesus about His departure, even claiming that he will give his life for Jesus (13:36–38). The prominence Peter had with his fellow disciples before the Crucifixion continues after the Resurrection.

Night fishing was common; nets with floats were set in the water throughout the night. John seems to include this note to depict Peter and the disciples as working in the dark; they are not yet living in the light of God's purpose.

> *But when the morning had now come, Jesus stood on the shore; yet the disciples did not know that it was Jesus. Then Jesus said to them, "Children, have you any food?" They answered Him, "No" (vv. 4, 5).*

Jesus appears at the shore but is not recognized by the disciples. This is not surprising. It is early and dark and Jesus is some distance away. Moreover, they would have been unfamiliar with His greeting: "Children." Before His crucifixion Jesus addressed them as friends (15:14).

It is likely that Jesus refers to the disciples as children in order to remind them of their new relationship to God as their Father. Though He has called them little children before (13:33), He has also called them friends. John began his gospel by observing that "as many as received Him, to them He gave the right to become children of God" (1:12). Jesus calls them children to affirm their new identity. One hundred times in John's gospel Jesus refers to God as His Father. Now He shares this privilege with His disciples who, as children of God, may relate to God in the same way.

The question Jesus asks is normal given the time and situation. It is early morning and the disciples have been working through the night.

> *And He said to them, "Cast the net on the right side of the boat, and you will find some." So they cast, and now they were not able to draw it in because of the multitude of fish (v. 6).*

The disciples respond to Jesus' encouragement by throwing their gill net on the right side of the boat and are rewarded with a catch of fish. So many fish, in fact, that the disciples struggle with the net. This miracle is indicated by the fact that the net thrown had floats attached to it and was used for overnight fishing. It was not a casting net. Yet it apparently fills with fish quickly. This miracle serves as a sign to the disciples—the first sign of the new creation apart from the Resurrection. It shows that Jesus will continue to provide for the disciples as they respond to His word. Even as the seven signs recorded by John in the first part of his gospel (chs. 2–11) reveal Jesus' identity as the One who gives eternal life to God's people and begins the work of new creation, so also this sign reveals that Jesus is the One who will provide for His followers as they continue this work.

Given the fact that the fish had become a symbol of the risen Jesus at the time John wrote his gospel, it is possible that he intends his readers to see in the miracle not only the provision for the human needs of the disciples but also an abundant response to their proclamation of the gospel as they are obedient to His word.

> *Therefore that disciple whom Jesus loved said to Peter, "It is the Lord!" Now when Simon Peter heard that it was the Lord, he put on his outer garment (for he had removed it), and plunged into the sea. But the other disciples came in the little boat (for they were not far from land, but about two hundred cubits), dragging the net with fish. Then, as soon as they had come to land, they saw a fire of coals there, and fish laid on it, and bread. Jesus said to them, "Bring some of the fish which you have just caught." Simon Peter went up and dragged the net to land, full of large*

fish, one hundred and fifty-three; and although there were so
many, the net was not broken (vv. 7–11).

The information that John provides in these verses point to an eyewitness account: the disciples throw the gill net on the right side of the boat; Peter quickly robes and throws himself into the water; the disciples are in a small boat and drag in a catch of 153 fish; the boat is 200 cubits from land; Jesus has prepared a fire of coals and cooks bread and fish on it. Such details indicate the importance of the event for John. It is proof that the Resurrection occurred and is not a mythical figment of their imagination. Jesus appeared to them and He continued to serve them as He had during His ministry. Though they did not recognize Him at first, the same Jesus who washed their feet the night before His crucifixion now serves breakfast to them.

One hundred fifty-three was a number that would have had significance for the disciples since it was the number of sections into which the Pentateuch was divided for reading in the synagogue over the course of three years. (Some early tradition indicates that there were 154 or 155 readings.) By reading through the Torah on a regular basis the Jewish people

THE PROMISED LAND AND THE PROMISED SPIRIT

God gave His Torah to Israel in the wilderness so that they might enter into Canaan and live as His people. It is important to note that the law was given before they reached the Promised Land so they could live according to the way of life outlined in it prior to their possession of God's promise. They were to be God's people by living according to the Torah before they engaged in the conquest of the land and settled it. At the same time, God provided quail and manna for them to eat. Thus, God sustained them while He formed them into His image as a people.

John draws on this story as he records the breakfast that Jesus prepares for the disciples. As God's Word, Jesus has manifested the life of God to His followers. He has shown them how they are to live. At the same time, He provides for their needs. And just as the Hebrew people were only to take some of the quail and manna provided for each day to show their faith in God's continued blessing (Ex. 16:16–19), so also the disciples are to take some of the fish for their breakfast. That is, they are to live by faith in His word just as they are to trust in the provision He makes. By including such details, John depicts Jesus as preparing the disciples to enter into the promise of the Spirit. The new creation has begun and will continue to unfold when the promise of the Spirit is manifested in their lives.

were reminded of the gift of the law and the provision of blessing that God had made for them through it. In fact, the first psalm of the Book of Psalms supports this idea since it indicates that God is to be praised for giving His people a way of blessing in His Torah. (The Hebrew title for the Book of Psalms is *tehillim*, תְּהִלִּים, which means "praises.") As the first psalm of the collection, it establishes the primary reason for which God should be praised. Likewise, the catch of 153 fish would represent the provision of blessing that Jesus will make for them as they give their devotion to Him and follow Him.

Jesus has made a fire of coals. The symbolism of this would not have been lost on Peter even as it is not lost on John's readers. During the night of Jesus' trial, Peter stood in the courtyard of the high priest and warmed himself by a fire of coals while he denied knowing Jesus (18:18). By building a similar fire of coals and not of dry wood or kindling, Jesus sets the scene for Peter's restoration.

> *Jesus said to them, "Come and eat breakfast." Yet none of the disciples dared ask Him, "Who are You?"? knowing that it was the Lord (v. 12).*

John says that the disciples were not daring (imperfect of *tolmaō*, τολμάω) to find out (infinitive of *exetazō*, ἐξετάζω) who speaks to them and prepares their breakfast. The Greek implies that they did not trust themselves or did not have the courage to inquire, "Who are You?" In Acts 7:32, Moses is said to be fearful (*tolmaō*) before the glory of God. The disciples' reaction to Jesus may be due to a changed appearance or to their continued wonder at His resurrection and their reverential deference to the One who is their Lord. Their response to Jesus at this time recalls their reaction to His conversation with the Samaritan woman (4:27). In any case, they know Jesus has come to them. The world may not know Him, but His followers do. These sheep know the voice of their Shepherd (10:2–5; 27–29).

> *Jesus then came and took the bread and gave it to them, and likewise the fish. This is now the third time Jesus showed Himself to His disciples after He was raised from the dead (vv. 13, 14).*

Jesus continues to serve the disciples. As before His crucifixion when He washed their feet and encouraged them to do the same, so now He provides food for them and implicitly encourages them to trust Him for what they need.

The Lamb of God and the Lambs of Jesus (John 21:15–17)

John begins his gospel by having John the Baptist introduce Jesus as the Lamb of God (1:29, 36). By announcing Jesus as God's Lamb who takes away the sins of the world, the Baptist prophetically speaks of His death, since lambs facilitate forgiveness (taking away sins) only if they are sacrificed. In this brief passage, the Lamb of God who has been sacrificed and resurrected commits the care of His lambs to Peter who denied knowing Him in the court of the high priest. Jesus does this because the new creation of God inaugurated through His ministry is by nature redemptive and defined by righteous judgment. Who better than Peter, a man restored to his place in Jesus' ministry of eternal life, to restore others in their relationship to God?

> *So when they had eaten breakfast, Jesus said to Simon Peter, "Simon, son of Jonah, do you love Me more than these?" He said to Him, "Yes, Lord; You know that I love You." He said to him, "Feed My lambs." He said to him again a second time, "Simon, son of Jonah, do you love Me?" He said to Him, "Yes, Lord; You know that I love You." He said to him, "Tend My sheep." He said to him the third time, "Simon, son of Jonah, do you love Me?" Peter was grieved because He said to him the third time, "Do you love Me?" And he said to Him, "Lord, You know all things; You know that I love You." Jesus said to him, "Feed My sheep" (vv. 15–17).*

Three times Jesus asks Peter, "Do you love Me?" And three times Peter responds, "Yes, Lord, You know that I love You" (21:15–17). After the third time Peter says, "You know all things" (v. 17). With these words he shows that he has grown in his understanding of Jesus. How so? Earlier in His ministry Jesus had said that He would be handed over to the temple leaders and the Romans, but Peter knew better (Matt. 16:21, 22); Jesus said that His disciples would abandon Him, but Peter knew better (Matt. 26:31–35; John 13:36–38). Now Peter knows that Jesus knows better. In view of his new confession, "You know all things," Jesus speaks prophetically and says, "Follow Me" (v. 19).

This exchange between Jesus and Peter is unusual in its language. The first two times Jesus asks if Peter loves Him the Greek word for *love* is "agapaō" (ἀγαπάω). The third time He inquires, "Do you love Me?" the word *love* is "phileō" (φιλέω) Peter responds each time by saying that he loves (*phileō*) Jesus. What are we to make of John's choice of words here? There are several possible answers:

- It may be that John uses different words for "love" simply because he enjoys word-play and variety in language.
- It may be that John intends to contrast Jesus' conception of love (*agapaō*) with Peter's (*phileō*). According to this view, Jesus asks if Peter is fully devoted to Him and Peter responds that he is devoted to Jesus. Since *agapaō* is used throughout the gospel to describe complete, unreserved devotion (like that of God in 3:16; 14:21–23; 17:23–26 and of God for Jesus in 3:35; 10:17; 15:15, as well as that of Jesus for His own in 11:5; 13:1, 34; 14:21; 15:9), Jesus wants to know if Peter is committed to Him in this way. He eventually acquiesces to Peter's confession, however, given Peter's humiliation.
- Another possibility is that Jesus simply asks if Peter has love (*agapaō* in a general sense) for Him and Peter responds by saying that he loves Jesus in a special way (*phileō*, like a brother, see 11:3, 36). When Peter repeats himself, Jesus asks if he, indeed, loves Him in this way. Since *phileō* is much less common than *agapaō* in the New Testament, occurring twenty-five times to almost 145 times (thirty-seven times in John's gospel alone), it is possible that John records Peter making an attempt to declare some kind of distinctive love for Jesus in light of his shameful renunciation of Him.

Each time Peter responds that he loves Jesus, Jesus commands him to "feed My lambs . . . feed My small sheep." Peter is given responsibility for all those who belong to Jesus. Jesus speaks as a sheep owner who entrusts the care of His flocks to under-shepherds. Just as He did not lose any that His Father had given to Him (17:12), so also His disciples are to keep those that He gives to them. The parable of the lost sheep cannot be far from Jesus' thinking at this point. Even the least of the flock is deserving of attentive and loving care. (See Matt. 18:10–14; Luke 15:4–7.)

The miracle catch is the first sign that Jesus gives to the disciples (and to Peter) after His resurrection. He will provide for His disciples as they follow Him. The second sign is the title Jesus gives Peter. He addresses him as "son of Jonah." Though early Greek texts of this passage read "son of John," there is good minority manuscript evidence for "son of Jonah." Given the theme of the passage (restoration) and the connection with Jesus' earlier identification of Peter as "Simon bar Jonah" (Matt. 16), it is certainly possible that Jesus referred to Peter at this time as "son of Jonah." But what does this designation mean? The answer is found in Matthew's gospel which records an encounter between Jesus and the Pharisees and their desire for a sign. Jesus refuses and says that the only sign He will give them is that of the prophet Jonah. Since Jonah remains swallowed in the fish for three days before being expelled (Jon. 1:17), the sign Jesus will give the Pharisees is His death and resurrection (Matt. 16:1–4). Following this, Jesus asks the disciples, "Who do they say that I am?" Several answers are given before Peter says, "You are the Christ, the Son of the Living God" (Matt. 16:16). Jesus responds by declaring that Peter could not conceive this truth apart from His Father in heaven and identifies him as "Simon bar Jonah," meaning "Simon son of Jonah." It is a mistake to think that Jesus is referring to Peter by his paternal name, however. It is unlikely that Peter's father was named Jonah since few Jewish people of the time would have been so named because of the prophet's unfavorable reputation as an obstinate man. Why does Jesus describe Peter in this way? It is to identify Peter with Himself. Jesus acknowledges that Peter is right: He is the Messiah (Christ); but He is not the Messiah as Peter and most other people of the time would expect. He is not a religious, political, or military figure who will forcibly establish His kingdom in the land. He is a Messiah who will inaugurate His kingdom through death or, in other words, through the sign of Jonah! Jesus is Jonah and Peter is a "son of Jonah" as a result of his confession that Jesus is the Son of the Living God.

Thus, by referring to Peter as Simon bar Jonah on the shore of the Sea of Galilee, Jesus draws his attention back to his revelatory confession at Caesarea Philippi. He affirms Peter's relationship with Him not only as the crucified Messiah, however, but as the resurrected Son of God, and He restores Peter as the rock upon which His church will be established (Matt. 16:18).

The Girding of Peter (John 21:18–19)

"Most assuredly, I say to you, when you were younger, you gird-
ed yourself and walked where you wished; but when you are old,
you will stretch out your hands, and another will gird you and
carry you where you do not wish" (v. 18).

John records the last emphatic statement made by Jesus, which begins with, "Most assuredly, I say to you." What is the meaning of the enigmatic words that follow? To answer this question it is necessary to recall what John has recorded up to this moment. When Peter realizes that Jesus is standing along the shore, he girds (*zōnnumi*, ζώννυμι) his outer garment and throws himself into the water (v. 7). The verb translated *gird* describes the act of tying or tightening. After they have eaten, Jesus asks, "Simon, son of Jonah, do you love Me?" Three times He poses this question to Peter. When Peter finally responds by saying, "Lord, You know all things" (v. 17), Jesus says that he will be girded yet again.

John's account indicates that Jesus noticed Peter's reaction to the news of His presence at the shore. He saw Peter tighten his tunic and plunge into the water. It would be apparent to Jesus, as to anyone who looked on, that people do not usually dress before jumping into the water. Likely, Peter puts his outer garment on so that he will not be half-dressed when he comes out of the water to Jesus. In doing this Peter means to show respect to his Lord. Jesus uses the opportunity to tell Peter that such honor and devotion to Him involves great responsibility.

The night before His crucifixion, Jesus "girded" (*diazōnnumi*, διαζώννυ-μι) His waist with a towel and in an act of humility and love honored the disciples by washing their feet (13:4–5). In this way He demonstrated how they should regard each other. "For I have given you an example, that you should do as I have done to you . . . If you know these things, blessed are you if you do them" (13:15, 17). This gesture of affection anticipates the great display of love He will show through His death. He washes their feet with water; He will wash their lives by His blood.

By telling Peter that he will be girded, Jesus describes Peter's present and future and once again identifies Peter with Himself. Simon son of Jonah, who has declared that Jesus is the Christ, the Son of the living God, now has responsibility for Jesus' lambs and little sheep and he must be prepared for the consequences of such responsibility. He has girded himself in coming to Jesus at the shore and he will be girded again, against his will however, as a result of his willingness to identify with Jesus.

This He spoke, signifying by what death he would glorify God. And when He had spoken this, He said to him, "Follow Me" (v. 19).

Jesus says that a time is coming in Peter's old age when he will stretch out his hands either to ward off those who will take control of him or to reach for help. According to John, Jesus' words anticipate the kind of death Peter will experience. Of course, by the time he writes his gospel, John and the people of his community would know how Peter died. According to early Christian tradition, Peter was crucified in Rome at the time of Nero. If the tradition is accurate, then Peter was indeed girded in the same way as Jesus and is a true son of Jonah.

"Follow Me" (John 21:19–25)

The last words that John reports Jesus speaking to His disciples (via the words He speaks to Peter here) resemble the first words that He spoke to them at the start of His public ministry: "Follow Me." At the beginning of His ministry, Jesus invites two of the Baptist's disciples to follow Him and see His residence with the words, "Come and see" (1:39). One of the disciples is Andrew who afterwards invites his brother Peter to meet Jesus. Later Jesus meets Philip and says, "Follow Me" (1:43).

> *Then Peter, turning around, saw the disciple whom Jesus loved following, who also had leaned on His breast at the supper, and said, "Lord who is the one who betrays You?" (v. 20).*

The command of Jesus, according to John, is to follow Him. It is to know Him as the One who came from the Father into the world to offer the eternal life of God to it and, in so knowing Him, also to go into the world with the same message and ministry by the Spirit. John presents the beloved disciple as responding to this command when he writes that Peter looks around and finds this disciple following (v. 20).

> *Peter, seeing him, said to Jesus, "But Lord, what about this man?" Jesus said to him, "If I will that he remain till I come, what is that to you? You follow Me" (vv. 21, 22).*

That each disciple's way in the world is the way that Jesus establishes for him or her is indicated by the fact that Peter's concern about the future of the beloved disciple is inappropriate. "If I will that he remain till I come, what is that to you? You follow Me" (v. 22). Peter's devotion and love for Jesus should make such a concern irrelevant. Jesus has given Peter a new name (1:42), restored him and given him new responsibility ("Feed My lambs . . . sheep"), and now issues a new command that is actually the first command He gave the disciples ("Follow Me"). Peter should not be distracted by concerns or questions that would detour him from the new way that Jesus has made for him.

> *Then this saying went out among the brethren that this disciple would not die. Yet Jesus did not say to him that he would not die, but, "If I will that he remain till I come, what is that to you?" This is the disciple who testifies of these things, and wrote these*

things; and we know that his testimony is true. And there are also many other things that Jesus did, which if they were written one by one, I suppose that even the world itself could not contain the books that would be written. Amen (vv. 23–25).

The disciple who follows Jesus—the beloved disciple—is the one who gives this testimony. As noted in the *Introduction*, this is John. John gives a true testimony to Jesus as the true one from God. He is the true Light that entered the world (1:9), the true Vine (15:1), and the very truth of God (14:6). Any other testimony to Jesus that contradicts that which John gives in his gospel cannot be true. Though there may be many testimonies and opinions about Jesus, John asserts that his is true.

The term *we know* may refer to those who, like John, were with Jesus or to those who have assisted him with his gospel. Just as Paul used secretaries or amanuenses to write his letters, so also John would have used the help of others to write and produce his testimony about Jesus.

The ministry of Jesus exemplifies the redemptive work of God in the books of the Old Testament. This cannot be recounted by all the books in all of the world. Such hyperbole is more than appropriate for the Light of God that entered the darkness but could not be controlled by the darkness. It aptly describes the Word of God that makes all other words possible.

Just as Jesus uses the expression, "Most assuredly I say to you," to emphasize teaching worthy of their attention, John uses the same term (*amēn*) to conclude his gospel. His depiction of Jesus is worthy of their belief.

QUESTIONS FOR PERSONAL REFLECTION AND GROUP DISCUSSION

1. What is the significance of the catch of 153 fish?
2. How does Jesus address Peter when they are beside the Sea of Galilee? What is the meaning of this name?
3. What is the result of Jesus' judging of Peter's failure?
4. Why does Jesus call Peter the son of Jonah?
5. What does Jesus mean when He says that Peter will be girded?

NOTES

1. *The Gospel according to St. John: An Introduction with Commentary and Notes on the Greek Text,* 2nd edition (Philadelphia: The Westminster Press, 1978), p. 102.

2. Barrett, p. 115.

3. See C.L. Blomberg, *The Historical Reliability of John's Gospel* (Downers Grove: InterVarsity Press, 2001), pp. 25–26.

4. See related observations by Blomberg, pp. 237–239.

5. *The Gospel according to St. John with Introduction and Notes* (London: John Murray, 1901), pp. v-xxv. See comments by Blomberg, pp. 27–29.

6. Barrett, pp. 43–45.

7. Rudolf Bultmann was the first to suggest that John drew from a collection of miracles or signs, among other collections, in writing his gospel. See *The Gospel of John* (Philadelphia: The Westminster Press, 1971).

8. *The Gospel according to John, 1–10,* eds. David W. Torrance and Thomas F. Torrance; trans. T.H.L. Parker (Grand Rapids: William B. Eerdmans Publishing Company, 1961), p. 6.

9. For further discussion, see Leon Morris, *Studies in the Fourth Gospel* (Grand Rapids: Eerdmans Publishing Company, 1967), p. 96.

10. The theme of knowledge in the Gospel of John is seen by a number of scholars as closely related to that of wisdom. For a comprehensive view of wisdom in the gospel see *John's Wisdom* by Ben Witherington, III (Louisville: Westminster John Knox Press, 1995). Also, for a specific look at wisdom and the Spirit in the Gospel of John see Max Turner's book, *The Holy Spirit and Spiritual Gifts in the New Testament Church and Today,* Revised Edition (Peabody, MA: Hendrickson Publishers, 1998), chapters 4–6.

11. Many John scholars believe that the author of the gospel writes on two levels when he refers to "the Jews." On one level, John writes of a group of people opposed to Jesus at the time of His ministry. On another level, "the Jews" refers to members of the synagogue at the end of the first century who reject the teachings of the church about Jesus. Thus, the author addresses both a reality during the ministry of Jesus as well as one in his own time. The classic formulation of this view is found in J. Louis Martyn's study, *History and Theology in the Fourth Gospel*, 3rd ed. (Louisville: Westminster John Knox Press, 2003).

12. A *chiasma* is a literary technique in which words or concepts are repeated in reverse order. This can be in the same or in modified form.

13. Jesus uses this expression throughout the Gospel of John. The word *amen* is usually made at the end of a statement, not at the beginning. By saying, "Amen, amen," at the beginning of certain statements, Jesus (according to John) alerts those who hear Him of the importance of the words He is about to speak.

14. There are several ways in which scholars understand the meal accounts in the synoptic Gospels and in John and answer the question, "Is the Last Supper a Passover meal?" For a careful summary of these approaches, see Leon Morris, *The Gospel according to John*, revised, NICNT (Grand Rapids: Eerdmans Publishing Company, 1995), pp. 684–695. Morris says that the synoptic Gospels depict the Last Supper as a Passover meal while John shows that Jesus is crucified at the time the Passover lambs were being sacrificed in the temple (and, thus, before the Passover meal was eaten). He believes that Jesus used one calendar (and considered the meal He ate with the disciples to be a Passover meal) while the temple authorities followed another. The view taken here, that Jesus ate the Passover meal with His disciples and, yet, was crucified while lambs were being slaughtered in the temple, which continued for several days to accommodate the thousands of pilgrims and worshipers to Jerusalem, is only one of several that sees agreement between the synoptic accounts of the meal and John's account.

Appendix

A Review of the
Theology of the Gospel of John

The theology of the Gospel of John may be briefly considered by addressing a few basic questions: What does John say about God? What is God's primary ambition, according to John? What does this mean for the world and the disciples of Jesus? and What does John believe to be the final achievement of God's work? Of course, these are the questions of *theology* (reflection on the person and nature of God)—which for John necessarily involves Christology and Pneumatology (reflection on Christ and the Spirit) —*soteriology* (salvation), *ecclesiology* (the people of God), and *eschatology* (the hope of the people of God).

A Trinitarian God

The being of God in the Gospel of John is manifestly Trinitarian. Though most students of the Gospel focus on the mutual relationship of Jesus the Son with God the Father, the person of the Holy Spirit is also emphasized by John.

Jesus says to His disciples and others who follow Him that He speaks only what He hears His Father say and He does only what He sees His Father do (5:19; 8:28, 29). He does nothing on His own (5:30). He tells Philip, "He who has seen Me has seen the Father" (14:9). But how does Jesus know what His Father is saying and doing? How can He say that His life is the perfect representation of God himself? As noted in the commentary, it is by the Holy Spirit. John observes that the Spirit came upon Jesus at the beginning of His messianic ministry and specifically points out, "He remained on Him" (1:32). From that moment, Jesus was enabled by the Spirit to know what His Father was saying and doing and empowered to speak the words of His Father and perform His mighty works. The signs recorded by John, therefore, point not only to Jesus and His Father but also to the present ministry of the Holy Spirit in the life of Jesus in fulfillment of the will of God the Father. The signs say to those who respond to them that God is fully present in the life and ministry of His Son by His Spirit.

This Trinitarian God is not merely an enigma but is knowable. He reveals himself through His Son by the Spirit. Jesus says in His Passion Prayer that He has made the Father known and that His disciples now know Him (17:25–26). They have come to know God through the Son. The teaching that Jesus has given about himself (the "I Am" statements throughout John) and the signs that He has shown have revealed the very nature of God to them. Not only the disciples, however, but all who will believe the teaching and signs of Jesus (as given by John in his Gospel) may know God as well. Thus, through Jesus, God has drawn near and taken upon himself human nature so that He might be known by all people.

God who makes himself known through the person and ministry of Jesus is a God of life (17:3). He has come near in the person of His Son by His Spirit not in anger and wrath for judgment, but so that the world may have abundant life (10:10). All of the self-declaration statements of Jesus show that God is a living God who gives life to His people. Jesus says that He is the Bread of Life, the Light of the World, the Good Shepherd of the flock, the Resurrection and Life, the Way, Truth, and Life, and the Vine of the Branches (6:34, 48, 51; 8:12, 9:5; 8:58; 10:7, 9, 11, 14; 11:25; 14:6; 15:1, 5). Each figurative self-description reveals that He has come to offer the very life of God to the people. God is a life-giving God.

Eternal Life (Soteriology)

God's chief ambition, according to John, is to give eternal life to His people. Jesus says to Nicodemus that God does not condemn the world, but He has sent His Son into the world to save it (3:17). This divine salvation, which comes through the life, death, and resurrection of Jesus, is not simply a reprieve from the ways and means of the world, or deliverance from the realm of the devil (depicted as darkness), but it is salvation for eternal life (3:16). Jesus says to the disciples, "I have come that they may have life, and that they may have it more abundantly" (10:10). He lays down His life so that His sheep may have such life (10:11, 15, 17). For John, salvation is the personal experience of the rich, vibrant, eternal life of God himself that is achieved through His Son's own immeasurable sacrifice.

Salvation is closely related to knowledge in the Gospel of John. God gives knowledge of himself and, in the process, banishes ignorance. John uses the imagery of light and darkness to describe knowledge of God on the one hand and ignorance of God's ways on the other (1:5f). Such knowledge comes through the very life and ministry of Jesus. He is the Light who makes God known (1:17). To know Jesus is to know God His Father. As He said to the disciples, "He who has seen Me has seen the Father" (14:9). This knowledge of God will continue after Jesus has left the disciples by the Spirit who will dwell with them and be in them (14:15–17).

The signs Jesus performs reveal God to be the Savior, Healer, Provider, and Life-Giver of His people. He who breathed into the man and made him into a living being (Gen 2:7) is the one who gives life to His people through His Son. Jesus says, "Lazarus, come forth!" and he whose body was as inert as the stone that covered the entrance of his tomb and as lifeless as the grave clothes that bound him steps out of darkness into light because the word of life has spoken! Out of the void emerges one who lives! The work of God is to give people an eternal living relationship with himself as in the beginning of Creation. This is the salvation that John describes.

Unity and Love (Ecclesiology)

Jesus is sent by His Father into the world so the whole world may experience the eternal life He offers. Though the immediate beneficiaries of Jesus' ministry were His own people, as a representative of His people He fulfills the call of ancient Israel to lead the nations in the worship of God and knowledge of Him (Ex.19:6). All who believe that Jesus was sent by God as His divine Son, who was crucified and resurrected, receive the promise of God's eternal life (20:31).

No one is excluded from this promise of God: Not wise and influential men like Nicodemus; not women who have been married five times; not powerless noblemen, and not lame men who despair of ever being whole; not innocent blind men and not guilty adulterous women; not even dead men like Lazarus! No one is beyond the life-transforming love of God! Not Philip who fails to understand that seeing Jesus is seeing God the Father; not Thomas who refuses to believe without seeing for himself; not Peter who sees too much and decides to abandon Jesus at the moment of His public humiliation. To Philip and all of the disciples Jesus exhorts, "Believe Me for the sake of the works themselves" (14:11); to Thomas, Jesus commands,

"Reach your finger here . . . reach your hand here. . . . Do not be unbelieving, but believing" (20:27); and to Peter, He says with love and finality, "You follow Me" (21:22).

Those who come to belief in Jesus and respond to His command ("Follow Me") will form a community that is marked by unity and love. It is Jesus' prayer the night prior to His crucifixion that His disciples, who now know God, will be one in unity together as He and His Father are one (by the Spirit), showing love for each other (17:26). Jesus desires that they will live together bound by the Spirit in the very way that He and His Father have lived in unity and love by the same Spirit (17:21–23). In this way the world that Jesus came to save may know that they are His people and that His offer of eternal life is real.

The Promise of the Spirit (Eschatology)

What is the result of Jesus' ministry, according to John? The disciples believe that He has come from God and is His divine Son (17:8). And what awaits these believing disciples? They will have the same Spirit that Jesus had during the course of His ministry among them (14:15-17, 25–26; 15:26–27; 16:13–15). The Spirit promised by the prophets who would come in the future and introduce a time of renewal and blessing for God's people (Joel 2; Ezekiel 11, 37; Isaiah 48:16; 34:16–35:2, 59:21–60:2), and who inaugurated such a time through Jesus, will be given to the disciples so they may continue His ministry into the future. They will experience the Trinitarian God of Father, Son, and Spirit, performing the will of the Father (as Jesus fulfilled the will of the Father) by the presence of the Spirit in the name of Jesus as they keep His words. In this way the intention of God to have a people who will worship Him by keeping the words of His commandments given by the Spirit will be accomplished. The life of God will continue to be manifested in the earth as the disciples live by His Spirit and follow Jesus.